UNIFORM PROBATE CODE

AND

UNIFORM TRUST CODE

IN A NUTSHELL

SIXTH EDITION

By

LAWRENCE H. AVERILL, JR.
Charles C. Baum Distinguished
Professor of Law Emeritus
University of Arkansas at Little Rock

MARY F. RADFORD
Catherine C. Henson Professor of Law
Georgia State University

WEST®

A Thomson Reuters business

Mat #40854864

Nutshell Series, In a Nutshell and the Nutshell Logo are trademarks registered in the U.S. Patent and Trademark Office.

COPYRIGHT © 1978, 1987, 1993, 1996 WEST PUBLISHING CO.
© West, a Thomson business, 2001
© 2010 Thomson Reuters

    610 Opperman Drive
    St. Paul, MN 55123
    1–800–313–9378

Printed in the United States of America

ISBN: 978–0–314–92692–0

To my brother, Richard W. Averill

To Lee

PREFACE

The two most dominant uniform laws in the area of trusts and estates are the Uniform Probate Code and the Uniform Trust Code. Both have had significant acceptance throughout the country either in complete enactments or piecemeal adoptions. The two Codes are inherently related and interconnected and thus it was a logical step to produce a single Nutshell that includes both of them.

To accomplish this in a reasonably compact text, it was necessary to compact and refine the UPC coverage in order to have space for the UTC coverage. This was accomplished without harming the basic comprehensiveness of the UPC portion. It required greater care to organization. The number of chapters has been reduced and the text in these chapters has been consolidated into a more efficient and reader friendly design. A few charts have been eliminated and most references to case law removed. Careful edition has reduced length to the benefit of the text.

Professor Averill has been primarily responsible for the UPC and its revision. Professor Radford has concentrated on the UTC. Both have tried to integrate the two Codes. Overlapping subject matter has been combined into single discussions. Superceded materials have been eliminated or cross-referenced.

This edition includes discussion of other uniform acts that have had an impact on and in some cases been integrated into the UPC or the UTC. These include: the Uniform Disclaimer of Property Interests Act, the Uniform Durable Power of Attorney Act, the Uniform Multiple–Person Accounts Act, the Uniform Nonprobate Transfers at Death Act, the Uniform Prudent Investor Act, the Uniform Simplification of Fiduciary Security Transfers Act, the Uniform Simultaneous Death Act, the Uniform Statutory Rule against Perpetuities, the Uniform Testamentary Additions to Trusts Act, the Uniform TOD Security Registration Act, and the Uniform Transfers to Minors Act.

LAWRENCE H. AVERILL, JR.

Hot Springs Village, Arkansas
July 1, 2010

MARY F. RADFORD

Atlanta, Georgia
July 1, 2010

OUTLINE

Page

PART THREE. PROBATE OF WILLS AND ADMINISTRATION

Chapter 10. Administration and Administration Avoidance Procedures 317

OUTLINE

PART FIVE.   NONPROBATE TRANSFERS

Page

OUTLINE

TABLE OF CASES

References are to Pages

TABLE OF CASES

TABLE OF CASES

TABLE OF CASES

TABLE OF COLLATERAL AUTHORITIES

COLLATERAL AUTHORITIES

Treatises and Law Review Articles	Citation, Page References
Roger W. Anderson, The Influence of the Uniform Probate Code in Nonadopting States, 8 U. Puget Sound L. Rev. 599 (1985)	Anderson, Influence of the Uniform Probate Code, 10
Thomas E. Atkinson, Wanted—A Model Probate Code, 23 J.Am.Jur.Soc'y 183 (1940)	Atkinson, Model Probate Code, 6
THOMAS E. ATKINSON, WILLS (2d ed. 1953)	Atkinson, Wills, 1, 70, 75, 90, 91, 98, 101, 104, 140, 161, 163, 173, 178, 179, 186, 194, 206, 225, 236, 263, 269, 272, 372, 409, 411, 412, 442, 446, 468, 550
Lawrence H. Averill, Jr., An Eclectic History and Analysis of the 1990 Uniform Probate Code, 55 Alb. L. Rev. 891 (1992)	Averill, An Eclectic History and Analysis, 4, 10
Susan T. Bart & Lyman W. Welch, State Statutes on Virtual Representation–A New State Survey, 35 ACTEC J. 368 (2010)	Bart & Welch, Virtual Representation, 604
Ira Mark Bloom, Perpetuities Refinement: There is an Alternative, 62 Wash. L. Rev. 23 (1987)	Bloom, Perpetuities Refinement, 300
G. T. BOGERT, TRUSTS (6th edition 1987)	Bogert, Trusts, 3, 615, 619, 623, 624, 634, 635
BLACK'S LAW DICTIONARY (Nolan–Haley rev. 4th ed., 1968)	Black's Law Dictionary, 1
Gerry W. Beyer & Jonathan P. Wilkerson, Max's Taxes: A Tax–Based Analysis of Pet Trusts, 43 U. Rich. L. Rev. 1219 (2009)	Beyer & Wilkerson, Pet Trusts, 619

COLLATERAL AUTHORITIES

COLLATERAL AUTHORITIES

Treatises and Law Review Articles	Citation, Page References
Lawrence A. Frolik & Mary F. Radford, "Sufficient" Capacity: The Contrasting Capacity Requirements for Different Documents, 2 NAELA Journal 303 (2006)	Frolik & Radford, Sufficient Capacity, 663, 665
Susan N. Gary, We Are Family: The Definition of Parent and Child for Succession Purposes, Winter 2008 AC-TEC Journal 171.	Gary, We Are Family, 69, 76
J. GRAY, THE RULE AGAINST PERPETUITIES (4th ed. 1942)	Gray, Rule Against Perpetuities, 298
Ashbel G. Gulliver & Catherine J. Tilson, Classification of Gratuitous Transfers, 51 Yale L.J. 1 (1941)	Gulliver & Tilson, Gratuitous Transfers, 153
Edward C. Halbach & Lawrence W. Waggoner, The UPC's New Survivorship and Antilapse Provision, 55 Alb. L. Rev. 1091 (1992)	Halbach & Waggoner, Survivorship and Antilapse, 207, 248
Adam J. Hirsch, Bequests for Purposes: A Unified Theory, 56 Wash. & Lee L. Rev. 33 (1999)	Hirsch, Bequests for Purposes, 621
Adam J. Hirsch, Revisions in Need of Revising: the Uniform Disclaimer of Property Interests Act, 2001 Fla. St. Univ. L. Rev. 109 (Fall).	Hirsch, Revisions in Need of Revising, 290
Adam J. Hirsch & Richard R. Gans, Perfecting Disclaimer Reform: Suggestions for a Revised Uniform Act, 31 Est. Plan. 185 (2004)	Hirsch & Gans, Perfecting Disclaimer Reform, 297
Sheldon F. Kurtz, Powers of Appointment Under the 1990 Uniform Probate Code: What Was Done—What Remains to Be Done, 55 Alb. L. Rev. 1151 (1992)	Kurtz, Powers of Appointment, 279, 287, 288

COLLATERAL AUTHORITIES

Treatises and Law Review Articles

Citation, Page References

Kevin D. Millard, Rights of a Trust Beneficiary's Creditors under the Uniform Trust Code, 34 ACTEC J. 58 (2008)

Millard, Trust Beneficiary's Creditors, 641, 644, 645, 648, 649, 650, 658

PAGE ON THE LAW OF WILLS (Bowe–Parker rev. ed., 1960) (8 vols.)

Page, Wills, 151, 189, 190, 194, 198, 199, 206, 553

PROBLEMS IN PROBATE LAW—A MODEL PROBATE CODE (1946)

Model Probate Code, 6, 180, 348, 403, 404, 496

Mary F. Radford, Postmortem Sperm Retrieval and the Social Security Administration: How Modern Reproductive Technology Makes Strange Bedfellows, 2009 Estate Planning & Community Property Law Journal 33 (Fall)

Radford, Postmortem Sperm Retrieval, 83

Eugene F. Scoles, Succession Without Administration: Past and Future, 48 Mo. L. Rev. 371 (1983)

Scoles, Succession Without Administration, 355, 360

AUSTIN W. SCOTT & WILLIAM F. FRATCHER, THE LAW OF TRUSTS (4th ed. 1987) (6 vols.)

Scott, Trusts, 431, 553, 603

David G. Shaftel, Newest Developments in Alaska Law Encourage Use of Alaska Trusts, 26 Est. Plan. 51 (1999)

Shaftel, Newest Developments in Alaska, 299

LEWIS M. SIMES, LAW OF FUTURE INTERESTS (2d ed. 1966)

Simes, Future Interests, 249, 280

Uniform Probate Code Notes (Joint Editorial Board for the Uniform Probate Code)

UPC Notes, 28

Lawrence W. Waggoner, Drafting Under the Uniform Statutory Rule Against Perpetuities and Related Generation–Skipping Tax Grand-

Waggoner, Drafting Under the USRAP, 305

Uniform Laws

Citation, Page References

TABLE OF UNIFORM PROBATE CODE SECTIONS

[References to Uniform Probate Code
Sections and Comments]

TABLE OF UNIFORM PROBATE CODE SECTIONS

TABLE OF UNIFORM PROBATE CODE SECTIONS

TABLE OF UNIFORM PROBATE CODE SECTIONS

TABLE OF UNIFORM PROBATE CODE SECTIONS

TABLE OF UNIFORM PROBATE CODE SECTIONS

TABLE OF UNIFORM PROBATE CODE SECTIONS

TABLE OF UNIFORM PROBATE CODE SECTIONS

TABLE OF UNIFORM PROBATE CODE SECTIONS

TABLE OF UNIFORM PROBATE CODE SECTIONS

TABLE OF UNIFORM PROBATE CODE SECTIONS

TABLE OF UNIFORM PROBATE CODE SECTIONS

TABLE OF UNIFORM PROBATE CODE SECTIONS

TABLE OF UNIFORM PROBATE CODE SECTIONS

TABLE OF UNIFORM PROBATE CODE SECTIONS

TABLE OF UNIFORM PROBATE CODE SECTIONS

TABLE OF UNIFORM PROBATE CODE SECTIONS

TABLE OF UNIFORM PROBATE CODE SECTIONS

TABLE OF UNIFORM PROBATE CODE SECTIONS

TABLE OF UNIFORM PROBATE CODE SECTIONS

TABLE OF UNIFORM PROBATE CODE SECTIONS

TABLE OF UNIFORM PROBATE CODE SECTIONS

TABLE OF UNIFORM PROBATE CODE SECTIONS

TABLE OF UNIFORM PROBATE CODE SECTIONS

TABLE OF UNIFORM PROBATE CODE SECTIONS

TABLE OF UNIFORM PROBATE CODE SECTIONS

TABLE OF UNIFORM PROBATE CODE SECTIONS

TABLE OF UNIFORM PROBATE CODE SECTIONS

TABLE OF UNIFORM PROBATE CODE SECTIONS

TABLE OF UNIFORM PROBATE CODE SECTIONS

TABLE OF UNIFORM TRUST CODE SECTIONS

[References to Uniform Trust Code
Sections and Comments]

TABLE OF UNIFORM TRUST CODE SECTIONS

TABLE OF UNIFORM TRUST CODE SECTIONS

TABLE OF UNIFORM TRUST CODE SECTIONS

TABLE OF UNIFORM TRUST CODE SECTIONS

TABLE OF UNIFORM TRUST CODE SECTIONS

TABLE OF UNIFORM TRUST CODE SECTIONS

TABLE OF UNIFORM TRUST CODE SECTIONS

TABLE OF UNIFORM TRUST CODE SECTIONS

TABLE OF UNIFORM TRUST CODE SECTIONS

TABLE OF UNIFORM TRUST CODE SECTIONS

TABLE OF UNIFORM TRUST CODE SECTIONS

TABLE OF STATUTES

TABLE OF STATUTES

UNIFORM PROBATE CODE

AND

UNIFORM TRUST CODE

IN A NUTSHELL

SIXTH EDITION

CHAPTER 1
GENERAL INTRODUCTION AND HISTORY

§ 1.01 General Introduction

The word "probate" in the English language has had a variety of meanings throughout the history of Anglo–American jurisprudence. Technically, the term "probate" refers to the process of proving and deciding the validity of a will before a court having competent jurisdiction; more generally, it refers to all matters appropriately before the probate courts. [Black's Law Dictionary]. Similarly, "probate courts" in the United States are granted jurisdiction not only over the probate of wills, but also the entire process of the administration of decedents' estates including their initiation, the collection of assets, the settling of creditors' claims and their closing and distribution. Some probate courts also have jurisdiction over the affairs and property of persons under a disability, such as minors and other incapacitated persons. Adding to this complexity several jurisdictions call probate courts "orphans' courts," "surrogate's courts," "courts of ordinary" or by the name of the court in the jurisdiction which has general or some other subject matter jurisdiction. [Atkinson, Wills § 4].

1

The Uniform Probate Code [UPC] adopts a very broad meaning and application to the word "probate." It not only includes law dealing with the affairs and estates of decedents and persons under a disability but also includes law dealing with specified nontestamentary transfers, contracts and bank deposits and with certain procedural and substantive rules of trusts and their administration. The theory of the Code is that there is a close interrelationship between these various areas of law and that they are all in need of unification, modernization, clarification and uniformity.

Unquestionably the UPC's content pertains to a cornerstone of our society. It is readily clear that the law dealing with the distribution and management of wealth at death or during disability is of profound concern and importance to our society. With the inevitability of death at some time and the inevitability of disability during minority and its reasonable possibility during the later years of life coupled with the present ability for people to possess or accumulate property the law dealing with these matters needs substantive rules which are relevant to modern societal needs and procedural rules which are efficient in time, cost and understanding. The UPC addresses itself to these principles.

The UPC is now complimented by the Uniform Trust Code [UTC] which was promulgated in 2000, over 30 years after the UPC. Although the early colonies imported the extensive trust law of England and trusts have been in common use in the

United States since the end of the 18th century [Bogert, Trusts, § 6], few states engaged in a systematic codification of the law relating to trusts. While the UPC contains some provisions relating to trusts, these provisions were somewhat fragmentary and did not answer many of the day-to-day questions pertaining to the operation of trusts. After the promulgation of the UPC, trusts came to be used even more extensively in personal and commercial transactions. [UTC, Prefatory Note]. Thus, the UTC was drafted to provide states with a comprehensive statutory framework for trust operation and management.

§ 1.02   History

The law of succession and estates is as ancient as civilization. Research indicates that the earliest law was family-oriented rather than individual centered. As societies became more complex, individual ownership and disposition law developed. Clearly by the time of the establishment of the United States, succession law gave significant recognition to individual ownership and freedom of disposition. The ancestor of our law is England, with Roman law and civil law of the European continent as shirt-tail relations. None of these relationships are pure. All descended concepts have been modified or reformulated. From a distance, broad similar characteristics are identifiable; but on closer inspection significant differences are patent.

Today, English history of wealth transmission is more significant for its underlying principles than for its rules. The recognition in the United States that the individual has power to determine her or his successors is one of the paramount legacies from English law. The creation of the trust device for holding property also persevered and flourished in our jurisprudence. Certainly, the intricacy and precision of future interest rules continued in our law. The idea of an administration of an estate was accepted by the States and cultured far beyond its original design and purpose.

In the United States, significant reform of succession law occurred when each state entered the union in the 18th and 19th centuries. England did not reform until the twentieth century and its reform was more dramatic and relevant to modern society than was the earlier reform in the States.

Major comprehensive reform did not really come to the states until the late 1960's when the UPC was promulgated. Many of the modern and improved rules and procedures presently existing under English law greatly influenced the draftsmen of the Uniform Probate Code. [Fratcher, Probate Can Be Quick and Cheap]. But the UPC is an amalgamation of many sources including state statutes, uniform acts and academic analyses. [See Averill, Eclectic History and Analysis, at 893–901]. Likewise, the UTC integrated a variety of trust-related uniform acts, state statutes, and analyses of trust law that appear in the Restatements of the law of trusts.

§ 1.03　Development of the Uniform Probate Code and Uniform Trust Code

In recent years, the word "probate" unfortunately symbolizes in the minds of some people the evils of graft, waste and delay. The source of much of the present dissatisfaction is in the laws themselves. First, there is insufficient uniformity between the laws of the fifty states. This fact may cause not only unjust results but also an inherent confusion and distrust among a very mobile lay populace. Second, some of the relevant laws in this area in many states are not contemporary; consequently, they do not take into account the material changes which have occurred in our society. Not only have we changed from a primarily rural to primarily urban society but also from one with a primary emphasis directed to ownership of real estate to one directed toward ownership of personal property and other contractual relationships. Furthermore, our society continues to progress from one educationally and sociologically provincial to one nationally and even internationally cognizant. In addition, the continued increase in the number of persons who have had multiple marriages and children with more than a single spouse creates a social phenomenon that much current succession law does not adequately address. Many of the present laws on these matters, therefore, do not adequately deal with the primary problems posed by the average person in regard to lifetime transfer and succession at death of wealth or in the management of that person's property during disability.

In 1946, a suggestion by Professor Atkinson to the American Bar Association Section of Real Property, Probate and Trust Law [hereinafter referred to as the Probate Section] that this organization prepare a Model Probate Code, [Atkinson, Model Probate Code, at 189] resulted in the publication of a Model Probate Code and accompanying studies. [Model Probate Code]. Although the Model Probate Code had a direct influence and effect on revisions in several states, it had neither the comprehensiveness nor the impetus to influence a majority of states to adopt it.

In 1962, the Probate Section and the Uniform Law Commission (formerly the National Conference of Commissioners on Uniform State Laws) [hereinafter referred to as the ULC] accepted a suggestion made by J. Pennington Straus of the Philadelphia Bar to revise and consolidate the Model Probate Code and other related and relevant uniform laws into a uniform probate law. In response, each organization formed a separate committee and Professor William F. Fratcher of the University of Missouri School of Law was appointed Research Director to conduct preliminary studies during 1963–64. Thereafter a Reporting Staff was recruited to draft the Uniform Probate Code under the supervision of the two committees. The late Professor Richard V. Wellman then of the University of Michigan and subsequently of the University of Georgia became the Reporting Staff's Chief Reporter.

After six drafts, six years of extensive research, consultation, and discussion, an official text was approved in August, 1969, by the ULC and by the House of Delegates of the American Bar Association. Although inspired and initiated as a project to redraft and update the Model Probate Code, the eventual finished product turned out to be much more. It not only is more comprehensive in coverage but also exhibits greater innovation and imagination. In addition, many of its basic philosophies are different. Consequently, the UPC offers a more viable package for influencing and affecting modern probate legislation.

Naturally, through the last forty years the UPC has been the subject of a great deal of legal commentary. A significant portion of it is cited throughout this Nutshell. One of the most important publications was the *Uniform Probate Code Manual* published by the Association of Continuing Legal Education Administrators in 1972 and edited by Professor Robert R. Wright. [UPC Practice Manual (1972)]. It contained a series of articles by recognized authorities on all parts of the UPC. Professor Wellman, as editor, updated and expanded this manual in a second edition published in 1977. [UPC Practice Manual]. Since that edition, the manual has not been updated.

In March of 1971 Idaho [Idaho Code §§ 15–1–101 to 15–7–401 (Effective July 1, 1972)] became the first state to adopt the UPC substantially in whole. Since that time, more than thirty percent of the fifty states have enacted laws that substantially conform to the UPC or major parts of it. Promotion and enactment of the UPC have not been easy in the states and have had varying degrees of success. Its primary detractors include what would appear to be bonding companies, loosely organized groups of older bar members and occasionally newspaper publishers. In some situations, these opponents have proved to be formidable adversaries and have shown considerable influence in state legislatures.

Even though the UPC succeeded in streamlining the probate process in many states, in the years following its promulgation, individuals and businesses began to expand the use of the trust as a vehicle for managing and transferring property. The use of the trust as a will substitute became prevalent at this time. As the use of trusts became more common, it became apparent that many states had no codified trust law at all and in those that did, the law was not usually not comprehensive. Exceptions to this were the states of California, Georgia, Indiana, Texas, and Washington, whose laws were studied during the drafting of the UTC. The major sources of trust law in most states was the Restatement (Second) of the Law of Trusts (1957) and two multi-volume treatises written in 1921 by Professor George Gleason Bogert [Bogert] and in 1939 by Professors Austin Wakeman Scott [Scott]. Although a number of Uniform Laws dealt with aspects of trust law, their treatment of this law was fragmentary. [UTC, Prefatory Note].

In 1993, a study committee was formed by the ULC for the purpose of determining whether the

ULC should consider drafting a comprehensive uniform trust law. The committee was chaired by Justice Maurice Hartnett of the Delaware Supreme Court, who had also served on the Delaware Chancery Court. At the study committee's recommendation, a drafting committee was appointed in 1994. [English, UTC Significant Provisions, p. 145]. The drafting committee was also chaired by Justice Hartnett. Professor David M. English of the University of Missouri Law School served as the drafting committee's Reporter. Professor Wellman (the Chief Reporter of the UPC) served on the drafting committee of the UTC along with Professor John Langbein of Yale and four distinguished lawyers. The drafting committee chose to keep the process deliberative in order to gather as much information as possible, so the UTC itself was not completed for six years. [English. UTC Significant Provisions, p. 145]. The drafting committee enlisted the aid of advisors from a number of professional organizations including the American Bar Association's Section of Real Property Probate and Trust Law, the American College of Trust and Estate Counsel ["ACTEC"], the American Bankers Association, and the California and Colorado State Bars. Members of the Joint Editorial Board for Uniform Trusts and Estates Acts and the ACTEC Committee on State Laws also attended the drafting meetings. [English, UTC Significant Provisions, p. 145].

The ULC approved the UTC on August 3, 2000 and recommended it for enactment in all the states. In 2001–02, the UTC was introduced into the legislatures of nine states. In May, 2002, Kansas became the first state to adopt the UTC. The UTC has been adopted in whole or in part by 22 states and the District of Columbia. The UTC was introduced in the New Jersey legislature in 2010.

The UTC incorporated or superseded a number of Uniform Laws. Among these was Article VII of the UPC, which at the time of the promulgation of the UTC had been adopted by about 15 jurisdictions. The drafters of the UTC intended it to supersede Article VII of the UPC. [UTC, Prefatory Note.] However, while some states that adopted the UTC have expressly repealed the trust provisions of the UPC (e.g., New Mexico), others have not. Some states make the UTC applicable only to trusts created after the date of enactment, so the UPC provisions may still be relevant for older trusts. Also, there are some states that have adopted the UPC but not the UTC, so the trust provisions of the UPC remain viable in those states. This Nutshell describes the UPC provisions relating to trusts in the context of the discussion of comparable provisions of the UTC.

§ 1.04 Promulgation and Maintenance of the UPC and UTC

For the purpose of promulgating the Uniform Probate Code, a Joint Editorial Board for the Uniform Probate Code was established in 1970. [See Averill, Eclectic History and Analysis, at 893–901]. It is now named the Joint Editorial Board for Uniform Trust and Estate Acts in order to reflect its broader responsibility. Its membership consists of five persons nominated by the ULC and five nominated by the Probate Section. Its responsibilities are: (a) to monitor literature dealing with the UPC; (b) to watch for problems that develop in the UPC itself and that arise in states which have enacted or are considering enacting it; (c) to educate the Bar and public about the UPC; and, (d) to reevaluate, alter and edit the UPC's text for the purpose of removing imperfections and improving content, both substantially and editorially. Professor Lawrence W. Waggoner, University of Michigan Law School, is the current Director of Research and Chief Reporter.

The UPC has been periodically updated and improved. During 1975–76, the ULC and the House of Delegates of the American Bar Association approved significant amendments called the "1975 Technical Amendments" promulgated by the Joint Editorial Board. Many of these amendments included suggestions and improvements made by various bar committees which have studied the UPC for enactment in their respective states. Other alterations were made in 1977, 1979, 1982, 1984, 1987, 1988, 1989, 1990, 1991 and 1993. [See UPC, at ix]. The 1990 revision substantially rewrote Article II. In 1993, significant Technical Amendments were introduced that substantially reorganized and reconstituted the UPC's elective share provisions that had been rewritten in the 1990 revision. In 2008, additional alterations were made to Article II.

When the initial enthusiasm and national effort to enact the Uniform Probate UPC as a comprehensive code lost much of its original momentum, the ULC altered its promotional approach regarding several new and old matters. In relevant, and appropriately separable, areas of probate law, the ULC developed freestanding acts from similar provisions integrated into the UPC as it existed at the relevant time. The reverse chronology also occurred. Some separate Uniform Acts have been subsequently integrated into the UPC in order to broaden its coverage. These techniques permitted the provisions to become law either as part of the whole Uniform Probate Code or as a separable and possibly more palatable distinct uniform act.

Accordingly, the Uniform Durable Power of Attorney Act was approved in 1979 and modified Part 5 of Article V; the Uniform Guardianship and Protective Proceedings Act was approved in 1982 and altered Parts 1, 2, 3, and 4 of Article V; the Uniform International Wills Act was approved in 1977 and added part 10 to Article II; and the Uniform Succession Without Administration Act was approved in 1983 from Sections 3–312 to 3–322 which had been added to Article III of the UPC in 1982.

The 1990 UPC added several more of them. The Uniform Statutory Rule Against Perpetuities Act, called USRAP, was promulgated separately in 1986 and was incorporated as Part 9 of the new Article II. The Uniform Nonprobate Transfers at Death Act which includes the Uniform Multiple–Person Accounts Act and the Uniform TOD Security Registration Act was promulgated in 1989 and mirrors Article VI of the 1990 UPC. The new Article II has been separately promulgated as the Uniform Intestacy, Wills, and Donative Transfers Act in 1991. Finally, Section 2–702 of the 1990 UPC was promulgated as the new Uniform Simultaneous Death Act in 1991. In 2002, UPC § 2–801 was replaced by the Uniform Disclaimer of Property Interests Act (1999), which is incorporated as Part 11 of Article 2. [§§ 2–1101 to 2–1117].

The existence of freestanding acts makes the UPC a more dynamic document. It permits those who advocate probate and related law reform to select the most palatable part for passage in their jurisdiction. This should increase the influence of the UPC on the law and motivate more jurisdictions to adopt its reform proposals.

The UTC has also undergone a series of amendments in 2001, 2003, 2004, and 2005. These amendments were developed as legislative committees in various states studied the UTC with an eye toward enacting it in whole or in part. Some of the provisions of the UTC proved controversial [e.g., the mandatory disclosure provisions of § 105(b)(8) and (b)(9), see § 17.08(M)]. The drafting committee gave careful consideration to these debates and made changes where it thought changes were warranted. In some cases, the amendment that was made was simply to bracket a Code section or a portion thereof, signaling to the states that they may or may not want to include that Code section or may want to amend it to coincide more closely with their own law.

As noted above, at the time the UTC was enacted, a variety of existing Uniform Acts covered various aspects of the law of trusts. The drafters of the UTC noted that the following Uniform Acts were not affected by the UTC and thus should continue to be available for enactment in free-standing form: Uniform Common Trust Fund Act (1938), Uniform Custodial Trust Act (1987), Uniform Management of Institutional Funds Act (1972) (which in 2006 was updated and renamed the Uniform Prudent Management of Institutional Funds Act), Uniform Principal and Income Act (1997) (which some states have incorporated into their trust codes), Uniform Probate Code (1969) (with the exception of Article VII, as discussed below), Uniform Statutory Rule Against Perpetuities (1986), Uniform Supervision of Trustees for Charitable Purposes Act (1954), and Uniform Testamentary Additions to Trusts Act (1960, 1991).

On the other hand, the UTC drafters intended that other Uniform Acts be incorporated into or superseded by the UTC and thus should be repealed by states that had adopted them. Most important of these is Article VII of the UPC, which dealt with some aspects of trust administration. Other superseded acts are: Uniform Prudent Investor Act (1994) (which the drafters suggest should be incorporated as Article IX of the UTC), Uniform Trustee Powers Act (1964) (the provisions have which have been updated and incorporated into the Article 8 of the UTC), and Uniform Trusts Act (1937) (which the drafters found to be an outdated act that addressed trust matters only in a limited way).

§ 1.05   Influence of the UPC and UTC

The influence and the use of the UPC is growing in a variety of ways. [See Anderson, Influence of the Uniform Probate Code]. The laws of nearly all if not all states have been affected by the UPC. The primary vehicles of influence are as follows:

(1) Enactment as a UPC in full with some amendments. Eighteen states fall into this category: Alaska, Arizona, Colorado, Florida, Hawaii, Idaho, Maine, Massachusetts, Michigan, Minnesota, Montana, Nebraska, New Jersey, New Mexico, North Dakota, South Carolina, South Dakota and Utah. [UPC, at p. 1 (Supp.2009)].

(2) Piece-meal enactment of segments or sections of the UPC for inclusion into another probate code or law. Nearly all the other states have enacted some part or section of the UPC. Sections of article II have been particularly popular. For example, California incorporated many provisions, in whole or in part, of the UPC into its recent revision of its probate code. In order to assure proper judicial construction of these UPC provisions, the new law requires that any portion of the California code which is derived "in substance" from the Uniform Probate Code, must be "construed as to effectuate the general purpose to make uniform the laws of those states which enact" provisions of the Uniform Probate Code. [West's Ann.Cal.Prob.Code § 2(b)]. The Georgia

Supreme Court held that because a local statute was identical to a provision in the UPC, the interpretation, cases, and comments on that section of the UPC should be adopted and applied to it. [Caldwell v. Walraven, 490 S.E.2d 384 (Ga. 1997)].

(3) Referred to as a model of modern policy by a court interpreting its own non UPC provision. [See, e.g., First Church of Christ, Scientist v. Watson, 239 So.2d 194 (Ala.1970)].

(4) Referred to as secondary or persuasive authority for determining proper rules of construction for the common law. [See, e.g., Russell v. Estate of Russell, 534 P.2d 261 (Kan.1975); Thompson v. Botts, 423 N.E.2d 90 (Ohio 1981); Smith v. Smith, 519 S.W.2d 152 (Tex.Civ.App. 1974)].

Even if comprehensive enactment does not continue, the UPC's influence over the law of probate and related matters will continue to increase.

As a newer act, the UTC has not yet enjoyed the influence of the UPC. However, its enactment to date in whole or in part by almost one-half of the states indicates that it already has become a respected compilation of trust law. Additionally, the proliferation of institutional trustees with multi-state presences will continue to put pressure on the states to enact a trust law that is similar to if not uniform to that of other states.

§ 1.06 Outline and Overview

A. UNIFORM PROBATE CODE

In order to get a proper perspective of the UPC, a brief summary of its content is appropriate. Article I contains what might be called the UPC's housekeeping and foundational provisions. A few examples include sections dealing with the UPC's purposes and rule of construction, important pervasive definitions, the court's subject matter jurisdiction and an inclusive method for and time of notice provision.

Article II contains twenty-three percent of the sections in the UPC which makes it the second largest article. It includes the substantive core of what is referred to as the law of wills, intestate succession, and donative transfers. In addition to provisions dealing with how to execute a will and with distribution under intestacy, it also includes provisions concerning the surviving spouse's elective share, family protections, rules of construction for wills and other donative instruments, disclaimers, the safekeeping of wills, the Rule Against Perpetuities, and other related matters.

Article III is the largest article in the UPC containing almost thirty-six percent of the sections. It consists of a comprehensive and flexible system for the probate of wills and the administration of decedents' estates. It includes, for example, provisions that: set a statute of limitations on probate and administration; create an administration system of

multiple techniques for accomplishing the various
desired actions; deal comprehensively with the status, function and activities of the personal representative; determine and settle creditors' claims; deal
with distributions, closings and the compromising
of controversies concerning estates; and, provide
several special procedures to deal with the very
small estate. Article IV is interrelated with Article
III and deals with foreign personal representatives
and ancillary administration.

Article V contains the third largest number of
sections in the UPC comprising approximately sev-
enteen percent. It comprehensively covers the area
of law concerned both with the protection of persons who are disabled either because of incapacity,
disappearance or minority and with the protection
of their property. Significantly, it also includes several escape devices so that elaborate formal procedures need not be used. The inclusion of guardianship provisions in a probate code is consistent with
current jurisdictional concepts of probate courts
under many court systems. In addition, because the
fiduciary relationships and administrative functions
of a guardian and a conservator are substantially
similar to that of a personal representative, it is
logical to include provisions on these matters in the
UPC.

The next two articles of the UPC are not as
obviously relevant to what would normally be conceived as probate matters. Article VI deals with
non-probate transfers including durable powers of
attorney, multiple-party bank accounts, transfer on

death security registrations and other types of documents that relate to the effect of death on property. It is beneficial to include provisions on these matters in the UPC due to the extreme state of confusion and lack of uniformity in the current law in most states and because they concern the succession of property at death. In addition, their validity and effect have a direct relationship to a personal representative's administration of a decedent's estate.

Finally, in Article VII the UPC includes provisions concerned with the administration of both inter vivos and testamentary trusts. Article VII is divided into three parts which include trust registration, jurisdiction of the Court concerning trusts and the duties and liabilities of the trustee. These provisions were included in the UPC for several reasons: (1) uniformity is needed as much in the area of trust administration law as it is in the area of decedents' estates law; (2) an obvious similarity exists between the relationship of a trustee to its beneficiaries and a personal representative to its beneficiaries; and (3) the full power Court concept of the UPC, made it logical to include trustees under the jurisdiction of this Court. If the UTC is adopted, Article VII is unnecessary. The discussion of the provisions of Article VII is integrated into the chapters of this Nutshell that discuss comparable provisions in the UTC.

Article VIII contains provisions concerned only with the UPC's effective date and repealer and therefore needs no further discussion in this Nutshell.

B. UNIFORM TRUST CODE

The UTC is comprised of 11 articles. Like the UPC, Article 1 contains definitions and foundational provisions. The article also contains provisions relating to miscellaneous topics that do not fit in any other article. The most important provision of Article 1 is UTC § 105. Although the UTC is primarily a "default statute" (that is, a statute whose provisions do not apply if the settlor manifests a different intent in the trust), there are some provisions of the UTC that were viewed by the drafters as ones that could not be modified by the settlor. These provisions are listed in UTC § 105. [See § 17.01(C)].

Although the drafters made no attempt to dictate blanket procedural rules for judicial proceedings involving trusts, Article 2 contains provisions that deal with selected issues such as jurisdiction and venue. Knowing that many trusts would have contacts with more than one state, the drafters felt it important to include a set of rules that would apply for such trusts.

Article 3 of the UTC is devoted completely to the rules that govern the circumstances under which a beneficiary or other interested party may be represented, either by another fiduciary or by virtual representation. This representation is important particularly in matters in which notice must be given or a beneficiary must give consent to a trustee's action. The concept of virtual representation is also covered in the UPC [1–403], although not as extensively as in the UTC.

Article 4 of the UTC contains the rules for creating trusts and for modifying and terminating them. The rules relating to trust creation include the common law requirements of capacity, ascertainable beneficiaries, trustee, trust property, and proper trust purpose. This article contains provisions for the creation of charitable trusts, trusts for benevolent but non-charitable purposes and trust for animals. The second half of the article contains provisions relating to the modification or termination of trusts that are designed to make these processes more flexible and to facilitate the carrying out of the settlor's intent. Included are provisions for allowing the beneficiaries and settlor to modify a trust without court intervention; petitioning a court to modify or terminate a trust; allowing a court to reform trust terms that were based on a mistake of law or facts; allowing for the termination of uneconomic trusts; and allowing the trustee to combine or divide trusts.

Article 5 deals exclusively with creditors' claims against both trust beneficiaries and settlors. This article describes valid spendthrift trusts and those creditors whose claims are exempt from the spendthrift protections. The article also contains provisions that address creditors' claims against trusts with discretionary distribution provisions and the access of the creditors of a settlor to trust property, both before and after the settlor's death.

Article 6 addresses a number of heretofore unsettled issues relating to revocable trusts. One of the developments that instigated the drafting of the UTC was the increasing use of revocable trusts as will substitutes. The basic approach of this article is to treat a revocable trust as the functional equivalent of a will. Importantly, this article contains a provision that reverses the long-established presumption that a trust could not be revoked or amended by the settlor unless the settlor expressly retained the power to do so in the trust instrument. The new approach is that a trust will be presumed to be revocable unless it contains terms that overcome that presumption.

Article 7 contains miscellaneous rules covering the office of trustee. These include provisions relating to the role of cotrustees, vacancies; removal of trustees; successor trustees; and trustee compensation.

Article 8 addresses the duties of trustees and enumerates the powers of trustees. The duties that are spelled out in this article expand to all trustee decisions and include many of the investment-related duties that are enumerated in the Uniform Prudent Investor Act. Unlike the UPC, which cross-referenced to the Uniform Trustees Powers Act, this article contains a provision that lists in exhaustive detail the powers of trustees and adds new powers relating to the management of property that may have environmental issues.

Article 9 deals exclusively with investment powers and is designed to encourage states that have already adopted the Uniform Prudent Investor Act to incorporate that act into the state's new trust code.

Article 10 deals in the first sections with claims against trustees for breach of trust. These provisions address remedies, damages, the statute of limitations, and defenses. The second portion of the article addresses the rights of third parties who deal with trustees with the purpose of providing protections that will encourage third parties to engage in commercial transactions with trustees.

Article 11 contains miscellaneous provisions, including the effective date and the application of the trust code to trusts established prior to the effective date.

PART ONE

GENERAL PROVISIONS, DEFINITIONS AND PROBATE JURISDICTION OF THE COURT

CHAPTER 2

GENERAL PROVISIONS, DEFINITIONS AND PROBATE JURISDICTION OF THE COURT

§ 2.01 Purposes, Rules of Construction, Policies and Definitions

A. PURPOSES AND RULES OF CONSTRUCTION

Article I of the UPC includes introductory provisions that generally define its purposes and rules of construction in conformance with the rules of good statutory draftsmanship. As is customary with uniform laws, it requests that courts liberally construe and apply the UPC in a manner which will best carry out and promote its underlying purposes and policies. [1–102(a)]. In their broadest sense, the most obvious purposes of the UPC are to make uniform and to improve the areas of law and procedure with which it is concerned among the several jurisdictions in the United States. [1–102(b)]. Hallmark principles for accomplishing this meritorious reform include simplification, clarification, efficacy, efficiency and serviceability. [See 1–102(b)(1)–(5)]. Only time and experience with the UPC's provisions will prove whether it can achieve its goals.

The UPC also includes the other housekeeping provisions typically found in modern statutes. These provide that general principles of law and equity are to supplement the UPC's own provisions [1–103; see UTC 106, § 17.01(C) for discussion of a similar provision in the UTC], that provisions held to be invalid are to be severed from those which are valid and effective [1–104], and that if reasonably avoidable, subsequent legislation shall not impliedly repeal Code provisions in whole or in part. [1–105].

B. OVERRIDING POLICIES AND PROVISIONS

Article I of the UPC includes several provisions that have pervasive and overriding application.

1. Fraud

Any person, who is injured by another's fraud perpetrated in connection with any proceeding or filing under the UPC, with the intent of circumventing the UPC's provisions or purposes, may seek and obtain appropriate relief from the perpetrator or may seek and obtain restitution from any person, innocent or otherwise, who benefitted from the fraud. [1–106]. Bona fide purchasers are expressly exempt from such liability, however. When an action is permitted under this provision, a special statute of limitations is substituted for all other statutes of limitation ordinarily applicable. This time limitation period requires that the proceeding be commenced within two years after the discovery of the fraud but if against one who was not a perpetrator of the fraud, no later than five years after the commission of the fraud. Frauds perpetrated against the decedent during the decedent's lifetime are not included within the scope of this provision.

The effect of this provision prevents the UPC's other limitation periods from protecting the fraud perpetrator or gratuitous beneficiaries. [1–106, Comment]. It also creates a remedy that is available directly against the perpetrator and other beneficiaries and that is supplemental to all of the other remedies and protections given under the UPC. An important limitation on the scope of this section is that if there are formal proceedings with notice and hearing before the Court, res judicata may prevent persons who were properly before the Court and subject to the jurisdiction of those proceedings from instituting any actions under it.

2. Perjury for Falsified Documents

In order to discourage misuse of the various UPC's procedures, the penalties of perjury are applicable to any deliberate falsification of any document filed with the Court. [1–310]. The mere filing of an application, petition or demand for notice is deemed to include a verification of its veracity. The threat of perjury prosecution under this provision has broad application. Although perjury penalties will in all likelihood never be strictly or conscientiously enforced, the provision will serve as a psychological bar against misuse of the UPC's procedures.

Significantly, verifications are apparently deemed to be a part of every filing even though the verification itself is absent from the document. This might mean, therefore, that the verification need not even be on the document thereby eliminating the need for notarization of documents filed with the Court. [See 18 Uniform Probate UPC Notes (Joint Editorial Board for the Uniform Probate UPC) 15 (Hereinafter cited as UPC Notes)].

3. Proof of Death or Status

The UPC establishes rules relating to the fact of death or of other status, such as one being missing or detained, because their determination can be a very important question arising during the course of proceedings under the UPC. [1–107]. Generally, the rules of evidence used in the court of general jurisdiction are applicable to determine death in a judicial proceeding. [1–107]. In addition the UPC contains the following specific provisions concerning evidence of death. First, the UPC defines the meaning of death as that determined either (1) by the Uniform Determination of Death Act, or (2) if the enacting state does not have that Act, by a determination in accordance with accepted medical standards that there is an irreversible cessation of all functions of either (a) circulatory and respiratory function, or (b) the entire brain, including the brain stem. [1–107(1)]. Second, a certified or authenticated copy of a death certificate establishes prima facie proof of death, the place, date and time of death and the identity of the decedent provided the certificate appears to have been issued by an official or agency of the purported place of death. [1–107(2)]. Third, a certified or authenticated copy of any record or report of either a domestic or foreign governmental agency establishes prima facie evidence that a person is missing, detained, dead, or alive and of the dates, circumstances, and places disclosed in the document. [1–107(3)]. Fourth, if the prima facie evidence of either the second or the third rules is not available, evidence of death may be proof by any evidence including circumstantial evidence if proof satisfies the clear and convincing evidence standard of proof.

Fifth, when the previous rules do not apply, a person is presumed to be dead if a person has been absent for a continuous period of five years. [1–107(5)]. This presumption applies only if during that time the absent person was not heard from and after diligent search or inquiry no satisfactory explanation is available to explain the absence. Unless evidence can prove that death occurred earlier, the date of death is presumed to be at the end of the five-year period. The question of status concerning whether someone is "missing" is important, for example, when determining whether a conservator or other protective order can be issued to protect that missing person's property. [See 5–401(c)].

Finally, if a certificate that constitutes prima facie evidence under either the second or the third rules mentioned above states a time of death, that time is evidence of the determination whether a person survived another person by 120 hours. [1–107(6); see 2–104 and 2–702; §§ 5.06, 11.02]. If it shows the person survived by the required 120 hours, the time on the certificate is clear and convincing evidence of that survivorship. The timing of death of the person whose death must be survived may be determined by any of the above rules.

4. Cost of Living Adjustment of Certain Dollar Amounts

In 2008 Section 1–109 was added to allow for an automatic adjustment for inflation of the dollar amounts included in Sections 2–102, [2–102A,] 2–202(b), 2–402, 2–403, and 2–405. The purpose is to make it unnecessary in the future for the Uniform Law Commission or individual enacting states to continue to amend the UPC periodically to adjust the dollar amounts for inflation. The Bureau of Labor Statistics of the U.S. Department of Labor reports each January on the CPI (annual average) for the preceding calendar year. The information can be obtained by telephone or on the Bureau's website.

The adjustment is not self-executing. The provision assumes that an appropriate state agency, such as the Department of Revenue, would issue an official cumulative list of the adjusted amounts beginning in January of the year after the effective date of the act. If an enacting state does not have a state agency that could appropriately be assigned the task of issuing updated amounts, the Comment suggest that that state might consider tasking the state supreme court to issue a court rule each year making the appropriate adjustment.

5. Definitions

The UPC contains a large number of definitions that are applicable throughout its content. [1–201]. These definitions are extremely important to an understanding of the UPC and any student of the UPC must gain a working knowledge of them. For the sake of clarity, comprehension and brevity, the meaning of each word will be provided only when the definition is relevant to the discussion in this text. For informational and overview purposes, Chart 2–1 lists them in alphabetical order.

CHART 2–1
GENERAL DEFINITIONS

Agent	Organization
Application	Parent
Beneficiary	Payor
Beneficiary designation	Person
Child	Personal representative
Claims	Petition
Conservator	Proceeding
Court	Property
Descendant	Protected person
Devise	Protective proceeding
Devisee	Record (2008)
Disability	Registrar
Distributee	Security
Estate	Settlement
Exempt property	Sign (2008)
Fiduciary	Special Administrator
Foreign personal representative	State
Formal proceedings	Successor personal representative
Governing instrument	Successors
Guardian	Supervised Administration
Heirs	Survive
Incapacitated person	Testacy proceeding
Informal proceedings	Testator
Interested person	Trust
Issue	Trustee
Joint tenants with the right	Ward
of survivorship	Will
Lease	
Letters	*Definitions for community*
Minor	*property states, only.*
Mortgage	Community property
Nonresident decedent	Separate property

Articles II, III, IV, V and VI also include separate definitions that control in particular sections, parts or articles. [See 2–106, 2–115, 2–120, 2–121, 2–201, 2–603, 2–706, 2–707, 2–709, 2–803, 2–804, 2–1001, 3–916, 4–101, 5–103, 5–501, 6–201, 6–301; see also 1–201, Comment].

The UTC also contains definitions, which are discussed at § 17.01(B).

§ 2.02 Jurisdiction, Venue and Courts

A. JURISDICTION AND MULTIPLE VENUES

The Court under the UPC is given subject matter jurisdiction over all subjects with which the UPC deals including the administration of the decedents' estates, interpretation of wills, determination of heirs and successors, the estates of protected or disabled persons, the protection of disabled persons and trusts. [1–302(a)]. The Court is also empowered to take all "necessary and proper" action for the purpose of administering justice in any matters properly before it. [1–302(b)]. The territorial reach of the Court's jurisdiction is based on one of the following factors: (1) the relevant person was domiciled in the state, (2) the relevant property of a non-domiciliary is located in the state, (3) the relevant property is under the control of a fiduciary who is subject to the laws of the state, or (4) the person, contractual device or fiduciary relationship is within the state. [1–301]. The latter relationships to the state refer respectively to minors or incapacitated persons residing within the state, to the existence of multiple party accounts and security registrations located in the state and to trusts being subject to administration in the state.

The UPC includes a detailed set of provisions dealing with the problems caused by the existence of multiple venues. When two or more courts are appropriate venues, the Court within which the proceeding was first commenced has exclusive right to continue its jurisdiction. [1–303(a)]. Furthermore, any issue concerning the venue must be determined by this Court and must be held in abeyance by any other court. [1–303(b)]. When the Court determines that in the interest of justice venue should be in another court, it may transfer the proceedings to another court of the same state. [1–303(c); see also 3–201(c)]. Although the parties do not need to re-initiate the proceeding when it is transferred under this provision, they will presumably be required to repeat some of the notices. [See 3–705, 3–801].

In addition to the above general provisions on jurisdiction and venue, the UPC includes special subject matter jurisdiction, personal jurisdiction and venue rules for the probate of wills and administration of decedents' estates under Article III [see § 10.02(C)], for the protection of persons under disability and their property under Article V [see § 15.04] and for the administration of trusts under Article VII. [See § 17.03].

B. THE COURT AND REGISTRAR

With respect to matters concerning the courts and practice before them, the UPC is extremely flexible and is designed to work within the framework of the state in which it is adopted. Generally, only two features appear to be essential: (1) the Court must be able to render binding adjudications in any civil litigation to which the fiduciary may be a party and (2) appeals from the Court must go to the same court to which appeals from courts of general jurisdiction go. [See 1–308, 1–309]. In other respects the UPC conforms to the practice and procedure rules of the court of general jurisdiction in the state. [See 1–304 to 1–306].

The UPC creates a new position or office in the Court. This position is called the "Registrar" and the person who holds this title will handle the informal proceedings to establish wills and to appoint personal representatives under Article III. [1–307; see 3–105, 3–303 to 3–311]. The Registrar's functions must be performed either by a judge of the Court or by a person so designated by a court order which must be filed and recorded in the office of the Court.

§ 2.03   Notice and Virtual Representation

A.   NOTICE

Although several provisions contain their own special notice procedures [see, e.g., 3–801 (Notice to Creditors)], the principal method and time for giving notice for a formal proceeding under the Court's exclusive subject matter jurisdiction is contained in the UPC in one inclusive provision. [1–401]. When notice of the time and place of a hearing on a petition for any hearing is necessary under this provision, it must be given to all interested persons or when appropriate to their attorneys. [1–401(a)]. The term "interested person" is broadly defined and basically includes any person with an interest in or against the estate involved in the proceeding. [1–201(24)]. The particular persons, who are considered interested and who require notice, may vary depending on the nature of each proceeding.

Three methods of giving notice of a hearing are provided and any one will, depending on the circumstances, satisfy the notice requirement. If the address and location of the person to be notified is known, then notice may be given either by registered or ordinary first class mail or by personal service. [1–401(a)(1)–(2)]. The mailing or the delivery of the notice must be accomplished at least fourteen days before the hearing date. If the address or identity of any person is unknown, notice must be made by publication once a week for three consecutive weeks in a county newspaper having general circulation. [1–401(a)(3)]. The last published notice must appear at least ten days before the hearing date. When good cause is shown, the Court is given the discretion to provide for a different method or time of giving notice for the hearing. [1–401(b)]. Petitioners must prove on or before the hearing that the appropriate notice was given and must file such proof in the proceeding. [1–401(c)]. Any person, including fiduciaries, may waive the required notice by filing a signed written waiver in the proceeding. [1–402]. Numerous provisions throughout the UPC either expressly or impliedly require use of this notice provision, including those concerned with decedents' estates, guardianships and protective proceedings and trusts. [See, e.g., 3–

106, 3–204, 3–403, 3–414, 3–502, 3–1001, 5–206(b), 5–304(c), 5–405, 7–206].

See 17.01(E) for the UTC treatment of notice. [UTC 109].

B. VIRTUAL REPRESENTATION

When formal judicial proceedings arise involving trusts and estates, it is common to have a large number of persons whose interests may be affected by the proceedings. Frequently these persons are not only numerous but also unknown, unborn or unascertainable. Notwithstanding, their interests need to be protected. It is desirable, therefore, to have some rules that permit certain persons of a large group with a common interest to represent other persons with the same interest. This is referred to as the doctrine of virtual representation. [See UTC 304, 305].

The UPC includes a comprehensive provision explaining the scope and application of the virtual representation doctrine in UPC proceedings. [1–403]. First, the doctrine applies solely to formal judicial proceedings involving trusts or estates and supervised settlements that are subject to the UPC's subject matter jurisdiction. [1–403]. Second, in order for the representation rule to apply, it is required that the pleadings describe the interests affected and give reasonable information to their owners either by name or class or by reference to the instrument creating the interests or in some "other appropriate manner." [1–403(1)]. Third, if the above two requirements are satisfied, the following virtual representation rules are applicable.

1.   Court orders that bind the sole holders or all co-holders of a general power of appointment or power of revocation bind all other persons to the extent that their interests are subject to these powers. [1–403(2)(i); see 1–108; § 9.06(C)].

2.   When no conflict of interest exists between a fiduciary and the persons for whom the fiduciary acts, Court orders binding the fiduciary may under some circumstances bind the person whose estate it controls. [1–403(2)(ii)]. This binding effect may occur between all of the fiduciary relationships dealt with in the UPC, including the conservator-ward, guardian-ward, trustee-beneficiary (in specified situations) [see § 17.03(E)], the personal representative-persons interested in the decedent's undistributed estate, and sometimes even in the parent-child relationships. In 1997, orders against holders of general testamentary power of appointment were made binding against others whose interests are subject to the power. Parents may represent minors who have no appointed conservator or guardian. [1–403(3)].

3.   An unrepresented, unborn or unascertained person is bound by court orders to the extent that person's interest was adequately represented by another participating person who had a substantially identical interest in the proceeding. [1–403(2)(iii)].

The final requirement in order for the above virtual representation rules to take effect is that notice must be given according to Section 1–401 to every interested person, to one of the specifically named persons who can bind other interested persons [1–403(4)(i)], or to all known persons who have interests substantially identical to those of the unborn or unascertained persons and who are not otherwise bound above. [1–403(4)(ii)].

If the Court determines that representation of an interest under the above rules would be inadequate, it has the discretion at any point in the proceedings to appoint a guardian ad litem to represent the interests of any person who is a minor, incapacitated, unborn, unascertained, or whose identity or address is unknown. [1–403(5)]. One guardian ad litem may be appointed to represent several persons or interests if these persons or interests do not between themselves raise conflicts of interests. When the Court exercises its discretion, the reasons for making an appointment of a guardian ad litem must become a part of the record of the proceedings.

See § 17.03 for a discussion of the representation provisions of the UTC. [UTC Ch. 3].

PART TWO

INTESTATE SUCCESSION, WILLS AND DONATIVE TRANSFERS

CHAPTER 3

INTESTATE SUCCESSION AND RELATED CONCEPTS

§ 3.01   Intestate Succession

A.   INTRODUCTION

Studies indicate that a substantial percentage of persons who have accumulated wealth during their lifetime die without creating effective or totally effective inter vivos arrangements and without making effective testamentary instruments for the disposition of their property. When this happens, decedent's property passes by intestate succession according to a statutory estate plan. [See 2–101(a)].

The theoretical purpose of intestate succession statutes is to distribute a decedent's wealth in a pattern that represents a close facsimile to that which an average person would have designed had that person's desires been properly manifested. Obviously, to accomplish this task on a general basis legislatures have developed objective rather than subjective programs that are necessarily subject to debate. Furthermore, any legislation on this matter naturally reflects the attitudes of the legislature of that moment under its contemporary societal ideals and policies. Attitudes change, of course, as these ideas and policies change.

When it comes to an estate planned by operation of law, the state has many options. The extreme systems might run from a system of no inheritance and confiscation of the entire estate by the state to a complex regulatory system that distributes the estate to designated relatives on the basis of need. England has a form of the latter model creating a statutory trust of the inheritable estate for the benefit of certain close relatives including the surviving spouse and minor children. No state in this country, however, has adopted either of these systems.

Intestate inheritance is recognized by all fifty states and territories at least for the benefit of certain relatives. The standard intestacy statute specifically apportions the intestate's property among a list of prioritized relatives. The surviving spouse, descendants and parents of the intestate are the standard preferred beneficiaries. In varying degrees, other ancestors and collateral relations are also protected after the preferred relations. Except for the surviving spouse, inheritance is usually limited to consanguine relations. Occasionally, the surviving spouse's consanguine relations may take if the decedent's consanguine relations cannot. [See 2–103(b); Ark. Code Ann. § 28–9–215]. The relational range of consanguinity necessary in order to take in intestacy varies among the states. Most intestacy statutes protect consanguine relations through grandparents and their descendants. Some even make no express relational cutoff point and if the specified relations in the statute cannot take, pass the intestate's estate to the determinable nearest of kin. All states recognized that the property escheats to the state if no one qualified under the intestacy provisions can take.

In recent times when intestacy statutes have been the subject of legislative reform, several policy disputes have arisen. For example, a policy controversy usually arises over the share of the surviving spouse. This controversy usually relates to the share that the surviving spouse takes when there are surviving descendants of the intestate and when there are no surviving descendants of the intestate but other consanguine relatives of the decedent survive. Many persons have urged that the share of the surviving spouse be enlarged from the share usually provided at common law and in many states, today. The 1969 version of the UPC adopted this approach and the 1990 UPC expands it further. 2008 revisions increased the monetary shares 50 percent and added a new cost of living adjustment section. [1–109].

Another common policy issue concerns the inheritance rights of nonmarital children and their genetic parents. The common law was very restrictive of such rights and the current trend is to eliminate restrictions and to base inheritance on maternity and paternity determinations. The increased use of assisted reproduction technologies has prompted efforts to address the status of children born from assisted reproductive technologies for intestacy purposes. [See Art 2, Subpart 2. Parent–Child Relationship].

B. GENERAL PATTERN

As with the vast majority of intestacy statutes, the UPC distributes the net intestate estate among decedent's relatives according to a set of contingencies. These contingencies divide the relatives into classes which are in turn scaled on a specific priority list. Except as will be explained under the concept of "representation," relatives included in a relational class of persons which is closer to the decedent, take to the exclusion of those in a relational class which is more distant from the decedent. The specific classes of relatives whose members are entitled to take as distributees under the UPC include the decedent's "surviving spouse," "descendants," "parents," "descendants of decedent's parents," "grandparents" and "descendants of grandparents." [2–102, 2–103]. In 2008, certain stepchildren were included in the classes of relatives as a last resort to avoid the intestate estate escheating to the state. [2–103(b)]. The UPC uses the term descendant instead of the term issue. In that the term "issue" has biological connotations, the term "descendant" is more appropriate because the UPC recognizes inheritance rights beyond biological relations, i.e., adoption. [2–102, Comment].

A key term in many of the classes of relatives described as taking a share is the word "descendant." [2–103]. This word is defined to include all of a person's lineal descendants at all generations. [1–201(9)]. Consequently, when the UPC refers to a decedent's descendants, it means the decedent's children, grandchildren, great grandchildren, etc. When it refers to the descendants of the decedent's parents, it means the decedent's siblings (i.e., brothers and sisters), nephews and nieces, grandnephews and grandnieces, etc. [See Chart 3–1]. A reference to the descendants of grandparents, of course, means the decedent's uncles and aunts, first cousins, first cousins once removed in the descendancy, etc.

CHART 3–1

Relationship Diagram

Great Great Grandparent (4)				
Great Great Aunt/Uncle (5)	Great Grandparent (3)			
First Cousin Twice Removed (6)	Great Aunt/Uncle (4)	Grandparent (2)		
Second Cousin Once Removed (7)	First Cousin Once Removed (5)	Aunt/Uncle (3)	Parent (1)	
Third Cousin (8)	*Second Cousin (6)*	*First Cousin (4)*	Sibling (2)	DECEDENT
Third Cousin Once Removed (9)	Second Cousin Once Removed (7)	First Cousin Once Removed (5)	Nephew/ Niece (3)	Child (1)
Third Cousin Twice Removed	Second Cousin Twice Removed (8)	First Cousin Twice Removed (6)	Grand Nephew/ Niece (4)	Grand- child (2)
Third Cousin Three Times Removed (11)	Second Cousin Three Times Removed (9)	First Cousin Three Times Removed (7)	Great Grand Nephew/ Niece (5)	Great Grand- child (3)
Third Cousin Four Times Removed (12)	Second Cousin Four Times Removed (10)	First Cousin Four Times Removed (8)	Great Great Grand Nephew/ Niece (6)	Great Great Grand- child (4)

Note:
a) Full cousins are in bold italics. Cousins above full cousins are "in the ascendancy"; Cousin below full cousins are "in the descendancy."
b) Numbers in parentheses constitute the degree of relationship to Decedent.

Chart 3–1 diagrams a decedent's family tree. The shaded area emphasizes the UPC's relational umbrella of covered relations. This protective umbrella has greater significance under the UPC than merely to take in intestacy. [See, e.g., the UPC's antilapse provision, 2–603; § 7.02].

If none of the above named classes of relatives include one or more persons qualified to take the estate, the UPC provides that the property escheats to the State. [2–105]. This latter contingency means that no matter what the circumstances are when a person dies, the contingencies will adjust and will eventually pass one's intestate property either to some person or persons or to the State.

Significantly, the UPC makes no distinction between real and personal property [1–201(39)] or between the sex of the surviving relatives. In addition, intestate distributions are made only from the net estate after all debts, family protections, taxes and other administration expenses have been paid. [3–807].

Chart 3–2 illustrates the application of the above contingency concept. The vertical left hand column lists the contingencies in order of priority. Note that within each numbered contingency the entire intestate estate is distributed. The top horizontal line designates the various classes of distributees that are relevant in the distribution pattern. The boxes descending in the vertical columns below each of these classes indicate the fraction or amount that persons who come within the classes will share or divide. In each box, the logotype, NS, indicates that no relative of the decedent qualifies within this class of distributees at the moment when the distribution shares are determined, and the logotype, 00, indicates that persons within this class would not take a share even if some of them qualified at the moment when distribution is made.

CHART 3-2

GENERAL PATTERN OF INTERSTATE SUCCESSION UNDER THE UNIFORM PROBATE CODE (2008)

Contingencies	Spouse [2-102, 2-102A]	Descendants [2-102(1)(ii), (3), (4), 2-103(1)]	Parents [2-102(2), 2-103(3)]	Parents' Descendants by Representation [2-103(3)]	Grandparents or their Descendants by Representation [2-103(4)-(5), 2-106(c)] Paternal	Grandparents or their Descendants by Representation [2-103(4)-(5), 2-106(c)] Maternal	Deceased spouses's children by representation [2-103(b)]	State [2-105]
1-A	All	00*	00	00	00	00	00	00
1-B	[$225,000] and ½ remainder	½ remainder**	00	00	00	00	00	00
1-C	[$150,000] and ½ remainder	½ remainder***	00	00	00	00	00	00

UNIFORM PROBATE CODE §§ 2-102, 2-102A, 2-103 (2008)

Chart 3-2

GENERAL PATTERN OF INTESTATE SUCCESSION UNDER THE UNIFORM PROBATE CODE (2008) — CONTINUED

AND	All Community Property						
2	[$300,000] and ¾ Remainder	¾ remainder	00	00	00	00	00
3	NS	NS	00	00	00	00	00
4	All	00	00	00	00	00	00
5	NS	All	00	00	00	00	00
6	NS	NS	All	00	00	00	00
7	NS	NS	NS	½	½	00	00
8	NS	NS	NS	All	NS	00	00
9	NS	NS	NS	NS	All	00	00
10	NS	NS	NS	NS	All	All	00
11	NS	NS	NS	NS	NS	NS	E

LEGEND: NS indicates that no relative of the decedent qualifies within this class of distributees at the time when distribution is determined; 00 indicates that persons within this class can not take a share even if some of them qualify within this class when distribution is made.

* If all of the decedent's surviving descendants are also descendants of the surviving spouse and the surviving spouse has one or more surviving descendants who are not descendants of the decedent.

** If all of decedent's descendants are also the surviving spouse's descendants and no other descendants of the surviving spouse survives the decedent.

*** If all of the decedent's surviving descendants are also descendants of the surviving spouse and the surviving spouse has one or more surviving descendants who are not descendants of the decedent.

C. SHARES OF THE SURVIVING SPOUSE, DESCENDANTS AND OTHER RELATIONS

1. Shares of the Surviving Spouse and Descendants

Under the UPC, depending upon the existence of specified relations to the decedent, a surviving spouse is accorded substantial shares if the decedent dies intestate. [See Chart 3–2]. The maximum share that a surviving spouse will take equals the total net intestate estate and the minimum share equals the first $150,000 of the net estate plus ½ anything exceeding that amount in the estate.

The surviving spouse takes all the intestate estate in two situations. First, the surviving spouse takes all the estate if the decedent is also survived by children who are all children of the decedent and the spouse. [2–102(1)(ii)]. This is a new provision and is derived from several studies that indicate testators usually follow this approach in their wills. Because intestacy portions should closely track the distribution patterns of the typical testator, the findings were incorporated into the UPC. Second, the surviving spouse takes all the estate if the decedent is not survived by descendants and parents notwithstanding other blood relations of the decedent survive. [2–102(1)(I)]. This is in line with the 1969 UPC and the law in many state intestacy statutes.

Between the above two situations lie three special familial circumstances that limit the surviving spouse's share. Notwithstanding the reduction, the share of the surviving spouse is substantial. If decedent's parents survive but no descendants of decedent survive, a surviving spouse takes the first $300,000 of the net estate plus $\frac{3}{4}$ of anything exceeding that amount in the estate. The large monetary prioritized amount insures that surviving spouses will take the entire estate in most cases.

Addressing the phenomenon of growing numbers of multi-relationship children, the UPC reduces the share of a surviving spouse in order to provide for descendants who are not the surviving spouse's descendants. If the decedent is survived by one or more descendants who are also descendants of the surviving spouse and by one or more descendants who are descendants of the surviving spouse but not of the decedent, the surviving spouse takes the first $225,000 of the net estate plus $\frac{1}{2}$ of anything exceeding that amount remaining in the estate. If decedent is survived by one or more descendants who are not descendants of the surviving spouse, the surviving spouse takes the first $150,000 of the net estate plus $\frac{1}{2}$ of anything exceeding that amount in the estate. Both these provision give limited protection in relatively large estates to decedent's descendants of relationships other than the one existing at death.

When it is realized that the above share of the surviving spouse is in addition to the family protection [see § 5.02] and other nonprobate assets that pass to the spouse, it is clear that the UPC will pass all of an intestate's estate in the predominant number of cases.

If no spouse survives but descendants of decedent survive, the descendants take the entire estate by representation. [2–103(1); see § 3.01(D)].

2. Shares of Other Relatives

If an intestate dies and is not survived by a spouse or descendants, the entire net estate passes to the decedent's parents equally or if only one survives, to the survivor. [2–103(a)(2)]. If both parents fail to survive, the estate passes to their descendants by representation. [2–103(a)(3)]. If an intestate dies and is not survived by a spouse, descendants, decedent's parents or their descendants, the entire net estate passes to the decedent's grandparents or their descendants by representation. [2–103(a)(5)]. Grandparental shares are divided into maternal and paternal categories if one of more appropriate persons in both categories survive decedent. One-half passes to the maternal grandparents or their descendants by representation and the other one-half passes to the paternal grandparents or their descendants by representation. All surviving grandparents share equally the share passing in the appropriate category. Any surviving grandparent in either category takes to the exclusion of any surviving descendants of either grandparent in that category. If no grandparent survives in one category, the share of that category passes to the descendants of either grandparent in that category. If neither grandparent nor any of their descendants survive in one category, the share for that category passes in a similar manner to the grandparents or their descendants by representation in the other category.

In a new subsection added in 2008, if no grandparents or their descendants can take, descendants of a deceased spouse or deceased spouses, but who are not also descendants of the intestate, take by representation. [2–103(b)]. These descendants are the decedent's step children and are not blood relatives. It adds one more class of relatives in order to avoid escheat.

3. Escheat

An important variation between the UPC and the law in many non-UPC states concerns the issue of distant relatives and their intestate inheritance rights. The UPC provides that the property will escheat to the State if there are no takers who qualify under its specific intestacy pattern. [2–105]. Consequently, decedent's grandparents and their descendants are the most distant relatives who can inherit under the UPC. [2–103]. [See highlighted portion of Chart 3–1]. This feature is designed not only to simplify proof of relationship but also to cut off so-called "laughing heirs" who, as very distant relatives, are far beyond the normal confines of the modern family unit and the probable donative intent of the decedent. It probably does not conform to the desires of the typical person because most persons, if they think about the issue, do not want property to pass to the state. Of course, a person is able to benefit such distant relatives if that person so provides in a valid will or will substitute. The relational limitation on inheritance has been held valid against an equal protection contention by an intestate's second cousin and closest heir. [Estate of Jurek v. State, 428 N.W.2d 774 (Mich.App.1988)].

4. Factual Illustrations
CHART 3–3
THE STAIRS OF INHERITANCE

Assumption:	In all of the following hypotheticals assume decedent, D, died intestate and the problem is to determine the respective shares of the named surviving persons. In all hypotheticals only D's closest relations are mentioned.
Hypothetical 1:	D is survived by spouse, S, and two children, A and B, who are children of both D and S.
Answer:	S takes the entire estate.
Hypothetical 2:	D is survived by spouse, S, and two grandchildren, G1 and G2, who are descendants of both D and S.
Answer:	S takes the entire estate.
Hypothetical 3:	D is survived by spouse, S, and two children, A and B; A is D's child by a prior relationship and B is a child of both D and S.
Answer:	S takes the first [$150,000] and ½ of the balance of the estate; A and B share equally the other ½ balance of the estate.
Hypothetical 4:	D is survived by spouse, S, and two grandchildren, G1 and G2, who are descendants of both D and S. G1 is D's grandchild by a prior relationship and G2 is D's grandchild of both D and S.
Answer:	S takes the first [$150,000] and ½ of the balance of the estate; G1 and G2 share equally the other ½ balance of the estate by representation.*

---

* The concept of representation is defined in the Code. [2–106; see § 3.01(D)].

Hypothetical 5:	D is survived by spouse, S, and two children, A and B, who are children of both D and S; D is also survived by C who is S' child from a prior relationship.
Answer:	S takes the first [$225,000] and ½ of the balance of the estate; A and B share equally the other ½ balance of the estate. C takes nothing directly from D's estate.
Hypothetical 6:	D is survived by spouse, S, and children, A, B, and C. A is D's child by a prior relationship, B is a child of both D and S. C is S' child from a prior relationship.
Answer:	S takes the first [$150,000] and ½ of the balance of the estate; A and B share equally the other ½ balance of the estate. C takes nothing directly from D's estate.
Hypothetical 7:	D is survived by spouse, S, and one or both parents but no descendants.
Answer:	S takes the first [$300,000] and ¾ of the balance of the estate; D's surviving parents share equally, or if only one survives the survivor takes, the ¼ balance of the estate.
Hypothetical 8:	D is survived by one or more descendants and one or more parents; no spouse survives.
Answer:	D's surviving descendants take the entire estate by representation. D' surviving parents take nothing from the estate.

| Hypothetical 9: | D is survived by one or more parents and one or more descendants of D's parents. |
| Answer: | D's surviving parents share equally, or if only one survives the survivor takes, the entire estate;

The descendants of D's parents take nothing from D's estate. |

| Additional Assumption: | The following hypotheticals assume that no spouse, descendants or parents of the D survived. |

| Hypothetical 10: | D is survived by one or more descendants of D's parents. |
| Answer: | The descendants of D's parents take by representation. |

| Hypothetical 11: | D is survived by one or more maternal grandparents and one or more paternal grandparents and one or more descendants of both maternal and paternal grandparents. |
| Answer: | D's surviving maternal grandparents share equally, or if only one survives the survivor takes, $\frac{1}{2}$ the estate;

D's surviving paternal grandparents share equally, or if only one survives the survivor takes, $\frac{1}{2}$ the estate;

None of the descendants' of the grandparents take from the estate. |

| Hypothetical 12: | D is survived by one or more maternal grandparents, one or more descendants of maternal grandparents, and one or more descendants of paternal grandparents but no paternal grandparents. |
| Answer: | D's surviving maternal grandparents share equally, or if only one survives the survivor takes, $\frac{1}{2}$ the estate; |

The descendants of paternal
grandparents take ½ of the estate by representation;

None of the descendants of maternal grandparents take from
the estate.

Hypothetical 13: D is survived by one of more descendants of both the maternal and the
paternal grandparents but no maternal
or paternal grandparent survives.

Answer: Descendants of the maternal
grandparents take ½ the estate
by representation;

Descendants of the paternal
grandparents take ½ the estate
by representation.

Hypothetical 14: D is survived by one or more maternal
grandparents but no paternal grand-
parents or descendants of paternal
grandparents.

Answer: D's surviving maternal grandparents share equally, or if only
one survives the survivor
takes, the entire estate;

Hypothetical 15: D is survived by one or more descendants of maternal grandparents but no
maternal grandparents and no paternal grandparents or descendants of paternal grandparents.

Answer: D's surviving descendants of the
maternal grandparents take
the entire estate by representation.

Hypothetical 16: D is survived by one or more descendants of paternal grandparents but no
paternal grandparents and no maternal grandparents or descendants of
maternal grandparents.

Answer: D's surviving descendants of the
paternal grandparents take
the entire estate by representation.

| Hypothetical 17: | D is survived by great-grandparents or descendants of great-grandparents or both. D is also survived by descendants of a deceased spouse to whom the D was married at the time of the spouses's death. |
| Answer: | The spouse's descendants (Decedent's step children) take the entire estate by representation. |

| Hypothetical 18: | D is survived by great-grandparents or descendants of great-grandparents or both. |
| Answer: | The estate escheats to the state. |

D. DESCENDANTS AND REPRESENTATION

When the UPC designates the descendants of a class of relatives as the takers in intestacy, it is frequently necessary to reclassify these descendants into two sub-classifications which further describe their relationship to the decedent. These subclassifications can be visualized schematically on vertical and horizontal graphic formats. The vertical classification refers to a descendant's family tree or stocks of lineal ancestors and descendants. The horizontal classification refers to a descendant's degree of relationship to the decedent. Each degree of relationship is a separate generation. These subclassifications can be better understood by examining Charts 3–4 and 3–5.

CHART 3–4

STOCKS IDENTIFICATION

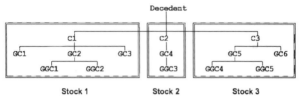

Stock 1   **Stock 2**   **Stock 3**

[LEGEND: C = Children; GC = Grandchildren; GGC = Great Grandchildren]

CHART 3–5

GENERATION IDENTIFICATION

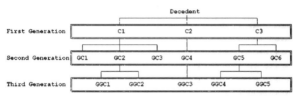

[LEGEND:C = Children; GC = Grandchildren; GGC = Great Grandchildren]

Because these charts deal with a decedent's own descendants, the starting point for examining the vertical-horizontal sub-classifications is with the decedent's three children. As Chart 3–4 indicates vertically, each child constitutes a separate stock within which that child's own descendant are listed and graphed on a generation by generation basis. Child C1, grandchildren GC1, GC2, GC3, and their more remote descendants constitute one stock. (Stock 1). The same description is applicable to C2 and C3 and their respective descendants. (Stocks 2 and 3). As

Chart 3–5 indicates horizontally, all of the decedent's descendants are classified also by degree or generation. Under this sub-classification the children constitute a separate generation, the grandchildren another and each generation of more remote descendants other generations. Therefore, C1, C2 and C3 are all in the same horizontal class, i.e., the First Generation. All the grandchildren would also constitute a horizontal class of their own, i.e., the Second Generation. The same type of vertical and horizontal analysis is also relevant to decedent's collateral relatives. [See Chart 3–1]. By using these two classification systems, it is possible under the UPC to determine the descendants who are to take and their individual shares.

Two general principles are important in the application of the above sub-classifications. First, with respect to descendants in the same stock, descendants of more remote degree from the decedent cannot inherit if their ancestor, who is related in a closer degree to the decedent, can take. In other words, using Chart 3–4 again as an example, GC1 will not be able to take anything by intestacy if C1 can take. The same rule would apply to the other grandchildren if their respective ancestor is able to take. Second, descendants of more remote degree from the decedent can inherit if their ancestor, who is related in a closer degree, cannot take even though there are other descendants of closer degree. In other words, using Chart 3–4 again as an example, GC1 will be able to take by intestacy if C1 can not take. GC1 can take even if C2 and C3 can take because GC1 is allowed to represent GC1's ancestor.

This is basically the application of the doctrine of "representation."

The concept of representation is recognized in some form or another in all common law jurisdictions. As indicated, it permits persons who are of more remote degree of kinship to an intestate to take some share from the estate even though there are relatives of closer degree of kinship to the intestate. Unfortunately, understanding the basic concept does not adequately explain what share each relative will take. Neither the commonly used terms of "per capita" and "per stirpes," nor the many statutory variations have adequately or consistently explained the meaning of the concept. The most common problem has been the determination of the generation which is to be considered the root generation for purposes of setting the stock shares of the more remote relatives who are able to represent their ancestors. For example, under a common but not uniform interpretation of the words "per stirpes," this root generation was always the generation closest in degree of relationship to the decedent even if none of those in the closest degree were able to take.

The antithesis of representation is a system of pure per capita with no representation. This system provides that all persons of the same degree of relationship who are in the closest degree relationship take an equal share. Descendants of the relation are not allowed to represent the ancestor. A pure per capita without representation system is not applicable in any state to resolve intestate inheritance issues of descendants of the decedent but has been used in some states to resolve inheritance issues in regard to distant collateral relations.

With the caveat that there are many variations, the concept of representation has been defined in three basic ways. For convenience, they will be call per stirpes, per capita with per capita representation, and per capita at each generation.

Per stirpes: Under a per stirpes system, the initial division of the estate is made at the generation nearest to the decedent, regardless of whether there are any members of that generation who are alive. The number of primary shares is the number of living persons in that nearest generation plus the number of deceased persons who themselves have living descendants. The latter are permitted to represent their ancestor.

Per capita with per capita representation: Under a per capita with per capita representation, the initial division of the estate is made at the first generation which left a living member. Representation is recognized for living descendants of that generation. The number of primary shares is the number of living persons in the first generation which has a surviving member, plus the number of deceased persons in that generation who have descendants who survive. The same approach is taken in dividing the share of each deceased member of that generation who leaves descendants surviving. This was the system adopted in the 1969 UPC.

Per capita at each generation: Under a per capita at each generation system, the estate is divided into primary shares at the first generation which contains one or more living members. Representation is recognized for living descendants of this generation. After the living members are allocated their shares, the remaining shares are combined and divided in the same way among the surviving descendants of the deceased descendants of the previous generation and so on. The UPC now officially adopts this system. [2–106].

Using Chart 3–4, the following example contrasts the three approaches. If C2 and C3 are alive, C1 is deceased and all grandchildren are alive, all three systems will distribute among the descendants in the same manner: the portion that the descendants receive will be divided into three stocks with C2 and C3 each receiving one-third and the grandchildren of C1 dividing their ancestor's one-third stock share equally. Accordingly, GC1, GC2 and GC3 will each receive one-third of one-third or one-ninth. None of the grandchildren (C2 and C3's children) will share in the estate because their respective ancestors, C2 or C3, survived and took their shares.

If all of the children (C1, C2 and C3) are dead, however, the per stirpes system will divide it differently from the other two systems. Here, per stirpes continues to designate the children as the root generation; consequently, the portion will be divided into three stocks again and the grandchildren of each child would divide their one-third stock equally. GC4 will obviously receive more than the others because there is no one else with whom to divide the one-third stock share. Under per capita with per capita representation and per capita at each generation, the distributable portion will be divided equally to each grandchild. Because all takers are of the same degree of relationship to the decedent, these systems ignore the stocks involved and distribute the estate on a per capita basis.

There are circumstances where per capita with per capita representation will operate in the same way as per stirpes, but per capita at each generation will be different. Generally, this will occur when there are three or more persons in a generation, of which one or more survived the decedent but two or more failed to survive leaving representatives.

Using Chart 3–4, presume that C3 survived but that C1 and C2 are deceased. As explained above under both the per stirpes and per capita with per capita representation systems, the distributable portion will be divided into three stock shares. C3 receives a full one-third, and the children of each deceased child (C1 and C2) divide their ancestor's one-third stock share. GC1, GC2 and GC3 take one-third of one-third or one-ninth and GC4 takes a full one-third. If the per capita at each generation method applied, the distributable portion is also divided into thirds and C3 would receive the one-third. The remaining two stock shares, however, are combined together and the children of the deceased children, C1 and C2, each share equally in the remaining two-thirds of the estate. In other words, rather than retaining the stock shares and dividing these shares depending on how many children each represented ancestor had, all of the persons in the same generation always receive an equal share. In our example, each grandchild representing an ancestor receives one-fourth of two-thirds or one-sixth. If several of these grandchildren are also unable to take and if they left surviving descendants, the same procedure is followed again by combining all of the shares for the deceased grandchildren into one share and then by dividing it equally among all of the great grandchildren who represent their ancestors.

The foundation for using the per capita at each generation system, lies in the belief that most decedents, if they thought about it, desire to divide the estate equally among living relatives of equal degree but to favor a living relative of a closer degree. [See 2–106, Comment]. The importance of the matter is relevant only when the descendants are of unequal degree. A notable feature of the per capita at each generation method is that it never allows a person of more remote degree to inherit more than a person of closer degree. In addition, the UPC carefully avoids the problem of share manipulation through the use of disclaimers. For example, in the last hypothetical, if C3 had three or more children or descendants of children, could C3, by disclaiming the share, cause a larger share to pass to C3's descendants than C3 would take directly? The UPC prohibits this because takers from disclaimant only receive the share the disclaimant would have received. [See § 9.02].

Chart 3–6 provides another hypothetical and its resolution under the most common representation methods including the ones discussed above.

It is important to emphasize that although the examples discussed were concerned with the decedent's own descendants, the UPC's methods are equally applicable to representation determinations concerning the descendants of decedent's parents or grandparents.

Chart 3–6
Representation Hypothetical and Resolution

Graphic Problem

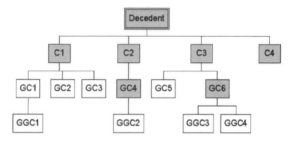

[LEGEND: C = Children; GC = Grandchildren; GGC = Great
            Grandchildren; Shaded = Deceased]

1. Assumptions and Problem
    a. Decedent is predeceased by the following: C1, C2, C3, C4,
        GC4, and GC6. Assume the net estate is valued at
        $108,000. Of the surviving descendants, who, in what
        fractions and amounts, will take under:
        i.   Per stirpes;
        ii.   Per capita without representation;
        iii. Per capita with per capita representation; and,
        iv.   Per capita at each generation. [2-106].

2. **Problem Resolutions**

Answers in Fractions		GC1	GC2	GC3	GC5	GCG1	GGC2	GGC3	GGC4
1.	Per Stirpes	1/9	1/9	1/9	1/6	0	1/3	1/12	1/12
2.	Per Capita without representati on	1/4	1/4	1/4	1/4	0	-0-	-0-	-0-
3.	Per capita with per capita representati on	1/6	1/6	1/6	1/6	0	1/6	1/12	1/12
4.	Per Capita at each generation [2-106]	1/6	1/6	1/6	1/6	0	1/9	1/9	1/9

3. **Fractions converted to Dollars**
   - a. 1/3   = $36,000
   - b. 1/4   = $27,000
   - c. 1/6   = $18,000
   - d. 1/9   = $12,000
   - e. 1/12   = $9,000

4. **Comments:**
   - a. GGC1 Takes nothing under all of the systems because that person's ancestor survived and took a share.
   - b. C4 does not figure into any of the problems because C$ predeceased Decedent and did not leave descendants who survived Decedent.

§ 3.02   Determination of Status

A.   INTRODUCTION TO STATUS

The UPC describes its intestate succession beneficiaries in terms of relational classification including
"parent," "grandparent," "descendant," "heirs"
and "surviving spouse." For distribution calculation
purposes, it is necessary to identify the person or
persons who qualify as members of these classifica-
tions. This determination is a problem of status.

Because of the importance of this problem for intestate succession and other related purposes, the UPC contains several specific provisions concerning the status of step-descendants, step-ancestors, half-bloods, posthumous heirs, adopted persons, persons born out of wedlock, persons conceived through assisted reproduction methods and spouses.

The common thread between these distinct categories is the reference to inheritance by, from and through a person. Using the Chart 3–7, if by, from and through inheritance is applicable, there is inheritance by C from P and through P from P's other descendants and PR, P's ancestors and collateral relations: conversely, there is inheritance by P from C and through C from CI, C's descendants.

CHART 3–7
BY, FROM AND THROUGH

PR	PR	=	Parents' Relations
P	P	=	Parents
C	C	=	Child with Status Concern
CD	CD	=	Child's Descendants

B. PARENT–CHILD RELATIONSHIPS

1. Introduction to the Parent–Child Relationship

The 2008 amendments to the UPC substantially reorganized, expanded and rewrote the sections concerning the issue whether one was a child or a parent for intestate succession purposes. The key to inheritance rights is whether a parent-child relationship exists. If under the provisions of the UPC, a parent-child relationship exists or is established, "the parent is a parent of the child and the child is a child of the parent for the purpose of intestate succession." [2–116]. There are exceptions that will be mentioned. [See § 3.02(B)(5)].

The parent-child relationship or parentage may be defined or established under the relevant state law, such as the Uniform Parentage Act [UPA], approved by the Uniform Law Commission in 1973, substantially revised in 2000 and amended in 2002. [UPA (2002); Susan N. Gary, We Are Family at 171]. The UPA defines "parent-child relationship" to mean the legal relationship between a parent and child and sets forth comprehensive rules for determining who should be treated as the legal parents of a child. [See UPA § 102(14)].

2. Adopted Persons

One's inclusion as a member of a relational classification may be based upon adoption. The issue of the consequences of an adoption has been a common subject of inheritance legislation. The legislation throughout the fifty-plus jurisdictions in this country varies in scope and content. The UPC, as revised in 2008, includes provisions for adopted persons that attempt to deal with the primary issues faced from an inheritance standpoint. [2–119–19]. The UPC does not define what adopted means. Assumably, it refers to a court proceeding set out in other statutes of the enacting jurisdiction. The question whether relationships of persons in the nature of adopted relationships will satisfy this provision is also unanswered by the UPC. Concepts of equitable adoption and other similar remedial inheritance devices would have to be developed by the courts aside from the specific terms of the UPC. [See, e.g., Atkinson, Wills § 23, at pp. 91–92]. The UPC specifically states its provisions do not affect the equitable adoption doctrine. [2–122]

The UPC recognizes that there are two primary types of adoption circumstances. For purposes of convenience these types might be called the "new family adoption," and the "stepparent adoption." They will be discussed separately.

New Family Adoption: The "new family adoption," concerns the situation where a genetic parent or both genetic parents voluntarily put their child up for adoption and an entirely new family, usually a husband and wife, adopt this child. [2–118(a), 2–115(5)–(7) (Definitions of genetic relationships)]. In this situation, the UPC adopts the policy of severing the relationship of the adopted child from that child's genetic parents [2–119(a)]: it grafts a new relationship between the adopted child and the adopting parents for inheritance purposes. [See Chart 3–8]. Under this analysis, the adopted person inherits by, from and through that person's adopting parents and vice-versa.* [2–118(a)]. On the other hand, no by, from or through inheritance rights continue between the adopted child and the genetic parents or vice-versa. [2–119(a)]. A total severance of the inheritance relationship is accomplished.

Using Chart 3–8 for reference, if any of AC's adopted family died intestate and AC was entitled to a share, AC, or AC's descendants if AC did not survive, inherit from AC's adopting parents, AP, and from the adopting parents' relations through AP if AP did not survive. The reverse is also applicable. If AC or AC's descendants died, AP would inherit from AC and from AC's descendants through AC if AC did not survive. In addition AP's other relations would inherit from AC through AP if AP did not survive. In the new family adoption situation, however, inheritance rights between AC and AC's genetic parents, NP, are severed. AC will not inherit from or through NP and NP will not inherit from or through AC.

* The 2008 added a provision that treats the adopted person as a child of an adopting parent who dies prior to the completion of the adoption processes if the processes are completed by the surviving adopting parent. [2–118(b)].

CHART 3–8
ADOPTED PERSON'S FAMILY TREE
NEW FAMILY ADOPTION

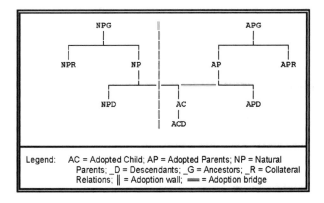

Legend: AC = Adopted Child; AP = Adopted Parents; NP = Natural
          Parents; _D = Descendants; _G = Ancestors; _R = Collateral
          Relations; ‖ = Adoption wall; ═ = Adoption bridge

Stepparent Adoption: The "stepparent adoption" is a more complex situation and requires greater elaboration from an inheritance standpoint. This type of adoption concerns the situation where one of the genetic parents continues as a normal custodial parent of the child, a new adopting parent or non-genetic parent adopts this child, and the other genetic parent is dead or continues in a noncustodial relationship. [See Chart 3–9]. In this situation, the UPC does not completely sever inheritance possibilities between the child and either of the child's genetic parents and their relations. [2–119(b)]. The child is permitted to inherit by, from and through the adopting parent and both of the genetic parents. The adopting parent (and that parent's family) inherit by, from and through the child. The child's genetic parent (and that parent's family) who has custody of the child and who married the adopting parent inherits by, from and through the child. Although the section is not as clear as it could be, its intent is to sever the relationship between the adopted child and the noncustodial genetic parents and that parent's family for purposes of inheritance by the other genetic parent and his or her relatives from or through the adopted child. [2–119(b)(2)].

CHART 3–9
ADOPTED PERSON'S FAMILY TREE

Stepparent Adoption

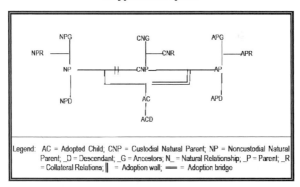

Legend: AC = Adopted Child; CNP = Custodial Natural Parent; NP = Noncustodial Natural Parent; _D = Descendant; _G = Ancestors; N_ = Natural Relationship; _P = Parent; _R = Collateral Relations; ‖ = Adoption wall; ═ = Adoption bridge

Using Chart 3–9 for reference, AC, who has been adopted by a new spouse, will inherit from three parents: the two genetic parents, CNP and NP, and the adopting parent, AP. AC is capable of inheriting from relatives of any of the three parents through the parent if any or all of these parents failed to survive. The adopting parent, AP, and the genetic parent, CNP, inherit from and through AC. Considered through the viewpoint of the adopted child, these provisions seem reasonable. Neither NP nor NP's relations will inherit from AC.

Special Situations: The 2008 amendments added two provisions that allow an adopted person to inherit from the non adopting genetic parent but not vice versa, if the adopted person is adopted by a relative of a genetic parent or the spouse or surviving spouse of a relative of a genetic parent [2–119(c)], or if the adoption occurs after the death of both genetic parents. [2–119(d)]. The parents of a parent-child relationship established between a child of assisted reproduction or a gestational child are treated the same as genetic parents when stepparent adoptions are concerned. [2–119(e)].

3. Afterborn (Posthumous) Persons

State inheritance laws have long recognized that a biological father may die while the woman who is carrying his child is pregnant. Inheritance statutes generally allow posthumous children (children born after decedent's death) to inherit from the parent or other relatives. Under the UPC, individuals who were conceived before the decedent's death but born after it, inherit the same as if they had been born during the decedent's lifetime. [2–104(a)(2)]. In order to qualify for inheritance status, it must be established by clear and convince evidence that the posthumous person lived 120 hours or more after the child's birth. The only relatives who might be able to fall within this category for intestacy purposes would be either decedent's descendants, parents' descendants or grandparents' descendants.

4. Nonmarital Issue

States have typically had special statutes dealing with the status of persons born out of wedlock or, using current terminology, nonmarital persons. [Atkinson, Wills § 22]. Although these statutes vary greatly in scope and context, generally they deal with inheritance by, from and through the parent and the nonmarital person. Recent judicial decisions have caused many states to review their present law.

The UPC provides that the marital status of parents as far as their children are concerned is irrelevant for inheritance purposes. [2–117]. In other words, within the meaning of the intestacy laws for purposes of determining succession, a nonmarital child inherits by, through, and from genetic parents so long as the parent and child relationship can be established. Inheritance from or through the child by a genetic parent or that parent's kindred is recognized unless inheritance is barred. [See 2–114; § 3.02(B)(5)].

5. Assisted Reproduction

Because of advances concerning assisted reproductive technology, the determination of parentage is substantially more complicated than in the past. The Uniform Parentage Act (2000 as amended in 2002) has provisions dealing with the matter. The UPA provides rules to determine legal parents in order to facilitate child support and to provide clear rules for determining who will make decisions about a child's welfare. The UPA, if adopted in a state, will define the parent-child relationship for all purposes in the state, unless the law of the state provides otherwise. [UPA § 203]. If adopted by a state, the 2008 UPC Amendments provide otherwise and will govern for intestacy purposes. There are some differences between the two uniform acts. [See Gary, We Are Family].

Under the UPC, assisted reproduction includes any method "of causing pregnancy other than sexual intercourse." [2–115(2)]. Modern technology has made it possible to use a variety of impregnation techniques. A wide range of scenarios are also possible. Stored gametic material can be used that may be from the intended parent or from a donor. A surrogate mother may help a couple create a child under a gestational agreement. A surviving spouse or partner may use the deceased spouse or partner's stored gametic material to conceive a child. Resolving how these procedures and circumstances affect intestacy and other property transfer methods has become more important as the number of cases increase. [Kurtz & Waggoner, The UPC Addresses the Class-gift and Intestacy Rights].

Chart 3–10
SOURCES, METHODS, SCENARIOS

CHART 3-10
SOURCES, METHODS, SCENARIOS

Sources of Gamete Material	Methods of Assisted Reproduction	Pregnancy Scenarios
Donation of eggs or sperm	Intrauterine insemination (previously and sometimes currently called artificial insemination).	The woman who becomes pregnant by one of these technologies may: intend to be the child's mother.
The sperm that fertilizes the egg may be	In-vitro fertilization.	be married to a man or a woman.
the sperm of a man who intends to be the child's father or	Intracytoplasmic sperm injection.	be in a civil union or domestic partnership with another woman.
the sperm of a third-party donor who has no such intention and probably was compensated for making the donation.	Donation of embryos (fertilized egg) Often frozen for later transfer.	may be unmarried with or without a partner of the same or opposite sex.
The egg that is fertilized may be		may be a surrogate who agreed to bear the child
the egg of a woman who intends to be the child's mother or		for a married or unmarried couple of the same or opposite sex, or
the egg of a third-party donor who has no such intention and probably was compensated for making the donation.		for an unpartnered man or woman.

New Section 2–120 deals with the inheritance rights of children conceived by assisted reproduction. New Section 2–121 deals with children born to gestational (surrogate) carriers. Both are complex and inherently intertwined into the rapidly changing medical area of reproduction technology. Modern reproductive technology will continue to change, at a pace more quickly than and in ways not yet imaginable.

The issues addressed by these sections are: who are the parents, both mother and father; what facts will presume parentage; what evidence is necessary to establish consent; and who are not parents. Although important in the vast majority of cases, the genetic origin of the child is not always important or even relevant. It is not necessary to find a mother and a father in each scenario. The key issue is whether a parent-child relationship is established. If women are always "mothers" and men are always "fathers," under the UPC assisted reproduction provisions, a child could have two "mothers" and no "father" or vice versa because of the circumstances. Under this system, a child can have more than two parents.

The drafters determined that it was necessary to take a global approach to the matter. Provisions are written anticipating a wide number of circumstances. It would be difficult to specifically list and explain every application to every circumstance. Assisted reproduction is broadly defined to include all human reproduction methods except sexual intercourse. The rules relate to the parties, their intent and conduct, not to the reproduction procedure used.

The goal is to provide a set of rules that will identify the proper person who should be considered to be parent or the parents of an assisted reproduction child and to appropriately apply the intestacy rules to that identified parent-child relationship. Intestate inheritance can be from or though the parent, to or through the child but also from or though the child, and to or through the parent.

In applying the provisions one must identify that there is an assisted reproduction child [ARC] involved in the steps of intestate inheritance. The most common case is that the ARC is an alleged child of the intestate. But, because inheritance is through the child, the child may be a link to other relatives who may take by intestacy. For example, can an ARC's child inherit by intestacy from ARC's parent's parent, assuming the ARC and putative parent predeceased the intestate? Yes, if a parent-child relationship is found between ARC and the putative parent. It matters not what method of assisted reproduction was used.

It needs to be emphasized that in a large majority of cases, the intricacies of these provisions will not be applicable. Where the parents are genetically the mother and father of the child, the method of impregnation is not going to be important. A parent-child relationship between this child and the genetic father and mother will be confirmed. If the parents are married, then parentage will be presumed. The difficult cases concern situations that go outside this scenario, e.g., where one or both of the parents are not the genetic parents or the parents are not spouses.

The UPC identifies a number of individuals who may be involved in the birth of an assisted reproduction child. These include:

1) The woman who gives birth to the child (the "birth mother") [2–120(a)(1)]. This woman may or may not be the genetic mother of the child. The term "birth mother" does not include a "gestational carrier."

2) A "gestational carrier" is a woman who is not intended to be the child's parent but who carries and gives birth to the child under an agreement with the intended parent or parents. [2–121].

3) A spouse who provides genetic material (sperm or eggs) for assisted reproduction by the other spouse. [2–120(a)(3)(A)].

4) A "third-party donor" of genetic material who will not have a parent-child relationship with the child. [2–120(a)(3)].

5) An individual other than the birth mother who consented to assisted reproduction by the birth mother and intended to be the other parent of the child. [2–120(f)].

No Parent–Child Relationship Exists: The UPC identifies several situations where a parent-child relationship is not established. A parent-child relationship does **not** exist between an assisted reproduction child and (1) a third-party donor who provides eggs or sperm for assisted reproduction [2–120(b)]; (2) a former spouse of the birth mother unless the former spouse had consented to be treated as the child's parent even if a divorce occurred before the placement of sperm, eggs or embryos; [2–120(I)]; and, (3) an individual who, in a record.

withdraws consent to assisted reproduction before placement of eggs, sperm, or embryos. [2–120(j)].

Parent–Child Relationship Exists: There are several situations where a parent-child relationship is declared to exist. A parent-child relationship exists between an assisted reproduction child and (1) the child's birth mother [2–120(c)]; (2) the husband of the child's birth mother if the husband, during his lifetime, provided the sperm that the birth mother used for assisted reproduction. [2–120(d)]; and (3) an individual other than the birth mother who consented to assisted reproduction by the birth mother with intent to be treated as the other parent of the child. [2–120(f)]. In the third category, although a parent-child relationship exists and inheritance is recognized to and through the child, inheritance by and through the intended parent may be limited. In order for that individual and any relative of that individual (who is not also a relative of the birth mother) to inherit from or through the child, that individual must have signed a record evidencing the intent to be treated as the parent within two years after the birth of the child or functioned as a parent of the child before the child reached [18] years of age. [2–120(g)]. "Functioned as a parent of the child" is defined in the UPC. [2–115(4)].

Parent–Child Relationship Presumptions: A presumption of a parent-child relationship exists between an assisted reproduction child and (1) an individual other than the birth mother who is identified on a birth certificate as the other parent, [2–120(e)]; (2) the birth mother's spouse if no divorce proceeding is pending, in the absence of clear and convincing evidence to the contrary; [2–120(h)(1)];

(3) the birth mother's deceased spouse if no divorce proceeding was pending, in the absence of clear and convincing evidence to the contrary. [2–120(h)(2)].

Consent and Intent: An individual will be declared a parent if that individual consented to assisted reproduction by the birth mother with intent to be treated as the other parent of the child. Consent to assisted reproduction by the birth mother with intent to be treated as the other parent of the child is established if the individual: (1) signed a record that evidences the individual's consent; [2–120(f)(1)]; (2) considering all the facts and circumstances, functioned as a parent of the child no later than two years after the child's birth; [2–120(f)(2)(A)]; (3) intended to function as a parent of the child no later than two years after the child's birth but was prevented from carrying out that intent by death, incapacity, or other circumstances; [2–120(f)(2)(B)]; or, (4) intended to be treated as a parent of a posthumously conceived child, if that intent is established by clear and convincing evidence. [2–120(f)(2)(C)].

Gestational Carrier: A gestational carrier is a woman who, under an agreement, agrees to carry a child for another person or persons. The latter are the intended parents. [2–121(a)(1)]. The gestational carrier is not the intended parent. The gestational child's genetic relationship to the gestational carrier or the intended parents is not determinative. Generally, there is a formal agreement that sets out the terms of the arrangement. These are commonly called surrogacy agreements.

The parent-child relationships related to these agreements can be a problem. If everything is normal, the intended parent(s) are the parents of the child and the gestational carrier is not. The gestational carrier will be found to be the parent only if a court under § 807 of the Uniform Parentage Act declares that existence or, if she is the child's genetic mother [2–115(6)] and a parent-child relationship does not exist under section 2–121 with an individual other than the gestational carrier. [2–121(c)]. A court order prevails over all the other rules of this section. The UPC takes no position on the legality of gestation agreements.

Posthumously Conceived Child: Sometimes a child is not even conceived until after one of the child's genetic parents has died. This situation occurs most commonly in the case of young husbands who are diagnosed with cancer and are encouraged by their doctors to bank sperm prior to undergoing chemotherapy. If the husband dies, the widow may still choose to become impregnated with her deceased spouse's sperm. The parent-child relationship for a posthumously conceived child can be established in the absence of a signed record, if the decedent's intent to be treated as a parent is shown by clear and convincing evidence. [2–120(f)(2)(C)]. Despite the evidence of intent, a posthumously conceived child must either be "in utero not later than 36 months after the individual's death or born not later than 45 months after the individual's death." [2–120(k), see Mary F. Radford, Postmortem Sperm Retrieval].

Section 2–121 deals with several situations when a gestational agreement is made after the death or incapacity of an individual. Whether that individual is in a parent-child relationship depends on two factors: (1) the child must have a genetic connection to the decedent, and (2) the individual must have "intended to be treated as the parent of the child." [2–121(e)]. Intent may be shown if: (1) the individual signed a record which shows the necessary intent considering all the facts and circumstances; or (2) other evidence establishes the intent by clear and convincing evidence.

In addition, subject to rebuttal only by clear and convincing evidence to the contrary, there is a presumption that a person intended to be treated as the parent of a posthumously conceived gestational child (1) if that person's sperm or egg was used, (2) the person was married and no divorce was pending when the sperm or eggs were deposited and (3) the person's spouse or surviving spouse functioned as a parent of the child no later than two years after the child's birth. [2–121(f)].

As with other posthumously conceived children, a posthumously conceived gestational child must either be "in utero not later than 36 months after the individual's death or born not later than 45 months after the individual's death." [2–121(h)]

6. Parental Exclusion

Despite the existence of a parent-child relationship, if a parent's parental rights were terminated, that parent will not inherit from or through the child. [2–114(a)(1)]. For if a child dies who is younger than 18 years, a parent will not inherit from or through the child if that parent's parental rights could have been terminated if a proceeding to terminate the parental rights could had been brought immediately before the death of the child. Grounds for termination include "nonsupport, abandonment, abuse, neglect, or other actions or inactions of the parent toward the child." [2–114(a)(2)]. The standard of proof is clear and convincing evidence. If terminated, the parent is treated as if the parent predeceased the child. [2–114(b)].

C. OTHER SPECIAL RELATIONSHIPS

1. Half–Blooded Persons

Half-blooded relatives are decedent's collateral relatives who share one common ancestor with that of the decedent but not both common ancestors. Descendants of parents and grandparents who are only "relatives" of the half-blood to the decedents inherit the same as they would if they were whole-blooded relatives. [2–107].

2. Relationships by Affinity

Under the UPC the most important relationship by affinity is the spousal relationship. This not only has importance in dealing with distribution in intestacy but also with elective share rights, the revocation of wills, the family protections and in priority for appointment as personal representative. Although the UPC leaves the requirements for a marriage to the law of domestic relations, it specifically explains how, what and when legal proceedings sever the relationship. [2–802]. An explanation of this provision is provided below. [See § 9.02].

With the exceptions of the surviving spouse and stepchildren to avoid escheat [see § 3.01(2)], relatives who are related to the decedent solely by affinity do not inherit under the UPC. [See In re Estate of Brewington, 568 P.2d 133 (Mont.1977)]. When the UPC uses the relational terminology parents, grandparents or descendants, persons classifiable in those groups as step or foster relations are excluded from these classes of persons. [1–201(5), (9), (33)]. California, however, now treats the relationship between a person and the person's foster stepparent the same as if it were an adoptive relationship under two conditions. The conditions are (1) that the relationship began while the stepchild was a minor and continued through the parties' joint lifetimes, and (2) clear and convincing evidence establishes that the foster or stepparent would have adopted the person except for a legal barrier. [West's Ann. Cal. Prob. UPC, Supp.1995, § 6454]. The comment to the section observes that the typical example satisfying the second condition would be where the parent of the foster or stepchild refused to consent to the adoption by the foster or stepparent. [West's Ann. Cal. Prob. Code, Supp. 1995, § 6454, Comment].

3. Aliens or Noncitizens

Despite their unconstitutionality, reciprocity or "Iron Curtain" acts still exist in some states. [E.g., Wyo. Stat. § 2–4–105]. These statutes usually state that a noncitizen heir cannot inherit from a domiciled decedent unless a domiciled heir may inherit from a decedent in the noncitizen's state or country. Under the UPC, persons who are aliens or noncitizen are not disqualified merely because of their alienage. [2–113].

D. SURVIVORSHIP AND SIMULTANEOUS DEATH

In order to inherit, an heir must survive the intestate. The general common law rule holds, however, that survival need not be for any specific length of time: any measurable length of time such as one minute or theoretically one second is sufficient. When the question of one's survival materially affects the distribution of the intestate's estate, the timing of death becomes an extremely disrupting and litigable issue. Many states attempted to alleviate the problem by enacting the original Uniform Simultaneous Death Act. [Uniform Simultaneous Death Act (1940)]. Section 1 of this Act provides that in an intestacy situation when "there is no sufficient evidence that the persons have died otherwise than simultaneously, the property of each person shall be disposed of as if he had survived. * * * " Unfortunately, this solution is only a partial one. It clearly implies that if there is adequate proof of the actual sequence of death in measurable time, the presumption does not apply and the "surviving" heir, no matter for how short a period of time, will be entitled to inherit that heir's intestate share from the intestate's estate. This issue alone has caused litigation over who survived, and unnecessary expense by requiring multiple administrations of the same property. [See, e.g., Janus v. Tarasewicz, 482 N.E.2d 418 (Ill.App.1985); Matter of Bucci, 293 N.Y.S.2d 994 (N.Y.Sur.1968); Schmitt v. Pierce, 344 S.W.2d 120 (Mo.1961)].

The UPC's survivorship provision for inheritance in intestacy eliminates these problems in the vast majority of situations. Drawing upon a frequently employed estate planning device, the UPC requires that in order to qualify as an heir, a person born before the decedent's death must survive the decedent for 120 hours. [2–104(a)]. The UPC creates a presumption of nonsurvival. It imposes a clear and convincing evidence standard of proof upon those who claim through the heir that the heir survived for the stated length of time. All failures of such proof are conclusively presumed to show failure to survive. [See § 2.01(B)(3)]. The only exception to this rule is that the survival time requirement does not apply if the decedent's property would escheat to the state because of a death of the only heir or heirs during this time period. In this situation, the common law's mere survivorship rule applies. [2–104(b)].

Although questions of the time of death might still present a problem, this provision will substantially reduce litigation over who has survived and avoid multiple administration of the same property where it is totally unnecessary. On the other hand, the provision could have an adverse tax consequence in a very large intestate estate, if the federal or other estate tax marital deduction is lost because a surviving spouse dies within the 120 hour period. Large estates of this nature, however, generally have received proper estate planning advice and consequently should include a will, which contains its own simultaneous death and survivorship requirements.

The UPC adopts as a default rule of construction the same durational survivorship technique for all types of gratuitous transfers including wills and all other governing instruments. [See 2–702; § 8.02]. The 120 hour survivorship requirement is now part of the 1991 version of the Uniform Simultaneous Death Act. [Uniform Simultaneous Death Act (1991)].

§ 3.03   Prior Gifts and Transactions

A. ADVANCEMENTS

At common law an heir's intestate share would be affected if the heir received an advancement from the intestate during the latter's lifetime. By common law definition, an advancement meant an irrevocable inter vivos gift of money or property, real or personal, to a child by a parent that enables the child to anticipate the child's inheritance from the parent to the extent of the gift. [Atkinson, Wills § 129]. If a child who received an advancement subjected the advancement to the "hotchpot,"* its value was added to the estate for calculation purposes only, and the child's distribution directly from the intestate's estate equaled the excess of the child's share over the value of the advancement received. If the value of the child's advancement exceeded the child's intestate share, the child would neither participate in the hotchpot nor receive an intestate share from the estate. The child, of course, kept the advancement. The theory of this doctrine is to bring about a degree of equality between the children of a decedent. Some states have extended the doctrine to other heirs in addition to the intestate's children.

The principal question raised when there has been an inter vivos gift by a donor to a prospective heir is whether the gift is intended as an advancement. Because the intent of the donor at the time of the gift is the determinative factor, not all such gifts are so characterized. Seldom, however, does one find that a donor has clearly indicated that intent. The transferring document, if there even is one, will seldom specifically indicate one way or the other. The result has been that the question of what constitutes proof of this intent has caused a substantial amount of litigation.

---

* A hotchpot is a fictional estate that is determined for calculation purposes only. It does not ever actually exist but is used to determine the proper distribution amount from estates that do exist.

The relevant UPC provision clarifies, expands, and restricts the application of the advancement doctrine. [2–109]. A gift is an advancement only if any one of several formalities is satisfied. A gift is a formal advancement if either the donor "declared in a contemporaneous writing" or the heir "acknowledged in writing" that the gift is an advancement. [2–109(a)]. The required writing may, rather than declaring the gift is an advancement, merely indicate that the gift must be taken into account in computing the division or distribution of decedent's intestate estate. No words of art such as "advancement" must be used by the donor. The gist of the declaration must indicate that the donor intended that the gift constitutes what lawyers call advancements. There is also no specific requirement that the written declaration of intent to make a formal advancement has to be communicated to the donee at the time of the gift. It could be a contemporaneous written note or indication that the gift is a formal advancement which is included with the donor's personal records. Of course, the writing must be available or provable after the donor's death when distribution decisions are made.

The UPC extends the application of the advancement concept to any individual who is an heir. This is a major extension of the doctrine from many state statutes that limit the doctrine solely to gifts to decedent's children or descendants. [Atkinson, Wills § 129, at p. 722]. In the UPC, the word "heirs" is defined to include all those who would be entitled to take by intestate succession the decedent's property including the surviving spouse. [1–201(21)]. Consequently, formal advancements may be made to collateral relatives and even to the surviving spouse and affect their intestate shares.

Although under the 1969 UPC, the advancee had to be both a "prospective heir" at the time of the gift and an heir at the decedent's death to cause a formal advancement to affect advancee's intestate's share, the 1990 UPC requires only that the advancee be an heir at decedent's death. [2–110(a) and Comment]. The scenario mentioned in the Comment concerns a written advancement to a grandchild at the time the grandchild's parent (the decedent's child) is still alive. If the donor dies and the child and grandchild survive, the child takes a full share and the advancement is of no consequence because the grandchild does not take anything in intestacy due to the survivorship of the grandchild's ancestor. If on the other hand the child died between the date of the gift and donor's death, the formal advancement now causes the grandchild to have his or her intestacy share reduced by the amount of the advancement.

Whereas the common law limited advancements to decedents who died totally intestate, the UPC applies its doctrine of advancement to decedents who die either totally or partially intestate. This is an extension of the doctrine and reverses the common law presumption that a testator who died with a will that passed a portion of the estate had revoked all advancements. This extension is justified considering the UPC's formality requirement and the interrelationship and consistency of the concept of advancement with the UPC's provision dealing with the related testacy doctrine of ademption by satisfaction. [See 2–609; § 10.05].

The UPC specifically provides that where a donee of a formal advancement fails to survive the donor, the formal advancement does not affect the shares that the donee's descendants take from the donor's intestate estate unless the donor's contemporaneous writing expressly provides that the gift affects the descendants' shares. [2–109(c)]. A donee's written acknowledgment that the gift affects the donee's descendants is not sufficient and will not rebut the statutory presumption. The latter limitation is a change from the 1969 UPC, which allowed either the donor's writing or donee's acknowledgment to bind the donee's descendants. The UPC prevents an advancee, however, from disclaiming his or her intestate share for the purpose of having a full intestate share pass to his or her descendants. This is accomplished through the disclaimer section which provides that only the disclaimant's interest not the share devolves to the disclaimant's descendants. [2–801(d)(1)]. The result is that the advancee's descendants take only the advancee's share from the decedent's estate less the value of the formal advancement if relevant to the issue.

The Comment states that a formal advancement need not necessarily be an outright gift. [2–109, Comment]. If the formality requirements are met, other will substitutes such as life insurance payable to the advancee could constitute an advancement under the UPC.

If a formal advancement exists, the provision's Comment explains how to adjust for it in distributing the decedent's intestate estate. [2–109, Comment]. [See also § 3.03(B)]. Valuation of a formal advancement is determined as of the time of the donee's possession or enjoyment or as of the donor's death, whichever occurs first. [2–109(c)].

Although the formality requirements probably coincide with modern estate planning practice and theory, because most gifts today are not thought of as transfers in anticipation of an inheritance, there are still pluses and minuses to consider. On the positive side, the rules alleviate the evidentiary problem of proving intent by requiring that the intent be in writing. Frequent litigation attempting to discover decedent's intent is precluded by the irrebuttable presumption. On the negative side, the provision precludes proof of intent unless a proper writing is present even where decedent clearly expressed intent in forms other than in writing. For example, the UPC's formality requirement may deny proof of decedent's clearly expressed oral intent. If the gifts are of a small nature, little real harm is done and the policy recognized by the UPC is meritoriously carried out. If, however, large gifts were made to an heir that were intended to be advancements, no amount of evidence showing that intent is admissible unless the statutory formality is satisfied.

It may be unrealistic to expect a person to put advancement intent in a proper writing when we know that person died intestate and probably did not seek legal counsel for his or her financial matters. It would not be unreasonable to assume that most persons would consider large gifts of $10,000 or more to have strings attached. Generally, most people desire equality among equals and the extra windfall of large gifts made to one and not to others during the intestate's lifetime is not consistent with that principle.

In a perfect society, persons would not make large gifts without advice of counsel, but we know this is not the case. It seems that a middle ground might have been created that applies the writing requirement to gifts under $10,000* but for gifts above $10,000 applies a presumption, either for or against, an advancement construction with the qualification that relevant extrinsic information, including declarations by the decedent, would be admissible to determine the intent.

* As adjusted for inflation, the federal gift tax law says that gifts of $13,000 or less per person per year are exempt from gift and estate tax consequences. I.R.C. § 2503(b). Therefore, similar to the UPC's no-advancement rule, gifts of that nature have no subsequent consequences. The reverse is true of gifts above the amount: they do have gift and estate tax consequences.

B. FACTUAL ILLUSTRATIONS

CHART 3–11

ADVANCEMENT CALCULATIONS

Hypothetical In all of the following hypotheticals assume decedent, D, made gifts to the named donees and these gifts were declared in a proper writing to be an advancement to the donee. Assume that D died intestate and D was survived by a spouse, S, two children, C1 and C2, and a grandchild, G1. G1 was C3's child; C3 did not survive D. C1 is D's child by a previous relationship. The problem is to determine the respective distributive intestate shares of the takers from D's estate.

Assumption 1: D made advancements of $20,000 to C2, $50,000 to C3, and $30,000 to G1. D's total distributable estate equals $350,000.

Answer:

Hotchpot	Amount	
Distributable Estate*	$400,000	
C2's Advancement	$ 20,000	
G1's Advancement	$ 30,000	
Total of Hotchpot	$450,000	
Distribution		
S's share equals		$300,000
Remaining estate	$150,000	
C1's 1/3 Share		$ 50,000
C2's 1/3 Share	$50,000–$20,000	$ 30,000
G1's 1/3 Share	$50,000–$30,000	$ 20,000
Total Distributed from Estate*		$400,000

Comment: Because C3 did not survive D and does not take from D's estate, C3's advancement is ignored. C1, C2 and G1 shares equal the balance of the estate after the surviving spouse share is deducted. The advancements received are deducted from the heirs who received them in order to equalize the gratuitous transfers to the heirs. Because C3's advancement did not specifically include G1, it does not affect G1's share from D's estate. The advancement directly to G1 affects G1's share even if G1 was not an heir at the time of the advancement because G1 is an heir at the time of D's death.

Assumption 2:   D made advancements of $20,000 to C2 and $50,000 to G1. D's total distributable estate equals $210,000.

Answer:

Hotchpot #1	Amount
Distributable Estate*	$260,000
C2's Advancement	$ 20,000
G1's Advancement	$ 50,000
Total of Hotchpot	$330,000

Distribution		
S's share equals		$240,000
Remaining estate	$90,000	
C1's 1/3 Share		$30,000
C2's 1/3 Share	$30,000–$20,000	$10,000
G1's 1/3 Share	$30,000–$50,000	($20,000)

Comment: Because G1 owes $20,000 to the estate if G1 participates in the hotchpot, G1 will not participate.

A second hotchpot must be completed.

Answer:

Hotchpot #2	Amount
Distributable Estate*	$260,000
C2's Advancement	$ 20,000
Total of Hotchpot	$280,000

Distribution		
S's share equals		$215,000
Remaining estate	$65,000	
C1's 1/3 Share		$ 32,500
C2's 1/3 Share	$32,500–$20,000	$ 12,500
Total Distributed from Estate*		$260,000

Comment: Because G1 did not participate, C1's and C2's intestate shares equal 1/2of the balance of the estate after the surviving spouse share is deducted. G1 does not take the normal intestacy share but G1 also does not have to return the advancement.

* The Distributable Estate and the Total Distributed from Estate amounts must be identical; otherwise, an error in calculation has occurred.

C. DEBTOR HEIRS

Although the UPC permits the debt owed to the estate by a debtor-heir to be charged against the heir's intestate share, it does not permit that debt to be charged against the share of the debtor-heir's descendants if the debtor-heir fails to survive the decedent. [2–110; see also 3–903; § 14.01].

§ 3.04 Negative Testacy Provision

The common law generally stated that one could not disinherit an heir by fiat. [Atkinson, Wills § 36, at p. 145]. Consequently, if a person executed a will that disinherited the person's heir but for whatever reason that will did not pass all of decedent's property, the heir would still be able to share. For example, if T wrote a will that stated "I give all my property to X. I intentionally disinherit my son C and do not want my son to take anything from this estate" C would be disinherited if X is capable of taking at T's death. But if X died prior to T and did not leave someone who could take in his or her place according to the law of lapse or antilapse, C would be able to take.

The UPC includes a provision recognizing what might be considered the negative will as far as intestacy is concerned. It provides that if a decedent has excluded or limited the right of an heir to succeed to that person's intestate property, the exclusion or limit is binding even if the decedent dies intestate. For example, using the above example, C would not take even if X's devise lapsed. The share of the disinherited heir passes as if the heir disclaimed the interest. [2–101(b)]. There may be situations where it is difficult to determine whether the decedent intentionally disinherited an heir. For example, mere omission from the will would probably not be considered the expressed disinheritance required under this section. On the other hand, a will that states that an heir is disinherited or that an heir shall only receive a certain amount from the estate and no more, would constitute the type of disinheritance for which this section would operate. As mentioned, the disinherited heir's share in intestacy passes as if that heir had disclaimed the interest. This means that the disinherited heir's descendants may take by representation but only the share the heir would have received. [2–101, Comment].

A recent problem in interpreting this provision concerns the situation where the testator expressly disinherits all heirs but dies intestate. Does the estate pass to the decedent's heirs or escheat to the state as if decedent died without heirs? The South Dakota Supreme Court held that the estate passes to the heirs and does not escheat. [Estate of Jetter, 570 N.W.2d 26 (S.D.1997)]. The court held that "an escheat can exist only where no heirs can be found. Here heirs have been found. As such the State's claim for escheat fails under the above statutes."

CHAPTER 4

ELECTIVE SHARE OF SURVIVING SPOUSE, THE AUGMENTED ESTATE, AND ELECTION PROCEDURE

§ 4.01 Elective Share of Surviving Spouse and the Augmented Estate Concept

A. INTRODUCTION TO SPOUSAL PROTECTIONS

If one were to build a spousal protection statute from the beginning, many difficult decisions would have to be made. The threshold question would be whether a spousal protection statute is needed at all. Studies indicate that the vast majority of married persons pass substantial portions of their estates to their surviving spouses and that spousal disinheritance is not a major problem. The problem, however, is that some circumstances and cases have arisen where people have attempted to disinherit their surviving spouses. Marital discord and other difficulties sometimes cause married persons to act like non-married persons. Consequently, it is worthwhile for the law to provide a safety net so that those who are unfairly disinherited will be able to protect their merited interest in the decedent's estate. On the other hand, its limited utility indicates that caution should be taken to limit protective provisions to situations deserving control and not to extend protection beyond its purpose and to cause interference with legitimate property allocations.

Assuming a spousal protection statute is desirable, there are numerous types of protection devices that might be selected. Anglo–American common law initially selected the dower/curtesy concept to protect spouses from disinheritance. This was primarily a real property protection device and typically was limited to a one-third life interest. Many states have expanded the concept to include personal property and have often enlarged the fractional interest in the estate from a life estate to one in fee.

The forced share is another common protection device enacted in many states. With wide variations, a typical forced share statute provides that if a decedent spouse does not pass a minimum arbitrary percentage, usually running from one-third to one-half, of that person's probate estate to the surviving spouse, the surviving spouse may elect to take that share under a spousal protection right. [Atkinson, Wills § 33]. The electing spouse takes the share in fee.

A third device, called community property, is found in nine states. This is a combined accrual and accumulation technique providing that property gained during a marriage is owned equally by each spouse. Community property goes beyond the typical spousal protection provisions that are found in common law states because it establishes a lifetime division of the property as well as a method for dividing an estate upon death of a spouse. It is actually a property division system among married persons and not merely a post-death safety-net minimum protection technique. Each spouse is treated in a sense as a tenant in common of the property earned by both spouses during the marriage. Community property operates as a protection from inter vivos disposition as well as testamentary disinheritance. States that have community property do not ordinarily need other spousal protection statutes although some have them to deal with noncommunity property acquired by the spouses before and during marriage.

A fourth device is a judicial share determined after death by some tribunal on the basis of set criteria. The financial needs of the surviving spouse and children are the primary considerations. The process empowers the appropriate judicial tribunal, usually a probate court, with the authority to entrust assets of the decedent's estate into a type of statutory trust for the benefit of the surviving spouse and other dependent persons. It springs from an assumed legal obligation on the part of the decedent to provide support for certain designated relatives. It suffers from indefiniteness as to application and result. A system of this nature prevails in England and other commonwealth countries. [See, e.g., Inheritance (Provision for Family and Dependents) Act 1975, c. 63].

Aside from the share, another consideration for a spousal protection provision concerns the coverage of the safety net. Dower and forced share have generally been limited to providing protection from the assets that are a part of the decedent's estate. Inter vivos transfers to others and the surviving spouse have, with a few exceptional circumstances, been excluded from the protective device. Other concepts developed to prevent this, such as permitting the surviving spouse to recover from intent to defraud transfers, or illusory transfers, have not operated satisfactorily and have not provided the necessary predictability for planning purposes. In addition, seldom did the law take into account assets the surviving spouse may have received by other devices. Consequently, there was frequently the potential for over-protection for the surviving spouse. If the spousal protection is a safety net, this is as much an evil of the law as the disinheritance technique constituted.

Another concern relates to the scope of the protected beneficiaries. Most current devices only protect the surviving spouse, although there are strong arguments for the protection of dependent children and dependent relatives or companions.With the exception of limited protection for certain descendants in Louisiana, the protection statutes in the states have not covered persons other than the surviving spouse.

Assuming an identifiable sum or share is protected for the surviving spouse, it is necessary to determine the method by which the share will be satisfied. Most protective devices favor the lump sum, distribute outright, approach. Periodic payments offer another alternative. This method would be particularly applicable if need were the primary determinant of the share. If periodic payments are made on the basis of need, the question of their duration arises.

Other factors might be relevant. Should the length of the marriage be a significant factor to the amount of the safety net protection? Should certain types of misconduct on the part of the surviving spouse cause a loss of the safety net? And finally, should the safety net be applied to the appropriate family unit regardless of the marital status of the persons.

With rare exceptions, states have enacted statutes which in some manner or other protect the surviving spouse from disinheritance by the decedent spouse. These statutes can be generally and broadly categorized into three types: statutory dower, forced share and community property. Within each category there is a large variety of methods and combinations. [Atkinson, Wills § 33]. The fractional interest among these categories range from one-third to one-half or is sometimes tied into the surviving spouse's intestate share. Depending upon the type, the shares are sometimes exempt from the decedent's creditors' claims and sometimes not exempt. They may also differ as to whether the surviving spouse must make an election against the will to obtain a share or must renounce the share in order to take under decedent's estate plan.

Although the UPC accepts the spousal protection concept and includes an elective share device, the scope and procedure of its provisions differ from anything existent in non-UPC states today. Significantly, the UPC's spousal protection provisions are intended only for common law jurisdictions which enact the UPC and not for community property states. [App. VII, Art. II, Pt. 2, General Comment].

The UPC's decipherable purposes for its spousal protection system are eclectic. They include desires: (1) to confer upon married persons broad freedom of disposition; (2) to provide a protective monetary safety net against spousal disinheritance; (3) to give recognition to the economic partnership of marriage by increasing the protective share for longer marriages than for shorter ones; (4) to adjust for the dispositional problems raised by multiple marriages and multi-family descendants; (5) to prevent will substitutes from defeating the prior purposes; (6) to prevent the surviving spouse from electing the forced share when decedent's estate plan adequately provides for the spouse or when the spouse's personal wealth compares to decedent's wealth; (7) to ease administration of the protective share processes; and (8) to provide predictability for persons who adequately plan their estates. It is clear that these purposes will not be consistently achievable in all circumstances. Because of potential conflict between them under specific circumstances, they point toward theoretical aspirations and not to subjective particular results.

B. ELECTIVE SHARE OF THE SURVIVING SPOUSE

The 1990 UPC made significant alterations to the elective share provisions of the 1969 version. In most respects, the new provisions built upon the 1969 version. 1993 Technical Amendments reorganized and renumbered the 1990 version and made several significant substantive changes. In 2008, another round of revisions were promulgated that further recognized and applied the partnership theory of marriage which recognizes "an unspoken marital bargain under which the partners agree that each is to enjoy a half interest in the fruits of the marriage." Consequently, the UPC now has an elective share that equals 50%. But also recognizing that this share needs to be tempered depending on the length of the marriage, the UPC applies the percentage according to the years of marriage.

Under the UPC, dower and curtesy are abolished. [2–112]. In addition, the UPC's election applies only if the decedent was domiciled at death in the UPC state; otherwise the spousal protection laws of the decedent's domicile control those rights. [2–202(d)]. If the domicile requirement is met, then the surviving spouse may elect to take a sliding scaled percentage of the "augmented estate." [2–202(a)]. Significantly, the surviving spouse is entitled to the family protections in addition to the elective share protection. [See § 5.02]. This means that a surviving spouse will be able to take the entire probate estate or $64,500 of it, whichever is less, as satisfaction of the family protection. [2–202(c)]. But as will be seen, the election extends beyond the probate estate.

The opportunity to take this elective share exists whether the decedent died intestate, testate with a will which disinherits the surviving spouse, or testate with a will which gives all or part of the estate to the surviving spouse. The decision to elect depends upon three determinations: (1) the elective share amount; (2) the determination of the augmented estate; and (3) the satisfaction of the elective share amount.

Whereas the elective share in the 1969 version of the UPC adopted an absolute one-third share of the augmented estate as the foundational protection for the surviving spouse, the 1990 UPC adopted an accrual-type elective share. [Art. II, Pt. 2, Gen. Comment]. The method of accrual employed a rational but arbitrary rising percentage scale based upon the length of the marriage. The elective share percentage ascended from a low of three percent of the augmented estate after the first year of marriage to a high of fifty percent of the augmented estate for fifteen or more years of marriage.

The 2008 revision comes to the same result but does it in a two step process. [Pt 2, Elective Share of Surviving Spouse, General Comment]. First, the elective share is set at 50% of the value of the marital-property portion of the augmented estate. Second, the UPC recognizes the importance of the length of the marriage in regard to the actual amount of the share. Similar to the 1990 version, the UPC sets a mechanically determined approximation system. There is a structured rising percentage scale to determine the Marital–Property portion of the augmented estate. The Marital–Property portion ascends from a low of three percent of the augmented estate after the first year of marriage to a high of one-hundred percent of the augmented estate for fifteen or more years of marriage. Third, there is no need to identify which of the couple's property was earned during the marriage and which was acquired prior to the marriage or acquired during the marriage by gift or inheritance. Fourth, the elective share dollar amount equals the fifty percent elective share multiplied by the Marital–Property portion of the augmented estate.

In addition, the UPC includes a supplemental or minimum safety-net monetary amount for a surviving spouse below which the elective share cannot equal regardless of the length of the marriage. Accordingly, any surviving spouse is entitled to a minimum elective share of $50,000, increased to an inflation adjusting $75,000 in 2008. [2–202(b), see 1–109]. The amount of the minimum amount is suggested and subject to alteration by an enacting state.

CHART 4–1
MARITAL-PROPERTY PORTION

Length of Marriage	Marital-Property Portion
Less than 1 year	3% of the augmented estate
1 year but less than 2 years	6% of the augmented estate
2 years but less than 3 years	12% of the augmented estate
3 years but less than 4 years	18% of the augmented estate
4 years but less than 5 years	24% of the augmented estate
5 years but less than 6 years	30% of the augmented estate
6 years but less than 7 years	36% of the augmented estate
7 years but less than 8 years	42% of the augmented estate
8 years but less than 9 years	48% of the augmented estate
9 years but less than 10 years	54% of the augmented estate
10 years but less than 11 years	60% of the augmented estate
11 years but less than 12 years	68% of the augmented estate
12 years but less than 13 years	76% of the augmented estate
13 years but less than 14 years	84% of the augmented estate
14 years but less than 15 years	92% of the augmented estate
15 years or more	100% of the augmented estate

The accrual approach theorizes that marriages are similar to economic partnerships and thus the partnership interest of one spouse should increase in the other spouse's assets as the marriage endures. [See Waggoner, Spousal Rights]. At the moment persons are married, little of their property has been earned as a result of the marriage in an economic partnership sense. The UPC provides that as the marriage continues each spouse earns an increasing percentage interest in the estate of the other spouse. This percentage constitutes the share that may be elected at the death of a spouse by the surviving spouse. This reciprocal maturing interest attaches to all of the assets of both spouses not merely the assets acquired during the marriage. This pervasive accrual approach differs significantly from community property states where the automatic one-half interest attaches only to assets earned during the marriage and not to "separate property" obtained prior to marriage or derived from third persons by inheritance or gratuitous transfer during marriage. Administrative efficiency is promoted because there need not be any tracing of assets to determine their source. It also roughly accords with the ways that married persons treat their assets: few distinguish separate from marital property when making gifts or devises to spouses.

After determining the appropriate elective share, it is necessary to identify an estate against which the elective share will be computed and funded. As indicated, the UPC calls this estate the "augmented estate." [2–203; § 4.01(C)]. It starts with the decedent's estate that is subject to administration through a decedent's estate and that passes at decedent's death either by intestacy or by testacy. To be fully effective, however, the spousal protection statute must take into account certain inter vivos transfers of the decedent spouse. Consequently, the UPC includes in the augmented estate what it calls the decedent's nonprobate estate. If this strategy is not effected, persons determined to disinherit their spouses could easily transfer their assets to third persons through the use of relatively frail inter vivos transactions or of probate estate purging transfers on their deathbed or in near deathbed situations. A law that permits easy and unburdensome avoidance establishes too vast a loophole and encourages disinheritance even in the most undesirable situation.

Concomitantly, the UPC prevents the surviving spouse from receiving more than the circumstances merit. Thus, the surviving spouse must include in the augmented estate both the assets derivable from the decedent as a result of the latter's death and all of the surviving spouse's personal assets including the surviving spouse's comparable nonprobate transfers to others. These latter inclusions discourage elections by surviving spouses in marriages of short duration and where the surviving spouse has substantial personal assets.

Finally, recognizing an underlying philosophy of freedom of disposition and clarity of title and ownership, the UPC excludes several categories of nonmarital interests and completed lifetime transfers made by either spouse.

The sum of the value of decedent's controllable estate plus the value of the surviving spouse's controllable estate, but excluding the value of nonmarital interests and completed transfers equals the augmented estate. [§ 4.01(C)].

For added protection from disinheritance, the UPC includes a monetary minimum for all surviving spouses. [2–202(b)]. Equal to a suggested $75,000, this provision guarantees that the surviving spouse will not take less than this amount from the augmented estate. It is claimed to be based on the support theory, that the spouses' "mutual duties of support during their lifetime should be continued in some form after death." [Art. II, Pt. 2, Gen. Comment]. If after funding the surviving spouse's elective share amount, the spouse takes less than $75,000, the spouse is entitled to take from the nonspousal beneficiaries of the augmented estate the difference between what the spouse took under the elective share and $75,000. The difference is satisfied from the nonspousal portions of the augmented estate in the same order as the elective share is satisfied. [2–209(b), (c); § 4.03]. This supplemental amount is calculated by subtracting from $75,000 the value of property interests attributable to the surviving spouse under the elective share process. Funding of this amount is discussed below. [See § 4.03].

In summary, the UPC's elective share recognizes the importance of the length of the marriage, adopts an efficient mechanical calculation technique, includes the appropriate parts of the assets from both the decedent and surviving spouse's estate plans, excludes completed transactions that should not be disturbed because of the death of a prior owner, and provides a fixed dollar minimum amount for support protection.

CHART 4–2

ELECTIVE SHARE COMPARISONS

Hypothetical: In all of the following hypotheticals assume that decedent, D, is married at D's death to the surviving spouse, S, and that D's estate plan passes nothing to S. No inter vivos transfers were made by either spouse. S takes the full value of the family protections, *i.e.,* $64,500.

Assumption 1:   D and S were married for ten years. At death D's net estate is valued at $300,000 and S's net estate is valued at $100,000. S petitions for the elective share in timely fashion. What result?

	Augmented Estate (AE) Hotchpot	**Amount**
	D's Estate (Segments 1 and 2)	$300,000
	S's Estate (Segment 4)	$100,000
	Total Value of AE	$400,000
	Marital-property Portion	60%
Answer:	Marital–Property Amount	240,000
	Elective Share Percentage	× 50%
	Elective Share of the AE	$120,000
	Less S's Chargeable Share (Fund 1)	
	S's Estate (Segment 4 ×(2 × 30%))	– $60,000
	Elective Share Deficiency	$60,000

Comment: Because the marriage lasted ten years the Marital-property Portion equaled 60% of the augmented estate. In this example, D's estate will have to pay S the value of the elective share deficiency, *i.e.,* $60,000. Although the surviving spouse, S, is protected to this degree, S had to credit against the total elective share, *i.e.,* $120,000, a comparable percentage of S's estate.

Assumption 2:   D and S were married for twenty years. At death D's net estate is valued at $100,000 and S's net estate is valued at $300,000. S petitions for the elective share in timely fashion. What result?

Augmented Estate (AE) Hotchpot	**Amount**
D's Estate (Segments 1 and 2)	$100,000
S's Estate (Segment 4)	$300,000
Total Value of AE	$400,000

Answer:	Marital-property Portion	100%
	Marital–Property Amount	$400,000
	Elective Share Percentage	× 50%
	Elective Share Amount of the AE	
	Less S's Chargeable Share (Fund 1)	$200,000
	S's Estate (Segment 4 × (2 × 50%))	− $300,000
	Elective Share Deficiency	− $100,000

Comment: Because the marriage lasted more than fourteen years, the elective share percentage equaled 50% of the Marital–Property Amount. In this example, D's estate will not have to pay S the value of the elective share deficiency which is a negative amount, *i.e.,* − $100,000. The Code does not require S to pay D's estate the elective share excess amount nor forfeit the value of the family protections. It does prevent S from taking even more from D's estate.

Assumption 3:   D and S were married for less than one year. At death D's net estate is valued at $80,000 and S's net estate is valued at $10,000. S petitions for the elective share in timely fashion.

	Augmented Estate (AE) Hotchpot	**Amount**
	D's Estate (Segments 1 and 2)	$80,000
	S's Estate (Segment 4)	$10,000
	Total Value of AE	$90,000
	Marital-property Portion	3%
Answer:	Marital–Property Amount	2,700
	Elective Share Percentage	× 50%
	Elective Share of the AE	$1,350
	Supplemental Amount	$75,000
	Less S's Chargeable Share (Fund 1)	
	S's Estate (Segment 4)	− $10,000
	Elective Share Deficiency	$65,000

Comment: Because the marriage lasted less than one year, the Marital-property Portion equaled 3% of the augmented estate. But the Code includes a Supplemental Amount, *i.e.* $75,000, to protect the surviving spouse in hardship cases when the surviving spouse would otherwise be left without sufficient funds for support. The supplemental amount is not based on the partnership of marriage but on the support theory. It protects only when the surviving spouse would otherwise be left without sufficient funds for support. Consequently, the length of the

marriage is irrelevant. In this example, D's estate will
have to pay S the amount of the supplemental amount.

C. THE AUGMENTED ESTATE
CALCULATION

Definition of the Augmented Estate: The augmented estate concept is the most complex part of the
UPC's elective share device and a thorough understanding of its meaning and scope is essential. [2–
203]. The augmented estate is a hotchpot estate in
that it does not really exist as a cohesive estate.
[See § 3.03(A)]. It is created for purposes of calculating the value of the elective share. Similar but
separate concepts deal with the funding of the
elective share amount. [2–209; see § 4.03].

Generally, the augmented estate includes all assets less liabilities owned or controlled by the decedent and by the decedent's surviving spouse plus
certain gratuitous transfers made by either spouse
to third persons. More specifically, it is composed of
four distinct segments. [2–203]. If the same property or interest is includable in more than one segment, it is includable in the segment that would
yield the highest value; however, the value for the
same interest may only be included in one segment.
[2–208(c)]. The Comments to the sections in this
part provide detailed information on how the augmented estate functions.

Segment 1 of the Augmented Estate: The first
segment (hereinafter called Segment 1) includes

what normally is thought of as the decedent's gross probate estate less enforceable claims, funeral and administration expenses, and the family protections. [2–204]. The probate estate is composed of all the property that passes by intestacy if a person had died intestate. [2–201(7)]. Claims include all of decedent's liabilities at death but do not include estate and inheritance taxes or title disputes over probate estate property. [2–204, Comment; see 1–201(6) (Claims)]. The valuation of Segment 1 property is determined at the date of death [2–204; see also 3–706].

Segment 2 of the Augmented Estate: The second segment (hereinafter called Segment 2) includes all properties over which decedent immediately prior to death retained certain interests, powers or relationships. [2–205]. The UPC refers to Segment 2 properties as the "decedent's nonprobate transfers to others." [2–205, Comment]. Although transfers of this nature pass outside the probate estate, they may be subject to reclaim if they are required to contribute to the funding of the surviving spouse's elective share amount. [2–205; see 2–209(b) and (c); see also § 4.03].*

The following interests are included as Segment 2 property:

(1) The value of all nonprobate transfers to others (third persons), including all types of property interests, no matter where situated but not

* Properties that have comparable relationships to the surviving spouse are includable in the augmented estate under Segment 4. [2–207].

including property included in Segment 1, in which decedent retained at the time of death a particular interest or power. The following transfers are included:

(A) Property over which decedent retained a personal, unshared, presently exercisable general power of appointment. [2–205(1)(i)]. A presently exercisable general power of appointment is defined as a power to create a present or future interest in favor of the decedent, decedent's creditors or creditors of decedent's estate and includes a power to revoke or invade the principal of the interest. [2–201(6)]. It makes no difference whether (1) decedent or someone else created the power, [2–205, Comment]; (2) the interest was created before or after the marriage to the surviving spouse; or, (3) at the time in question, the decedent had capacity to exercise the power. [2–201(6)]. This provision does not apply, however, to a general testamentary power held by decedent at death. [2–205, Comment]. A typical example of a property interest includable under this provision is property in a trust which the decedent may unilaterally revoke. This provision prevents the revocable inter vivos trust and other forms of revocable property transfers from being effective spousal protection avoidance devices. A power of this nature is equivalent to full ownership; therefore, its inclusion in the augmented estate is reasonable. The value of the included property is the value of the property subject to the power to the extent there was a transfer to a third person at decedent's death.

(B) Property in which decedent held a fractional interest in joint tenancy with right of survivorship with one or more third persons other than the surviving spouse. [2–205(1)(ii)]. It makes no difference whether (1) decedent personally or someone else created the fractional interest in decedent, [Cf. 2–205, Comment]; or (2) the interest was created before or after the marriage to the surviving spouse. It applies to all joint tenancies with right of survivorship interests even if the decedent does not hold a unilateral power to sever the joint tenancy but merely holds an equal voice in such decision. [2–205, Comment]. It is the fractional interest coupled with the right of survivorship that triggers the inclusion of these interests. A joint interest in a survivorship interest is equivalent to full ownership as to the fractional part. The value of the includable property equals the value of the decedent's fractional interest to the extent it passed by right of survivorship.

(C) Property in which decedent held an ownership interest in any property, account or registration held in POD, TOD, or co-ownership with right of survivorship. [2–205(1)(iii)]. It makes no difference whether the interest was created before or after the marriage to the surviving spouse. It applies to all types of financial arrangements in which decedent held accounts or other financial devices in decedent's own name with a survivorship interest in one or more third persons other than the surviving spouse. The value of the includable interest is the extent of the decedent's ownership interest that passed at death to or for the third persons named on the account. Typical examples of property interests includable under this provision consist of multiple-party financial and security TOD registration accounts. [See §§ 16.02, 16.03] An ownership interest in one of these account is equivalent to full ownership; therefore, its inclusion in the augmented estate is reasonable.

(D) The proceeds of any type of life insurance policy on decedent's life that decedent owned immediately prior to death or over which decedent retained a personal, unshared, presently exercisable general power of appointment over the policy or its proceeds. [2–205(1)(iv)]. Ownership is not defined but probably includes any incident of ownership such as a power to change the beneficiary. A power includes the power to designate the beneficiary of the policy. [2–201(5)]. Life insurance is broadly defined to include accidental death insurance. It makes no difference who originally purchased the policy or whether the policy was purchased before or after the marriage to the surviving spouse so long as the decedent owns the policy or holds a presently exercisable power of appointment over it. The value of the includable amount equals the value of the proceeds to the extent that value passes to third persons at decedent's death. As part of the surviving spouse's nonprobate transfers to others, however, policies on and controlled by the surviving spouse are valued at their adjusted interpolated terminal reserve value as of decedent's date of death. [2–207, Comment; see Treas. Reg. § 20.2031–8]. The control over a life insurance policy required by this provision is equivalent to full ownership of the policy.

It is important to note that this provision does not specifically include other types of policy arrangements such as annuities and retirement agreements. [See 2–205(2)(i)]. It also does not include the life insurance owned by the decedent on others' lives. To the extent these policies have value, they will be valued as part of the decedent's probate (Segment 1) estate.

(2) The value of property that the decedent gratuitously transferred to third persons during marriage to the surviving spouse but in which the decedent retained specified interests or powers. The following transfers are included:

(A) Property irrevocably transferred by decedent to the extent the decedent retained a right to possession or enjoyment of or the income from the property at the time of decedent's death. [2–205(2)(i)]. A right to income includes payments under annuity and other similar contractual arrangements. [2–201(9)]. When this provision applies, the value includable in the augmented estate is the value of whatever portion of the property to which decedent's retained interest related. It is important to distinguish the situation covered by this provision from the situation where decedent holds or retains only a life interest in an interest created by someone else or transferred by decedent prior to the marriage to the surviving spouse. In the latter situation, no portion of the value of the property is included in decedent's augmented estate because decedent did not transfer the interest and retain a life interest during the marriage.

(B) Property transferred by decedent to the extent the income or principal of the property remained at the time of the decedent's death subject to a power exercisable either by decedent alone or in conjunction with any other person, or by a nonadverse party, for the benefit of decedent, decedent's creditors or creditors of decedent's estate. [2–205(2)(ii)]. The scope of this inclusion is different from the inclusion of the property subject to an unshared presently exercisable power of appointment. The power covered by this provision includes only powers created or retained in regard to decedent's transfers. It includes, however, not only unshared powers retained by decedent but also powers decedent shared with others and even powers exercisable by nonadverse person. A nonadverse person is one who does not have a substantial beneficial interest in the property.

[2–201(4)]. In addition, the property is included whether the power extends over the property's principal or the income or both. The value of the includable property equals the value of the property or its earnings that are subject to the power to the extent (1) the power was exercisable at decedent's death to or for the benefit of any third person, or (2) the property subject to the power passed at decedent's death by exercise, release, lapse, in default, or otherwise to or for the benefit of any third person.

(3) The value of property irrevocably transferred to third persons by decedent during marriage to the surviving spouse and within a two year period preceding decedent's date of death that would otherwise have been included within Segment 2 if it had not been transferred or that exceeds a certain amount. The following transfers are included:

(A) Property that passes as a result of the termination of a right or interest in or power over any property that would have been included in Segment 2 of the augmented estate under (1)(A), (B), and (C) or (2)(A), above, if the right, interest, or power had not terminated before the decedent's death. [2–205(3)(i)]. A termination means the right or interest was (a) terminated by the terms of the governing instrument, or (b) transferred or relinquished by decedent. [2–205(3)(i)]. A power terminates when it is exercised, released, lapsed, defaulted or otherwise ended, but a presently exercisable general power of appointment terminates only when exercised or released and not merely by lapse, default or otherwise. The value of the includable property under this provision equals the same value that the property would have had if the transfer had not occurred except that the valuation date is the time of the termination of decedent's power or interest and that the value is limited only to the extent the property passed upon termination to or for the benefit of any third person.

(B) Any transfer of insurance on the decedent's life if the proceeds would have been included under (1)(D) had the transfer not occurred. [2–205(3)(ii)]. The value of the includable amount equals the value of the proceeds to the extent they passed at decedent's death to or for the benefit of any third person.

(C) Property irrevocably transferred to or for the benefit of third persons but only to the extent the aggregate value of all transfers to any donee exceeds $10,000 in either year. [2–205(3)(iii)]. This provision protects the surviving spouse against large near death gifts but recognizes a significant small gift exclusion. Irrevocable transfers prior to the two years before death are excluded in total and regardless of value.

Segment 3 of the Augmented Estate: The third segment (hereinafter called Segment 3) includes all of decedent's nonprobate property which the surviving spouse gratuitously received or derived from the decedent by reason of the latter's death. [2–206]. This includes property received by the surviving spouse from decedent by way of survivorship, appointment, benefits of life insurance on decedent's life, benefits from retirement plans in which decedent participated and of any other property that would have been included as parts (1) and (2) of Segment 2, described above, had it passed to a third person. Social security system survivorship benefits are, however, specifically exempt. Segment 3 also does not include any Segment 1 properties received from the decedent's estate or the value of the spouse's family protections. [2–202(c); see § 5.02].

Segment 4 of the Augmented Estate: The fourth segment (hereinafter called Segment 4) includes (1) all of the surviving spouse's individual property and (2) the surviving spouse's Segment 2 property (the spouse's nonprobate transfers to others) as if that spouse predeceased decedent, to the extent these properties are not included in Segments 1 and 3. [2–207]. This Segment is all inclusive and supplemental to the other segments. It includes not only assets earned during the marriage but also assets acquired prior to marriage and assets derived gratuitously from the decedent and other persons. It also includes the spouse's fractional interests in survivorship property, the ownership interests in financial accounts and security registrations and property passing to the spouse by reason of the decedent's death. In addition, it includes the commuted value of income and other future interests. [2–208(b)(2)].

Property included under Segment 4 is valued at the decedent's death except that the value of spouse's fractional and ownership interests in survivorship property and in financial accounts and security registrations are valued immediately before decedent's death. [2–207(b)]. The value of enforceable claims against any property or against the spouse are deducted from the value of the property included. [2–207(c)]. Life insurance on the spouse's life that is includable in Segment 4 is valued at its present value and not its value as of the surviving spouse's death. [2–207(b)]. Segment 4 guarantees that surviving spouses will have to account for their own estate and estate plan in opting for the elective share.

Summary of the Augmented Estate: The sum of the value of these four segments equals the augmented estate and the surviving spouse's elective share equals the elective share percentage times the augmented estate. A comprehensive hypothetical graphically outlining the parts of the augmented estate and the necessary calculations can be perused at Averill, UPC Nutshell 121–30 (5th Edition, 2001).

For income and other partial interests includable under Segment 3 and Segment 4, value equals the commuted value of any amounts payable to the surviving spouse either currently or after decedent's death under trusts, life insurance settlement options, annuity contracts, public or private pensions, and disability compensation arrangements. [2–208(b)(2)]. This means that the date of death value must be determined for serial payments of income to the surviving spouse in the future. The method of determining such value is not specified and will be part of the advocative process when an elective share is sought and will have to be determined by the court under the particular circumstances of the case. [See Langbein & Waggoner, The New Uniform Probate Code, at 883].

§ 4.02 Exclusions From the Augmented Estate

Several qualifications and exclusions to the augmented estate deserve special mention. Because the nonprobate transfers to others of both spouses concern gratuitous transactions by the spouses, transfers for which either spouse received adequate and full consideration in money or money's worth are excluded from the augmented estate. [2–208(a)]. The augmented estate also excludes all nonprobate transfers made with the written consent or joinder of the other spouse.

Antenuptial and postnuptial contracts, agreements and waivers of a right of election of a surviving spouse are also specifically recognized so long as they are (a) in writing, (b) voluntary, and (c) not unconscionable. [2–213(a)]. The family protection allowances may similarly be waived. The surviving spouse who contests a waiver has the burden of showing that the waiver was not executed voluntarily or it was unconscionable when executed and lacked fair disclosure prior to execution. [2–213(b); see, e.g., Lopata v. Metzel, 641 P.2d 952 (Colo. 1982)]. Fair disclosure is explained. It must be either (a) a "fair and reasonable disclosure" of the decedent's assets and liabilities, (b) a voluntary and express waiver of any disclosure, or (c) knowledge of the decedent's assets and liabilities was possessed or reasonably available. [2–213(b)(2)(i)–(iii)]. Unconscionability is a question of law and is not a jury question. [2–213].

If the relevant agreement waives "all rights" or contains equivalent language, each spouse waives all rights to elective share and the family protections in the other spouse's estate and renounces all interests passing from the other spouse by intestacy or by a will executed before the agreement. [2–213(d)].

In addition, certain gratuitous transfers by the spouses are excluded. First, transfers made prior to the marriage with the other spouse are excluded even if interests are retained so long as the retained interests are not characterizable as certain types of Segment 2 powers. [2–205; see § 4.03]. Examples of common interests that might be retained in pre-marriage transfers and not cause inclusion include life interests and nongeneral powers of appointment. An example of a retained interest that would cause inclusion in the augmented estates is an unrestricted, unshared power to revoke held at death. [2–205(1)(i)]. Second, irrevocable and outright gifts to third persons up to $10,000 per donee per year are excluded whenever they are made. [2–205(3)(iii)]. The first exclusion assists in clearing titles and reduces disruption to finalized gratuitous transfers that an elected share petition can cause.

The second exclusion protects normal donative transfers from elective share attack. Both exclusions may be occasionally abused by spouses and might propel a court to ignore the literal application of the UPC and apply inherent equitable powers over abusive spousal share avoidance transfers. [See Langbein & Waggoner, New Uniform Probate Code, at 881 n.12].

Finally, the UPC permits third persons, e.g., parents, grandparents and other relatives, to transfer property in trust for the benefit of a person who is married or may get married and still protect the property from the elective share of the person's surviving spouse. Unless the trust beneficiary holds an unshared presently exercisable power to appointment, a fractional share held in joint tenancy with right of survivorship, or the remainder of the trust estate passes as part of the beneficiary's probate estate at death, the trust assets will not be part of the augmented estate if the beneficiary's surviving spouse seeks an elective share against the beneficiary's estate. This trust is exempt even if the beneficiary holds any one or more of the following interests: a life interest, an inter vivos or testamentary nongeneral power of appointment, and a presently exercisable general power of appointment if the latter power is limited by an ascertainable standard or is exercisable only with the consent of an adverse or nonadverse person. The exclusion from the augmented estate of interests in trusts that are created by third persons protects family estate plans from the disruption of elective share petitions by surviving spouses. If the property were transferred outright to the beneficiary, however, the property would be part of the augmented estate. If these same interests are held by the surviving spouse, they must be included in Segment 4 of the augmented estate as "property owned" by that spouse. [2–207; see 2–201(7)]. In this situation, the interests would be valued at their commuted valued. This distinction between the inclusion in the augmented estate for interests held by the decedent as compared with those held by the surviving spouses may impose an unequal economic burden on the surviving spouse.

The UPC includes provisions protecting payors, and other third persons who dealt with a beneficiary prior to notice that the surviving spouse intends to file or has filed a petition for the elective share. [2–214; see § 9.04].

§ 4.03 Funding the Elective Share

The third step in analyzing the elective share processes is the matter of funding the elective share amount or the supplemental elective share. Once the elective share percentage and the augmented estate are determined, a monetary amount is set by multiplying the elective share percentage times the augmented estate. For example, if the spouses have been married 11½ years, the Marital–Property Portion equals 68%, and if the augmented estate equals $500,000, the Marital–Property equals $340,000 and elective share amount equals 50% of that amount or

$170,000. [See § 4.02, Chart 4–1]. How that amount is going to be funded is the subject of this section.

For funding purposes, the UPC divides the augmented estate into three separate hotchpots or funds. Each fund is composed of property interests that are included in the augmented estate depending on certain characterization decisions that will be explained. The ultimate goal is to fully fund the elective share amount. To accomplish this goal and to allocate the necessary contribution from each fund, the funds are arranged in an order of priority. Fund 1 interests must contribute first to satisfy the elective share amount and must be exhausted before seeking contribution from Fund 2 interests. Fund 3 interests are required to contribute if the previous two funds do not fully satisfy the elective share amount.

Fund 1 is composed of the amounts of the augmented estate that are received or attributable to the surviving spouse** and includes the following amounts:

** The 1993 Technical Amendments eliminated the provision that required the surviving spouse to deduct interests in the augmented estate that passed to the spouse but were disclaimed. Although the removal of this provision is defended as further recognition of the economic partnership of marriage, it may cause the UPC's elective share system to have much greater application. It alters the emphasis of the UPC's elective share provisions from protection from disinheritance to a form of community property ownership. The change means that adequate provision for the surviving spouse is not enough, it must be adequate ownership in fee. Under the change, trusts, such as the QTIP trust, for the surviving spouse will be at risk of full or partial destruction if the surviving spouse elective ownership

1. The intestate and testate portions of Segment 1 that pass to the surviving spouse from the decedent;

2. The amounts included in Segment 3;

3. The marital property portion times the amounts of Segment 4 of the augmented estate.

[2–209(a)]. If after deducting the value of the surviving spouse's share, the elective share amount is satisfied, this is the end of the process and thus the surviving spouse will take nothing further.

If there remains an elective share deficiency, Fund 2 must be calculated and it includes the following amounts: (1) the amounts of the non-spousal portions of Segment 1; and (2) the amount of Segment 2 of the augmented estate less the value of certain irrevocable transfers made by decedent within the two year period prior to death. [2–209(b); 2–205(3)(i) and (iii); see § 4.01(C)]. The third person beneficiaries of these included amounts must contribute to the funding of the elective share deficiency. All contributions from these beneficiaries are made on a pro rata basis. A pro rata share

share is not otherwise satisfied by the estate plan. In the multi-family situations, the destruction of these types of trusts, in whole or in part, may fuel the litigation fires between surviving spouses and decedent's surviving descendants of a prior marriage. It was this type of litigation that the UPC intends to avoid. Notwithstanding the increased litigation, removal of the disclaimer limitation will increase the number of estates where the surviving spouse might seek the elective share because the surviving spouse finds it desirable to take decedent's augmented estate in fee rather than in trust. Concomitantly, it will impose the complexity of the elective share procedure, and thus higher costs of administration, on a larger number of estates.

equals the value of the recipient's interest divided by total value of Fund 2. Fund 2 transfers must be fully exhausted before proceeding to Fund 3.

If interests in Fund 2 assets are exhausted and the elective share amount still remains unsatisfied, Fund 3 must be calculated. It includes the irrevocable transfers made by decedent within the two year period prior to death that are included in Segment 2 except for life insurance proceeds of policies irrevocably transferred by decedent during this period of time. [2–209(c); 2–205(3)(i) and (iii)]. The insurance proceeds are included in Fund 2. [2–209(b); 2–205(3)(ii)]. The recipients of Fund 3 must contribute to the remaining unsatisfied portion of elective share amount. All contributors of Fund 3 contribute on a pro rata basis. A pro rata share equals the value of recipient's interest divided by the value of Fund 3. The elective share amount should be fully funded after the three contribution steps are completed.

Only the original recipients and their gratuitous donees are liable for contribution. [2–210]. In addition, a recipient may either pay the value of the amount of contribution due or give up the proportional part of the nonprobate reclaimable asset received. No recipient or gratuitous donee of a recipient is required to contribute more than the pro rata portion as determined through the above funding process even though the elective share amount is not fully satisfied because some recipients are unable to contribute or are jurisdictionally unavailable. [2–211(d); see also 2–209(b) and (c)]. For example, if a recipient of Fund 2 interests is unable or unavailable to pay the pro rata portion, the other recipients of Fund 2 amounts do not have to make up the difference. Fund 3 recipients must contribute only if Fund 2 is insufficient to satisfy assuming all recipients in Fund 2 contributed their full pro rata portion. These limitations on funding mean that some surviving spouses will not be able to collect their full elective share amount.

The funding procedures require valuation determination similar to those required for the augmented estate procedure. A difference may apply in regard to determining the value of Fund 1. If the surviving spouse takes a partial or future interest from the decedent spouse's will, these interests will be valued at their commuted value. [2–208(b)(2)]. A life interest, e.g., a QTIP trust, for the benefit of the surviving spouse in a trust in the will of the decedent spouse is a common example of such an interest. Otherwise the valuation determinations are the same.

§ 4.04   The Election Procedure

In order to take the elective share, the surviving spouse must file in court and mail to the personal representative a petition for such share within nine months after the date of death or within six months after decedent's will is probated, whichever limitation last expires. [2–211(a)]. Notwithstanding these overall limitation periods, Segment 2 assets will only be included in the augmented estate if the petition is filed within nine months after the date of death. For good cause shown and if requested before the nine month limitation expires, the surviving spouse may seek and obtain an extension of the time for election from the Court. If the petition is filed within the time set for the extension, the Segment 2 assets are included.

The elective share procedure under the UPC requires that there be full notice and a hearing. Notice of time and place of the hearing must be given by the surviving spouse to all persons interested in the estate and to Segment 1 distributees and Segment 2 recipients whose interests will be adversely affected by the elective share petition. [2–211(a)]. The Court, then, has the responsibility for determining the elective share, its satisfaction and the liability of recipients for contribution. [2–211(d)].

A petition demanding the elective share may be withdrawn by the surviving spouse any time before entry of a final determination. [2–211(c)]. In addition, the right of election is personal to the surviving spouse and cannot be exercised by anyone else before or after the surviving spouse's death; however, it may be exercised on behalf of the surviving spouse by a conservator, guardian or agent under a power of attorney. [2–212(a); see 5–407(b)(3)].

The UPC's provisions attempt to strike a balance between encouraging and restricting a surviving spouse from petitioning for the election. [Art. II, Pt. 2, General Comment]. In addition, they definitely will encourage persons concerned about potential election problems to seek counseling. Because many of these questions cannot be determined within filing limitation periods, and because an election petition may be withdrawn without adverse consequences, petitioning for the elective share as a matter of course in uncertain cases might be advisable in order to protect the surviving spouse's elective option. On the other hand, retention of the assets received by the recipients until the limitation period expires might be desirable because it puts a ceiling upon their contribution. If a will exists, Segment 1 recipients will definitely want to start the six-month statute of limitations running by probating it.

If the surviving spouse is incapacitated and the election is exercised by a proper person representing the spouse, amounts received by the fiduciary in satisfaction of the elective share amount from Segment 1 and Segment 2 must be placed in a custodial trust under the Uniform Custodial Trust Act or, if the enacting state does not have that Act, under the terms of a custodial trust established in the UPC. [2–212(b)]. Under the statutory custodial trust, the fiduciary electing for the surviving spouse is the trustee, the surviving spouse is the beneficiary, the decedent spouse is the settlor, and the date of the trust is the date of the decedent's death.

The trustee is required to administer the trust for the benefit of the beneficiary. [2–212(c)(2)]. The trustee has discretion to expend trust property for the use and benefit of the beneficiary and others who were supported by the beneficiary when the incapacity occurred or who are legally entitled to support from the beneficiary. The trustee may without court order determine when, how and what is expended. The trustee must, however, take into account the beneficiaries' other support, income and property including government benefits such as social security and medicare. [2–212, Comment]. If the enacting state provides, the trust may have to consider need qualification limits set for other government assistance programs such as medicaid.

Unless the incapacitated surviving spouse regains capacity and terminates the trust, no one including the incapacitated spouse may terminate the trust. [2–212(c)(1)]. The trust automatically terminates on the death of the incapacitated spouse. On termination at the surviving spouse's death, the remaining trust property passes according to the estate plan, if any, of the predeceased spouse against whose estate the surviving spouse had elected the elective share. The property passes as if the predeceased spouse died immediately after the surviving spouse rather than before. If the predeceased spouse had a will, the will controls if it effectively disposes of the estate. If the will fails to dispose of the property or there is no will, the property passes to the predeceased spouse's heirs determined at the time of the surviving spouse's death. [2–212(c)(3), 2–711, 2–105; §§ 8.05(D), 3.01(C)].

CHAPTER 5

FAMILY OMISSIONS AND PROTECTIONS

§ 5.01   Pretermitted Spouses and Children

A.   PRETERMITTED SPOUSE

A situation related to disinheritance of a spouse concerns the spouse who is not provided for as a spouse in the will because the marriage to testator occurred after the execution of the will. Most states do not specifically protect the spouse but rely on their spousal protection provisions against disinheritance. The UPC contains a special remedy for this situation.

Under the UPC, if a surviving spouse is a pretermitted spouse, the spouse is entitled to a spouse's intestate share valued at no less than the value the spouse would have received if the testator had died intestate. [2–301(a)]. The provision's application is dependent only upon the fact that the marriage occurred after the will was executed. This is not an election on the part of the surviving spouse but an intestacy right. It is not avoided merely because the spouse was a devisee under the will. The only consequence of the spouse being a devisee is that the spouse must deduct the devise from the intestacy share required by the statute. This intestate share is limited, however, to the portion of the testator's estate that is not devised to one or more children of the testator who were born before the marriage to the surviving spouse and who are not children of the surviving spouse. Devises to children or descendants of the child who take under the antilapse provisions of Section 2–603 or 2–604 are also exempt from this share.

The UPC recognizes several important exceptions to this intestacy share right. First, there is no intestacy right if the will or other evidence indicates it was made in contemplation of the testator's marriage to the surviving spouse. Second, the testator may express an intention that the will is effective notwithstanding subsequent marriage or marriages. Third, the share does not apply if the testator provided for the surviving spouse by way of transfers outside the will and these transfers were intended in lieu of a testamentary provision. The latter intent may be shown by statements of the testator or from reasonable inferences from the nature of the transfer or other evidence. The burden of proof of satisfying any or all of the exceptions is placed upon the moving party urging the application of one or more of the exceptions. [2–301, Comment].

It is not clear whether transfers outside the will act as advancements and therefore as deductions from the intestacy share or whether they must be only in total substitution for the share. For example, consider the situation where the calculated intestacy share equals $100,000. How would a life insurance policy in favor of the surviving spouse for $50,000 be treated? Does the testator's intent to make the transfer in lieu of a testamentary provision relate only to a full satisfaction, i.e., the $50,000 is in place of the $100,000, or might the surviving spouse have to treat the $50,000 as an advancement and bring it into the hotchpot for subsequent recalculation? The latter approach would seem to be a more equitable approach both in terms of a share of the surviving spouse and in terms of the consequences of this intestate's share coming out of gifts to other persons.

The justification for this provision is that it attempts to do what most testators probably would want to do had they contemplated the prior will and the changed marital circumstances. [2–301, Comment]. In addition, it may reduce the number of elections against the estate under the elective share provisions. With the stated liberal extrinsic evidence rules and relatively complete elaboration of differing situations, the UPC exceptions should provide sufficient barriers to the application of this section where it was not intended. On the other hand, although the provision attempts to address the variables and to protect against misuse of the provision, it does not contain the explicit limitations and procedures imposed by the elective share provisions designed to address these problems.

In calculating the surviving spouse's share it is necessary to create an internal hotchpot in the estate. First, the net distributable estate is calculated and the devises to the qualified children or descendants of children are subtracted from that estate. The spouse's intestate share then would be calculated against the remaining amount. Abatement, therefore, is suffered only by the beneficiaries of the will who are not in the preferred class of children or descendants of children. The general abatement provision of the UPC is applicable to abatement of these devises caused by the application of this provision. [2–301(b); 3–902; § 14.01].

B. PRETERMITTED CHILDREN

Except in the State of Louisiana, no other jurisdiction within the United States has an effective forced kinship provision in favor of descendants and other heirs; consequently, if one desires, one may disinherit one's children. [Atkinson, Wills § 36]. Although this disinheritance power may be partially altered by the statutory family protections [see § 5.02], the closest and most common facsimile to forced kinship provisions is one that protects pretermitted descendants. The general rationale behind such provisions is that it is presumed the testator did not intend to disinherit the descendant who is omitted in the testator's will. Among the states which have such provisions, their contents vary greatly as to who, when and how they are to be applied.

Because pretermitted heir statutes are intended and designed to prevent injustice and reduce will contests when unintentionally omitted heirs survive a testator, the statute should be designed to accomplish these goals. Unfortunately, some statutes that exist in non-UPC states have actually produced the opposite results. Accordingly, the UPC's provision contains very precise prerequisites and limitations that are designed to reduce this litigation and judicial misinterpretation.

The UPC establishes conditional thresholds against which each applicable situation must be tested. [2–302(a)]. First, the protection is limited to pretermitted children and does not protect disinheritance of other descendants and relatives. Second, the child must be born or adopted after the execution of the will that disinherits the child. Third, intent to disinherit must not appear on the "face of the will." Fourth, the disinherited or omitted child must not have been provided for by transfers outside the will intended to be in lieu of testamentary provision. [2–302(b)]. A liberal admissibility of extrinsic evidence rule is adopted in regard to proof of intent to use nontestamentary transfers in lieu of testamentary transfers. Extrinsic evidence may include the testator's declarations, the value of the transfer vis à vis the estate and "other evidence" that is relevant to proof of intent.

If the threshold requirements are satisfied, the omitted child must then test the section's protection against two factual circumstances. The first standard applies to situations where the testator had no children living when the will was executed. [2–302(a)(1)]. The second standard applies where the testator had one or more children living when the will was executed. [2–302(a)(2)]. In the first situation the omitted child takes an intestate share from the estate unless the natural or adopted child's parent is "devised all or substantially all" of the estate, survives the testator and is entitled to take under the will. The last condition concerns whether the will might have been revoked by other law. Several matters are left unanswered. Assumably, the child's parent does not have to be the spouse of the decedent: marriage between the decedent and that child's other parent would not seem to be necessary.

The general abatement provision of the UPC is applicable to abatement of devises caused by the application of this provision. [2–302(d); 3–902; § 14.01].

If testator had one or more children living when the will was executed, the pretermitted child takes only if one or more of those existing children at the time of the will's execution received a legal or equitable interest in the estate from the will. [2–302(a)(2)]. If pre-will children take, the pretermitted child takes a representative pro rata share from the total value of the interests devised to the pre-existing children. The interest of the pre-existing children's devises abate pro rata according to their respective interests. The nature of the interest accorded, e.g., legal, equitable, present, future, to the omitted child must conform to the extent possible to the character to the devises to the pre-existing children. In general, the character of the estate plan must be preserved to the maximum degree possible.

In other words, the pretermitted child does not take a separate share from the estate but is a forced devisee among the gifts given to the pre-existing children. Chart 5–1 uses a hypothetical to illustrate the process.

CHART 5–1
Computation of a Pretermitted Child's Share

Hypothetical 1: Testator has two living children, A and B, when will was executed. Will provides nothing for A and B. Subsequent to will execution, C is born. Testator dies.

Answer: Under the Code's pretermitted children section, the pretermitted child C would not be entitled to take anything from the estate because pre-existing children of the testator were not devised property under the will. Thus, all children are treated equally even if decedent's children are born both before and after the will is executed. Some pretermitted heir statutes give C a share although A and B would take nothing.

Hypothetical 2: Testator has two children A and B when will is executed. The will gives $9,000 to A and $9,000 to B. Subsequent to the will execution, C is born. Testator dies.

Answer: C takes a portion of the devises to A and B. C does not take from other assets in the estate. In this example, C takes $6,000. A and B each take $6,000. Their $9,000 devises are abated $3,000 apiece.

Hypothetical 3: Assuming the same condition as hypothetical 2 except that the will gives A $6,000 and B $12,000. Testator dies.

Answer: C takes a pro rata share of the total of the gifts to A and B. As one of the three children, C takes one-third of $18,000 which equals the total gifts to A and B. In other words, C takes 6,000. Since B received two-thirds of the total of those gifts, two-thirds of the $6,000 will come from B's share. Concomitantly, one-third of the forced share of C will come from A's devise. This means that A's interest will be abated by $2,000 and B's interest will be abated by $4,000. The final distribution of these gifts will be A will take $4,000, B will take $8,000 and C will take $6,000. Although this solution does not result in perfect equality, it addresses the pretermitted heir problem, it attempts to address the presumed intent of the testator due to the pretermission, and it attempts to provide basic equality among those who do take. Although A now takes less than C, the loss was a pro rata portion of the abatement. In addition, the satisfaction of the pretermitted child's forced share has no effect on the other devises made in the will. Consequently, the total estate plan suffers minimal disruption and abatement problems are greatly diminished.

The UPC also incorporates a specific exception to the general exclusionary evidence rule concerned with mistake in the inducement. This provision treats a child living when the will was executed who is omitted because the testator believed the child to be dead as an omitted after-born or after-adopted

child. [2–302(c)]. The admissibility and sufficiency
of evidence concerning such a belief are controlled
by the general rules of evidence and burden of proof
of the UPC state. [See 2–601, Comment]. The provision does not protect the omitted child if the child
would have been omitted had the child been alive,
or if the child had been provided for by transfers
outside the will intended to be in lieu of testamentary provision. [2–302(b), and Comment]. The share
from the estate is limited in the same manner as
the share of an omitted child. [See 2–302(a) and
(b)].

§ 5.02   The Family Protections

It is common for states to have statutes that
attempt to financially protect a decedent's family
unit. These statutes typically provide specified surviving family members of a decedent with a mini-
mal amount of protection both from the decedent's
creditors and from the decedent's own intentional
disinheritance. Although these statutes come in a
variety of kinds and names, they are commonly
broken down into three categories: (1) homesteads,
(2) exemptions and (3) allowances. The UPC contains a representative for all three categories of the
above family protections. In 2008, the suggested
dollar amounts were adjusted for inflation. The
dollar amounts are subject to annual cost-of-living
adjustments under UPC 1–109.

Although the UPC's provisions on homestead [2–
402], exemptions [2–403] and allowance [2–404] differ in many respects, there is a significant degree of

similarity and a definite interrelationship between all of them. Significantly, all three limit their benefits only for relatives of a decedent who died domiciled in the UPC state. [2–401]. To qualify under any of the categories the protected beneficiaries must survive the decedent by 120 hours. [Art. II, Pt. 4, General Comment; see 2–104]. Although all benefits received under all three provisions are ordinarily in addition to any share passing to the beneficiaries by intestacy, by elective share of the surviving spouse and by will, a testator may specifically in his will make devises to these beneficiaries in lieu of any or all family protection benefits. For example, the will might state "This devise to my [surviving spouse or children] is expressly in lieu of [his, her or their] right to the homestead allowance, exempt property and the family allowance; any acceptance of such benefits shall be charged against this devise." Although a decedent in a will may thus limit devises to the protected beneficiaries to an amount no greater than the amount provided by these family protections, the decedent cannot by will take away or limit these amounts below the statutory minimum without a prior waiver. [See 2–213; In re Estate of Peterson v. Moore, 576 N.W.2d 767 (Neb. 1998)]. Consequently, the UPC's family protections preclude disinheritance to the extent of their monetary limitations.

These provisions also provide their beneficiaries with protection against a decedent's unsecured creditors: they are all expressly exempt from, and are in priority to, all unsecured claims against the estate. The family protections have priority even over expenses of administration. [Compare Art. II, Pt. 4 with 3–805; see In re Estate of Hutchinson, 577 P.2d 1074 (Alaska 1978)]. If the estate is not sufficient even to satisfy all of the family protections, the UPC interrelates these three protective devices so that an order of priority of payment is established. [See also § 16.02(F)]. The homestead allowance is satisfied first, followed by the family allowance which under these circumstances may not last for more than one year, and finally followed by satisfaction of the exempt property allowance. Finally, the monetary value of these family protection provisions is the benchmark for application of the UPC's summary administration procedures for the small estate. [See 3–1203, 3–1204; § 10.03(B)].

A. PROTECTIVE AMOUNTS AND THEIR BENEFICIARIES

Homestead Allowance: The UPC provides for a specific monetary homestead allowance either for the surviving spouse or, if there is no surviving spouse, an equal share of the allowance for each minor child and each dependent child of the deceased. [2–402]. The suggested amount, which is alterable by enacting legislatures, is $22,500. The UPC also includes an optional provision that coordinates its homestead allowance with any existing state constitutional homestead right tied to the family home, i.e., the value of the family home is charged against the UPC's monetary homestead allowance. [2–402A].

Exempt Property Allowance: The UPC also provides a $15,000 exempt property allowance in favor of either the surviving spouse or the decedent's children if there is no surviving spouse. [2–403]. Significantly, the children need not be minors or dependents of the decedent. The exempt property allowances will ordinarily first be charged against household furniture, automobiles, furnishings, appliances and personal effects. [3–906(a)(1)]. If the value of these assets, less security interests held by third parties against them, does not equal the specified monetary amount, however, the protected beneficiaries are entitled to other assets of the estate to the extent necessary to make up the difference.

Family Allowance: For purposes of support and maintenance during the period of administration, the UPC provides for the payment from the estate of a reasonable monetary allowance for the benefit of the surviving spouse, minor legal dependents and other actually dependent children. [2–404]. The allowance may be paid either to the surviving spouse or, if there is no surviving spouse, to the children or dependents or their guardians. When a child or dependent does not live with the surviving spouse, however, the allowance may be apportioned between the surviving spouse and the child or other dependent as their respective needs require. Any allowance may be paid in a lump sum or in periodic installments. If the estate is insolvent, an allowance cannot continue for more than one year from the decedent's death. A protected person's death terminates the right to the family allowance including even approved unpaid amounts. [2–404(b)].

B. PROCEDURAL PROVISIONS

Ordinarily, the determination and distribution of the family protection rights will be accomplished informally by the personal representative and the protected persons without the need of court proceedings or supervision. [2–405; see 3–901]. The Court is empowered to give appropriate relief, however, when a personal representative or any aggrieved person requests such by petition. For example, whether a family allowance should be extended is a matter within the discretion of the trial court. [Dandrea v. McCarty, 577 P.2d 1112 (Colo.App. 1978)].

Several important limitations are imposed upon the personal representative and the determination of the family protections. [2–405(a)]. First, the homestead and the exempt property allowance may not be satisfied with property specifically devised when other assets of the estate are otherwise sufficient. Second, the personal representative, without court order, may not set and distribute a family allowance which exceeds a lump sum of more than $27,000 or periodic payments of more than $2,250 per month for one year. Third, the homestead and the family allowance cannot be satisfied in kind with assets out of the residue that a residuary devisee requests remain in the estate. [3–906(a)(2)(iii)].

If the surviving spouse is incapacitated and the spouse's representative elects to exercise the elective share, unexpended portions of the three family protection provisions may be added to the custodial trust created under the elective share procedure. [2–405(b); see 2–212; § 4.04].

CHAPTER 6
WILL AND DONATIVE TRANSFERS

§ 6.01 Wills and Related Doctrines

A. INTRODUCTION

1. The Statute of Wills

A fundamental device for distributing wealth upon death is the will. Presently, a will is a creature of statute. To constitute a valid will, these statutory provisions customarily require that a will must: (1) be voluntarily executed; (2) be executed by a competent person; (3) appear in a written or other specifically approved form; (4) be intended to take effect only after the testator's death; and (5) dispose of property, or make other directions, or both. [See 1 Page, Wills § 1.2]. Wills are ambulatory in the sense that they apply to the situation that exists at the testator's death rather than that which was present at the time of the execution. [See 2–602]. Wills are also revocable by a competent testator who follows the proper revocation procedure. [See 2–507; § 9.03].

A codicil is a will with a special purpose. Normally the special purpose is to amend a primary will. Even if there is a primary will, the codicil must be properly executed according to a valid will execution procedure. Because it must be executed as a will, it may be able to stand on its own if the "primary" will is not effective.

Although all jurisdictions by statute provide methods for making and revoking wills, execution requirements unfortunately vary greatly between them. This lack of uniformity results in a serious lack of predictability for persons whose estates cross state lines or who change domiciles during their lives.

2. UPC Policy and Devices

The UPC's will provisions have three primary objectives: (1) to make uniform among the jurisdictions the execution requirements for wills; (2) to reduce execution requirements to their indispensable minimum; and (3) to validate as often as possible instruments purporting to be wills.

For basic validity, the UPC recognizes four separate and alternative will execution techniques, the successful satisfaction of any one of which produces a probatable will in the UPC state. For convenience, the four techniques result in four types of wills called the ordinary witnessed will [2–502(a)], the holographic or handwritten will [2–502(b)], the foreign will [2–506], and the international will. [Art. II, Pt. 10, Uniform International Wills Act]. The UPC also includes a special procedure for executing a fifth kind of will called the self-proved will, which although not essential for basic validity is useful to follow for purposes of easing proof of execution requirements in contested will cases. [2–504]. Significantly, the UPC does not include recognized procedures for nuncupative or other types of special wills.

3. Formality Analysis

Legal scholarship is rife with discussions of the merits, demerits and proper utility for formalities. [See, e.g., Gulliver & Tilson, Gratuitous Transfers; Langbein, Substantial Compliance]. Several purposes have been identified including purposes to protect and safeguard the testator, to provide reliable proof and evidence, to provide an event that emphasizes the finality of intent and of the act of execution, to result in a document that will receive the anticipated legal response and recognition and to provide administrative judicial efficiency. The purposes present a good case for requiring certain formalities to take place before one should be said to have satisfied the requirements. Considering the solemnness, importance, and finality of a will, it has been common for states to set out elaborate formalities necessary to be followed in order to satisfy and to produce a recognizable and valid will.

Generally, a will is an intent enforcing type of document. The goal of the instrument is to identify and explain the desires of the testator. It is assumed that if these desires and intent are adequately expressed, they will be obeyed. The difficulty is that they have no effect and are a nullity unless the instrument can be proven and thereby probated. To probate one must satisfy the execution formalities set out in the statute that recognizes a will as a transfer device. The dilemma created by legal formalities is that if a formality is not obeyed and it is considered a crucial formality, the failure to satisfy the formality may cause the instrument to fail and thus cause an intent denying rather than intent enforcing result.

Because the validity or invalidity of an instrument such as a will may be so important in terms of the distribution of an estate, the determination of validity has been a highly litigated issue. Opponents of wills will offer any reason to deny probate. Consequently, the formalities of the execution statute have been fertile fodder for these arguments. Courts that face this litigation are put in a policy bind. On the one hand, the court is conscious and respectful of legislative intent as expressed in the appropriate wills statute. If the legislature has set out a particular formality to follow, it is not for the court to ignore. On the other hand, the finding of invalidity of a will on a failure on the part of the testator to conform to a technical formality may appear extremely picayune and callous when the result dashes what is clearly expressed and finalized intent of the testator. Recently, significant efforts have been taken to reduce the necessary formalities for the execution of wills. This is in part in response to some very technical decisions applying a strict construction concept.

4. Strict Construction

Generally, the courts have followed the concept of strict construction: i.e., an instrument must satisfy all the formalities set out in the statute. Consequently, when analyzing the validity of the instrument, one has to dissect the statute word by word to see if and what formalities are satisfied. In an effort that the policy of strict construction be kept within its legitimate domain, courts have adopted the doctrine that formalities not included in the statute will not be added. Generally, one must only satisfy the formalities required and no more. [See, e.g., Lemayne v. Stanley, 3 Lev. 1 (1691) but cf. Estate of McKellar, 380 So.2d 1273 (Miss.1980)]. In addition, courts do not object to greater formalization than the statute requires.

Even where strict construction is the court's philosophy, some have been willing to ignore or to generously interpret some incidental formalities in the statutes. For example, a statute might require the testator to "request" the witnesses to witness the will. The word "request" may be liberally interpreted to mean the circumstances must indicate that the testator wanted the witnesses to witness the will. The testator need not have actually verbally requested the witnesses to do so. [See, e.g., Hollingsworth v. Hollingsworth, 401 S.W.2d 555 (Ark. 1966)]. This might be referred to as a reasonable compliance standard for these incidental formalities.

It is difficult, however, to distinguish between a formality that is going to receive a strict construction versus one that will receive a reasonable construction. Advocates of more liberal analyses of will formalities have determined that courts will not, on their own, adopt a more reasonable approach with regards to most formalities set out in will statutes. [Langbein, Substantial Compliance; see also Estate of Voeller v. Voeller, 534 N.W.2d 24 (N.D.1995); Taylor v. Estate of Taylor, 770 P.2d 163 (Utah App.1989)]. Consequently, it is urged that a statutory substantial compliance or dispensing power be included.

5. The Substantial Compliance and Harmless Error Doctrines

The substantial compliance standard is a judicially developed approach to the will execution problems. It permits probate of an otherwise defectively executed will if the proponents prove that the document adequately expresses the decedent's testamentary intent, and the execution procedure actually completed sufficiently approximates the execution requirements and purposes of the relevant statute of wills. Rather than an afterthought, the doctrine is a positive approach to execution issues. [Cf. In re Ranney, 589 A.2d 1339 (N.J.1991)].

The Restatement (Third) of Property expressly adopts a harmless error rule for will execution formalities. Adopting the philosophy that will formalities are meant to facilitate intent-serving purpose, not to be ends in themselves, the Restatement provides that "A harmless error in executing a will may be excused if the proponent establishes by clear and convincing evidence that the decedent adopted the document as his or her will." [Restatement (Third) of Property, § 3.3]. The harmless error rules is based on the principle that mistake in execution should not defeat intention nor work unjust enrichment. The question is whether an execution defect was harmless in relation to the purpose of the statutory formalities, not in relation to an isolated individual statutory formality. In evaluating the purposes of all of the execution formalities, the Restatement recognizes "a hierarchy" among the formalities. While a writing is essential and excusing testator's signature is difficult but not insuperable, excusing attestation defects may be an easy matter. [See Restatement (Third) of Property, § 3.3, Comment b].

6. Dispensing Power

The 1990 UPC does not adopt the substantial compliance standard but includes a dispensing power provision which is now titled "Harmless Error." [2–503]. Basically, this provision permits a court to dispense with one or more of the statutory formalities even if they have not been followed so long as the proponents of the document or writing establish by clear and convincing evidence that the testator intended the document to constitute the decedent's will or other will related instructions. [2–503]. An example of this would be a will that requires two witnesses but the testator only had one witness. If the standard of proof could be met, a court could dispense with the second witness and permit the

will to be probated. This provision does not encourage testators to disregard the letter of the execution
statutes: it merely provides a remedy in those cases
where a rejection of the will causes significant intent denying results to occur notwithstanding the
available proof of that intent. In addition, it is not
designed to convert incomplete plans into finalized
plans. Its purpose is to convert ineffective attempts
at finalized intent into effective, finalized plans if
the standard of evidence can be satisfied.

The provision is unspecific as to which formalities
may be dispensed. With the exception that there
must be a document or a writing added upon a
document, all other formalities are subject to the
dispensing remedy. Considering the uniqueness of
wills validity situations, the dispensing power will
be exercised on a case by case basis. Decisions on
this issue will generally be too factually restrictive
and therefore not provide precedent for later cases.

7. Overall Approach

Some have argued that the law should abolish
major formalities other than the merest physical
evidence of the instrument. [See, e.g., Lingren, Fall
of Formalism (urges abolition of attestation requirement)]. The sole question should be an evidentiary
matter concerning testamentary intent. Advocates
of this approach would add a suggested model that
follows a more precise formality. The point is the
model would not be required but would be the
preferred planning and practice technique.

The UPC adopts a middle ground approach to these issues. First, the UPC includes several types of formal wills and has pared the actual formalities for each type down to minimum levels. Most instruments that are executed as wills will satisfy one or more of the types of formalities. Second, the UPC provides an escape device in that the court is accorded a dispensing authority for formalities not followed so long as the standard of proof is met. This covers the occasional case where clear unfairness occurs if the will is not recognized. Third, the UPC provides a model form to follow. This is the self-proved will and it has its own attributes and advantages if proper practice follows its formalities to the letter.

§ 6.02 Execution Requirements

A. TESTATOR'S CAPACITY

A pervasive execution requirement under the UPC for all recognized types of wills is that the testator must possess testamentary capacity. This capacity means that the testator must be of a certain age and possess the necessary mental ability. [2–501]. For uniformity purposes, the UPC sets the age of eighteen or more years as the age a person must be in order to be able to execute a valid will. This age conforms to the age for will execution in the vast majority of states in this country and a single uniform age for will execution is desirable. The UPC also continues the universal rule that a testator must be of sound mind in order to make a probatable will. Although the term ''sound mind'' is not defined in the UPC, prior law is well developed in this area and should provide a definition.

B. THE ORDINARY WITNESSED OR NOTARIZED WILL

Consistent with its purpose to keep execution requirements as simple as possible, the UPC requires that only the bare essentials be satisfied in order to execute the ordinary witnessed will. [2–502]. In addition to the age and sound mind requirements discussed above, the UPC requires the following:

(1) a writing;

(2) the testator's signature or a proxy signature in testator's presence and by testator's direction;

And either

(3) two witnesses;

   (a) the witnesses must be competent at the time of witnessing;

   (b) the witnesses must sign the will; and

   (c) the witnesses must witness either the signing process or the testator's acknowledgment of that signature or the testator's acknowledgment of the will. [2–502(3)(A)]

Or

(3) the testator must acknowledged testator's signature before a notary public or other individ-

ual authorized by law to take acknowledgments. [2–502(3)(B)].

The UPC does not require: (1) a signing at the end of the will; (2) the witnesses to sign in the testator's presence; (3) the witnesses to sign in each other's presence; and (4) a statement in all cases by the testator that testator publishes the document as testator's will. Mention of these nonrequirements is important because although strict compliance with the stated formalities required by a will statute is mandatory, generally no additional ones are required. [Atkinson, Wills § 62; see § 6.01]. On the other hand, although the UPC is silent on when a witness must sign the will as witness, several decisions have refused to probate wills where the witnesses signed outside the normal execution process. In one case after the testator signed the will in the hospital, it was taken to a residence where the necessary witnesses signed the will. This was held to be ineffective. [Estate of McGurrin v. Scoggin, 743 P.2d 994 (Idaho App.1987)]. In another case, it has held that necessary witnesses must sign prior to the testator's death. [Estate of Royal, 826 P.2d 1236 (Colo.1992)].

The 2008 revision allows notarized wills. It is a safe and reasonable execution technique that has worked in several jurisdictions. Its validity as an execution technique will reduce confusion and chance of error.

Because wills under the UPC are valid even if one follows these extra requirements, or in other words over-executes the will, it will be common for many attorneys in UPC states to continue their old practice of having their clients over-execute their wills.

The UPC also specifically defines who is eligible and competent to be a witness to a will. Under this provision, the test of competence is whether at the time of witnessing the witness of the will was generally competent to testify as a witness in court. [2–505(a)]. Significantly, the UPC completely eliminates the prohibition or penalty imposed under non-UPC law on persons witnessing a will who receive an interest from the will. [2–505(b)]. Consequently, a will is valid even if an essential witness is interested and the interested witness can also take any devise provided in the will regardless of any rights of the witness to take an intestate share. The UPC leaves all underlying questions of undue influence to a direct attack in a will contest. It is important to emphasize, however, that by this rule the UPC is not intended to encourage the use of either minors or devisees as witnesses but is designed to prevent injustices that have occurred under the contrary current law. For example, the UPC's rule will not invalidate a will because a witness, unknown to the testator, was under the age of majority or take away or reduce the interest of a devisee under a will because the innocent and unknowing devisee signed as witness. [2–505, Comment]. In order to further discourage volitional witnessing by a devisee, California added to its similar provision a clause that creates a presumption of undue influence against the devisee-witness with regard to that devisee's share. [West's Ann.Cal.Prob.Code § 6112(c)]. Evidence the witness did not know of the devise in the will should be relevant and admissible to rebut the presumption.

C. THE HOLOGRAPHIC WILL

Approximately one-half of the states have provisions authorizing the holographic or unwitnessed handwritten will. The UPC also includes a provision giving recognition to holographic wills. [2–502(b)]. Such recognition is consistent with modern will policies which generally are to increase recognition and to reduce the number of denials of probate. In addition, many of the old fears with regard to fraud and undue influence have either not materialized or are not relevant today because the holographic procedure satisfactorily protects a person from these dangers.

The UPC's holographic execution procedure has only two requirements: (1) material portions of the document must be in the testator's handwriting; and (2) the instrument must be signed by the hand of the testator. [2–502(b)]. The UPC's "material portions" terminology must be compared to the "entirely written" terminology found in most holographic statutes today. The UPC's terminology is specifically intended to counteract a strict statutory construction applied by some courts to the words "entirely written." [2–502, Comment; see Atkinson, Wills § 75]. These courts have held holographic wills invalid if they contain any printed matter on their faces provided that the testators intended the printed matter to be a part of the wills. By contrast, the "material portions" terminology should permit a holding of validity for a holographic will executed on a printed will form if the printed portions can be eliminated and if the handwritten portions still adequately describe the testator's testamentary scheme. [2–502(b), Comment; see Estate of Fitzgerald, 738 P.2d 236 (Utah App.1987)]. Although testamentary intent might not be present from the handwritten portion, it should be provable by the admission of extrinsic evidence provided by the printed portion. [Estate of Muder v. Muder, 765 P.2d 997 (Ariz.1988)].

Significantly, the UPC neither requires that a holographic will be dated nor prescribes the location of the testator's signature. The primary question arising when there is no date or when the signature is in an unusual place, or when both of these facts are present, is whether the person intended the instrument to be a will or nothing more than a statement of what would be done if executed as a will. This is, of course, an evidentiary problem dealing with testamentary intent and properly is not an execution formality problem. [See Estate of Erickson, 806 P.2d 1186 (Utah 1991)]. The UPC allows the printed portions of the holographic will to be used to prove testamentary intent if necessary. [2–502(c)]. Without this provision, it has been held that it is necessary that "the handwritten portion of the . . . the will clearly expresses testamentary intent." [Estate of Foxley v. Hogan, 575 N.W.2d 150 (Neb.1998)].

California, which adopted the UPC's "material provisions" language, adopted two limitations if the holographic will is not dated. [West's Ann.Cal.Prob. Code § 6111]. First, if the provisions of an undated holographic will are inconsistent with those of another will, the holographic will is considered invalid unless it can be established that the holographic will was executed after the other will. [West's Ann. Cal.Prob.Code § 6111(b)(1)]. Second, the will is also invalid if it is established that the testator lacked testamentary capacity during any period of time when the undated holographic will might have been executed unless it can be established that the holographic will was executed while the testator had testamentary capacity. [West's Ann.Cal.Prob.Code § 6111(b)(2)].

D.   THE FOREIGN AND INTERNATIONAL WILL

In our modern mobile society, the question of the validity of wills executed according to the wills execution laws of other states or countries is an important consideration. The principal problem is how to protect a person's reasonable expectations concerning an instrument that the person believes to be a valid will. The UPC includes two statutory devices to deal with this problem. The first is a special choice of law rule with regard to the probate of foreign wills properly executed according to the wills' execution laws of other states or countries. [2–506]. The second establishes a special execution procedure for executing a will that will be valid in all jurisdictions that join an international convention or that enact the appropriate act. The latter procedure is incorporated in Part 10 of Article II of the UPC and also constitutes the provisions for the freestanding Uniform International Wills Act (Hereinafter referred to as the International Wills Act).

Based upon the existence of any specific contact between the testator and the foreign jurisdiction, the UPC adopts a broad choice of law rule as to execution. [2–506]. In addition to recognizing the validity of any foreign instrument that happens to be executed according to any of the UPC's will execution techniques, a will is also valid if executed in compliance with the law of any of the following jurisdictions: (1) the place of execution; (2) the testator's domicile at the time of execution; (3) the testator's place of abode at the time of execution; (4) the place of the testator's nationality at the time of execution; (5) the testator's domicile at the time of death; (6) the testator's place of abode at the time of death; or (7) the testator's nationality at the time of death. [2–506]. If an instrument is a valid will under the laws of any of these jurisdictions, then the will is valid and may be probated in the UPC state.

In effect, if a relevant contact is satisfied, the UPC literally incorporates by reference the execution statute of the relevant jurisdictions. Consequently, the execution procedures of these other jurisdictions represent additional methods of executing a proper will. In addition, the reference to the laws of these other jurisdictions presumably includes all aspects of the actual execution process. The only expressed limitation placed by the provision on this reference to the execution laws of other jurisdictions is that the will must be "written"; consequently, nuncupative wills will not be recognized in the UPC state even if recognized by the law of the jurisdiction having a relevant contact. It is not clear whether the reference to the other jurisdiction's law includes its rules with regard to the testator's and witnesses' capacities.

It is important to emphasize that the terms of this provision apply to wills being offered for probate for the first time and are not restricted to wills that have been previously probated in the foreign jurisdiction. This provision anticipates probate of the foreign executed will in the testator's domicile. Ancillary procedures are separately dealt with in the UPC. [See § 26.04].

The distinction between the International Wills Act and the choice of law provision is significant. Whereas the choice of law rule attempts to validate wills executed under the laws of other jurisdictions, the Act anticipates an execution intended to be valid in jurisdictions that recognize it. By following the Act, the testator selected a procedure that anticipates probate in different jurisdictions. The expectation that this execution process will be valid for probate of the will wherever necessary is greater than the expectation of the testator who, at death, happens to have an estate requiring probate in several jurisdictions. Enactment of the International Wills Act is crucial to the protection of these expectations. Unless the federal government adopts the Act in the form of an international will convention, it will be up to each state individually to approve this legislation. [Art. II, Pt. 10. International Wills Act, Prefatory Note, 88–89]. At least fourteen states have enacted the free standing uniform act. [Id.].

The application of the International Wills Act is not dependent upon the place of execution, the location of assets or the nationality, domicile or residence of the testator. [2–1002(a)]. Its procedures are independent of those circumstances. If the proper execution procedure is followed, the will is presumed to be valid under the Act. On the other hand, the fact that a will is not validly executed under the Act does not affect its formal validity under other will statutes and acts. [2–1002(b)]. Nor would execution under the Act preclude the probate of such will under other wills' acts or provisions including the choice of law provision.

The basic requirements of an international will are as follows:

(1) The will must be in writing. [2–1003(a)]. This writing requirement covers any form of expression made by recognizable signs on a durable substance. Any language can be used.

(2) The testator must declare that the document is testator's will and that testator knows its contents in the presence of three people, i.e., two witnesses and another "authorized person." [2–1003(b)]. The contents of the will need not be revealed to these persons.

(3) The testator must sign the will or acknowledge testator's signature if testator had previously signed it in the presence of these three persons. [2–1003(c)].

(4) If the testator indicates a reason for testator's inability to sign, any other person may sign as proxy for the testator if the authorized proxy signs the testator's name at the latter's direction and makes note of this on the will. [2–1003(d)].

(5) The witnesses and the authorized person must attest the will by signing it in the presence of the testator. [2–1003(e)].

An "authorized person" is defined as a person who has been admitted to practice law before the courts of the state and who is in good standing as an active law practitioner in the state [2–1009], or as a person who is empowered to supervise the execution of international wills according to the laws of the United States. [2–1001(2)].

Several other points of form are set out in the Act but the failure to comply with them will not cause the will to be invalid. [2–1004(d)]. These requirements include:

(1) All signatures must be placed at the end of the will; [2–1004(a)]

(2) On multiple page wills, each sheet must be signed by the testator or proxy and must be numbered; [Id.]

(3) The date of the execution of the will must be noted at the end of the will by the authorized person; [2–1004(b)] and

(4) The authorized person must ask the testator whether testator desires to make a declaration concerning the safekeeping of the will, and that expressed desire must be mentioned in the certificate attached to the will. [2–1004(c)].

The International Wills Act sets out a form of a certificate that must be signed by the authorized person and that recites the requirements under the Act for valid execution of an international will. [2–1005]. Similar to an attestation clause, or self-proved will affidavit [see § 6.02(E)], the certificate contains all of the elements necessary for the identification of the parties to the execution process including the testator, the witnesses and the authorized person and expressly outlines the necessary formalities to obtain the protection and recognition under the act. Three copies of this certificate must be executed.

Probate of the will with a certificate attached should be immediate since the certificate is conclusive of the formal validity of the instrument as a will. [2–1006]. Of course, such a will can be contested under formal testacy proceedings on the grounds of lack of capacity, fraud, undue influence, revocation, substantive ineffectiveness, and even forgery and genuineness. [2–1005, Comment; 2–1007; 2–1006; 2–1006 Comment]. The authorized person must retain one of the executed copies of the certificate, deliver another to the testator and attach the third to the will itself. [2–1005]. This multi-certificate execution process is touted to provide a reminder to the authorized person of the terms of its content, a document that may be found with testator's papers to inform interested persons of the existence of the will and its location, and to protect against unauthorized alterations to the certificate. [2–1005, Comment].

E. THE SELF–PROVED WILL

The UPC adds an execution technique for a special will called the "self-proved will." [2–504]. Applicable only to the ordinary witnessed will, it adds a notarized affidavit executed by the testator and the witnesses. It also adds to the ordinary witnessed will execution process the following three execution formalities: (1) the testator must declare to the witnesses that the will is testator's last will; (2) the witnesses must sign as witness to testator's will; and (3) the witnesses must sign in the testator's presence and hearing.

The forms for two alternative affidavits are included in the UPC. In a manner similar to the technique of the attestation clauses typically included in wills today, the affidavits describe the formalities and facts that were followed and observed in execution. Because they are affidavits, however, they both must be notarized. The first affidavit form permits the self-proved will affidavit to be a part of the will itself and actually constitutes the execution thereof. [2–504(a)]. In using this form, the testator and the witnesses execute the affidavit and the will simultaneously. [2–504, Comment]. The second affidavit form is to be executed separately from and subsequently to the execution of the ordinary witnessed will. [2–504(b)]. When using this form, the testator and the witnesses execute the will separately and then subsequently in a continuous or separate proceeding complete and sign the affidavit.

The effect of executing a self-proved will is not very significant. In most respects, when a self-proved will is offered for probate, it is subject to the same treatment as any other validly executed will. Its principal distinguishing feature is to permit the will to be admitted to probate in a formal testacy proceeding without the necessity of testimony of one of the subscribing witnesses [3–406(a)] and the signature requirement is conclusively presumed. [3–406(b)]. The will, however, still is subject to contest for grounds such as revocation, undue influence, lack of testamentary capacity, fraud and even forgery. [3–406, Comment; see § 11.02(B)(6)]. Notwithstanding its limited significance, use of one or the other of these forms should become standard practice for attorneys who draft and supervise the execution of wills.

§ 6.03   Revocation of Wills

A.   GENERAL REVOCATION PRINCIPLES

An inherent characteristic of a will is the power of the testator to revoke it. [2–507]. Just as statutes specifically prescribe the procedure by which wills must be executed, statutes typically prescribe the procedure by which wills must be revoked. The three generally accepted revocation methods are: (1) by physical act; (2) by subsequent instrument; and (3) by operation of law due to changed circumstances. [Atkinson, Wills § 84]. The first two methods require three principal elements that must occur concurrently: (1) an authorized act or instrument; (2) an intent on the part of the testator to revoke; and (3) a testator possessing legal capacity. Revocation by operation of law springs not from intentional acts on the document or subsequent testamentary documents but from changed circumstances between the date of the will's execution and the date of the testator's death. It springs automatically from the happening of these events. The UPC recognizes and defines all three of these methods.

Each revocation method creates a formality against which testator's intent must be evaluated and compared. If the conditions of these methods of revocations are not obeyed, the will will not be revoked and the identifiable intent of the testator defeated. The best example would be a testator who has verbally expressed to many, including non-interested persons, that the testator presently revokes a previous will but the testator performs neither a physical act nor executes a subsequent revocatory instrument. Although it may be argued that since no physical act or subsequent instrument was executed the testator's intent was merely formative and not determinative, one may also conclude that the testator's intent was not followed. Consequently, just as with execution formalities, revocation formalities must be limited to the minimum degree necessary to protect the purposes of the formalities.

B. REVOCATION BY PHYSICAL ACT

The UPC permits a testator to revoke a will or any part of a will by performing certain revocatory acts on the will. [2–507(a)(2)]. These acts must be performed with the intent and for the purpose of revoking the will or a part of it. The revocatory act may be performed by another person if that person performs the act in the testator's conscious presence and by the testator's direction. A "conscious presence" test was specifically adopted in order to eliminate a line of sight test some courts have applied when "in the presence" is required by the statute. [2–507, Comment].

A revocatory act includes the typical laundry list of physical acts. [2–507(a)(2)]. The list includes burning, tearing, canceling, obliterating, and destroying. Usually, revocation statutes do not explain the degree to which each act must be performed on the will. This statutory omission causes interpretative problems for courts when the physical act performed by the testator fails to clearly match the statutory list of revocatory physical acts. On occasion, courts have refused to recognize a revocation when testator's act did not technically fit the court's definition of what is necessary to constitute a revocatory act. [See, e.g., Thompson v. Royall, 175 S.E. 748 (Va.1934)]. The UPC attempts to prevent restrictive interpretations of the revocatory acts by providing specifically that a burning, tearing, or canceling is a revocatory act notwithstanding the burning, tearing, or canceling does not touch actual words of the will. Assumedly, this means that although some form of physical evidence of revocation must appear on the will itself, front or back, the act need not deface the printed words on the instrument.

Revocation of a will by physical act may raise greater risks of fraud than execution raises because the appearance of revocatory acts on a will is inherently ambiguous as far as the testator's actual intent is concerned. Consequently, courts must be cautious about claims of physical revocation and should require adequate proof with extrinsic evidence, including the testator's statements, if any, that the testator intended a revocatory act to constitute a physical revocation.

C. REVOCATION BY SUBSEQUENT INSTRUMENT

Revocation by subsequent instrument is also recognized by the UPC when accomplished by an instrument executed with the same formalities as any valid will. [2–507(a)(1); see § 6.02]. Revocation of any prior will by this method may also be accomplished in whole or in part. A valid can not be revoked by the decedent's act of signing a nontestamentary written instrument stating that it is his intent to revoke his prior will. [Estate of Martinez, 985 P.2d 1230 (N.M.App.1999)].

One of the most litigated situations concerning the revocation by subsequent instrument is when a testator executes a subsequent will which is inconsistent in whole or in part with a prior will, but which does not specifically revoke the prior will. [See Restatement (Second) of Property, § 33.2]. The relevant issue which arises is whether the subsequent inconsistencies revoke the prior will or its provisions, or whether the prior will or its provisions are merely superseded by the subsequent inconsistent will or its provisions. Of course, if both wills are probated after the testator's death, the provisions and terms of the subsequent will prevail. If, however, the subsequent will is revoked before the testator's death, the determination of the issue whether the prior will was revoked or merely superseded is important. If the subsequent will merely superseded the prior will, revocation of the subsequent inconsistent will or its provisions reinstates the prior will or its provisions. If the prior will is held to have been revoked, however, that will or its provisions will be effective again only if reexecuted or the doctrine of revival is applicable. [See § 6.04(B)].

The UPC attempts to give some meaning to the concept of revocation by inconsistency. [2–507(b)–(d)]. It begins with the general proposition that a previous will is revoked by inconsistency if the testator intended the subsequent will to replace rather than supplement the previous will. Clearly, an expression of such intent in the subsequent will would be effective to do this. Unfortunately, an expressed intent does not always appear in the subsequent will and courts may be faced with the responsibility of evaluating extrinsic evidence, if any, or to employ relevant evidentiary presumptions.

The UPC deals directly with these evidentiary problems. First, the UPC recognizes the general admissibility of extrinsic evidence to prove this intent. [2–507, Comment]. It then sets certain presumptions depending on the circumstances of the two or more wills. A testator is presumed to have intended revocation rather than supplementation of the previous will if the subsequent will makes a complete disposition of the testator's estate. [2–507(c)]. On the other hand, the testator is presumed to have intended a subsequent will to be merely supplemental rather than revocatory of a previous will if the second subsequent will does not make a complete disposition the testator's estate. [2–507(d)]. Either presumption may be rebutted on a clear and convincing standard by extrinsic evidence. If not rebutted, the presumption stands. If a subsequent will entirely disposes of testator's estate, the burden of overcoming the presumption falls on those who wish to argue that the subsequent will is merely supplemental. On the other side, if the will is merely inconsistent in part, the burden of proving that the subsequent will revoked the prior will falls on those who want to argue revocation.

The application of the presumption may be important to the operations of the revival provision.

D.   REVOCATION BY OPERATION OF LAW

At common law, revocation by operation of law was recognized in two situations: a single woman's will was revoked when she subsequently married, and a single man's will was revoked after his marriage and birth of an issue. [Atkinson, Wills § 85]. No other change of circumstances would revoke a will by operation of law.

The UPC characterizes the issue as one of changed circumstances. [2–508]. It limits the revocatory effect of changed circumstances on wills to divorce by a spouse and to the testator's homicide by a devisee. The scope and application of these particular circumstances are discussed separately. [See §§ 9.03, 9.04]. No other change of circum-

stances shall be deemed to revoke a will by operation of law.

E. THE LOST OR DESTROYED WILL

Another problem related to revocation concerns
the effect of a lost or unintentionally destroyed will.
The general rule has been that in the absence of
statutory provisions to the contrary, the lost or
destroyed will may be admitted to probate upon
adequate proof of its content and due execution.
[Atkinson, Wills § 97]. If such proof cannot be
maintained or if a statute restricts the proof of such
wills, the lost or destroyed will has been in a sense
revoked. Many non-UPC states have statutes that
specifically apply to the probate of such wills. A
typical provision which is found in some of these
statutes is that the lost or destroyed will cannot be
probated unless it is "proved to be in existence at
the time of the death of the testator, or is shown to
have been fraudulently destroyed in the lifetime of
the testator." [E.g., Ark.Code Ann. § 28–40–302].
The quoted phrase has caused litigation where the
will was lost or destroyed during the testator's
lifetime but not by testator's action or authority
and not fraudulently by another person. According
to the literal language of the quoted phrase, such a
will cannot be probated and has thereby in effect
been revoked by a means not approved by the
revocation statute. Several courts have circumvent-
ed this result by giving the key words, "existence"
or "fraudulently" unusual meanings. [See, e.g., In

re Fox's Will, 174 N.E.2d 499 (N.Y.1961); In re Estate of Havel, 194 N.W. 633 (Minn.1923)].

The UPC contains no special limitation on the probate of a lost or destroyed will other than to require that such will be probated in a "Formal Testacy" proceeding. [3–402(a); see § 11.02]. The apparent rationale is that specific guidelines either create a rigidity which prevents appropriate adaptation in all cases or cause interpretations of the statutes which are direct affronts to the literal meaning of the language. [See Model Probate Code, at 20]. The UPC avoids these problems by leaving this matter to the rules of procedure and evidence of the probate proceeding itself. Legal presumptions concerning lost wills may also be relevant. For example, some jurisdictions have a presumption that if a will is traced to the testator decedent and cannot be found, there is a presumption of revocation. This rule may be applicable under the UPC as well. [In re Estate of Hartman, 563 P.2d 569 (Mont. 1977)]. Of course, the rules concerning overcoming the presumption would also be applicable. [Id.].

§ 6.04 Supersession, Revocation and Revival

A. SUPERSESSION

The UPC is relatively precise in its coverage of the procedural interrelationship of the will doctrines of supersession, revocation, and revival. Supersession deals with the situation where a subsequent testamentary clause or instrument suspends the effectiveness of a prior testamentary clause or instrument if all instruments and circumstances remained the same until testator's death. If relevant matters remain the same at the death of the testator, the subsequent or superseding provision will control and the prior disposition is effectively revoked. A supersession characterization is important, however, if, for some reason or event, the subsequent clause or instrument fails, the removal of the superseding disposition automatically reinstates the superseded disposition's effectiveness if possible under the circumstances. On the other hand, if a subsequent clause or will is characterized as revoking rather than superseding the prior clause or will, the removal or ineffectiveness of the subsequent clause or will does not reinstate the prior disposition unless the prior disposition is revived under the UPC's revival provision. The UPC's revival provision has its own presumptions concerning this matter. [2–509].

B. REVIVAL OF REVOKED WILLS

The revival of revoked wills provision originally promulgated in the UPC was significantly reworked in the 1990 version. Similar to the approach taken in the revocation by subsequent instrument provision, the UPC adopts separate rules depending upon whether the subsequent will wholly revokes the previous will or merely partly revokes the previous will. [2–509]. In regard to revival of the previous will if the subsequent will is physically revoked, the UPC creates different evidentiary requirements to prove revival. If a physically revoked subsequent will wholly revokes the previous will, revival occurs only when those who seek revival present evidence that the testator intended the previous will to be revived. [2–509(a)]. This puts the burden on those seeking revival of the previous will. The UPC permits extrinsic evidence including statements by the testator to be admissible to prove intent. Accordingly, if no evidence is introduced or if the evidence is inconclusive, the prior will will not be revived. For example, if T executed Will 1 and wholly revokes it by express terms in Will 2, T's physical revocation of Will 2 is presumed not to revive Will 1 unless adequate proof of T's intent to revive is admitted into evidence. [2–509(a)]. Extrinsic evidence including statements by T is admissible to determine T's intent. Revival intent means an intent that the previous will will take affect as executed. Information concerning the testator's knowledge of the contents of the previous will is relevant evidence. [See Langbein & Waggoner, New Uniform Probate Code, at 886–87].

With regard to a physically revoked subsequent will that only partly revokes the previous will, the UPC adopts the rule that revival is presumed unless those who contend that no revival occurred introduce evidence showing the testator did not intend revival of the prior instrument. [2–509(b)]. This puts the burden on those seeking nonrevival of the previous will. The UPC permits extrinsic evidence including statements by the testator to be admissible to prove intent. If no evidence is introduced or if the evidence is inconclusive, however, the prior will will be revived. For example, if T executed Will 1 and only partially revoked it either by inconsistency or by the express terms of Will 2, T's physical revocation of Will 2 is presumed to revive Will 1 unless the person, who contends that T did not intend to revive the prior will, introduces evidence of that contrary intent. Again extrinsic evidence including statements by T is admissible to determine T's intent.

From the above examples, it is crucial to determine whether the subsequent will wholly or partially revokes the prior will. [See UPC 6.04(A)]. In litigation on these types of issues, it is common that the party who must rebut the presumption loses because the extrinsic evidence is inadequate or inconsistent.

The UPC's revival provision does not apply to the situation where the prior will has also been physically revoked by the testator. For example, if T executed Will 1 and revoked it by physical act and by the express terms in Will 2, T's physical revocation of Will 2 will not revive Will 1. No extrinsic evidence, including statements by T, is admissible to determine T's intent. Revival of Will 1 will occur only if the testator reexecutes Will 1 or executes Will 3 that incorporates by reference Will 1 into Will 3. [See 2–510; § 6.05(A)].

Revival is also limited if the subsequent revoking will is in turn revoked by a later will. In this situation it makes no difference whether the subsequent will wholly or partially revokes the prior will. In either case, the revoked portions of the prior will are revived only if testator's intent to revive them appears from the terms of the latest will. [2–509(c)]. For example, if T properly executed Will 1 but partially revoked it by properly executed Will 2, the revocation of Will 2 by properly executed Will 3 will not revive the portions of Will 1 revoked by Will 2 unless the revival of the revoked portion appears from the terms of the Will 3. Evidence of intent is limited to the words on the face of the will unless some other evidence admissibility rule applies. Assumably, statements by T regarding revival are also inadmissible.

Although conditions for revival may not be present, one must not forget the potential application of the dispensing power concept in regard to execution, revocation, alteration and revival of wills. [2–503; § 6.01(C)]. A document, writing or even interlineation on a will might be treated as executed in compliance with the UPC's will statute, if proponents of the document, writing or interlineation prove by clear and convincing evidence that the testator desired it to constitute a revival of a prior revoked clause or will. Because the full range of this provision has not been explored by the drafters in the comments or by the courts, it is difficult to craft an example that will definitely apply the principle. For purposes of further reflection consider the following example:

T properly executed Will 1 that is partially revoked by properly executed Will 2. As indicated above, the revocation of Will 2 by Will 3 will not revive the portions of Will 1 revoked by Will 2 unless the revival of the revoked portion of Will 1 appears from the terms of the Will 3. Evidence of intent will be limited to the face of the will and statements by T regarding revival are assumably inadmissible. If T wrote a personal letter to a beneficiary of Will 1 expressing the belief that Will 1 was revived because Will 2 had been revoked by Will 3, the holographic letter may satisfy the dispensing power requirements, i.e., it is a writing and it expresses the intent to revive the prior will. This letter may not qualify as a valid will under section 2–502 because it is not signed or is not witnessed or lacks testamentary intent. If the letter and other relevant extrinsic evidence constitutes sufficient clear and convincing proof that the testator intended the revival, the letter might be admitted to probate the same as a properly executed will would be and it would be given the effect it exhibits.

Treating this writing as the equivalent of a will is not inconsistent with the exclusion of extrinsic rule as would be applicable if revival were the basis of the revival. In this situation, the dispensing power under section 2–503 is being used not the revival concept under section 2–509. These are separate concepts each to be applied under its own scope and limitations.

As indicated, the UPC provides for the automatic revocation of provisions in favor of a spouse who the decedent divorced and in favor of the spouse's relatives. [2–804(b); see § 9.03]. If decedent remarries the prior spouse or the divorce is nullified, the provisions for spouse or relatives are automatically revived by operation of law. [2–804(d)].

When a testator physically revokes a will or a part thereof with the immediate present intent of making a new will or of substituting a new partial alteration and when the will or alteration is not made or is ineffective for any reason, many courts under the "dependent relative revocation" doctrine have presumed that the testator would prefer to die testate than intestate. Consequently, the revoked will or its provisions, if the contents can be ascertained, have been admitted to probate in the absence of evidence overcoming this presumption. [Atkinson, Wills § 58]. The UPC takes no official position on the scope and extent of this doctrine. It merely makes an affirmative reference to the doctrine in the Comment to Section 2–507 and leaves the doctrine's recognition and development to the courts. There may be occasional situations where this doctrine would produce the better result than revocation or revival would. [See Langbein & Waggoner, New Uniform Probate Code, at 887].

C. SUPERSESSION, REVOCATION AND REVIVAL COMPARED

The interrelationship of the above concepts may create a progression of procedural issues to resolve in some situations. Consider the following problems:

CHART 6–1

Supersession, Revocation and Revival Compared

Assumption 1:   A. T properly executes Will 1 that provides:
"The grandfather's clock to A,
$10,000 to B, and
the residue to C."

B. T later properly executes Will 2 that has no revocation clause and only provides,
"The grandfather's clock to D."

C. T subsequently physically revokes Will 2.

D. A wants the grandfather clock; C contends it is part of the residuary.

Analysis: If a prior clause or will is only partially altered by inconsistency, two presumptions under the Code are potentially applicable. First, the subsequent inconsistent provision is presumed merely to supersede the former: both provisions are in effect at death unless otherwise revoked. If the subsequent provision is revoked or becomes ineffective, the former provision is automatically effective. This presumption of supersession, however, may be rebutted by clear and convincing evidence. This means that those contending revocation rather than supersession may prove by the appropriate standard of proof that the testator intended revocation rather than supersession. Second, notwithstanding revocation of the prior clause or instrument, those desiring effectiveness for the prior clause or instrument can still argue and prove revival. Under the revival provision when the previous will or clause is only partially revoked by inconsistency, revival is presumed if the subsequent will or clause is revoked by physical act. [See § 6.04(B)]. This presumption is rebuttable by a preponderance of evidence propounded by those who argue no revival. Consequently, the person seeking effectiveness for the prior clause can use both affirmative presumptions. An intent to revoke is not the same as an intent not to revive because these intent issues concern the testator's state of mind at different times. The person contending revocation of the prior clause by the subsequent clause or will and nonrevival of the prior clause upon physical revocation of the subsequent clause is faced with a double burden of proof.

Assumption 2:   A. T properly executes Will 1 that provides:
"The grandfather's clock to A, $10,000 to B, and the residue to C."

                 B. T later properly executes Will 2 that has no revocation clause and provides,
"The grandfather's clock to D. $10,000 to B, and the residue to C."

                 C. T subsequently physically revokes Will 2.

                 D. A wants the grandfather clock; C contends it is part of the residuary.

Analysis: When the inconsistencies are characterized as revocation, the presumptions are reversed. Because the second will makes a complete disposition of the testator's estate, it is presumed that the testator intended revocation rather than supplementation of the previous will unless the revocation is rebutted by clear and convincing evidence. If rebutted, the previous terms prevail automatically as indicated in the previous illustration. Even where the subsequent clause or will is presumed to have revoked the prior will, however, A may submit evidence that the revoked will was revived. The standard of proof is by a preponderance of evidence standard. If this proof is met, the former instrument will be revived and the former gift will prevail. This assumes a revocation of the subsequent instrument or clause by physical act. [See § 6.03].

The above two examples and analyses clearly indicate that the Code is very favorable to reinstatement under supersession or revival of prior provisions. This is often justified because otherwise testator will die intestate.

§ 6.05   Nonexecuted Documents and Events Affecting Wills

A.   INCORPORATION BY REFERENCE

The overwhelming majority of American courts recognize the doctrine of "incorporation by reference." [Restatement (Second) of Property, § 33.1]. Generally, this doctrine holds that an unexecuted document or instrument may be incorporated for specific purposes into a validly executed will. [2 Page, § 19.17]. In order to avoid obvious possibilities of fraud, generally six prerequisites must be satisfied in order for the doctrine to apply. They include: (1) a validly executed will; (2) a distinct reference to the unexecuted document in the will itself; (3) a showing or statement in the will that the document is in existence at the time the will is executed; (4) proof that the document was actually

in existence at the time of execution; (5) a showing
of intent on the part of the testator to incorporate
the document into the will; and (6) a showing that
the document offered is the one referred to in the
will. The courts have not adhered to the above
requirements consistently. For example, requirements 1 and 4 have been strictly adhered to whereas 2 and 5 have sometimes been liberally applied. If
a document is held to have been incorporated by
reference into a will, it is treated as part of the will
for the specific purpose it is to serve and as if it had
been fully recited in the will itself but not as a
physical part of the will that needs to be probated.
[2 Page, § 19.32].

The UPC substantially codifies the doctrine of
incorporation by reference as described above. [2–
510]. The one exception is that requirement 3 is not
a prerequisite. Consequently, so long as there is
proof that the document was actually in existence at
the time of execution (requirement 4), the UPC
does not require that there be a showing or statement in the will that the document is in existence
at the time that the will is executed.

The essence of the doctrine is the determination
that the testator intended to incorporate the document into the will. The UPC requires that the
language of the will "manifest" this intent. The key
word "manifest" when used as a verb means "to
show plainly: make palpably evident or certain by
showing or displaying." [Webster's Third New Int'l
Dictionary 1375]. This means that although there
must be some indication of an intent to incorporate

by reference another document on the face of the will, it is not necessary that precise language be used such as "I intend to incorporate" as a means of showing this intent. The intent can be derived from the total meaning of the relevant clauses in the will. For example, under this provision, it would be feasible to find that a testator intended to incorporate a previously improperly executed "will" into a subsequent codicil merely by reference to the previous instrument. This would be true even though technically, the testator did not intend to incorporate the previous document into the codicil but intended merely to modify it.

Contrary to interpretations in some states, the UPC permits a valid holographic will to incorporate a non-holographic instrument into it. [2–510]. The problem posed is whether the incorporation of a non-holographic instrument, which provides the primary information concerning the testator's estate plan, into the holographic will constitutes an infringement upon the requirement that the "material portions of the document" must be in the testator's handwriting. Although the UPC does not specifically state the theory underlying its incorporation by reference provision, it may be assumed in this situation that the incorporation is for purposes of admissible evidence and not for purposes of integrating the instrument into the incorporating will. Because a holographic will is capable of being interpreted by extrinsic evidence, it follows that a non-holographic instrument incorporated into the holographic will which qualifies under the incorporation by reference provision should be a proper form of admissible evidence.

B. TESTAMENTARY ADDITIONS TO TRUSTS

For purposes of drafting and administrative convenience and for the benefit of future flexibility, it is a common estate planning technique to include a devise in a client's will that passes property from the estate to a trustee of a trust for the benefit of beneficiaries named in the trust. This type of clause is called a "pour-over" clause. Before statutes were enacted to validate these devises, a question might arise whether the beneficiaries had been adequately identified in the will when their identity is found only in the trust. If the trust existed when the will was executed and remained unchanged at testator's death, the devise usually satisfied the requirements of incorporation by reference. [§ 6.05(A)]. Even if the trust had been changed, if it possessed a substantial corpus, the doctrine of independent significance could be used to validate the devise. [§ 6.05(C)]. Estate planning techniques, however, have become much more sophisticated and reliance upon a trust not being changed or a trust actually possessing a corpus is too restrictive and might cause some pour-over devises which do not satisfy either circumstance to fail. [See, e.g., Atwood v. Rhode Island Hospital Trust Co., 275 F. 513 (1st Cir.1921)]. This is a very undesirable possibility where planning and expectations are involved.

The UPC protects these planning and expectation factors. [2–511]. Its provision not only validates the simple pour-over devise into an existing trust, but also addresses the validity issues concerning more sophisticated techniques. In regard to the threshold question, the devise is not invalid because the trust is amendable or revocable or even if it is actually amended after the execution of the will or the testator's death. The pour-over trust may be established in either of two methods. First, the trust can be established during the testator's lifetime either by the testator, or by the testator and some other person, or by some other person. Second, the trust can be established at testator's death if the trust is identified in the testator's will and the trust's terms are (a) recited in a non-testamentary written instrument that was executed at any time before, with or after the testator executed the will or (b) recited in the will of another individual who has predeceased the testator. If the trust is created during the testator's lifetime, it may be a funded or unfunded life insurance trust even if the trustor has reserved all rights of ownership in the insurance contracts. If the trust is created at the testator's death, the devise is valid notwithstanding the existence, size or character of the corpus of the trust during the testator's lifetime.

The testator is given the option whether to treat the trust as a testamentary trust under the testator's will or to allow it to be governed by the terms of the trust and by its terms and provisions including amendments made to the trust before or after the testator's death. The presumption is that unless the testator's will indicates otherwise, the property devised will be administered under the terms and conditions of the trust and not as a new testamentary trust. If the trust is revoked or terminated before the testator's death, the pour-over devise lapses unless the testator's will provides that it does not lapse.

The UPC's provisions have been converted into Section 1 of the Uniform Testamentary Additions to Trusts Act (1991). [2–511, Comment].

C. EVENTS OF INDEPENDENT SIGNIFICANCE

One doctrine of the law of wills that is typically not codified but which is absolutely essential to its proper functioning is the doctrine of "events of independent significance." Basically, this doctrine permits certain evidence outside the will to be admitted in order to determine who receives and what property passes under the testator's will. [2 Page, § 19.34]. A statement of its principle is that if a fact, be it an act or event, has significance other than to pass property at death, this significance entitles that fact to control and to determine the disposition of the property. Significantly, the above principle applies regardless of whether the testator or third persons can affect the act or event subsequent to the will's execution. [Atkinson, Wills § 81]. Typical examples of the application of the doctrine are the common use in wills of such terms as "children," "cousins," "brothers and sisters," the "residue" and "all my property." In order to determine the meaning of each of these words or phrases, it is necessary to look at facts outside the face of the will; however, because these words have obvious significance other than to pass property at death, extrinsic evidence is admitted to show their meaning.

Apparently for uniformity and clarity purposes, the UPC includes a provision that codifies a broad statement of the common law rule. [2–512]. This provision is applicable to acts or events that occur not only before or after the execution of the will but also that occur after the testator's death. Under its test, testamentary dispositions may be controlled by these acts and events only if the latter "have significance apart from their effect upon the dispositions made by the will." Although the UPC generally leaves to the Court the determination of what comes within its test, it does expressly state that under the test the execution or revocation of another's will constitutes such an event. This separate and specific rule permits a testator to dispose of testator's property according to the terms of another's will notwithstanding that the other's will was executed before or after the testator's will.

D. REFERENCES TO SEPARATE WRITINGS

The UPC permits, under limited circumstances and with explicit restrictions, a written statement or list to dispose of certain tangible personal property notwithstanding that the writing does not satisfy any will execution procedure, the incorporation by reference doctrine or the events of independent significance doctrine. [2–513]. The requirements for such a writing are as follows:

(1) The writing must be signed by the testator;

(2) The items disposed of and the devisees must be described with reasonable certainty;

(3) The items disposed of must be tangible personal property;

(4) The tangible personal property items disposed of must not otherwise be specifically disposed of by the testator's will; and

(5) There must be a reference to this writing in a properly executed will of the testator.

If these requirements are satisfied, it makes no difference whether the writing comes into existence before or after the execution of the will, whether the writing is actually altered by the testator after the execution of the will, or whether the writing has significance other than its effect on the dispositions made in the will.

One important limitation on the use of this type of transfer device is that it is limited to the disposition of tangible personal property. The provision specifically prohibits the use of this device for the disposition of money. This limitation inferentially also bars the device's use to dispose of evidences of indebtedness, documents of title, securities, and property used in trade or business under this device. [2–513, Comment].

The writing and signature formalities put a relatively high burden on users of this device. Unsigned holographic writings do not qualify. To be effective, the latter instruments would have to be probatable under the UPC's formality dispensing provision. [2–513, Comment; see 2–503; § 6.01(A)(6)]. Although the absence of a dating requirement removes a barrier to validity for these devices, the possibility that undated and partially or wholly conflicting signed writings may be found among a decedent's records after death may cause serious construction problems. A disadvantage from such misuse of the device might cause the underlying will to be denied informal probate. [See 3–304].

On the whole, the recognition of such a device is justified on the grounds that it is in line with the policies of giving effect to the testator's intent and of relaxing execution formalities. [2–513, Comment; see § 6.01(A)]. Considering the limitation placed upon the type and extent of property that may be disposed of in this manner, problems of fraud, duress and undue influence are not serious considerations. One of the most beneficial aspects of this provision is to provide a convenient and simple device for persons who desire to change their wills frequently with respect to devises of tangible personal property and effects. This new device appears to be popular both with laymen and with practicing attorneys.

§ 6.06 Peripheral Issues

A. NO CONTEST OR CLAIM CLAUSES

The UPC also codifies the rule in many states that an anti-contest or anti-claim clause in a will is unenforceable against an interested person if that person had probable cause to institute the proceeding. [3–905; replicated in 2–517]. For example, under the probable cause standard, this clause protects devisees in a will from automatic forfeiture of the devise for instituting a contest proceeding against the will. Since the devisee obviously lost the contest it is usually difficult to establish probable cause. The provision is unclear on how the probable cause standard applies to a devisee who is a creditor of the estate and who submits a claim against the estate despite the forfeiture provision in the will. If the devisee succeeds on the claim, does this constitute probable cause and permit the devisee to take a devise also? Is this not what the testator might have desired to prohibit? How this provision resolves the above questions and other similar ones will have to wait for court decisions. Fortunately, litigation over forfeiture clauses is not common. At best, this provision provides a residual remedy to prevent injustice.

B. SUCCESSION CONTRACTS

Contracts concerned with the succession of property have generally been held to be valid and enforceable. [1 Page, § 10.1]. In their broadest general categories, these contracts include contracts to make a will or to devise, contracts not to revoke a will or devise, and contracts to revoke a will or to die intestate or both. The substantive requirements for such contracts are determined by the law of contracts, not by the law of succession. Contract law, therefore, determines such issues as offer and acceptance, certainty of terms, consideration, capacity, and any formality requirement such as the Statute of Frauds. The formality requirement issue, however, raises significant interrelationship concerns between the law of contracts and the law of succession. Obviously, succession contracts may effect the determination of who succeeds to the property after the death of the deceased promisor.

One of the most common problems concerning succession contracts is whether oral succession contracts may be proved. [1 Page, §§ 10.10–10.11]. Because the Statute of Wills is not applicable, in most states the basic question has been the applicability of the Statute of Frauds. Unless the state has a specific provision dealing with succession contracts that adequately limits the proof of oral succession contracts, the Statute of Frauds constitutes no significant limitation on the proof of these oral contracts. Even where the Statute of Frauds' provision relating to the sale of real estate applies to a succession contract dealing with transfers of real estate, the courts commonly apply exceptions to the statute such as part performance and other presumptions to circumvent the Statute's proof restriction and permit the oral contracts to be proved.

Depending upon one's viewpoint toward formality requirements, this circumvention of the Statute of Frauds may or may not be beneficial. Notwithstanding this value judgment, the ineffectiveness of the Statute of Frauds as a bar to proof of a succession contract has significantly encouraged litigation over these matters.

In order to reduce the uncertainties and litigation caused by oral succession contracts, the UPC tightens the proof requirements for all three categories of succession contracts. [2–514]. It provides that a succession contract can be established against a decedent's estate only if (1) material provisions of the contract are stated in the decedent's will, or (2) an express reference in the will is made to such a contract that is supplemented by other admissible extrinsic evidence proving the terms of the contract, or (3) evidence of the contract appears in a writing signed by the decedent. In addition, the UPC specifically provides that no presumption of a contract not to revoke a will can be created by the mere execution of a joint will or mutual wills. Otherwise, this provision is not intended to alter the rules of evidence with regard to the proof of such contracts. [2–514, Comment].

Clearly, this provision intentionally limits the proof of succession contracts and washes away all of the authority and decisions dealing with the application of the Statute of Frauds and its exceptions. [Orlando v. Prewett, 705 P.2d 593 (Mont.1985)]. As with the adoption of any new formalistic requirement, the expectations of some persons will be destroyed. [See § 6.01(A)]. Considering that one of the parties to the contract is no longer available to testify, however, it would appear to be good public policy to require some form of written evidence that the contract actually exists. In addition, the limitations themselves leave adequate room for the courts to develop reasonable interpretation of the requirements so that harm will not be caused to a substantial number of persons. The terms "material provisions" and "evidencing" and the admissibility of extrinsic evidence where the will makes reference to the contract are three concepts in the provision that give the courts adequate interpretive flexibility.

Significantly, the UPC makes no attempt to restrict or delineate what otherwise is necessary to prove succession contracts; nor does it attempt in any way to deal with the problem of the appropriate remedy when such contracts are proved. In addition, so that these new formalities do not interfere with pre-existing rights, this provision specifically applies only to succession contracts made after the effective date of the UPC. [2–514]. Pre-existing succession contracts will be tested by the previously applicable formality requirement, if any.

C. CONFIDENTIAL PUBLIC DEPOSITORY

Under rules to be established by each court, the UPC provides that a testator or testator's agent may deposit a will with any court for purposes of protective preservation. [2–515]. So that as much confidentiality as is feasible is maintained, the UPC provides that only the testator or the agent, authorized in writing, may obtain repossession of the will. Although the testator's conservator may also be allowed to examine the will, the Court is to set strict procedures designed to maintain the confidentiality of the will. Under such procedures, for example, the conservator is not to be given possession of the will but only to be permitted to examine it. Upon the completion of this examination, the will must be resealed and left on deposit.

When the Court is informed of the testator's death, it is to notify any person who is designated to receive the will and to deliver the will to that person on request. In the alternative, the Court may deliver the will to the appropriate court.

Under the Uniform International Wills Act reproduced in Part 10 of the UPC, a registry system is created for the international will. [2–1010]. The system provides a location where authorized persons can file for safekeeping specific information concerning the international will. The information filed, which will be preserved in confidence until death, is limited to the name, social security and any other individual identifying number established by law, address, and date and place of birth of the testator, and the intended place of deposit or safekeeping of the international will. The official, which the UPC suggests be the Secretary of State, may make this information available only to persons who present a death certificate of the testator or satisfactory evidence of the testator's death to the central information center.

D. WILL CUSTODIANS

A custodian of a will of a testator who has died is on request of an interested person under a duty to deliver with reasonable promptness any will of the testator either to a person who is able to secure its probate or to an appropriate Court if no such person is known. [2–516]. Willful failure to deliver a will causes the custodian to be liable to any person who suffers damages as a consequence of that failure. A custodian may also be subject to the penalty of contempt of court if the custodian willfully refuses or fails to deliver a will, although required to do so by a court order issued as a result of a proceeding specifically brought to compel delivery.

CHAPTER 7
RULES OF CONSTRUCTION APPLICABLE TO WILLS ONLY

§ 7.01 Rules of Construction for Wills

A. Introduction to Construction: Inherently, a will is nothing more than words structured so as to communicate the testator's desires. In order to carry out the will's purposes and effects, it is necessary to ascribe a meaning to the words. When determining the meaning of words used in a will, the cardinal principle is that the subjective intent of the testator, as expressed in testator's will and if not against public policy, controls the legal effect of the will's dispositions. [Cf. 2–601]. Consequently, a testator may ascribe a meaning to a word different from the ordinary meaning. If the testator's own meaning can be determined, it should control. When the testator's meaning cannot be determined or is inadequately expressed, the interpreters must seek the meaning of the word from other sources. [2–601; see also 2–701; § 8.01].

As with any area of law, there are frequently used words of art or common recurring situations. Because of the frequency of the use of these words or of the occurrence of the situation, the law must develop uniform and set definitions and interpretations. These definitions and interpretations serve two purposes: (1) they provide a rule of construction for wills where the testator's expressed intent is inadequate or lacking; and, (2) they provide a set of uniform rules that drafters of wills may incorporate by reference either explicitly or implicitly. The UPC not only includes a long list of general definitions that are useful for these purposes, [see § 2.01(B)(4)] but also incorporates rules of construction for many of the most common problems concerning will interpretation and construction. [Art. II, Pt. 6]. Presumably, these rules of construction are based upon what the drafters determined the typical testator would desire if the testator had expressly indicated that intent. Significantly, they do not apply if evidence indicates testator had a contrary intention. [2–601].

Because many of the rules of construction in this chapter and in other parts of the UPC are applicable only to particular types of testamentary gifts, definitions of the various classes of testamentary gifts are important. Due to the absence of definitions of these terms in the UPC, the common law definitions are relevant. Generally, testamentary gifts are classified into four different categories, i.e., specific, general, demonstrative and residuary devises. A specific devise is a gift of a specific item or portion of the estate. A general devise is a gift of a set value or generally described property which is to be charged against the whole estate and not a specific portion. A demonstrative devise is a gift payable out of the whole estate but which is in the first instance charged against certain parts of the estate. A residuary devise is a gift of the remainder of the estate. [See 6 Page, Wills §§ 48.1–.10].

§ 7.02 Devisee Lapse

A. INTRODUCTION

Common law holds that when a devisee (including a legatee) died between the execution of the will and the death of the testator, the devise to that person lapses. [6 Page, Wills § 50.20]. If a devisee died before the execution of the will, the devise is void. [6 Page, Wills § 50.22]. These characterizations generate a constructional presumption providing that neither the dead devisee nor that devisee's estate can take the devise. A lapsed or void devise passes to others according to a set of other presumptions. [Atkinson, Wills § 140]. First, the devise passes to one or more devisees named as alternative devisees including survivors of survivorship type devises such as class gifts. If no alternative devisee is named, the devise passes to the residuary devisee, if any. If no residuary devisee is named, or if the residuary devise becomes void or lapses, the devise passes by intestacy. All of these presumptions yield to a testator's expressions of contrary intent.

The following methods are commonly used by testators to avert or resolve these problems: (1) a testator makes the devise to several persons as joint tenants expecting the survivorship of one or more of the joint tenants to prevent lapse; (2) a testator specifically provides for alternative devises to other persons until the likelihood of total failure of the devise is negligible; or, (3) a testator uses class gifts with their built-in survivorship presumptions.

Because lapse occurs more often than many testators have anticipated and because lapse causes disinheritance of the devisee and the devisee's relational stock, nearly all of the jurisdictions in this country have enacted what are commonly referred to as "antilapse statutes." [See Restatement (Second) of Property Statutory, Note to § 34.6]. Although called "antilapse statutes," they do not prevent lapse but actually create a statutory substitute devise to the devisee's descendants. [2–603, Comment]. Generally, these statutes permit the descendants of certain classes of dead devisees to stand in their ancestor's place for purposes of taking under a testator's will. They create a rule of construction that may be altered by the testator. If a testator intends that lapse occurs, it will occur and the devise will fail. None of the statutes apply to all testamentary gifts and they vary greatly as to their scope.

Cognizant that the lapse and voidness of devises are common, unanticipated occurrences in wills, the UPC contains a comprehensive, although restricted, set of constructional rules concerned with lapse and its related problems. [2–603, 2–604]. Due to the multiplicity of issues that concern lapse, the UPC's provisions are relatively complex. [See Halbach & Waggoner, Survivorship and Antilapse, at 1099–1125]. Three levels of concern must be digested for a proper understanding of these provisions: one must determine (1) the scope and limitations of the provisions; (2) the application to relevant lapse problems; and, (3) how a testator may override their application.

B. SCOPE AND LIMITATIONS OF THE ANTILAPSE PROTECTION

As with other similar statutes, the UPC's substitute devise protection does not apply to all devisees. This protection is only provided for (1) devisees who come within the relational classification of being a testator's grandparent or a lineal descendant of a grandparent [See the UPC's relational umbrella of covered relations highlighted in Chart 3–1, § 3.01(B)] and (2) devisees who are stepchildren of the testator or of the donor of a power of appointment exercised by the testator's will. [2–603(b)]. If a devisee is not a person who comes within the relational umbrella or a stepchild, the common law rule of lapse applies and there is no substitute devise. For example, descendants of devisees who are uncovered relatives related by marriage or who are legal strangers would not be protected by this provision. When testator's spouse is a devisee, the spouse's descendants also are not protected by the provision. This situation is to be compared to the case when the spouse's child, a stepchild of testator, is the devisee. When the stepchild is a devisee, the stepchild's descendants are protected by the provision but if a devise is made to a surviving spouse and no one else, the spouse's descendants, including a possible stepchild, are not protected under the provision.

If a devisee is a qualified devisee and the devise lapses, a substitute devise is created for the devisee's surviving descendants. [2–603; see also 2–106, § 3.01(C)]. Descendants who take the substitute devise share only the interest the devisee would have taken if the devisee had survived the testator and whatever they take, they take by representation. [2–603(b)(1), (2); see also 2–106 (Representation defined)]. Significantly, only the devisee's descendants receive this substituted devise; other relatives of the devisee, such as spouses, ancestors and collaterals, are not accorded a substitute devise under the provision. Furthermore, in order for the substitute descendants of deceased devisees to take under the provision, they must survive the testator by 120 hours although they need not survive the deceased devisee by any specific length of time. [See 2–702; § 8.02]. If descendants of a qualified devisee fail to survive, the common law rule of lapse applies and there is no substitute devise.

The UPC's antilapse provision is expansive in regard to the timing of the lapse and to the types of devises covered. Its rules apply to all types of devises including specific, general, demonstrative and residuary. It applies notwithstanding that the qualified devisee died before the testator's will was executed or died between the execution date and the testator's death. [2–603(a)(4)(ii)]. Beyond actual death of a devisee, the provision applies in all circumstances where the devisee is deemed under the UPC to have predeceased the testator. [See 2–702, 2–801(d), 2–803, 2–804]. The antilapse provision also specifically applies to descendants of devisees of class gifts regardless whether the common law treats the devise as lapsed or void. [2–603(b)(2)]. Class gifts include, for example, devises to one's children, siblings, cousins and similar single generation relational groups. Because of an inherent substitute devise effect, the UPC's provision does not apply to class devises such as devises to one's issue, descendants, heirs, next of kin and other multi-generational relational groups.

In a significant clarification of the law of lapse, the UPC specifically applies its substitute gift protection to the exercise of powers of appointment. [See § 9.06; see also, e.g., French, Application of Antilapse Statutes]. Under the UPC, the exercise of a testamentary power of appointment is a devise and an appointee of an exercised testamentary power of appointment is a devisee. [2–603(a)(3), (4)]. Exercised testamentary powers are protected by the substitute gift presumption if the appointee either comes within the class of being a grandparent or a lineal descendant of a grandparent [See the UPC's relational umbrella of covered relations highlighted in Chart 3–1, § 3.01(B)] or is a stepchild of the donor of a power of appointment exercised by the testator's will or of the testator who is donee of the power. [2–603(b)]. For example, if D devised or deeded property "to T for life, remainder to G's children as T shall appoint," and T exercised the power in favor of A but A predeceased T leaving surviving descendants, A's surviving descendants would take a substitute devise if A is a member of the covered relations of either D or T. It makes no difference whether the power of appointment is a general or special power so long as the appointee's relational threshold requirement is met. The exercise may be to an individual or a class. If the substitute gift presumption applies, it does not matter that the substitute taker is not a member of the class of permissible appointees so long as the appointee is a permissible appointee and meets the relational threshold requirement.

C. APPLICATION TO RELEVANT LAPSE PROBLEMS

Beyond the threshold determination of substantive relevance, one is faced with a range of application problems that run from simple to complex. The Comment to section 2–603 contains excellent illustrations explaining the operation of this provision. In the simple case the answers are easy. For example, if T devised property to A and A died before T or did not survive T by 120 hours or more, A's surviving descendants, if any, will take the devise as substitute devisees if A falls within the relational umbrella protected by the UPC and if a contrary intent is not established. Another simple example would be the will that makes a devise to A's children, where at T's death, two of A's children survived and one predeceased T but left descendants who survived T. The descendants of the predeceased child collectively receive a substitute devise equal to the shares of A's two children who survived T. These descendants share the devise among themselves by representation. In both examples, it makes no difference to the result whether the nonsurviving devisee died before or after the will was written.

More complex problems concern wills in which the testator has created alternative devises. For example, who takes if T devised property "to A, but if A does not survive T, to B" and assuming A does not survive T but leaves descendants who do? Under the UPC, B will take because the alternative devise prevails. Taking the same example further, who takes if B also predeceases T but leaves no descendants who survived T? In this situation A's surviving descendants will take a substitute devise because the alternative devise failed and the substitute devise presumption prevails. [2–603(b)(4)]. Continuing one step further, who takes if B also predeceased T and like A left descendants who do? Again, the UPC provides that A's descendants will take a substitute devise to the exclusion of B's descendants because A's descendants were the primary substitute gift as A held the primary devise. [2–603(c)(1), 2–603(c)(3)(ii)]. The primary devise is the one that will be effective if all nonsurviving devisees had survived the testator which in this example will always be A. [2–603(c)(3)(I)].

A third group of circumstances that cause lapse problems are the devises that include an alternative gift to the person or persons who would have been the substitute taker under the antilapse provision. [2–603(c)]. For example, consider the lapse problem raised when T devised property "to A, but if A does not survive T, to A's children" and assuming A does not survive T but leaves a child, B, who survived T and two grandchildren, F and G, who survived T but whose parent, C, predeceased T. The devise to the children, B and C, is a "younger generation devise" because it is to a descendant of the primary devise, A, it is an alternative devise to the primary devise, it is one for which a substitute gift is created and it would have gone into effect if all deceased devisees had survived except for the primary devisee, A, who predeceased the testator. [2–603(c)(3)(iii)]. In this situation the "younger-generation substitute gift" to F and G takes precedence over the primary substitute gift to B and C; consequently, F and G, collectively, take one half of the estate and B takes the other half. [2–603(c)(3)(iv)]. If this priority of substitute gifts did not apply, it would be possible to conclude that B takes one-half of the devise plus one half of the devise to A and F and G would share only the one-half of one half rather than one-half of the whole devise. The UPC's approach to this matter conforms to the probable intention of most testators.

If a devise lapses and the substitute devise provisions are inapplicable, the UPC has a special provision designating to whom the lapsed devise passes. Significantly, the following rules apply to all lapsed devises regardless of who the devisee is. All lapsed devises other than the residuary devise become part of the residue and pass to the residuary devisees. [2–604(a)]. When the residue is devised to two or more devisees and one share fails for any reason, that devisee's share passes to the other residuary devisee or devisees. [2–604(b)]. This is a meritorious rule of construction because it will frequently avoid part of the estate passing in intestacy. Of course, if all of the residue fails for any reason, the residuary estate passes by intestacy to the testator's heirs.

D. TESTATOR'S EXPRESSED CONTRARY INTENTION

As with all of the UPC's rules of construction, the provision does not apply if the testator, by the terms of the will, indicates that the provision does not apply. Section 2–603 sets the presumption that mere statements of survivorship such as "if he survives me" are not, "in the absence of additional evidence," sufficient indications of an intent to override the statute's presumption. [2–603(b)(3)]. The justification for this boiled down to two primary arguments. First, the statute is said to be remedial in that it favors family and thus deserves broad interpretation and second, the issue has been litigated enough to have a firm rule. [2–603, Comment]. The Comment notes the conflict among the cases and cites several examples.

It is clear that if the testator adequately expresses an intent to require survivorship, this expression will be given effect. [2–601; 2–603, Comment]. The comment to section 2–603 states that "foolproof" drafting techniques of expressing a contrary intent include adding an additional phrase to a devise that states "and not to [the devisee's] descendants" or a separate clause that states "all lapsed or failed nonresiduary devises are to pass under the residuary clause," or an addition to the residuary clause that states "including all lapsed or failed devises." [2–603, Comment]. Where or how the line is to drawn between "mere words of survivorship" and "express contrary intent" is not explained.

In many lapse situations, no actual intent will be available and the court will be left with only the words of the will to decipher. As mentioned, the UPC's substitute devise presumably applies unless a contrary intent is found. When a testator uses survivorship words, however, a presumption stand-off arises: the presumption of statutory application against an expression of contrary intent. In such situations presumptions are frequently and properly used, in a sense, to break the tie. The drafters correctly contend that something has to be said to break the new tie and they opted for testator's "express contrary intent" to rebut the statutory presumption while testator's "mere words of survivorship" will not rebut it.

Without relevant extrinsic evidence to explain the testator's actual intent, however, interpreters of the will are flying blind. In these situations, presumptions and rules of construction should conform to the desires of the average person because there is nothing else on which to rely. Analysis whether the presumption concerning survivorship language conforms to average intent may depend on the class of devisee involved in the devise. For example, it is one thing to say that most persons probably want grandchildren to take by representation in the place of deceased children and quite another to say they probably want their nephews and nieces to take by representation in the place of deceased brothers and sisters. For example one might give an entirely different interpretation to a will that devised "$100,000 to surviving brothers and sisters, and the residue to X charity," than to one that devised "$100,000 to surviving children, and the residue to X charity," One might conclude that testator in the first situation did not want nephews and nieces to take the devise unless all brothers and sisters died[1] *and* unless the charity was incapable of taking but in the second situation might reach the opposite conclusion and allow descendants of predeceased children to take by representation in the place of deceased children and to the exclusion of the charity. The UPC does not make this distinction and applies the same rules to collateral relatives as it does to descendants. From an inheritance stand-

---

1. The illustration raises two substitute devise issues under the UPC. The first is whether descendants of a predeceased brother or sister take under the section if one or more brothers or sisters survive. The second is whether descendants of predeceased brothers and sisters can take if no brother or sister survives or whether the charity takes instead. If the words "surviving brother and sisters" are mere words of survivorship, the presumption of section 2–603(b)(3) would apply and the descendants of predeceased brothers and sisters might share with surviving brothers and sisters and take in lieu of the charity. [2–603(b)(3)].

point, one's descendants are vastly different from one's collaterals and the statutory presumption should probably recognize this.

E. FACTUAL ILLUSTRATIONS

CHART 7–1

APPLICATIONS OF ANTILAPSE PROVISIONS[2]

Assumption 1: A. T's properly executed Will provides:
"The grandfather's clock to A, $10,000 to B, and the residue to C."

B. A is a neighbor and friend; B is a second cousin; and C is a first cousin.

C. A, B, and C predecease T, each leaving surviving descendants.

Question: Who takes what property?

Analysis: A's devise lapses because A predeceased T. A's descendants do not take a substitute gift because A is not a member of the relational umbrella. A's lapsed devise becomes part of the residue.

B's devise lapses because B predeceased T. Although B is a blood relation, B's descendants will not take a substitute gift because B is not a member of the relational umbrella. B's

2. When a person is said to survive, it means the person satisfies all requirements of survivorship including the 120 hour rule [2–702] and is not treated as having predeceased. [See 2–702, 2–801(d), 2–803, 2–804].

lapsed devise becomes part of the residue.

C's devise lapses because C predeceased T. C's descendants will take a substitute gift because C is a member of the relational umbrella. C's descendants take the entire residuary estate including the above lapsed devises.

Assumption 2:   A. T's properly executed Will provides:
"My 100 shares of XYZ stock to A and B or to the survivor, $10,000 to C's surviving children, and the residue to D and E."

B. A and B are T's siblings; C is a first cousin; and D and E are friends of T.

C. A, C, and D predecease T, each leaving surviving descendants: C had three children, F, G, and H. F predeceased T leaving M and N as descendants. M died 100 hours after T leaving no surviving descendants.

Question: Who takes what property?

Analysis: B takes the entire devise of 100 shares. A's devise lapses because A predeceased T. A's descendants are not substituted for A although A is a member of the relational umbrella because the words "or the survivor" create an alternative gift of A's ½ to B. The alternative devise takes precedence over both the substitute gift and the residuary devise.

The devise to C's children is covered by the presumption. The presumption of a substitute devise applies to class devises such as to children and here the children are members of the protected relational umbrella. Consequently, F's descendants, M and N, are eligible to take by representation the substitute devise in place of their ancestor F. The words "surviving children" are considered to be mere words of survivorship and do not on their own rebut the substituted devise. M died without surviving descendants 100 hours after T and under 2–702 failed to survive T; consequently, M is no longer a substitute devisee leaving N as F's only substitute devisee. The end result is that N, and G and H will share equally the devise. The substitute gift takes precedence over the residuary devise.

D's devise lapses because D predeceased T. D's descendants will not take a substitute devise under 2–603 because D is not a member of the relational umbrella. Even though E is not a member of the relational umbrella, E takes the entire residuary devise including D's lapsed share of the residuary devises because 2–604(b) applies and it does not require a particular relationship to the testator. It is a presumption that applies from the circumstance and in order to avoid intestacy.

Assumption 3: A. T's properly executed Will provides:
"$10,000 to A, but if A does not survive me, to A's descendants, $10,000 to B, but if B does not survive me, to C, and the residue, including all lapsed or failed nonresiduary devises, to D, if he is

living at my death, if not then to X Charity."

B.   A, B and T are siblings; C is B's spouse; and D is T's stepchild.

C.   A, B, C, and D predecease T, each leaving surviving descendants. A's three children, E, F, and G, predecease T but left one, three, and four grandchildren, respectively, who survived T.

Question: Who takes what property?

Analysis: A's devise lapses because A predeceased T. A's grandchildren will take, by representation or ⅛ each [see 2–705; § 8.05], as alternative devisees. The devise to A's descendants does not become part of the residuary even though the residuary devise specifically includes lapsed devises because devisees take directly as alternative devisees and not as substitute devisees. The substitute devise presumption is not used to protect the grandchildren since the devise is to a multigenerational class gift and such gifts inherently include an antilapse avoidance technique by employing the concept of representation.

B's devise lapses because B predeceased T. C's devise lapses because C predeceased T. The lapsed devises become part of the residue. Although B is a member of the protected relational umbrella and a substitute devise is presumed in favor of B's descendants, the devise lapses into the residuary because the specific language included in the residuary clause captures lapsed devises. For this provision to apply, however, there has to be an "expressly designated devisee" who takes. In this situation, D is an expressly designated devise, but he predeceased T and cannot take X Charity is also an expressly designated devisee and can take as an alternative devisee. C's descendants are not entitled to a presumptive substitute devise because C is not a member of the protected relational umbrella; consequently, C's devise would fail even if the residuary devise did not specifically include lapsed devises. Or there was no expressly designated devisee to take.

D's devise lapses because D predeceased T. Although D is not a member of the protected relational umbrella, D is separately protected under 2–603 as a stepchild of the testator. The alternative devisee, X Charity, is qualified and capable to take. X Charity take the entire residuary estate including the above lapsed devises. The specific language concerning lapsed devises applies only to nonresiduary devises and does not apply to residuary devises. The substitute devise presumption will not apply to this residuary devise because of the alternative gift to X Charity ..

Assumption 4:   A. T's properly executed Will provides:
"$10,000 to A, but if A does not survive me, to A's children, $10,000 to B's children, and the residue, including all lapsed or failed nonresiduary devises, to C."
B. A and B are siblings; C is T's spouse.

C. A, B, and C predecease T, each
leaving surviving descendants. A's
three children, E, F, and G, predecease T but left one, three, and
four grandchildren, respectively.
Of B's three children, H, I, and J,
H predeceased T but H's child,
M, survived T. C's two children
survived T but are from a prior
marriage and are only T's stepchildren. D, T's adopted child,
survived T.

Question: Who takes what property?

Analysis: A's devise lapses because A predeceased T. The alternative devise to A's
children also lapses because none survived T. Although A is covered by the
relational umbrella and A's grandchildren would be entitled to a substitute
devise under the statutory presumption that covers class gifts to children,
is the presumption rebutted by specific
inclusion of lapsed devises into the residuary devise? The specific inclusion
of lapsed devises into the residuary devise clause applies in this situation
only if the there is to be an "expressly
designated devisee" who takes. In this
situation, D is an expressly designated
devise, but he predeceased T and cannot take. The substitute devise to A's
grandchildren would be entitled to a
substitute devise under the statutory
presumption that covers class gifts.
None of this devise lapses into the residuary.

The devise to B's children does not
lapse because two of B's children survived T. They take as surviving mem-

bers of the class thus no part of the devise passes to the residuary devise. A secondary question arises, however, whether M, the child of B's predeceased child, H, may take under the statutory presumption for a substitute devise. Because none of the devise lapses, the specific language in the residuary devise is not applicable to this devise. But does the existence of this language rebut the application of the statutory presumption within the confines of the class gift? All requirements for the substitute devise are satisfied. Considering the remedial nature of the antilapse provision, the provision should be interpreted to protect M, and M should be able to share equally with I and J.

C's devise lapses because C predeceased T. C's children do not take a substitute devise because they are not members of the protected relational umbrella. The protection for a stepchild does not apply because it only applies when a stepchild is the named devisee not a substitute devisee under the statutory presumption. Unfortunately, this means the residue will pass by intestacy and the disinherited adopted child of T will take the entire residuary estate as sole surviving child. [See 2–103; § 5.02]. It is doubtful that the negative will provision of 2–101(b) would apply since the disinheritance was silent. Even if applicable, it would pass the residue to T's collateral relation, by representation and not to T's stepchildren.

Assumption 5:   A.   D's properly executed and probat-
                       ed Will devised, in relevant part,
                       the residue to T in trust for E's
                       life, remainder to any person or
                       persons E shall appoint by will but
                       in default of such appointment the
                       remainder goes to Charity C.
                 B.   E's properly executed and probat-
                       ed Will, in relevant part, exercises
                       the above power and appoints the
                       trust estate to A.
                 C.   A predeceased E but A's descen-
                       dants survived E.
                 D.   Charity C is a legally recognized
                       entity capable of holding property.

Question: Who takes what property?

Analysis: As an appointee under a power of ap-
                 pointment, A is a devisee under E's
                 will. If A is a grandparent or descen-
                 dant of a grandparent, or a stepchild,
                 of either D, the donor of the power, or
                 E, the donee and testator, A's descen-
                 dants may take by representation a
                 substitute devise under the will be-
                 cause they survived E, the relevant tes-
                 tator.

                 If A is not a member of the protected
                 relations of either D or E, or is not
                 survived by descendants, the devise
                 lapses and Charity C will take the
                 property as taker in default. Note that
                 in this situation, the property subject
                 to the power of appointment does not
                 pass through the donee's estate if the
                 donee has not effectively exercised the
                 power. It passes directly to the takers
                 in default under the terms of E's in-
                 strument, the person who created the
                 power.

§ 7.03 Ademption and Nonademption by Extinction

Common Law Ademption by Extinction: The common law rule of construction regarding ademption by extinction asserts that when a specifically devised item of property is not identified as part of the testator's estate at the time of the testator's death, the devise fails. [Atkinson, Wills § 134]. Although this rule is merely a rule of construction and is subject to control by the testator, many courts severely limit the proof of testator's intent by refusing to admit extrinsic evidence of it. In these decisions, testator's intent to override the rule must be expressed on the face of the will: the will must anticipate the problem and express a solution. For example, T's will might read, "I devise my diamond ring to A, but if I do not own a diamond ring at my death, I devise $10,000 to A." Here, the testator has anticipated ademption by extinction and if the ring is not in the estate, A would take the $10,000 substitute devise. Unfortunately, most testators do not anticipate ademption, and the common law rule precludes A from taking anything from the estate for the devise unless the ring is there regardless of T's intent.

Ademption by Extinction Escape Devices: Often courts that follow the strict identity theory employ escape devices to avoid forfeiture for a devisee when the court does not believe testator intended ademption. These devices include tracing efforts to find the asset that testator holds at death which is traceable to the asset described by the specific devise. This worked in situations where the subject of the devise exists in testator's estate but it does not exactly conform to the devise. For example, if T devised "my 1999 Chevrolet to A" but at death owns a 2000 Cadillac, A may be able to take the Cadillac if a court is willing to trace the original devise to the currently owned asset.

Another related and sometimes overlapping escape device concerns changes in form. The common law ademption rule did not cause forfeiture if the specifically devised asset merely changed in form and not in substance between the date of the will and the date of death. The asset as changed passes to the devisee. Depending on the attitude of the court toward the particular devise in question, this approach could often save a devise. For example, if T devised "my 100 shares of XYZ common stock to A," and the corporation converted the shares to preferred stock, A might successfully contend that the 100 shares of common stock had only changed form and, therefore, A should take the 100 preferred shares. Application of this approach might depend on the degree of actual change and whether the change was caused by voluntary or involuntary action by the testator. [See § 7.04].

Ademption by Extinction under the UPC: The UPC significantly alters and clarifies the common law rules concerning ademption by extinction of specific devises.*** [2–606].

First, the specific devisee has a right to specifically devised property or any part of it that exists in testator's estate at death. [2–606(a)]. Concomitantly, the specific devisee has a right to assets that represent, in part or in whole, the remaining interest which the testator retains at death in the specifically devised property. [2–606(a)(1)–(5)]. The provision delineates the following five situations as constituting a testator's remaining interest at death: (1) the unpaid balance of the purchase price, plus any accompanying security agreement, owed to the testator; (2) the unpaid amount of a condemnation award owed to the testator; (3) the unpaid fire or casualty insurance proceeds or recovery for injury to the specifically devised property; (4) the property received by foreclosure or obtained in lieu of foreclosure on a specifically devised obligation; and, (5) the real or personal property acquired by testator as a replacement for the specifically devised property. These rules are not subject to contra-

*** The 1990 revision originally reversed the presumption of ademption. Under this version, if the specifically devised property was not in the estate at testator's death, the devisee was presumptively entitled to a general pecuniary devise equal to the value of the specifically devised property less the value of any actual portion of the devise remaining in the estate at testator's death and of the five representative remaining interests described in the text following this note. [2–606(a)(6) (1990)]. The presumption was rebuttable either when the facts and circumstances indicated testator intended ademption, or if ademption was consistent with the testator's manifested plan of distribution. The current version was adopted in 1997.

diction by extrinsic evidence of testator's unexpressed intent.

Second, to the extent the specifically devised property is not in the testator's estate at death, the devisee is entitled to a general pecuniary devise equal to the value of the specifically devised property (less the value of any actual portion of the devise remaining in the estate at testator's death and of the five representative remaining interests described above), if it is established by clear and convincing evidence that ademption would be inconsistent with the testator's intent. UPC § 2–606(a)(6) (as amended in 1997).

Extrinsic Evidence: The UPC adopts a broad extrinsic evidence rule to permit proof of testator's intent concerning ademption. The presumption for ademption in (a)(6), as revised, may be rebutted either when the facts and circumstances indicate testator did not intend ademption, or if ademption is inconsistent with the testator's manifested plan of distribution. The latter proviso permits extrinsic evidence to be admitted to determine testator's intent and to permit the court to consider the entire estate plan in order to determine what the testator desired.

Third, the UPC provides a special rule concerning transactions made for an incapacitated testator by or with a court appointed lifetime conservator or an agent acting within the authority of a durable power of attorney. [2–606(b)–(e)]. The three specific situations covered by the provision include when a conservator or agent: (1) sold the specifically devised property; (2) received a condemnation award for the specifically devised property; and (3) received insurance proceeds for loss of the property due to fire or casualty. [2–606(b)]. In all three situations, the specific devisee is entitled to a general pecuniary devise equal to the net sale price, condemnation award or the value of the insurance proceeds. This right exists even when the conservator or agent has already received the amounts and has integrated these amounts into the testator's other assets. These rules are not subject to contradiction by extrinsic evidence of testator's unexpressed intent. If the testator survives a judicial termination that testator's disability ceased for one year or more, however, the protection provided to the specific devisee by this provision is no longer applicable. [2–606(d)]. Protecting the specific devisee from conservator and agent transactions is consistent with the concept that ademption or nonademption should be related to testator's intent. Acts of a third person, including a testator's conservator or agent under a durable power, do not reveal testator's desires and should not materially and unfairly affect a specific devisee's interest.

Consider the following problems:

CHART 7–2
ADEMPTION BY EXTINCTION UNDER UPC

<u>Assumption 1</u>:   a.   T's properly executed Will provides:

"The grandfather's clock I own at my death to A, but if I do not own one, $1,000 to A;

> my automobile to B;
> my residence to C;
> my 100 shares of XYZ, Inc., common stock to D;
> the residue to E."

   b. T sold the grandfather's clock and did not replace it.
       T's automobile was destroyed in a major accident; the insurance company has agreed to pay $2,000 but had not paid at T's death.
       T sold the residence moved into an apartment and took $20,000 cash and a note and mortgage for $80,000 from P as payment. P paid the cash but still owes $75,000 on the note and mortgage.
       T sold the XYZ, Inc., stock and used the proceeds to buy WVU, Inc., stock.
       T's residue is valued at $100,000.

   c. All devisees survived T.

Question: Who takes what property?

Analysis: The specifically devised grandfather's clock is adeemed and T's expressed intent devises A the alternate $1,000.

   B is entitled to the unpaid insurance proceeds on the totaled automobile. Subject to a finding of contrary intent on the part of T, if the unpaid insurance proceeds do not equal the value of the devise, B would be entitled to a pecuniary devise equal to the difference between the value of the devise less the unpaid insurance proceeds from the estate.

C is entitled to the unpaid balance of the sale price and the security interest held in the estate on the residence. Subject to a finding of contrary intent on the part of T, if the unpaid purchase price and security interest do not equal the value of the devise, C would be entitled to a pecuniary devise equal to the difference between the value of the devise less the unpaid purchase price and security interest.

D is entitled to the WVU stock as T's replacement for the XYZ stock. Subject to a finding of contrary intent on the part of T, if the WVU stock does not equal the value of the devise, D would be entitled to a pecuniary devise equal to the difference between the value of the devise less the value of the WVU stock from the estate.

E is entitled to the residue which is the remaining estate after the deductions for expenses of administration and the payment of all the above devises. If facts and circumstances indicate or it is found that the will manifests an intent to apply ademption, the specific devises will adeem to the extent they are not satisfied by the property remaining in the estate and the adeemed portion would pass to E as part of the residue.

Assumption 2:   a.   T's properly executed Will provides the same devises as indicated in Assumption 1, above.

                 b.   Rather than T, all the actions and events in Assumption 1 were performed by T's conservator or

attorney in fact under a valid
durable power of attorney.
T's residue is valued at $100,000.

c.   All devisees survived T.

Question: Who takes what property?

Analysis: The analysis in Assumption 1 is the
same with two exceptions. First A
would take the greater of the value of
the grandfather's clock or the $1,000.
The other specific devisees will take
what ever remains of their devise plus
a general pecuniary devise of the difference of the value of the devise less
the value of the remaining portion of
the devise. When a conservator or attorney in fact carries out the adeeming
action, there is no residual relevance of
T's intent. Therefore, the general pecuniary devises would be absolute and
not rebuttable with extrinsic evidence.

§ 7.04   Accessions Regarding Devises of Secu-
rities

A significant amount of the litigation concerning
ademption by extinction [see § 7.03] deals with
devises of securities that, between the time of the
will's execution and the testator's death, have undergone changes of form such as stock splits, refor-
mulations or other accessions. [See, e.g., Mandelle's
Estate, 233 N.W. 230 (Mich.1930)]. The UPC provides answers to the common issues raised by such
devises. [2–605]. The UPC's provision concerns only
devises of securities which are broadly defined to

include not only all types of notes, stocks, bonds and loans but also mineral interest agreements and leases as well as "any interest or instrument commonly known as a security" and the right to purchase any of the above. [1–201(43)]. The threshold requirements of the provision are:

(1) Testator's will devised securities;

(2) At the time the will was executed, testator owned securities that meet the description of the devised securities;

(3) The additional securities owned by testator at death were acquired after the will was executed; and,

(4) The additional securities owned by testator at death were acquired as a result of testator's ownership of the devised securities.

[2–605(a)]. It makes no difference whether the devise is characterized as specific or general. [2–605, Comment]. If these conditions are satisfied, the devisee, in addition to being entitled to as many of the devised shares of the security as are part of the estate at the testator's death, is entitled to additional or other securities in the following three situations:

(1) When the additional securities of the same entity were issued by reason of action initiated by the entity but not including securities acquired by the exercise of purchase options;

(2) When securities of other entities are the result of a merger, consolidation, reorganization or other similar action; or,

(3) When securities of the same entity are acquired as the result of reinvestment. [2–605(a)(1)–(3)].

There are exclusions from the protective rule. Cash distributions prior to death are not part of the devise. [2–605(b)]. The latter limitation means that distributions such as cash dividends declared prior to death, although not paid until after death, are not part of the specific devise. [2–605, Comment].

The provision also does not apply to nonsecurity devises that may be subject to accessions. The Comment states that the section is not intended to be exclusive as to accessions affecting securities and assumably it would not preclude similar accession interpretations in regard to other nonsecurity devises that raise similar problems.

Consider the following factual illustrations.

CHART 7–3
APPLICATIONS OF SECURITY ACCESSIONS PROVISION

Assumptions:		
	a.	T's properly executed Will provides: "100 shares of W Corporation stock to A, 100 shares of X Corporation stock to B, 100 shares of Y Corporate bonds to C, 100 shares of Z Mutual Fund shares to D the residue to E."
	b.	T owned the above securities at the time the will was executed.
	c.	Between the date of execution and death, W Corporation declared a three for one stock split. Although T sold 200 shares of W Corporation Stock after

the stock split, at T's death, T owned 200 shares of W Corporation stock.

d. Between the date of execution and death, X Corporation merged with I Corporation and the combined corporation reissued two shares in the new XI Corporation for each share of the X Corporation stock. At T's death, T owned 200 shares of XI Corporation stock.

e. Between the date of execution and death, Y Corporation converted its outstanding bonds to preferred stock. For every ten bonds, Y Corporation issued one share of preferred stock. At T's death, T owned 10 shares of Y Corporation preferred stock.

f. T held the Z Mutual Fund shares in a reinvestment plan where all earnings, both of income and principal, were reinvested in the fund and the share accumulated. At T's death the 100 shares had grown to a total of 200 shares.

Question: Who takes what property?

Analysis: A will take the 200 shares of W Corporation stock remaining in T's estate. The devise qualifies under section 2–605. It makes no difference whether T sold the original shares devised or some of the dividend shares because A receives what is left of the shares in T's estate. A will not take the 200 shares that T sold before death or their value unless section 2–606 is applicable. [See § 10.04].

B will take the 200 shares of the new XI Corporation because the issuance of the new corporate shares as a result of the merger are protected under section 2–605(a)(2). All actions were initiated by the entity and not be T. It would make no difference to this answer if T had never converted the shares so long as the conversion was by entity action and could be done after T's death.

C will take the 10 shares of Y Corporation preferred stock. Despite the change in security type, the devisee is protected under section 2–605 so long as the conversion was done as a result of entity action.

D will take the full 200 shares of Z Mutual Fund shares owned at T's death because these shares constitute the original 100 shares plus the reinvested shares acquired from the reinvestment plan set up by the entity. It would make no difference if the shares were of an entity other than a mutual fund so long as there is a reinvestment plan.

––––––––––

§ 7.05   Ademption by Satisfaction

The ademption by satisfaction doctrine is the testamentary counterpart of the advancement doctrine under intestate succession. [See § 3.03(A)]. Under the common law, the doctrine provides that a general or residuary devise is adeemed in whole or in part when a testator makes an inter vivos gift to the devisee after the execution of the will. [Atkinson, Wills § 133]. As with advancements, the purpose of the doctrine is to prevent a devisee from receiving a double share. Although its application in any situation depends on proof of the testator's intent, that intent is difficult to judicially establish. When intent is not clearly manifested, courts use presumptions to settle the issue. Under some circumstances a gift might be presumed to be satisfaction; under another situation, it might be presumed to be an unencumbered gift. Unfortunately, the presumptions have not been applied with any significant degree of consistency.

The UPC codifies the ademption by satisfaction doctrine and formalizes its proof requirements. [2–609]. Paralleling its provision concerning advancements, the UPC provides that a gift is satisfaction of a devise only if one of several formalities is satisfied. A gift is a formal satisfaction if either (1) the will provides for the deduction, or (2) the testator "declared in a contemporaneous writing," or (3) the devisee "acknowledged in writing" that the gift is in satisfaction of the devise. [2–609(a)]. The required writing may, rather than declaring the gift is in satisfaction, merely indicate that the gift must be deducted from the value of the devise. No words of art such as "satisfaction" need be used by the testator. The gist of the declaration must indicate the testator intended that the gift constitutes what lawyers call a gift in satisfaction of a devise. It is also not specifically required that the written expression of intent to make a formal satisfaction be communicated to the devisee at the time of the gift. A qualified formality could be a contemporaneous written note or indication that the gift is a formal satisfaction which is included with the testator's personal records. The writing must be available or provable after the testator's death when distribution decisions are made. It cannot be a blanket written statement that attempts to categorize future gifts as satisfaction. [Estate of McFayden v. Sample, 454 N.W.2d 676 (Neb.1990)].

Several other features of the UPC's provision deserve mention. There is no requirement that the gift must be made to the devisee: if the formality of satisfaction is satisfied and the necessary intent is declared, a gift to someone other than the devisee will be satisfaction of the devise. [2–609, Comment]. Although required by common law, the UPC does not require that the relevant actions take place in a certain chronology. Formal satisfaction might be accomplished before the will is executed although most cases will concern the reverse chronology. The Comment states that formal satisfaction need not necessarily be an outright gift. Other will substitutes such as life insurance payable to the devisee may constitute a satisfaction under the UPC. [2–609, Comment].

The UPC specifically provides that where a devisee of a formal satisfaction fails to survive the donor, the formal satisfaction affects the share that the devisee's descendants take from testator's estate if the descendants take as substitute devisees under the UPC's antilapse provisions, unless the testator's contemporaneous writing expressly provides that the gift is not to affect the descendants' devise. [2–609(c); see 2–603, 2–604]. This is the opposite rule from the UPC's advancement provision. The distinction is justifiable on the basis that satisfaction concerns the testator's intent whereas advancement concerns intestacy and therefore legislative intent. The gift in satisfaction does not affect the devisee's descendants if they take as alternative devisees unless the testator's contemporaneous writing expressly provides that the gift affects that descendants' devise.

Valuation of formal satisfaction is determined as of the time of the devisee's possession or enjoyment or as of the testator's death, whichever occurs first. [2–609(c)].

Consider the following problems:

CHART 7–4
SATISFACTION CALCULATIONS

Hypothetical: In all of the following hypotheticals assume decedent, T, made gifts to the named devisee and that these gifts were declared in a proper writing to be a satisfaction to the devisee.

Assumption 1: Assume that T's will provided: "I devise $50,000 to each of my children and the residue to my spouse."
  a. T made gifts in satisfactions of $20,000 to A, $30,000 to B, and $50,000 to C.
  b. T was survived by a spouse, S, two children, A and B, and a grandchild, G. G was C's child: C did not survive T.
  c. T's total distributable estate equals $400,000.

Question: Who takes what property?

Analysis: A will take $30,000 or the $50,000 de-
                   vise less the $20,000 satisfaction. A
                   question may arise whether the
                   $30,000 constituted full satisfaction of
                   the devise. If the satisfaction formality
                   expresses the intent in that the gift is
                   full satisfaction, then A would take
                   zero. Because the gift was less than the
                   devise and without outward expression
                   that full satisfaction was intended, a
                   presumption of partial satisfaction
                   would be compatible with the purposes
                   of the Code's provision.

                   B will take $20,000 or the $50,000 de-
                   vise less the $30,000 satisfaction. The
                   same analysis is applicable to B's de-
                   vise as discussed above regarding A's
                   devise.

                   Because C did not survive T, C does
                   not take from T's estate, but C's satis-
                   faction is not ignored. It affects G's
                   substitute devise because G takes C's
                   devise under the Code's antilapse pro-
                   vision, 2–603. Consequently, because
                   C's devise is apparently fully satisfied
                   by the gift which equals the amount of
                   the devise, G will take zero from the
                   estate.

                   S takes the residue of $350,000 which
                   now equals the total distributable es-
                   tate less the devises to A and B. In this
                   situation the reduction of the gifts in
                   satisfaction ran to the benefit of the
                   residuary devisee.

Assumption 2:   a. Assume that T's will provided: "I
                       devise $200,000 to my spouse
                       and the residue to my children
                       but if a child

does not survive me to that child's descendants.''

b.   T made gifts in satisfactions of $20,000 to A, $30,000 to B, and $50,000 to C.

c.   T was survived by a spouse, S, two children, A and B, and a grandchild, G. G was C's child: C did not survive T.

d.   T's total distributable estate equals $300,000.

Question: Who takes what property?

Analysis: S, who takes a general devise, takes $200,000 from the estate leaving a residue equal to $200,000.

Neither C nor C's estate will take for T's estate because C did not survive T.

G is entitled to a full share of the residue as a direct alternative devisee. Because G does not take under the antilapse provision but takes personally, the gift in satisfaction to C, G's ancestor, does not affect G's share.

The calculation of the shares of A, B, and G from the residue requires the construction of a hotchpot.

Satisfaction Hotchpot	Amount	Distribution
Distributable		
Residuary Estate*	$100,000	
A's Satisfaction	$20,000	
B's Satisfaction	$30,000	
Total of Hotchpot	$150,000	
Distribution		
A's ⅓ Share	$50,000–$20,000	$30,000
B's ⅓ Share	$50,000–$30,000	$20,000
G's ⅓ Share	$50,000	$50,000

Total Distributed
Residuary Estate* $100,000

---

§ 7.06   Miscellaneous Rules of Construction

The UPC codifies several other rules of construction that deserve mention. All of the following, of course, are subject to a finding based on the terms of the will or by admissible extrinsic evidence of a contrary intention by the testator. [2–601].

A.   AFTER–ACQUIRED PROPERTY

The UPC provides that a will may pass all the testator's property owned at death and acquired by the estate after testator's death. [2–602]. This rule codifies a part of the ambulatory nature of wills. [See § 6.01]. The provision also recognized that decedents' estates may become entitled to property after a testator's death such as inheritance to the estate of a decedent and retirement or other post employment benefits and awards. [See 2–602, Comment].

B.   RIGHT OF NONEXONERATION

The common law rule of right of exoneration of a mortgage on specifically devised real and personal

---

* The Distributable Estate and the Total Distributed Residuary Estate amounts must be identical; otherwise, an error in calculation has occurred.

property is abolished regardless of a general directive in the will to pay debts. [2–607]. Consequently, property specifically devised is distributed subject to any mortgage interest attached to it that exists at the testator's death. With the common current practice of mortgaging equity on residences for general borrowing needs because of the current income tax deduction for interest paid on mortgages but not deductible for other paid interest, the non-exoneration rule may be contrary to testator's intent. Extrinsic evidence of such a situation should be admissible to rebut the rule of construction.

CHAPTER 8
RULES OF CONSTRUCTION APPLICABLE TO WILLS AND TO OTHER GOVERNING INSTRUMENTS

§ 8.01   Introduction to Rules of Construction for All Governing Instruments

The UPC contains several important provisions dealing with issues raised by questions of survivorship, lapse and related problems. Because of the estate planning importance of will substitutes, the UPC extends these constructional rules beyond testamentary instruments and includes constructional rules concerning any "governing instrument." [2–701]. A governing instrument includes deeds, wills, and trusts, life insurance and other related policies, POD accounts, TOD security registrations, pension, retirement and other related plans; any other "dispositive, appointive, or nominative instrument." [1–201(19)]. The UPC establishes a set of rules of construction that apply in default but are subject to alteration either by proof of clear and convincing evidence of intent contrary to the default rule or by explicit language superseding the default rule in the governing instrument. [2–701].

For additional discussion of rules of construction, see § 7.01. As discussed in § 17.01(G), the UTC contains an optional provision that provides that the enacting state should apply to trusts the rules of construction that apply in that state to the construction of wills. [UTC 112].

§ 8.02 Survivorship Duration Determinations

The UPC adopts the rule that a beneficiary under any governing instrument must survive the date and time of the relevant event that determines ownership by 120 hours. [2–702]. This provision applies to a wide range of transfer devices including wills, life insurance policies, multiple-party accounts, transfer on death (TOD) security registrations, and other joint ownership with right of survivorship interests. [See 1–201(19)]. Persons who claim the beneficiary survived by the 120 hours must prove that the beneficiary survived the time period by clear and convincing evidence.

The 120 hours rule for all gratuitous transfer documents including wills, deeds, trusts, appointments and other beneficiary designations tracks the same rule that is applicable in the intestacy situation. [See 2–104; § 3.02(D)]. The difference between these concepts is that in regard to intestacy, the requirement is a rule of law and is not rebuttable whereas the rule applicable to voluntary transfers is alterable by the terms of the document. The UPC is very specific, however, in regards to what is necessary to rebut the statutory rule of construction. [2–702(d)]. The UPC itemizes four general situations where the statutory rule of construction will not apply. First, it will not apply if the governing instrument contains language that deals explicitly with simultaneous death or with deaths in a common disaster and that language is operable under the facts of the case. Second, the rule of construction is rebutted if the governing instrument expressly indicates that the beneficiary is not required to survive to a particular time or event, by any specific length of time or that expressly requires the individual to survive an event or time by a specific period. The specific period in the above exception includes a reference to the death of another individual. Third, the rule of construction does not apply if application of the rule would cause the transfer to fail to qualify as a valid transfer under the Uniform Statutory Rule Against Perpetuities. [See 2–901]. The fourth rebuttal for the rule of construction applies in the situation where the rule would result in an unintended failure or unintended duplication of a disposition. Notwithstanding the waiver of the 120 hour survivorship requirement, survival of an event or time must be established by clear and convincing evidence.

Third parties dealing with and bona fide purchasers from transferees who subsequently fail to survive the necessary period of time are protected under the UPC. [See § 9.04].

The 120 hour survivorship requirement is now part of the new version of the Uniform Simultaneous Death Act of 1991. This Act incorporates the relevant portions of the UPC and covers all types of gratuitous transfers. [§ 3.02(D)].

§ 8.03   Antilapse of Beneficiary Designations in Nominative Instruments

The common law rules concerning lapse of testamentary devises and the UPC's modifications to them are discussed previously. [2–603, 2–604; § 7.02]. Many of the same issues may arise regarding the interpretation of beneficiary designations in modern will substitutes, e.g., the unanticipated death or failure of a named beneficiary in a governing instrument. The UPC incorporates a provision that provides guidance and stability to the interpretation of these beneficiary designations. [1–201(4)]. The UPC applies the same substitute gift presumption to these designations as it does to beneficiary designations in wills. [2–706] The range of documents to which the provision applies is set out in the UPC's general definitions. [2–706(a)(2), and Comment]. It applies to beneficiary designations included in all insurance and annuity policies, all POD accounts, all TOD security registrations, all pension, profit-sharing, retirement and other benefit plans, and all other nonprobate transfers that occur at death. [1–201(4)]. The last reference is a catch-all reference that makes the provision applicable to all nontestamentary gratuitous transfers that arise at death and that are evidenced by a governing instrument. On the other hand, the 1993 Technical Amendments made it clear that it does not apply to persons who hold interests held in joint tenancy with right of survivorship or to parties of multiple-party joint accounts held with right of survivorship. [2–706(a)(2); see § 16.02(E)].

This provision gives needed substance and predictability to the many types of inter vivos documents that are lacking under current law in most states. For example, if the beneficiary designation on a life insurance policy reads: "to my spouse, but if my spouse does not survive me, to my children," but the insured is survived only by a child and a grandchild of another child that predeceased the insured, this provision creates a substitute gift for the grandchild and allows that person to share equally with the surviving child unless the terms of the policy designate an alternative beneficiary. [2–706, Comment]. This result clearly accords with the intent of most insureds.

The substantive scope and application of the provision are the same as those matters related to lapse of devises in wills. The same protected group, timing and types of designation are employed. A perusal of the text discussing section 2–603 provides the reader with an explanation of how this provision is to be applied and to operate. [See § 7.02; Halbach & Waggoner, Survivorship and Antilapse, at 1125–30].

Because of potential liability for third persons who rely on the named designations, the UPC protects third persons who pay proceeds to, receive proceeds in payment for enforceable obligations from, or purchase for value assets from the beneficiary. [See 2–706(d)–(e); § 9.04]. The beneficiary and other gratuitous transferees are not protected and remain liable for the proceeds received.

§ 8.04 Relational Terminology for Dispositive Purposes

A. BENEFICIARY STATUS

In dispositive instruments it is common to use class gifts as a means of describing certain beneficiaries. For example, testators or settlors may use terms of relational classification including "children," "grandchildren," "descendants," "issue," "brothers and sisters," "uncles and aunts," "nephews and nieces" and "cousins." Gifts using this type of terminology are commonly referred to as "class gifts" about which a long list of rules of construction have developed at common law. [See Simes, Future Interests §§ 101–04]. Class gift terminology is used not only for convenience, but also to allow the members in the particular class to fluctuate in number. For example, members in a class may be born and thereby included within, or some may die and predecease the testator and thereby excluded from, the above terminology when distribution is made.

The meaning of this class terminology is as important and determinative when used in dispositive instruments, as it is in defining relational terminology in intestacy situations. Consequently, when a testator in a will uses terms such as "children" or "brothers," it becomes necessary to determine who is to be included within such classes of persons. For full-blooded marital persons the problem of being included within the terminology is merely one of proof of relationship and survivorship. For half-bloods, adopted persons, nonmarital persons, assisted reproduction persons and persons related by affinity, the problem of proof of intended inclusion is problematic. In order for these persons to be included in such class terminology, they must show that the testator or donor intended that they be included. Unfortunately, there is usually no specific indication of intent in the dispositive instrument itself and disputes have developed. The resultant litigation has not only been costly and bitter but has also resulted in uncertainties and inconsistencies.

This determination is a problem of status. Because of the importance of this problem for distribution purposes under the terms of dispositive instruments, the UPC includes a specific provision concerning the status of adopted children, children of assisted reproduction, gestational children, nonmarital children, half blooded individuals and individuals related by affinity. [2–705]. Subject to alteration by the creator of the instrument and to two exceptions and a special rule for class gifts, a rule of construction is set that class gift language in dispositive instruments is to be construed in a manner similar to the meaning given to similar terms under the status definitions for intestacy. [2–705(b); See § 3.02]. Consequently, relations of the half blood are included in class gifts to collateral relations but relations by affinity are excluded from class gifts that refer to relationship by blood whether or not the term commonly differentiates between blood and affinity relationship. [2–705(c)]. For example, class gifts to "brothers" or "aunts" will exclude persons who fit the category because of marriage regardless whether the phrase "in law" is commonly added when making reference to the relationship. On the other hand, half blooded brothers or aunts are included in such gifts. Added in 2008, a class gift that uses a term of relationship to identify the class members includes a child of assisted reproduction, a gestational child and respective descendants, if appropriate to the class, in accordance with the rules for intestate succession regarding parent-child relationships.

Whereas under intestacy, adopted and nonmarital persons are included with other blood relations, in an effort to address the concern of the over extensions of this provision, the UPC incorporates two exceptions from this inclusion. In both situations, the UPC includes within appropriate class gift language such persons only if certain conditions are met. [2–705(e), and (f)].

In understanding these exceptions it is helpful to distinguish between class gift language used in three situations. The first concerns class gift language used in the instrument of a person who is directly involved in the relationship in question, e.g., a devise to one's "children" in the will of a person who adopted or who is the genetic parent of a person. The second concerns a transfer instrument of a person who is not directly involved with the particular relationship situation, but who is an ancestor, collateral, or descendant of a person who is directly involved, e.g., a devise to one's "grand-children" in the will of the parent of the adopting parent of an adopted child or of the parent of a nonmarital child. The third circumstance concerns the transfer instrument of a person who is neither directly involved nor related to the person directly involved in the relationship situation, e.g., a devise to a nonrelation "A or if A does not survive to A's descendants" in the will of a person where the nonrelation is an adopting parent or parent of a nonmarital child. The issue in all three situations is whether the class gift language includes adopted or nonmarital persons.

If the interpretation of the class gift concerns an instrument executed by the adopting or natural parent, an adopted or nonmarital child of that parent takes unless an intent to exclude is discovered. If the interpretation of the class gift concerns an instrument executed by someone other than the natural parent, however, a nonmarital child of that natural parent will not take under the instrument of a nonparental donor unless such child is express-ly included or unless the child lived while a minor with the natural parent or that parent's parent, brother, sister, spouse or surviving spouse. [2–705(e)]. Similarly, if the interpretation of the class gift concerns an instrument executed by someone other than the adopting person, dispositive provi-sions in instruments made by a stranger to the adoption do not include an adopted person unless the adopted person was either a minor at the time of the adoption, or the adoptive parent was the adoptee's stepparent or foster parent, or the adoptive parent functioned as the adoptee's parent while the adoptee was a minor. [2–705(f)]. These provisions attempt to accord what some contend conforms to the desires of most people faced with these situations. [2–705, Comment (e), (f)]. Most nonparental transferors do not want to include the adopted or nonmarital persons of others as members of class gifts unless the persons were raised in a manner reasonably similar to that as a child of the parent.

In addition to the inclusion as part of the relational words to describe the beneficiaries, class gifts require that a member of the class must also qualify under the class-closing rules. Generally, that means the child must be in being or be treated as in being on or before the distribution date. [Restatement (Third) of Property, § 15.1]. If a member of the class is born after the distribution date, that person is not included within the class. The UPC includes three exceptions to the class closing rule. If the child was conceived before the death of the person whose death triggered the closing of the class, that child may take as a class member if the child lives 120 hours after birth. A more difficult issue concerns the child conceived after the class closing date. The UPC permits inclusion of that person but puts a time limit on inclusion. The child is treated as living on the distribution date if the child lives 120 hours after birth and was conceived not later than 36 months after the deceased parent's death or born not later than 45 months after the deceased parent's death. Finally, if a person is in the process of being adopted, that person is includable as an adopted person if the adoption is finally granted even if the final adoption occurs after the class closes.

Significantly, these rules only establish a rule of construction regarding class gifts, not a mandatory rule. A rule of construction is a default rule that applies in the absence of a contrary intention. The document drafter can alter a rule of construction in order to give effect to the transferor's individual preferences.

B. MULTIPLE GENERATION CLASS GIFTS

Consistent with the UPC's adoption of the per capita at each generation definition of representation for intestacy, it adopts the definition as a rule of construction for class gifts made to "descendants," "issue," and "heirs of the body" for all dispositive instruments that do not otherwise specify the manner of distribution. [2–708; see § 3.01(D)]. In effect, the UPC treats the designated ancestor as if the person died intestate as to the property transferred to the class. This definition rejects the per stirpes definition found in the Restatement of Property. [Restatement (Second) of Property, § 28.2 (1988)]. It probably conforms, however, to the desires of the typical testator. [See 2–106, Comment].

C. DETERMINATION OF REPRESENTATION

The terms "representation," "per capita at each generation," and "per stirpes" are used in several provisions in the UPC [See 2–603, 2–706, and 2–707] and possibly in other statutes and may also be found in various dispositive instruments. For the purpose of determining their applications, it is necessary to give meaning to them. [2–709]. "Representation" and "per capita at each generation" are given identical definitions and it is the same one provided for these terms in intestacy, i.e., per capita at each generation. [2–709(b), 2–106; see § 3.01(D)]. Per stirpes is given the predominant definition that uses the first generation as the root generation for purposes of the initial and subsequent divisions of the estate distributed even if none survives the ancestor. [2–709(c), and Comment; see § 3.01(D)].

Three other definitions of words used in the provision are also important. The UPC defines "deceased" child or descendant to mean a member of the particular class who fails to survive the distribution date by 120 hours. [2–709(a)(1); 2–702]. The UPC defines "surviving" ancestor, child or descendant to mean a member of the particular class who neither predeceases the distribution date nor is deemed to predecease within 120 hours of the distribution date. [2–709(a)(3); 2–702]. The "distribution date" means the actual time when the interest in question takes effect in possession or enjoyment, be it the beginning, end, or other time of the day. [2–709(a)(2)].

§ 8.05   Constructional Rules for Future Interests

A.   INTRODUCTION TO FUTURE INTERESTS

The trust device is a common estate planning tool. Inherent in the trust is the future interest. The typical trust is established for the term of one or more persons' lives with the undistributed corpus to be transferred free of the trust to the remainder beneficiaries or to the settlor or the settlor's estate as a reversion. Although life interests, remainder interests and reversions are present interests, they are called future interests if they are not also presently possessory or currently enjoyed. Other interests similarly characterized include executory interests, possibilities of reverter and rights of entry. Any of these interests may have problems of construction at the time the interest becomes possessory or ready for present enjoyment, i.e., identifying the particular beneficiaries who will take. As with most matters of construction, the expressed desires of the transferor will be followed if determinable. Unfortunately, the expressed intent is often not expressed, inadequately expressed, or inapplicable because of changed circumstances. It then is necessary to fill the intent gap with rules of construction. Generally, these rules should conform to the desires of the average transferor. The common law developed rules of construction for these circumstances but they are often inconsistently applied and result in distributions that many would contend are not consistent with the desires of the average transferor.

The UPC, recognizing the importance of future interest in modern estate planning, addresses the major constructional problems that arise when expressed intent is absent and distribution decisions must be made.

B. FUTURE INTERESTS IN TRUST

1. Survivorship

The survivorship of the life interests is not a problem. If one is not alive or does not survive the creation of the trust or the interest in trust, the life beneficiary does not take from the trust. Survivorship is most often a problem of the remainder beneficiaries because their interests do not mature in possession or enjoyment until the death of those who hold the life interests. The question of survivorship arises after the death of the transferor or the date of creation of the trust when the life interest or interests end. Must the remainder beneficiaries survive the time of distribution or merely the time of creation? Courts have had numerous problems with this question.

If the transferor clearly indicates that survivorship to the date of distribution is or is not required, the expressed intent will be obeyed. The problem arises when intent is not clearly expressed. What is the default rule? The general common law rule holds that survivorship to date of distribution is not presumed: that is if the remainder beneficiary died between date of creation and date of distribution, the interest passes to the beneficiary's estate for distribution according to the beneficiary's will or by intestacy if no will. This construction requires reopening of estates and the consequent complexities. Because of this, courts sometimes strained to avoid application of the general rule but have not developed a consistent response to the problem.

The UPC adopts a new rule of construction concerning the survivorship requirement for future interests in trust. [2–707]. It reverses the presumption and provides that there is an implied requirement of survivorship to the date of distribution for future interests held in trust. [2–707(b)]. In addition, the survivorship requirement is extended to 120 hours after the time of distribution. [2–702]. For example, under the UPC's provision a simple trust that provides "to T in trust for A for life, remainder to B," B must survive A's death, the date of distribution, by 120 hours in order for B to take the remainder interest.

The new presumption is only applicable to future interests in trust and therefore does not apply to nonequitable interests such as "to A for life, remainder to B." [2–707, Comment]. The common law rule would continue to apply in those cases. Despite the limitation, the new rule will apply to most future interests created today because of the dominance of the trust device as an estate planning tool. One of the arguments for the nonsurvivorship rule is the desire to permit free alienation of property as soon as possible. If persons who hold remainders do not have to survive anyone to take, the interest is more readily transferrable in comparison with a contingent remainder dependent on survivorship to an unknown date. Survivorship contingencies in regard to trust interests are not barriers to property transfer because the trustee may transfer the property of the trust during its administration.

If beneficiaries fail to survive the date of distribution and the antilapse presumption is unavailable, the UPC specifies how the lapse will be treated. [2–707(d)]. If there is a residue devise in transferor's will, the trust corpus passes to those beneficiaries. If no residue exists or the residue is in trust and its remainder beneficiaries fail to survive the date of distribution, the trust corpus passes in intestacy. The 1993 Technical Amendments added that for future interests created by the exercise of a power of appointment, the lapsed property interest passes to the donor's takers in default clause, if any, which is treated as creating a future interest in trust. [2–707(e)(1)]. If still no takers then, the lapsed interest passes as an ordinary future interest except the transferor means the donor of a nongeneral power and the donee of a general power. [2–707(e)(2)].

2. Antilapse

The presumption that survivorship is necessary may cause interests to fail and if the nonsurviving beneficiary cannot take, might cut off the beneficiary's stock. The problem of forfeiture served in part as the reasoning behind the common law presumption against a survivorship requirement. Unfortunately, the common law remedy of passing the remainder interest through the nonsurviving beneficiary's estate did not depend upon the existence of descendants surviving the beneficiary. The UPC resolves the forfeiture problem by providing an "antilapse" presumption in favor of nonsurviving beneficiary's descendants.

The UPC provides that if a remainder beneficiary fails to survive the date of distribution, a substitute gift arises for the beneficiary's descendants, if any survive. [2–707]. This is an "antilapse" rule for future interests in trust. It protects descendants of all remainder beneficiaries regardless of their relationship to the transferor. [See 2–603; § 7.02(B)]. One does not have to be a grandparent or descendant of a grandparent to be entitled to the presumption of the substitute gift. It applies to remainders to specific individuals and to remainders left to classes of persons who are all in a single generation. Examples of single generation class gifts include gifts to "children," "grandchildren," "siblings," and "nephews and nieces." It does not apply to multiple-generation class gifts that inherently possess a nonlapsing affect because representation is allowed for descendants of predeceased ancestors in the class. Examples of such class gifts include gifts to "descendants," "issue," "heirs" and "next of kin." In a sense, the UPC converts all single generation class gifts in remainder to multiple generation gifts in remainder. It applies both to irrevocable inter vivos trusts and to trusts that are created at death.

The antilapse protection is merely a rule of construction subject to revision by the transferor. Similar to the rule as applied to decedent's estates, a mere survivorship requirement in the instrument will not rebut the presumption.

The common law rule of lapse and the UPC's modification to it are discussed previously. [2–604; § 7.02]. A perusal of the text discussing the application of Section 2–603 provides the reader with an explanation of how this provision basically operates. [See § 7.02(C), and (D)]. In addition, the Comment to Section 2–707 contains a comprehensive explanation with illustrations.

C. WORTHIER TITLE

In an effort to clarify an otherwise confused and varied area of the law of future interests, the UPC abolishes the Worthier Title doctrine both as a rule of law and of construction. [2–710]. In other words, transfers that pass interests to the transferor's "heirs," "heirs at law," "next of kin," "relatives," "family," and analogous terms do not create, by law or presumption, a reversionary interest in the transferor. The default rule is that a remainder is created. [See 2–710; § 8.05(D)]. Fundamentally, the abolition merely means the transferor's intent must be determined without the assistance of the Worthier Title presumption or rule. Assumably, when specific intent is not indicated, intent may be established by extrinsic evidence. [2–701].

D. DEFINITION OF "HEIRS"

The UPC provides a rule of construction for terms such as "heirs," "heirs at law," "next of kin," "relatives," "family," or analogous terms used in applicable statutes or governing instruments. [2–711; see also 1–201(21)]. It applies to both present and future interests. [See Restatement (Second) of Property, § 29.4, Comments c and g]. The UPC simply and properly provides that these terms when used in relation to a designated individual pass the interests covered by the transfer to those who would take the designated individual's property according to the intestate succession law of the designated individual's domicile. The date to determine this distribution is the time when the disposition takes effect in possession or enjoyment. If applicable under the law of the domicile, the state may take by escheat if other relations can not take. One specific exception in the provision bars a surviving spouse of a designated individual from being an heir if the surviving spouse is remarried at the time of distribution.

§ 8.06 Reformations and Modification of Instruments for Mistake or Tax Error

The 2008 Revision included two sections that concern reformation and modification of Governing Instruments. These sections are modified versions of similar sections in the UTC. [415, 416, see § 18.01(B)(2)(c), (d)]. Section 2–805 empowers the court to reform governing instruments to conform to the transferor's intent if it is proved that the testator's intent and terms were affected by mistake of fact or law. The proof must satisfy the clear and convincing evidence burden of proof. Governing instrument include deeds, wills, trusts, and dispositive instruments of any type. [1–201(18)]. The terms do not need to be ambiguous and the mistake can be in expression or inducement. This section broadens the scope of UTC 415 to apply to all governing instruments. [See § 18.01(B)(2)(c)].

The court may prospectively or retroactively modify a governing instrument to achieve transferor's tax objectives, so long as the modification is not contrary to the transferor's probable intentions. [2–806]. Whether the IRS will recognize the modification depends on federal law and will be probably limited to modification made prior to the tax event in question. [See Restatement (Third) of Property, § 12.1, Comments. and Reporter's Notes]. This section broadens the scope of UTC 416 to apply to all governing instruments. [See § 18.01(B)(2)(c)].

§ 8.07   Choice of Law

Choice of law determinations for testamentary and other donative transfers frequently depend upon the type of property involved, the donor's domicile, and the situs of the property. [Atkinson, Wills §§ 94, 145]. Although the UPC does not alter the ordinary choice of law rules, it provides that any

governing instrument may select the law of the
state that is determinative of the meaning and legal
effect of the instrument. [2–703; see 1–201(19); see
also UTC 107, § 17.01(D) and UTC 401,
§ 18.01(A)]. Thus, the UPC permits the transferor
by the terms of the governing instrument ordinarily
to select and specify what local law shall be applied
in determining both the meaning and the legal
effect of a testamentary disposition of his property.
This power in the transferor to select the controlling law is effective regardless: (1) whether the
disposition is of personalty or of realty; (2) where
the property is located; and (3) whether the testator
was domiciled in the state whose law was selected
either at the time when the will was executed, at
the time of death, or at any time.

The only general limitation is that the law of the
selected jurisdiction cannot be contrary to the applicable public policy of the UPC state. [A similar
limitation appears in UTC 107, § 17.01(D) and
UTC 401, § 18.01(A)]. In addition, the provision
specifically prohibits a locally domiciled transferor
from making a choice of law that circumvents the
UPC's elective share [see Art. II, Pt. 2; §§ 6.01–.07]
or family protection provisions. [See Art. II, Pt. 4;
§§ 8.01–.03]. Other policies that might fit within
the general public policy limitation include attempts
to avoid taxation, future interest rules with respect
to real property, and creditor avoidance devices
such as spendthrift clauses.

This provision promotes several policies of the
UPC. First, by permitting transferors to select the

rules and laws to be applicable to their donative instruments, it improves the chances that the transferors' intentions will control the legal effect of their dispositions. Second, it aligns testamentary choice of law rules with what is generally permitted in dealing with inter vivos transactions including trusts. The removal of differences between the way inter vivos transactions and testamentary transactions are treated is one of the goals of the UPC and of recent Conflict of Laws theory. [See Restatement (Second), Conflict of Laws, §§ 139, 140, 263, 264]. And third, the overall effect of this provision should encourage the use of the will as a dispositive device.

CHAPTER 9
GENERAL MISCELLANEOUS PROVISIONS AND TOPICS

§ 9.01   Introduction to Miscellaneous Matters

Part 8 of Article II of the UPC contains four sections that not only are applicable to intestate and testate succession but also have application to other parts of the UPC, or to other transfer devices not covered by its content. Briefly, these sections deal with the following matters: (1) the disclaimer of property interests devolving by all means; (2) the effect of various divorces, annulments, and separation decrees upon the issue whether a person is a surviving spouse; (3) the disqualification effect of homicide on intestate succession, wills, trusts, joint survivorship ownership, multiple-party accounts, TOD security registrations, life insurance and other beneficiary designations, and fiduciary nominations; and, (4) the revocation of probate and nonprobate transfers due to divorce of the transferor and the beneficiary.

Another concept that crosses subject matter lines is the protection of bona fide purchasers and third persons who deal with persons whose interests in property or assets in question are extinguished under the UPC. The UPC contains provisions in several areas dealing with this matter. The meaning and interrelationship of these provisions is discussed in this chapter. [See § 9.04].

Finally, provisions concerning powers of appointment are scattered throughout various parts of the UPC. For purposes of clarity and in recognition of the importance of powers of appoint, the discussion of many of these provisions are collected in a single section. [See § 9.06].

§ 9.02   Termination of Marital Status

A.   INTRODUCTION

The UPC contains two provisions that concern the termination of marital status. The first concerns the determination when a person is a surviving spouse for purposes of receiving the benefits conferred upon a surviving spouse by the UPC in Parts 1–4 of Article II and Section 3–203 of Article III. [2–802]. The second concerns the consequences of the termination of a marital relationship on benefits conferred in dispositive instruments. [2–804].

B.   DEFINITION OF A SURVIVING SPOUSE

A person's marital status is very important in determining many rights and responsibilities set by the UPC. These rights and responsibilities include, for example, distribution in intestacy, elective share rights, revocation of wills, family protection rights, priority for appointment as personal representative, and appointment of a guardian for an incapacitated person. [See 2–802(b)]. Although the UPC leaves the requirements for marriage to the law of domestic relations, it includes provisions setting the scope and effect of legal proceedings and other actions which sever the relationship.

Under the UPC, a person is not a surviving spouse of the decedent if the person and the decedent have been divorced or their marriage annulled. [2–802(a)]. This rule does not apply, of course, if they remarry and are married on the date of the decedent's death. It also does not apply to a decree of separation that does not terminate the husband-wife status. Notwithstanding the absence of a final divorce or annulment, unless a contrary intent appears on the agreement, a complete property settlement entered into after or in anticipation of separation or divorce operates as a disclaimer of the spouse's elective share, family protections, rights under intestate succession and provisions in wills executed before the property settlement. [2–213].

In addition to a spouse who has obtained a valid divorce or an annulment, the term "surviving spouse" also does not include: (1) a person who obtained or consented to a final decree of divorce or of annulment even though the decree is not valid in the UPC state, unless that person has subsequently remarried the decedent, or subsequently lived together as husband and wife [2–802(b)(1)]; (2) a person who participated in a marriage ceremony with a third person following a valid or invalid decree of divorce or annulment [2–802(b)(2)]; or (3) a person who participated as a party to a valid proceeding which terminated all marital property rights. [2–802(b)(3)]. The three above situations recognize a kind of estoppel concept. In each one the surviving person has either consented, participated in, sought or completed some volitional act other than the "divorce" that causes the marital relationship to be terminated as far as the surviving spouse's rights under the UPC are concerned. Because the rights of a surviving spouse under the UPC are substantial, it is very important that only those who legally and equitably should be considered a surviving spouse are able to take these benefits.

C.   REVOCATION OF INTERESTS AND POWERS BY OPERATION OF LAW

At common law, revocation of wills by operation of law was recognized in two situations: a single woman's will was revoked when she subsequently married, and a single man's will was revoked after his marriage and birth of an issue. [Atkinson, Wills § 85]. No other change of circumstances would revoke a will by operation of law.

Taking the modern approach to revocation by operation of law as its guide, the UPC rejects these common law situations. In their place it includes a ground for revocation relevant to current societal problems, i.e., termination of the marriage. [2–804]. In addition, recognizing that the problem of a for-

mer spouse taking an unintended benefit from a
prior spouse's estate arises in more than merely
testamentary situations: all gratuitous transfers
may include such a result, particularly inter vivos
trusts. In response the UPC expands the revocation
concept due to divorce to these instruments. The
UPC specifically restricts revocation of covered instruments by operation of law to divorce, annulment and homicide. [2–804(f); see 2–803;
§ 6.03(D)].

By the terms of this provision, a testator's divorce
or annulment which occurs after the execution of a
will, trust or contract revokes any disposition or
appointment of property made by that instrument
to the former spouse. [2–804(b); see 2–508]. In
addition, divorce or annulment revokes any grant of
a general or special power of appointment to the
former spouse as well as any nomination of the
former spouse as executor, trustee, conservator, or
guardian. Any grant of a power or nomination for
fiduciary office is interpreted and carried out as if
the surviving former spouse predeceased the testator. Similar provisions in the instrument in favor of
the former spouse's relatives [2–804(a)(5)], who are
not the decedent's heirs, are also revoked. [2–
804(b)(1)]. In addition, property held by decedent
and the former spouse at the time of the divorce as
joint tenants with right of survivorship is converted
to equal tenancies in common. [2–804(b)(2)]. All
revoked dispositive provisions are treated as if the
former spouse or spouse's relatives disclaimed
them. [2–804(d)]. This permits the property to pass

according to the rules relating to the type of transaction or interest involved. Under a will for example, a disclaimer of a general devise is treated as a lapse of the devise and the normal lapse and anti-lapse provisions of the will or the UPC apply to determine the devisee. [See §§ 7.02, 9.02]. Also, for example, disclaimed proceeds under a life insurance policy will be paid to the alternative beneficiaries, if any. [See § 9.02].

The meaning of divorce or annulment under this provision is cross referenced to Section 2–802(b) discussed in the previous part of this section.

Several limitations on the scope and application of this provision are important. First, if by the terms of the instrument the testator anticipates divorce or annulment and still desires to benefit, empower or nominate the former spouse notwithstanding the divorce or annulment, the terms of the provision will be carried out. [2–804(b)]. Second, the testator's remarriage to the former spouse revives all provisions for the former spouse which were revoked solely because of this provision. [2–804(e)]. And third, a mere separation decree does not terminate the marriage and is not a divorce. [2–804(a)(2)]. The latter limitation is not to be confused, however, with the situation where there has been a complete property settlement between the testator and the spouse. Unless the property settlement provides otherwise, such a settlement constitutes a disclaimer by the spouse of all benefits under any prior will. [2–213].

For an explanation of the UPC's treatment of the rights between those who claim the property because of the divorce and third persons who dealt with the former spouse, see § 9.05.

§ 9.03   Effect of Homicide

Generally, a person's misconduct does not disqualify the person from inheriting property or from taking property passing from other persons. [Atkinson, Wills § 31]. Consequently, for example, desertion, conviction of a felony, or adultery will not cause a forfeiture of the wrongdoer's property or rights to property passing from those harmed. There are exceptions. A parent is barred from inheriting frmo or through a child of the parent if the parent's rights had been terminated or could have been terminated immediately before the child's death due to nonsupport, abandonment, abuse, neglect or other similar actions or inactions. [See 2–114(a); § 3.02(B)(6)].

The most pervasive exception to the general rule concerns statutes or court decisions that bar murderers from inheriting or taking property from their victims. The rationale for this rule is to prohibit a wrongdoer from profiting from the wrongful act done to the victim. The substantive and procedural rules for this forfeiture greatly differ among the states which recognize it. In addition, substantial omissions in the rules are commonly present. For example, it is common for a state to bar a murderer from taking in intestacy, testacy and from receiving life insurance proceeds on the victim's life but to ignore other forms of property transfers. Sometimes courts have filled in some of the gaps, but many still exist.

For the sake of clarity and uniformity, the UPC includes a substantively and procedurally comprehensive provision concerning the effect of homicide on the rights of murderers to take property from, or assume other privileges granted by, their victims. [2–803]. This provision is applicable, however, only when similar concepts are not in the relevant instruments. [Wilkins v. Fireman's Fund Am. Life Ins. Co., 695 P.2d 391 (Idaho 1985)]. Basically, the UPC prohibits a person who feloniously and intentionally kills another from accepting any benefits derived from the victim. The UPC deals specifically with statutory benefits conferred as a result of death, benefits conferred in all the decedent's revocable governing instruments, and rights of survivorship in jointly held or community property. [2–803(b), and (c)]. The UPC also includes a catch-all clause providing that the same principles are to be applied to the murderer's acquisition of any property or interest from the victim. [2–803(f)]. In addition to forfeiture of property interests, the UPC revokes nominations of the murderer in governing instruments to serve in fiduciary or representative capacities such as personal representative, trustee or agent.

The murderer forfeits all statutory benefits conferred on the murderer by the UPC in regard to a decedent's estate. [2–803(b)]. This means the murderer forfeits any intestate share, elective share, pretermitted spouse or heir share, or family protection amounts normally conferred upon a person with the murderer's status due to the death of the decedent.

Concomitantly, due to the wrongful act, the UPC's provision revokes all benefits conferred on the murderer by the terms of any and all revocable governing instruments executed by the decedent. [2–803(c)(1)]. This all inclusive application of the forfeiture concept includes benefits bestowed in wills, trusts, contractual agreements, multiple-party accounts, and TOD security registrations. An instrument is revocable if the decedent, alone, held a power at the time or immediately before death to cancel the benefit for the murderer. [2–803(a)(3)]. The decedent, however, need not possess the power to designate the decedent in place of the murderer or the capacity to exercise the power at the time of the murder. This means that the murderer forfeits any testacy share, gift in a revocable trust, POD or TOD survivor benefits, proceeds of life insurance and benefits from other contractual arrangements. [2–803(c)(1)].

Finally, the UPC converts an interest held as joint tenancy or community property with right of survivorship into equal tenancies in common. [2–803(c)(2)]. Consequently, the victim's share passes as part of the victim's estate and the murderer forfeits the right to survivorship but retains the personal interest in the property. To bind a purchaser of the survivorship property from the murderer, however, persons interested in the decedent's

estate who contend a severance of title occurred
must file a writing declaring the severance in the
appropriate recording office for the type of property
in question. [2–803(d)]. For real estate, this means a
notice of severance must be filed where deeds to the
real estate are filed. If the notice of severance is not
filed, a third party purchaser for value may acquire
the property without forfeiture consequences. Because survivorship titles are usually confirmed easily and quickly by filing an affidavit and a death
certificate and because there is usually significant
delay between the time of the murder and the
development of a case accusing a successor of the
crime, accused murderers may often have an opportunity to sell the asset to a third person and avoid
the claim of severance. Of course, for whatever it
may be worth, the murderer would remain liable for
the value of the severed interests.

Under the UPC, nonrevoked provisions of a governing instrument are given effect as if the mur-
dered disclaimed all revoked provisions. [2–803(e)].
The consequence of disclaimer permits the property
to pass according to the rules relating to the type of
transaction or interest involved. [See § 9.06]. Under
a will, for example, a disclaimer of a general devise
is treated as a lapse of the devise and the normal
lapse and antilapse provisions of the will or the
UPC apply to determine the devisee. [See §§ 7.02,
9.06]. Also, for example, under a life insurance
policy the disclaimed proceeds would be paid to the
alternative beneficiaries, if any. [See § 9.02]. Re-

voked nominations are treated as if the murderer predeceased the decedent.

The UPC also deals with the problem of proof. [2–803(g)]. First, for purposes of forfeiture under this provision, it makes a judgment of conviction, which establishes criminal accountability, after all rights of appeal have been exhausted, conclusive evidence that defendant killed decedent. Second, notwithstanding an absence of a conviction or even with the presence of an acquittal, the UPC permits, on petition of an interested person, a civil proceeding against the murderer to take place and adopts the "preponderance of evidence" test as the relevant burden of proof that the accused is criminally accountable for the felonious and intentional killing of the decedent. If the court determines the accountability for the murder is proved, the determination conclusively establishes wrongdoing for purposes of the application of this provision. Two particular consequences of these provisions deserve mention. First, because conviction is not required for application of the forfeiture provisions, suicide by the murderer does not preclude their application if the crime can be proved in the civil proceeding. Second, criminal accountability includes acting as an accomplice or co-conspirator as well as the actor or direct perpetrator. [2–803, Comment].

In addition to the notice requirement to bind purchasers of property sold by a surviving joint tenant with right of survivorship [2–803(d)], the UPC includes provisions protecting other payors, bona fide purchasers and other third persons who deal with the murderer prior to notice of the claim against the murderer. [2–803(h), and (i); see § 9.04]. This protection for bona fide purchasers and other unknowing third persons recognizes that there may be a long delay in instituting proceedings accusing a person of murdering another and even after institution of the case, the result may be in doubt for a long period of time.

§ 9.04 Protection of Payors and Third Parties

Because the UPC creates circumstances that in effect suspend ownership of assets for a period of time after a decedent's death, it is concerned with the validity of transfers between those who hold these suspended ownership interests and third parties. These third parties are payors who either hold the interest for or are bona fide purchasers of the interest from those who hold this suspended ownership. The UPC seeks to protect these third persons from liability for payment or purchase of the property. The UPC contains five sections specifically dealing with this problem in relationship to particular property ownership situations. These include: (1) the problem of the nonprobate transfers to others under the augmented estate concept, [2–214, 2–210(b); see § 4.01(C)]; (2) the problem of a beneficiary not surviving the necessary 120 hours, [2–702(e), and (f); see § 8.02]; (3) the problem of transactions with a murderer who is a beneficiary of the victim's estate, [2–803(h), and (i); see § 9.03]; (4) the problem of revoked clauses and rights due to divorce, [2–804(g), and (h); see § 9.02]; and, (5) the problem of the substitute gift due to lapse in life insurance, retirement plans and similar transactions, [2–706(d), and (e); § 8.03]. The provisions are in two parts. The first provision protects persons who are obligated to pay or transfer assets to a named individual under a governing instrument. The second provision protects bona fide purchasers of property from the recipient whose ownership is in suspension.

The protection for payors and other obligated third parties is not unlimited but is considerable. If a payor or a person who is obligated to transfer or deliver property to another, pays or delivers to the person designated in the appropriate governing instrument or agreement, the payor or person making the transfer is protected from liability unless that person received written notice of the adverse claim by another. Conversely, the payor who received written notice of the claim is liable for making payment or delivery.

Written notice requirements are specified in each of the sections. Generally, they require that notice of the claim or triggering event or action must be a written notice mailed to the payor or third person by registered or certified mail or served upon that person as a civil action summons would be served. A mailed notice may be sent to the payor's main office or home. After receipt of written notice, the payor may pay the amount or property over to the proper court for safe keeping purposes. The proper court is defined as the court in which the decedent's estate is being administered or if there is no administration in the court in which the administration could be instituted due to decedent's residency. Payment to the court discharges the payor or person holding the property. Once the court determines the proper ownership or particular time periods expire that settle the ownership, it may transfer the property to the appropriate beneficiaries.

Purchasers for value and without notice and payees of payments or other property items in partial or full satisfaction of legally enforceable obligations are not obligated to return payment or the property. On the other hand, persons who receive payment or property gratuitously are obligated to return the payment or property and are even personally liable for the payment of property to the person who is determined to be entitled to the property. This rule applies even if federal law preempts the underlying property title or ownership provision. The federal preemption relates to the Employee Retirement Income Security Act of 1974 which preempts state law in regard to any employee benefit plan. The drafters of the UPC believe that the provision conforms with this preemption. [See 2–804, Comment].

§ 9.05   Powers of Appointment

A.   INTRODUCTION AND DEFINITIONS

Because the UPC's provisions concerning powers of appointment are scattered among several Articles, a single amalgamated discussion of them is helpful for their comprehension. [Kurtz, Powers of

Appointment]. Although a complete explanation of the law of powers of appointment is beyond the scope of this Nutshell, a short review of powers and the UPC's references to them is appropriate. [See generally, Simes, Future Interests §§ 55–60].

As defined by the Restatement of Property, Second, a power of appointment is the "authority, other than as an incident of the beneficial ownership of property, to designate recipients of beneficial interest in property." [Restatement (Second) Property, § 11.1]. There are five principal persons who are inherently involved in a power: (1) the donor, who is the creator of the power; (2) the donee, who is the person who holds the power; (3) the objects, who are the persons for whom an appointment can be exercised; (4) the appointees, who are the persons for whom the power has been exercised; and, (5) the takers in default, who are the persons who will take the property to the extent that the power is not exercised. [Restatement (Second) Property, § 11.2]. Persons may function in more than one category. In addition, a power is personal to the donee and may not be exercised by other persons. If a donee does not exercise it, it expires. Two property interests need identification: (1) the appointive assets which compose the assets that are subject to the exercise of the power; and, (2) the donee's personal beneficial interest in the appointive assets other than as an object of the power. [Restatement (Second) Property, § 11.3].

There are several types of powers that are relevant to the UPC's provisions. [Restatement (Second) Property, § 11.4]. First, a general power is defined as a power that permits the donee to appoint the property to the donee, personally, to the donee's creditors, to the donee's estate, or to creditors of the donee's estate. If a power contains no restriction on whom may be an appointee, it is presumed the power is a general power. Second, a nongeneral power, or what is sometimes called a special power, is unhelpfully defined by the Restatement as any power that is not a general power. Usually the donee of a nongeneral power is permitted to appoint only to a particular group of persons, such as one's children or descendants. Because of federal gift and estate tax benefits, nongeneral powers may include as objects everyone except the donee, the donee's creditors, the donee's estate, and the creditors of the donee's estate.

Powers are also categorized as to when they may be exercised. [Restatement (Second) Property, § 11.5]. A power of appointment is presently exercisable if the donee may immediately exercise it at the time in question. It is stated that the donee may exercise it by deed. A "deed" is merely any legally operative act or instrument effective during the donee's lifetime. A power of appointment is not presently exercisable if it may only be exercised by a will (testamentary power) or at the time in question cannot be exercised until some event or passage of time occurs. All powers must be in existence before they are exercisable. [Restatement (Second) Property, § 11.5, Comment a]. A power of appointment created in a living person's will does not come into existence until that person dies and the will becomes effective.

Two other characterizations are also relevant. [Restatement (Second) Property, § 11.4, Comment c]. The donee may hold a purely collateral power if the donee holds no interest in the property except the power. On the other hand, the donee may hold a power in gross if the donee holds both an interest in the property and a power that if exercised would dispose of the interest that the donee does not hold.

The UTC contains specific provisions relating to a "power of withdrawal," which is a presently exercisable power that allows the holder to appoint some or all of the trust property to himself or herself. This is the essential equivalent of a general power of appointment. The UTC discusses explicitly how such a power, when held by a beneficiary of a trust, affects the rights of that beneficiary's creditors to reach the beneficiary's interest in the trust. [UTC 505; see § 18.02(B)(2)(e); see also UTC 302, § 17.03(A); UTC 603, § 18.03(C)].

B. EXERCISE OF POWER OF APPOINTMENT

When a testator holds a testamentary power of appointment at death, it becomes essential to determine whether the testator, as donee of the power, has exercised it in testator's will. Most often the instrument that creates the special or general power of appointment specifically names a taker or takers in default of the appointment by the donee.

Occasionally, the power does not name takers in default and if a general power is not exercised by the donee, the property reverts to the donor's estate for distribution according to the distribution pattern determined for that estate. The UPC includes rules of construction to resolve these issues when a testator's intent is not clearly expressed.

There are several situations that must be distinguished. The following three factors guide the application of the rules of construction adopted in the UPC: (1) whether the governing instrument that created the power of appointment expressly requires that a power is exercised by the will only if the donee makes a reference to the power or its source in the will; (2) whether the power of appointment is a general or a nongeneral power; and, (3) whether the testator-donee's will expresses an intention to exercise the power of appointment.

No Specific Reference Requirement: If the document creating a power of appointment is nonexplicit in that it does not include a requirement that the power may only be exercised "by a reference, or by an express or specific reference" to the power in the exercising document, a will that contains a "general residuary clause" or that makes a "general disposition of all the testator's property," exercises the power only if one of two conditions are met. First, a will containing a general residuary clause or a comparable clause exercises a general testamentary nonexplicit power if the document creating the power fails to contain an effective gift in default of exercise. This rule permits the donee's will to control the disposition of the property subject to the power rather than allowing the takers of the donor's estate to take. A contrary rule can create unintended and unanticipated results, including the need to reopen a donor's closed estate and to cause estate tax consequences to an otherwise settled estate. Second, any general and nongeneral nonexplicit testamentary power is exercised if the testator's will manifests an intention to include the property that is subject to the power as part of the residuary or general disposition clause. [2–608].

These rules prevent unintended exercises of powers from occurring merely because a residue clause is included in a donee's will but provide a broad exception if admissible evidence indicates that the testator desired to exercise the power. The distinction between interpretations can be illustrated by comparing its application to two typical drafting examples: (1) if the residuary clause in testators's will merely devises "all the rest, residue and remainder" of testator's estate, presumably the power is not exercised; but (2) if the residuary clause in testators's will devises "all the rest, residue and remainder, including any property over which a power of appointment is held," of testator's estate, presumably the power is exercised. [2–608, Comment]. The latter is called a "blending" or "blanket" clause. The inclusion of such a clause in a will raises a presumption under the UPC that testator intended to exercise a power if that power does not require a particular reference to it to be exercised. When the residuary clause omits the reference to powers of appointment, the presumption is that testator does not intend to exercise a power. Either presumption is subject to rebuttal with extrinsic evidence under the principle of Section 2–601. [2–608, Comment; § 10.01].

Specific Reference Requirement: If the document creating a power of appointment is explicit in that it includes a requirement that the power may only be exercised "by a reference, or by an express or specific reference" to the power in the exercising document, the language is presumed to indicate the donor did not desire inadvertent exercise of the power. [2–704] This presumption relates to the exercise of all explicit powers whether they are general or nongeneral and to all exercising documents whether they are wills or other will substitutes. The exact meaning of this provision is not clear on its face. The Comment to the section explains that the section creates a mere presumption against exercise that prevents, for example, a blending clause from automatically exercising the power as such a clause would do when the power is nonexplicit. Beyond the mere presumption, the questions of the donor's intent as to the requirements for exercise, and the donee's intent as to the exercise, of the power, is left to extrinsic evidence. [See 2–701]. Relevant extrinsic evidence may swing the determination either way: in one direction it may show that the donee intended exercise although the donee did not make an otherwise sufficient reference to the power; or, in the other direction, it may show that the donor desired a specific reference to the power and any reference that fails to satisfy this requirement fails to exercise the power. The provision has the apparent purpose of both preventing inadvertent exercise but leaving open the question of proof of intent by inferentially relying on extrinsic evidence to supply that intent.

C. VIRTUAL REPRESENTATION AND GENERAL POWERS OF APPOINTMENT

The UPC gives special treatment to the acts of, and to formal court orders binding, the sole holder or all co-holders of a presently exercisable general power of appointment. [1–108, 1–403(2)(i)]. A general power is described as any power of appointment in which the holder of the power is capable of drawing absolute ownership to the holder, personally. [1–108, Comment; see § 9.05(A)]. Although a "holder" of such a power is commonly a donee of a general power of appointment created by the donor, the term is also applicable to the settlor or beneficiary of a trust in which the settlor or beneficiary retains a power to revoke the trust.

A holder or the unanimous co-holders of a presently exercisable general power of appointment can, by granting consent or approval, relieve personal representatives or trustees from a liability or a penalty which these fiduciaries would ordinarily suffer due to a failure to perform a particular duty required by the UPC or other law. [1–108]. Similarly, the holder or unanimous co-holders of a general power may consent to modifications or terminations of a trust or to deviations from its terms. The effect of approval or consent of the holder or unanimous co-holders of a general power is to bind the beneficiaries to the extent that the beneficiaries' interests are subject to the power notwithstanding that no court order is obtained. This virtual representation capability can be of crucial significance in nonjudicial settlements of estates and trusts where consent of all those with interests is essential to effectuate the settlement.

The UPC also provides that orders resulting from formal court proceedings which bind a holder or all co-holders of such a general power bind other persons to the extent that these persons' interests are subject to the power. [1–403(2)(i)]. This provision has the effect of eliminating the ordinary requirements for notice to and jurisdiction over numerous and unknown, sometime unborn, beneficiaries when litigation occurs. It would not apply, however, if the validity of the general power itself is the issue involved because the power holder or holders cannot represent the others in this type of litigation. [1–403, Comment]. The justification for this ability to bind others is that the holders of presently exercisable general powers of appointment possess the equivalent of full ownership. Furthermore the financial interests between the holder of the power and those persons who have interests subject to the power are sufficiently compatible to satisfy fairness and due process concerns. [Kurtz, Powers of Appointment, at 1154–1155].

The virtual representation power of holders of presently exercisable general powers of appointment does not apply under the UPC to holders of nongeneral powers such as special powers and general testamentary powers. [See § 2.03(B)]. There are valid arguments, however, that the donee of a nongeneral power of appointment should have virtual representation capabilities except in limited circumstances. [See Kurtz, Powers of Appointment, at 1155–62].

See § 17.03(A) for a discussion of virtual representation for the holder of a power of withdrawal under the UTC.

§ 9.06   Uniform Disclaimer of Property Interests Act (1999)

Disclaimer Definition: A disclaimer is any refusal to accept an interest in or power over property. [2–1102(3)]. It is an important estate planning device. A disclaimer is usually made to avoid some burden or obligation that the person does not want to assume or cause. These burdens include, for example, the avoidance of taxes, creditors, spendthrift provisions, Medicaid or other public assistance disqualification and sometimes spousal protections.

Common Law Disclaimers: At Common Law a person could not disclaim an interest passing by intestacy, but one could disclaim an interest passing by will. Beyond those rules the Common Law is uncharted, if not nonexistent.

Federal Disclaimer Law: In 1976, Congress passed of the Tax Reform Act of 1976 which included IRC section 2518. Section 2518 revolutionized disclaimer law by recognizing disclaimers as a valid method to avoid transfer taxes. Section 2518 provided a uniform federal rule of timeliness for disclaimers that would be effective for tax purposes, and, would not result in a taxable transfer by the disclaimants. It led the states to enact disclaimer laws in order to provide their residents with a means to make tax qualified disclaimers. State law governs to whom disclaimed interests pass, and provides the mechanisms for recognizing the disclaimer.

In outline terms Section 2518 provides that a disclaimer is effective for estate and gift tax purposes if (1) disclaimant disclaims in a writing, (2) the writing is received by the transferor within nine months after the later of creation day, or the day disclaimant reaches 21, (3) the disclaimant has not accepted any interest or benefit therefrom and (4) the interest passes without directions to decedent's spouse, or to nondisclaimant. There are special rules for disclaimers of less than an entire interest and of powers.

If disclaimers are being used for estate and gift savings purposes, disclaimants must scrupulously obey the requirements of I.R.C. Section 2518 as well as state law. A consistent issue with state enactments has been the degree to which the two systems coincide. There have been conflicts. For example, under some state disclaimer acts, significant differences exist concerning the timing of disclaimers particularly in the disclaiming of future interests. [See Medlin, An Examination of Disclaimers; Hirsch, Revisions in Need of Revising].

UDPIA Promulgation: In 2002, the UPC added the first sixteen sections of the Uniform Disclaimer of Property Interests Act of 1999 [Hereinafter the UDPIA] to the UPC. [UPC, Pt. 11]. It replaced the Uniform Disclaimer of Property Interests Act of 1978. The UDPIA is more than a mere revision: it is a new act. It is comprehensive, complex and supported with extensive comments. It is not without controversy. [Hirsch, Revisions in Need of Revising].

With an Act of this complexity, a Nutshell discussion can only offer a cursory review of its provisions. The reader is urged to peruse the provisions and their comments. Generally, disclaimer statutes typically cover common ground. They deal with what interests can be disclaimed, the formality for executing a disclaimer, the necessary procedure(s) to follow, the destination for the disclaimed interest, when a disclaimer is barred, and usually set a time limit or time frame within which a disclaimer must be made. The UDPIA conforms to this litany of issues.

Scope of UDPIA: The UDPIA permits, under defined procedures, persons or fiduciaries, to whom interests in or power over property devolve by whatever means, to disclaim, in whole or part, their interests or powers in the property. [2–1105(a)(b)]. Except for fiduciaries whose right to disclaim may be limited by law or by the granting instrument, the right to disclaim exists regardless whether the transfer instrument permits disclaimers and even if the transfer instrument restricts transfers or prohibits disclaimer or both.

The UDPIA sets no time limit on a disclaimer. If a qualified tax disclaimer is desired, however, disclaimants must meet the deadlines set by IRC § 2518. The UDPIA also does not restrict disclaimers depending on the motive for the disclaimer or the financial situation of the disclaimant.

The disclaimer may be made either personally by any competent person, or by persons who represent the disclaimant. [2–1104, Cmt.]. A representative of a person includes not only a conservator for a disabled person but also a guardian for a minor or incapacitated person, an agent under a durable power of attorney and a decedent's personal representatives. A disclaimer may be made for an incapacitated or protected person or by that person's representative if made according to applicable procedures for protected persons.

Disclaimer Formality: A valid disclaimer may be made only by a written instrument that describes the property or interest disclaimed, declares the fact and extent of the disclaimer and is signed by the person renouncing or that person's proper representative. [UPC § 2–1105(c)]. They must be properly delivered and are irrevocable when delivered. Partial disclaimers may be expressed in fractions, percentages, dollar amounts, terms of years, power limitations. [2–1105(d)]. According to the UDPIA, a valid disclaimer is not "a transfer, assignment or release." [2–1105(f)].

Effectiveness date: The UDPIA has specific rules on when a disclaimer become effective and depends upon the type of interest disclaimed. [2–1106]. Generally, the disclaimer becomes effective as of the time the interest became irrevocable or in the case of an interest that is acquired due to intestate succession, at the decedent's death.

Disclaimed Interest Beneficiary: The disclaimed interest passes: (1) according to the terms of the relevant instrument if any; (2) as if the disclaimant did not exist for a non individual disclaimant; (3) as if the disclaimant had died immediately before the time of distribution, in the case of an individual disclaimant; or (4) if by law the disclaimed property would pass to the disclaimant or disclaimant's estate, the interest passes to the disclaimant's descendants who survived to the time of distribution. [2–

1106(b)(3)(A)–(C)]. Disclaiming supporting estates accelerates the remainder but disclaiming future interests does not. [2–1106(b)(4)].

Jointly Held Property: One of the most complex areas of disclaimer law concerns the disclaiming of joint interests with right of survivorship. The possibility of three or more coholders, the variety of interests that are included, e.g., real property, bank accounts, brokerage accounts, and that coholders may not have contributed a pro rata share, make it difficult to design a disclaimer provision that will accommodate all policy concerns. The UDPIA recognizes disclaimers for jointly held property. Jointly held property is defined as "property held in the name of two or more persons under an arrangement in which all holders have concurrent interests and under which the last surviving holder is entitled to the whole of the property." [2–1102(5)].

When a holder of jointly held property dies the UDPIA gives the surviving holder a choice. [2–1107]. The holder can disclaim the greater of the fractional interest that is passing because of the death of the holder or all the interest less than disclaimant's attributable contribution. For example, if A and B are joint tenants in an asset and A contributed 60% of the original contribution, upon B's death, A can disclaim either a full 50% of the interest or 40% of it. If a qualified tax disclaimer is desired, the disclaimant must meet the conditions of Section 2518 and its regulations. [See Treas. Reg. 25.2518–2(c)(4)].

The disclaimer of a joint interest is effective as of the death of the holder and the interest disclaimed passes as if the disclaimant predeceased the decedent holder. [2–1107(b),(c)].

Trustee Disclaimer: Compatible with a fiduciary's fiduciary obligation, a trustee can disclaim property passing to the trust. [2–1108]. The disclaimed property does not become trust property but passes to alternate beneficiaries under the transfer instrument or to the donor under the resulting trust doctrine.

Powers of Appointment: The UDPIA has a set of sections dedicated to the effective dates for disclaiming power of appointment interests. [See § 9.05] The effective time for disclaiming a non fiduciary power depends on whether the power had ever been exercised by the holder. [2–1109] If not, the effective date is when the power became irrevocable. If it had been exercised previously, the effective date is immediately after the last exercise.

A disclaimer by an appointee takes effect when the instrument exercising the power becomes irrevocable. A disclaimer by an object or taker in default takes effect when the instrument creating the power becomes irrevocable.

A previously unexercised fiduciary power takes effect when the instrument creating the power becomes irrevocable. [2–1111]. A previously exercised fiduciary power takes effect immediately after the last exercise. Cofiduciaries are bound if the disclaimer so provides and the disclaimant has authority to bind the entity or cofiduciary.

Delivery of Disclaimer: The UDPIA permits any method of delivery that is "likely to result in its receipt" including first-class mail. [2–1112(b)]. The UDPIA has a long list of the recipients to whom a disclaimer needs to be delivered or filed. The purpose is insure that the person who is responsible for distributing the disclaimed interest will receive notice of the disclaimer. The list of the most appropriate person or entity is quite detailed. For example, if the interest concerns intestacy or testacy, the disclaimer must be delivered to any appointed personal representative or if none, filed with the proper court, but if there is a testamentary trust, delivery must be to any active trustee. [2–2112(c)(d)].

Chart 9-1
DISCLAIMER DELIVERY UNDER § 2-1112

Subsection	Disclaimer Delivery Designatee	
(c)	Intestacy	Personal Representative or Court
(d), (e)	Testamentary or Inter Vivos Trust	Active Trustee or court with jurisdiction
(f)	Instrument containing beneficiary des-ignation—prior to irrevocability	Person making designation
(g)	Instrument contained beneficiary des-ignation—after irrevocability	Person obligated to distribute
(h)	Jointly held property	Person to whom interest passes
(l)	Power of Appointment—object or taker in default	1. Holder of the power or instrument Fiduciary or 2. If none, the appropriate court
(j)	Power of Appointment appointee	1 Holder of the power or instrument or holder's personal representative 2. If none, the appropriate court
(k)	Fiduciary power	As provided in (c)-(e) above
(l)	Power held by agent	The principal or principal's representative

Disclaimers Barred or Limited: Certain specified actions or conduct by the person attempting to disclaim will bar the right to disclaim. [2–1113]. Even if the disclaimer is barred, it takes effect as a transfer to the person who would have taken the interest from a valid disclaimer. [2–1113(f)].

A disclaimer is barred if disclaimant, prior to the disclaimer, waived in writing the right to disclaim; or voluntarily accepted, assigned, pledged, transferred or contracted with the interest; or the property subject to the interest was sold at a judicial sale by the personal representative. [2–1113(b)]. Fiduciary powers are not barred by previous exercise. [2–1113(c)]. General powers of appointment are barred if previously exercised, but all other nonfiduciary powers are not. [2–1113(d)]. In a change from earlier disclaimer acts, other state law may limit or bar disclaimers. [2–1113(e)].

Tax Qualified Disclaimer: In order to validate all qualified tax disclaimers under the law of the enacting state, the UDPIA incorporates current and future provisions of IRC § 2518 and its regulations. [2–1114]. Disclaimers that are qualified for estate and gift tax purposes are declared valid disclaimers under the UDPIA even though they do not otherwise meet its more specific requirements. Although generally the UDPIA recognizes the validity of qualified disclaimers, there may be situations when the tax law goes beyond its rules. [See Hirsch & Gans, Perfecting Disclaimer Reform, 193].

Recording Disclaimer: The UDPIA permits the recordation of a disclaimer of an interest for which there is a recording system. [2–1115]. This allows disclaimants to establish the chain of title to real property, and to ward off creditors and bona fide purchasers.

§ 9.07 Uniform Statutory Rule Against Perpetuities

A. INTRODUCTION

The common law Rule Against Perpetuities has perplexed students, professors, lawyers and judges for centuries. Although the Rule is easy to state, its complexity developed from difficulties in its application. A common formulation of the Rule provides: "No interest is good unless it must vest, if at all, not later than twenty-one years after some life in being at the creation of the interest." [Gray, Rule Against Perpetuities, § 201, at 191]. Its chief purposes are stated to be a desire to curtail the deadhand control of wealth and to facilitate the marketability of property. [Lynn, Modern Rule Against Perpetuities, at 10]. Few would question its goals but many have criticized its methods. Several facets of the Rule's application engender the criticisms.

First, the Rule is really not a rule concerned with the duration of an interest but is concerned with a technical property concept of the vesting of an interest. Comparatively speaking, a relatively short twenty-five year suspended interest could violate the Rule for failure to vest within its confines whereas a suspended interest tested against lives in being could be valid under the Rule even though it actually will last for ninety years or more. This inconsistency in application justifies criticism.

Second, the Rule is enforced with psychic anticipation of contingencies coupled with a draconian "all or nothing" remedy if the contingencies violate the Rule. According to the common law, an interest created in a governing instrument, whether a will or other transfer device, had to be tested against the Rule at its creation. All contingencies in the interest created are tested to see whether they will become vested within the term of the Rule. There must be an initial certainty of vesting of all of the interests. If an interest is not certain of vesting within the Rule, the concept of infective invalidity might cause the entire transfer to fail. Commentators belabor these points in emphasizing the Rule's inconsistency, nonsensical approach, draconian remedy and unjust result. [See, e.g., Leach, Perpetuities in Perspective; Waggoner, Perpetuity Reform].

Despite these compelling criticisms, the Rule proves to endure against reform. A major reason for the lack of reformation derives from disagreements over what form the reform should take. Reformation proposals include: (1) total repeal of the Rule,[1] (2) creation of an immediate judicial reformation power for interests that will not vest within the Rule, (3) creation of wait and see or deferral judicial reformation power for interests that do not vest within the Rule, and (4) substitution of a specific period of time or period in gross within which all

---

1. Alaska, Arizona, Delaware, Idaho, Illinois, Maryland, South Dakota, and Wisconsin have abolished the Rule. See Shaftel, Newest Developments in Alaska.

conditional interests must vest. [See generally, Fellows, Testing Perpetuity Reforms, at 602–08].

Checkerboard reform among the states creates more problems than it solves. The multi-state property owner is more numerous than ever before. The possibility that interests will cross state lines has increased significantly during the last fifty years and the need for greater uniformity has concomitantly increased. The force of reform finally gained some momentum in 1979 when the American Law Institute accepted a wait and see doctrine as part of the Restatement (Second) of Property. [See Restatement (Second) of Property, § 1.4]. The Restatement nurtured additional discussion over the Rule and its modifications and this renewed interest reached a crescendo when the National Conference adopted the Uniform Statutory Rule Against Perpetuities Act (hereinafter USRAP) in 1986. Since its promulgation, twenty-five states have enacted it as their law.[2] Clearly, it constitutes the best and most politically viable reform proposal made to date. It is important to note that the Act is not without its opponents. [See, Dukeminier, Ninety Years in Limbo; Bloom, Perpetuities Refinement].

In 1990, the USRAP was made a part of the Uniform Probate Code and is found in Part 9 of Article II. Although the comments concerning the

2. Enacted in Alaska, Arizona, Arkansas, California, Colorado, Connecticut, District of Columbia, Florida, Georgia, Hawaii, Indiana, Kansas, Massachusetts, Michigan, Minnesota, Montana, Nebraska, Nevada, New Jersey, New Mexico, North Carolina, North Dakota, Oregon, South Carolina, Tennessee, Virginia and West Virginia.

provisions are extensive in the UPC, the comments and prefatory note materials incorporated into the separate Uniform Act are even more extensive and constitute one of the best sources of information concerning how the act works. For anyone who wishes to peruse the details of USRAP provisions, reference to these materials is essential. The following is but a brief outline of the relevant concepts promoted by the USRAP as well as a brief description of its provisions.

The purposes of the USRAP are broad. Obviously, as part of the Uniform Probate Code and as a separate uniform act, it is designed to bring uniformity of the law to the various states in this country. In addition, promulgation of the provisions reaffirms that there is a need for a Rule Against Perpetuities. Abolition of the Rule was rejected. Another important factor and feature of the provisions is that transfer language in instruments effective prior to enactment of the USRAP continues to be valid after enactment. The USRAP does not enlarge the range of invalidity. It is designed to recognize devices currently valid and to expand the scope of validity to other drafting techniques. Consequently, those who are well versed in the old law will not have to learn new law in order to qualify their transfer techniques.

Finally, a primary purpose of the USRAP is to reduce, and even eliminate in many situations, much of the litigation concerning perpetuity problems. With some limited exceptions, litigation over perpetuity questions cannot arise until the Rule as defined by the statute is violated. Consequently, all transfers which over time become effective despite their technical potential invalidity under the old common law Rule will not produce litigation. Only a transfer device that violates both period testing arms of the USRAP will come before the court except as noted. Even when litigation does occur, the nature and purpose of the litigation will be dramatically different from much litigation under the current common law Rule. Much litigation under the current Rule derives its motivation from a desire to destroy the contingent interest. Actions are brought by those who will gain by the destruction of the transfer device. Under the USRAP, this type of litigation is eliminated. The only litigation that will arise will be litigation to reform an instrument to conform to the Rule. Consequently, only those who wish to settle legitimate concerns and to terminate or to settle ownership of ancient trusts will be able to seek court review. This feature of the USRAP should abolish the common law attribute of granting unjust enrichment to nonintended beneficiaries due to technical failure of transfers due to perpetuity violations. [See Waggoner, Perpetuities Reform].

B. STATUTORY RULE AGAINST PERPETUITIES

The core of the USRAP is found in its definition of the period of time within which a non-vested interest must vest in order to be valid. Phrased in the disjunctive, a non-vested interest is valid if it is certain to vest or terminate either no later than twenty-one years after the death of a living individual or within ninety years after its creation. [2–901]. The first arm of the rule is merely a codification of the common law Rule. The second arm is a form of a wait and see approach tied to a specific length of time. The combination of these two alternate standards can be summarized as follows:

(1) A transfer which is valid under the common law Rule is valid under the USRAP's provision and no modification is necessary to forms or instruments that satisfy this standard;

(2) Notwithstanding the existence of a question concerning validity under the common law Rule, no interest is contestable as to validity until ninety years have passed from its creation;

(3) The common "savings" clause which specifically terminates an interest within the common law Rule will also qualify under this provision.

The rules are specifically applicable to non-vested property interests, general powers of appointment that are not presently exercisable because of a condition precedent, and non-general powers of appointment which generally are testamentary powers of appointment. [2–901(a), (b), and (c)].

There is a distinct judicial and practice advantage in validating current methods of estate planning. The positive results will be a decline in litigation concerning previous instruments and techniques used in wills subject to the provision after its enactment. Practitioners will not create invalid transfers under the Rule merely by following old practices. In addition, the second arm of the rule is a remedial safety net for provisions not properly drafted. It basically incorporates a fail-safe rule for improper drafting. No interest will fail due to the rule but may require reformation in order to be valid. The draconian remedy of the common law Rule is abolished.

Because of the broad protection provided by the provision, the USRAP specifically restricts the application of lives in being as that definition concerns post-death procreation. In determining whether an interest vests or not, the USRAP disregards the possibility that an individual may have a child born after the individual's death. This exclusion is primarily directed toward the problem raised by post-death procreation due to advances in medical science. [2–901(d), Comment]. It also, however, eliminates the common law lives in being extension granted to children en ventre sa mere. The common law rule was intended to validate interests that might otherwise have been invalid due to the birth of a child after the death of a life in being or transferor. The new rule makes this extension unnecessary for purposes of validating interests under the perpetuity rule and therefore is eliminatable.

Concern has been expressed that the alternative perpetuity periods might be used by drafters using clauses which provide that the maximum time of vesting or termination of an interest or trust must occur no later than the later of the two testing periods. For example, an instrument might use a clause that stated the following or similar to the following: "The non-vested interest is to vest on the later of (a) twenty-one years after the death of the survivor of specified lives in being at the creation of the trust or (b) ninety years after the creation of the trust." To avoid this misuse of the alternate perpetuity periods, the UPC converts this type of "later of" clause into a traditional perpetuity saving clause. [2–901(e)]. Basically that limits the length of time to the common law Rule. [Fellows, Testing Perpetuity Reforms, at 657–63]. This section does not apply, however, to a later than clause which does not tack the twenty-one years on to the specific lives in being. [2–901, Comment]. For example, a transfer that creates an interest that is to vest upon "the later of the death of my spouse or thirty years after my death" would not be converted to the common law Rule but would be permitted to vest within the ninety year rule. In addition, it does not prohibit a clause that terminates the trust after 90 years, although this approach is discouraged. [Waggoner, Drafting Under the USRAP, at 248].

C. DATE OF CREATION OF INTEREST

Because the perpetuity period refers to the time of creation of the non-vested interest, it is necessary to define when that interest is created. The USRAP codifies the common law on this matter with some clarification. The time of creation for most non-vested property interests or powers of appointment is determined under general principles of property law. [2–902(a)]. This means that a non-vested interest created in a will will have the date of the testator's death as its creation date. In regard to inter vivos transfers, an interest or power is created as of the effective date of the transfer. In addition, two special circumstances are resolved. If by the terms of the instrument a person alone and without the consent of any other person may exercise a power to become the unqualified beneficial owner of the property subject to the interest, the non-vested interest or power of appointment is created for purposes of the perpetuity period when that unqualified power terminates. For example, if a person has a power to revoke an inter vivos or testamentary trust, the perpetuity period does not begin to run and is not created until the person no longer is able to exercise the power of revocation. The period then runs from the termination of this power over the interest subject to the USRAP. [2–902(b)].

Occasionally, property arrangements such as trusts, which include interests subject to the USRAP, may provide that additional property can be added to them during their existence. The question in such situations is at what point do you evaluate the perpetuity period for these new interests transferred to the existing trust. The USRAP, taking the efficient course of action, provides that its perpetuity period begins when the instrument or trust was created not from the date of subsequent transfers to it. [2–902(c)]. Considering the nonforfeiture approach and generous duration of the USRAP's perpetuity periods, this limitation should not deny intent or cause harm to intended beneficiaries.

D. REFORMATION

As mentioned previously, the USRAP includes a judicial reformation procedure exercisable by the courts concerning transfers which are found to violate its perpetuity period. [2–903]. Although this will not occur in most situations because experience informs us that most transfers will qualify under the general rule, the reformation power is reserved to correct those circumstances in which a perpetuity error has indeed been made. The USRAP adopts a deferred rather than prospective reformation power in the court. This means that there is no power to reform until the transfer is invalid under the perpetuity period. [2–903]. Durationally speaking, this means the non-vested interest has not vested within either of the durational periods of the perpetuity period.

A deferred reformation power was selected for several reasons. First, it will significantly reduce "temperature testing" law suits over a perpetuity question. Second, it permits the transferor's plan to fully work out. As indicated previously, most transfers will vest within one or the other period and thus a law suit is unnecessary. Third, it rejects the prospective analysis of vesting determinations and adopts the retrospective analysis approach. At the time of reformation, the court will know more about how the donor would reform the instrument had the donor known the instrument created an invalid transfer. Should it be when the instrument first is created with a more or less prospective reformation or should it be after the instrument is no longer valid and we know what the actual facts are of the potential distribution? The USRAP elects the latter.

Two exceptions to the post-validity reformation requirement are recognized. The first exception concerns class gifts in which the vesting may still be endowed but the time for actual possession or enjoyment of a share of the estate in a class member has arrived. This exception permits those of the class entitled to immediate possession or enjoyment to seek reformation of the instrument so that their possession or enjoyment may occur immediately. [2–903(2), and Comment].

A second exception concerns the ability to institute a reformation action although the perpetuity periods have not expired if it is clear they will expire before the property vests. [2–903(3)]. This exception would cover the unlikely case where a donor created a transfer that would not vest until a period of time has passed clearly beyond the Rule. For example, consider a transfer of property into a trust from which the income is to be paid by representation among the donor's descendants, from time to time, living for one hundred years: at the end of the one hundred year period the trustee is to distribute the corpus and accumulated income to the donor's living descendants by representation but if none to a charity. It is clear that this transfer violates the USRAP including its ninety year rule.

In this situation a prospective reformation action should be permitted to correct the clear undenied violation of the Rule.

When a reformation action is permitted, the court must reform the document. It does not have the discretion to hold that the transfer is invalid.

The USRAP provides information concerning what the court should consider in making the reformation. The statutory requirement is that the court must reform the transfer in a "manner that most closely approximates the transferor's manifested plan of distribution." [2–903]. This provision effectively revokes the common law doctrine of infectious invalidity. [2–903, Comment]. Generally, the recommendation is that courts make as little alteration to the disposition as possible. The goal is to use a scalpel and not a butcher knife. This means that (1) the maximum number of persons who could take at the time of reformation should be permitted to take even though their interests technically were not vested within the period of the rule, and (2) other prohibitory provisions should be altered as little as possible, e.g., an age requirement above twenty-one should be reduced only to the point where it will satisfy the rules. [USRAP, Section 3, Comment].

One of the advantages of the delayed reformation is the opportunity to see how the donor's plan operated and to apply any reformation necessary to the situation as it exists at the current time. There is no need to predict the future. The decision needs to be made at the time it needs to be made and it is final.

E. EXCLUSIONS FROM THE RULE

The USRAP specifically excludes certain transactions and powers from application of its rule. [2–904]. First, the provision provides that all exceptions recognized at common law or excluded by statute are excluded under the USRAP. The US-RAP then defines particular situations that also are excluded. Generally, non-donative transfers are not subject to the Rule. [2–904(1)]. Although not excepted at common law the position of the drafters of the USRAP is that this is the preferred law because a perpetuity rule that concerns gratuitous transfers is not appropriate to apply to transactions with consideration. So that the exclusion is not interpreted beyond its intent, the USRAP excepts from the exclusion certain transactions that are in the nature of donative transfers despite their nongratuitous characterization. This would include prenuptial and postnuptial agreements, separation or divorce settlements, surviving spouses' elections, and other similar types of devices specifically enumerated.

The USRAP codifies the common law determination that nonvested charitable interests held in trusts or by governmental entities are not subject to the perpetuity period so long as they pass from one charitable entity to another charitable entity. [2–904(5)]. Furthermore, with some particular exceptions, nonvested property interests or powers of attorney in regards to trusts or other arrangements dealing with pension, profit sharing, stock bonuses and other types of employee benefit arrangements are excepted from the Rule as well. [2–904(6)].

Purely administrative or management powers that are not related to distribution are excepted from the rule. [2–904(2)]. In addition, a power to appoint a fiduciary [2–904(3)], and a discretionary trustee's power to distribute principal to an indefeasibly vested beneficiary are excepted. [2–904(4)].

The purpose of these exclusions is to draw particular divisions between the types of transfers to which the Rule should apply versus those to which it should not. The USRAP does not indicate that other durational limitations should not be imposed on the excepted transfers. The point being that the Rule Against Perpetuities is the wrong policy to apply against these devices and that particular specialized durational limitations need to be developed for them.

F.   DATE OF APPLICATION

The USRAP's provisions do not apply retroactively and will not apply prospectively to transfers that occurred before its effective date. [2–905]. Nonvested interests created by the exercise of a power of appointment after the effective date are covered by the USRAP's rule even though the original transfer occurred prior to the effective date. In addition, any power of appointment created subsequent to the effective date is covered by the USRAP rule if exercised after the effective date or if a power to revoke expires after the effective date.

For transfers not covered by the USRAP, the court is encouraged to adopt equitable principles that will incorporate the principles of the Act in order to avoid failure of the transaction. [2–905(b)]. The USRAP also includes a ministerial provision in which a state enacting it would have to repeal or supersede certain other laws in the state.

G. ILLUSTRATIONS USING
THE USRAP

The following Chart 9–2 illustrates how the US-RAP deals with several specific situations.

CHART 9–2
USRAP ILLUSTRATIONS

Comment: The following three hypotheticals are merely illustrative of the application of the USRAP. The first hypothetical concerns a conveyance that would be valid under the common law Rule Against Perpetuities. The second and third hypotheticals concern conveyances that would violate the common law Rule but which are validated under the US-RAP.

Hypothetical 1:   D devises the residue of the estate to T, in trust, with the income to D's children for life, the remainder passes to such of D's grandchildren as attain the age of twenty-one. D's will contains no savings clause. D is survived by three children, ages 12,

7, and 3 years of age, and no grandchildren.

Answer: This trust is valid under the common
law Rule. It must vest, if at all, within
lives in being (D's children) plus twenty-one years. All interests in the grandchild will vest no later than twenty-one
years after the death of the last child
to die. The USRAP does not change
this analysis. The common law Rule is
allowed to play out its requirements.
Under this example, if one of the children were to live more than ninety
years after D's death, absolute vesting
of the transfer will not be known for a
longer period than the USRAP's alternative ninety year rule. Because the
devise is valid under the common law
Rule, the ninety year limitation does
not apply.

Hypothetical 2:   D devises the residue of the estate
to T, in trust, with the income pay-
able to D's children for life. The
trust terminates when D's youngest
grandchild reaches the age of twenty-five. D's will contains no savings
clause. D is survived by three children and seven grandchildren
whose ages ranged from eleven to
twenty-nine.[3]

Answer: This trust violates the common law
Rule Against Perpetuities, because it is
possible that D's youngest grandchild
may be born after D's death and this
grandchild might not reach the age of
twenty-five until more than twenty-one

3. The facts of this hypothetical are basically similar to the
facts of Merrill v. Wimmer, 481 N.E.2d 1294 (Ind. 1985).

years after all the lives in being (D's children and grandchildren living at D's death) are dead. Although the remainder interest probably would vest within the length of the common law rule, it is invalid because of the mere possibility that it will not vest. The USRAP, however, validates the trust. Even if the slim possibility occurred it is likely the remainder interest in the trust will vested within ninety years of D's death and thus the trust will complete its full duration. Even if it has not vested within the ninety year period, the USRAP will cause the interests to be vest at that time by court order. In addition, the USRAP would not permit litigation over the perpetuity period until the later of its two limitation periods passed.

Hypothetical 3:   M transferred into an irrevocable inter vivos trust assets the income from which to be paid to M's child, D, for life; D was given a testamentary power of appointment to the remainder. D died thirty years after the date of creation of M's trust. In D's valid will, the power was exercised by transferring the assets into trust. The income and principal from the trust was payable to D's children in the discretion of the trustee. Upon the death of each child, that child's share would be distributed to that child's then living descendants or if none were living, to that child's then living siblings, per stirpes. D was survived by three children ages 24, 22, and 21.

All were born after the creation of M's trust.[4]

Answer: This trust violates the common law Rule Against Perpetuities because the trust does not vest until the death of each child of D and D's children are not lives in being. At common law the perpetuity period in this hypothetical would run from the date of the irrevocable inter vivos trust created by M rather than from D's date of death. As the facts state, none of D's children were lives in being at that time. One or more of D's children might not die and thus vesting might not occur until more than twenty-one years after all the lives in being are dead. If held to be invalid, the entire trust might fail. Under the USRAP the trust would be allowed to function for the lives of D's children or sixty years (ninety years less the thirty years that had expired from the running of the perpetuity period) whichever period is shorter. If all of D's children die within the sixty year period, the trust will function and terminate without court involvement according to D's expressed desires. If one or more of D's children lived sixty years beyond D's death, then the Act's alternative ninety year rule applies and the trust will have to be reformed. In this situation, the court would probably vest the income interest in the living children and the remainder of each living child's share on death in that child's descendants, per stirpes, living

4. The facts of this hypothetical are basically similar to the facts of Arrowsmith v. Mercantile–Safe Deposit & Trust Co., 313 Md. 334, 545 A.2d 674 (1988).

at that time. [See Waggoner, USRAP in Oregon, at 271–72]. This approach discourages litigation because the trust retains validity, no costs of litigation occur until the relevant periods expire, and thus the donor's intent is carried out in substantial part, if not in whole.

H.   HONORARY TRUSTS

See § 18.01(A)(4)(c), (d) for a discussion of the UPC and UTC treatment of honorary trusts.

PART THREE

PROBATE OF WILLS AND ADMINISTRATION

CHAPTER 10

ADMINISTRATION AND ADMINISTRATION AVOIDANCE PROCEDURES

§ 10.01 Introduction to the Flexible System of Administration

A. INTRODUCTION TO THE PROCESS OF ADMINISTRATION

The process of administration of an estate can be better understood if one knows what matters have to be resolved. A person's financial relationship with his or her property might be characterized as a partnership between the person and the estate. The death of the person causes a dissolution of the partnership and a liquidation of the assets of the estate is necessary. The following outlines the usual necessary steps for this liquidation:

(1) Take care of funeral and burial arrangements;

(2) Gather information concerning the status of the decedent's estate and the extent of the property held;

(3) Make an inventory of the assets in the estate;

(4) Identify creditors and obligations owed to other persons;

(5) Provide basic support for surviving family members during the liquidation process;

(6) Determine taxation obligations and complete and file necessary tax returns;

(7) If necessary, manage the assets of the estate during liquidation;

(8) Liquidate sufficient portions of the estate to pay obligations, debts, and taxes;

(9) Pay obligations, debts and taxes;

(10) Determine shares of eventual successors;

(11) Distribute remaining assets and funds to successors in appropriate shares;

(12) Complete final accounting of transactions during the administration process;

(13) Discharge the personal representative;

(14) Terminate the liquidation process.

The above outlines the basic steps. Most estates will require something more or less.

One of the principal issues in the determining how this process is to operate is who should have control over it. Should the law assume that everyone must follow a specified and standardized process or should the persons in interest control what actions should be taken? The former technique will raise transactional costs for a larger number of estates than will the latter. The latter approach is said to increase the risk of misappropriation and fraud on those who need to be protected. The traditional technique in this country favors the former approach. The UPC and similar laws in other jurisdictions take the latter approach.

The current law in most jurisdictions concerning the administration of decedents' estates is typically monolithic, inflexible and formalistic. By contrast the UPC provides persons interested in a decedent's estate with substantial flexibility and numerous procedural alternatives and combinations. Reduced to their conceptual characteristics, the three basic types of procedures available are called "informal," "formal" and "supervised." Generally, the informal proceedings for the probate of a will or appointment of a personal representative are administrative in nature and ordinarily require no prior notice to interested persons. [1–201(23)]. They are initiated by an application to the Registrar who either denies it or issues a written statement of approval. At this moment, the Registrar's decision is considered nonadjudicative and is not appealable. If the application is approved by the Registrar, it permits certain processes to function without continual court involvement and will mature into a final adjudication after the passage of a specific length of time. Formal proceedings are initiated by a petition to the

Court and become effective and operational only after notice to interested persons, a hearing and an order of court. [1–201(18)]. They are final adjudications subject only to vacation on limited grounds and reversible only on appeal. In addition, once the order of court is rendered, the Court's involvement ends. Supervised administration functions much as the procedures now existing in non-UPC states. [1–201(4)]. Briefly, it is a single continuous proceeding requiring formal procedures and frequent court involvement.

The above three types of proceedings form the framework for the operation of the UPC's procedure for the administration of decedents' estates. Significantly, all three proceedings are self-sufficient and interrelated depending upon the desires of the persons interested in the estate. In addition, except for supervised administration, each application to the Registrar or proceeding requiring court action is independent in nature. [3–107]. This attribute of independence permits interested persons to seek judicial review when necessary without affecting the other procedures selected. [See Estates of Brown v. Dickinson, 999 P.2d 1057 (N.M.App. 2000)]. Naturally, when an informal proceeding and a formal proceeding are in direct conflict, the formal proceeding supersedes its corresponding informal procedure.

In greater detail, the system is composed of the following specific procedural devices: informal appointment, formal appointment, informal probate, formal testacy, formal closing, and supervised administration. Within the above structure, the UPC also includes other significant procedural devices and concepts which increase flexibility and predictability. These include, for example, a comprehensive set of statutes of limitations, comprehensive provisions establishing title to property, affidavit and summary procedures for handling very small estates, universal succession, informal procedures, which are in the nature of informal proceedings, for the purposes of accomplishing various tasks such as inventory and appraisement, termination of appointment and closing, and efficient procedures for dealing with the multi-state estates. In addition, after notice and a hearing, the Court may issue formal orders on any range of matters limited only by the court's substantive jurisdiction and the desires of the petitioner. [3–107, Comment]. Except for supervised administration, all proceedings are independent of each other.

The theory behind the UPC's proceedings and procedures is to provide interested persons with the option to formalize and seek court action only to the extent they desire. The Court is not involved unless those persons petition for its involvement. If they do so petition, the Court is given the power to deal with the issue or problem presented. Although control is primarily within the domain of those concerned about the decedent's estate, the UPC has meaningful provisions for protecting those who may be harmed by wrongful and devious activities of others. The UPC was not conceived with any naive thoughts that all persons are honest and fair. An important point to emphasize, however, is that each interested person must exercise affirmative action to be fully protected. One's own self interest is considered a better guardian than is the Court.

Some of the factors that will be considered by interested persons when determining which procedures or devices to use are: (1) the value of the decedent's administrable estate; (2) the statute of limitations applicable; (3) the degree of trust, cooperation and agreement among the interested persons; (4) the testator's express testamentary wishes; (5) the complexities of the administration; (6) the degree of protection from liability needed by the successors or by the personal representative or both; and (7) proof of title to property requirements.

B. ILLUSTRATIVE TECHNIQUES

An understanding of the UPC's procedures and operation for decedents' estates can best be acquired by examining and applying the provisions to hypothetical problems. The following five hypothetical problems demonstrate how many of the UPC's numerous procedures deal with the opening and closing of both a testate and intestate estate, with protective devices available and with the contest of wills. Because two of the UPC's outstanding features are its pervasive flexibility and multiplicity of techniques, it is not desirable to structure procedures unnecessarily. To do so would reincarnate much of the evil contained in non-UPC probate systems. Consequently, the following suggested techniques should be viewed as mere guideposts and not as dogma.

1.   Estate Valued at Less Than $5,000

Hypothetical: Decedent's estate subject to administration is valued at less than $5,000. Decedent is survived by a spouse or a sole heir or a sole devisee.

One obvious course of action for a sole successor is to take no official action under the UPC. Presumably, if the successor personally pays off the decedent's creditors, the successor could pocket the remainder of the estate. In fact, if third persons hold possession or title to personal property of the decedent, thirty days after death the title or possession or both can be obtained by the sole successor on the force of a special affidavit so long as no administration has been applied for. [3–1201(a)]. With a similar affidavit, even titles to securities can be changed in this manner. [3–1201(b)]. It also makes no difference whether the decedent died intestate or testate. The effect of the affidavit, however, is merely to protect the third person, not the successor. [3–1202]. Without much additional effort the procedures suggested in the next hypothetical would also be available and may frequently be more desirable.

2.   Estate Valued at Less Than Family Protections and Expenses

Hypothetical: Decedent's estate subject to administration after subtracting liens and encumbrances is valued at less than the total of the relevant

family protections, reasonable funeral and administration expenses and reasonable medical and hospital expenses of the last illness. Decedent is survived
by heirs who are entitled to the relevant family
protections.

a. *Intestacy*

According to the hypothetical, if the appropriate
heir or heirs survive the decedent by 120 hours,
they are entitled to the whole estate. [See
§ 3.01(B)]. The UPC contains a variety of devices
by which the surviving heirs can take the estate.
Although, they could do nothing other than to take
possession of the estate, it is not practical under
this hypothetical if any question of title may be
involved. If creditors are the only concern, doing
nothing is feasible because after the passage of one
year from the date of the decedent's death, unsecured creditors are barred under the limitation on
creditor claims provision. [3–803(a)(1)]. There are
better alternatives, however.

One alternative for the parties in interest would
be to seek universal succession. This procedure permits decedent's heirs or testator's devisee to accept
the estate assets without administration by assuming responsibility for discharging those obligations
that normally would be discharged by a personal
representative. [Art. III, Pt. 3, Succession Without
Administration, Prefatory Note to 3–312 to –322].
Although an application to and a written statement
of Universal Succession from the Registrar is required, no personal representative is appointed, no

administration process is conducted, and no court proceedings are required. [3–313, 3–314]. Universal succession cannot be approved by the Registrar until five days from the decedent's death has passed. [3–315]. Once approved, successors must take upon themselves the responsibility of paying the family protections, reasonable funeral and administration expenses and the reasonable medical and hospital expenses of the last illness. [3–316]. In addition, they may prove title to those assets if requested by purchasers or transfer agents. If our hypothetical small estate is solvent, the universal succession alternative is very appropriate and desirable. If the amount of creditor claims and thus the solvency of the estate is in question, universal succession is not going to satisfy the successors' needs because there will be a definite desire on their part to identify and terminate these creditor claims. Although creditor claims can be paid under universal succession, no procedure is provided for identifying them or for protecting the successors from possible insolvency of the estate. [3–317, Comment]. Consequently, under universal succession there would be no method available for the successors to take advantage of the family protections which protect against such insolvency.

In that case, a sensible alternative is for the heirs to have a person with priority file an application for an informal appointment of a personal representative. [3–301(a)(1), and (4)]. Approval of the application by the Registrar may be obtained five days after decedent's death. [3–307(a)]. Even if nothing else is done, this procedure gives the personal representative full status. [3–307(b)]. The personal representative may make transfers and bona fide purchasers are fully protected even if the transfer is later found to be invalid. [3–714]. In addition, the personal representative is empowered to settle and distribute the estate without court order or supervision. [3–704].

Normally, within thirty days of appointment the personal representative must give notice to all heirs of that appointment. [3–705]. If after inventory and appraisal, however, it appears that the value of the entire estate will not exceed the value of the family protection, costs of administration, reasonable funeral expenses and reasonable and necessary last illness medical and hospital expenses, the personal representative may immediately disburse and distribute the estate to the appropriate persons without giving the normally mandatory notice to creditors. [3–1203]. In this example, therefore, the personal representative could quickly pay the necessary bills, and distribute the remainder to the heirs in satisfaction of their family protection provisions. After the assets are distributed or disbursed, the personal representative can then close the estate by filing a verified statement which recites that to the best of the personal representative's knowledge the value of the entire estate did not exceed the family protection and the other deductible expenses, that disbursement and distribution is complete and that a copy of this statement was sent to all distributees and known un-

paid creditors. [3–1204]. The consequences of this
filing are that successors and unbarred creditors
have only six months from the date of that filing to
commence a proceeding against the personal representative and that the personal representative's appointment terminates one year after the filing if no
proceedings are pending. [3–1204(b)–(c); see 3–
1003(b), 3–1005].

If there is a possibility that additional assets may
be discovered that would cause the estate to be
valued above the amount permitted under the summary administrative procedure, the personal representative should definitely publish notice to creditors. [3–801]. Publication is advantageous because it
reduces the relevant statute of limitations applicable to creditors from one year after death to the
later of sixty days after actual notice to known
creditors or four months from the date of first
publication. [3–803(a)(2)]. Furthermore, publication
will not delay administration because the family
protection may still be paid before the nonclaim
period runs. [2–404, 3–906(a)(2)]. Anytime six
months after the date of the original appointment,
the personal representative can and should informally close the estate by filing with the Court a
certified statement reciting that notice to creditors
has been published more than six months before
the date of this statement, that the estate has been
fully administered and settled (noting claims that
remain unpaid), and that a copy of the full accounting of the administration has been sent to all distributees and creditors. [3–1003]. The consequences

of this filing are exactly the same as under the summary procedure, that is, successors and unbarred creditors have only six months from the filing to commence a proceeding against the personal representative and the personal representative's appointment terminates one year after the filing if no proceeding is pending. [3–1005, 3–1003(b)].

b. Testacy

With the following three exceptions, the fact that decedent died testate rather than intestate would not change the above described procedure. First, if settlement of the estate will be by universal succession, a request for informal probate should be joined with the initiation application. [3–313]. Second, if an executor is nominated in the will, the executor has priority for appointment. [3–203]. Third, if administration is desired, the person who has priority to be personal representative should file an application simultaneously for both informal probate and informal appointment. [3–301(a)(1), (2)]. So long as superseding proceedings are not instituted within the later of three years from death or one year from the date of informal probate, devisees under the will are provided proof of title. [3–108, 3–301(a)(1)(vi), 3–314(a)(5)]. Informally probating the will, therefore, will protect devisees' titles and rights if additional property is discovered.

Although the suggested procedures employed for this hypothetical may be all classified as informal or summary procedures, under the circumstances presented, they should be sufficient for efficient administration. The more formal procedures available would seem best used only when necessary. Nonessential use of formal procedures impairs much of the flexibility, efficiency and other benefits of the UPC.

3. Estates Valued in Excess of Family Protections and Expenses

Hypothetical: Decedent's estate is valued above the total of the relevant family protections, if any, reasonable funeral and administration expenses and medical and hospital expenses of the last illness. Presume there is harmony among the appropriate successors, and there is no disagreement about distribution and administration.

One of the outstanding features of the UPC is that except for the summary procedures previously discussed for the very small estates, the UPC's efficient and flexible procedures are as applicable to the very large, e.g., $1,000,000 plus, estate as it is to the moderate, e.g., $50,000 or less, estate.

a. Intestacy

Because universal succession is not limited by the value of the estate, it is available to the successors in this hypothetical as well as in the previous hypothetical. Even very large estates may be able to use this technique. As before, the heirs or devisee must be harmonious and serious problems with creditors or claims should not be present. The application to the Registrar would be the same. [3–313]. Once approved, there would be no further proceedings before the court unless desired by the successors or other interested persons.

There may be one or more difficult creditor or tax issues involved, however. The successors may want a conclusive determination of claims and settlement. Therefore, some kind of administration will be required. The UPC includes the necessary procedures to satisfy this desire without unduly involving the court.

As with the previous hypothetical, to begin the administration of the estate, the first course of action will be to select the personal representative. Presuming harmony among the heirs, the appropriate or agreed upon person should file an application for informal appointment. [3–301(a)(1), and (4)]. Appointment by the Registrar is probably all that is necessary for administration of the estate. [See 3–307(a)]. Upon approval of appointment by the Registrar, acceptance by the personal representative and issuance of letters, the personal representative possesses full powers to administer the estate without further court approval. [3–307(b)].

Although the personal representative may use only the informal closing procedure, as discussed in the subsection B hypothetical, a more comprehensive alternative, formal closing, would probably be desired. [3–1001(a)]. This procedure is particularly advantageous when there is more than one heir involved. It is desirable both for the protection of the personal representative and for settling various potential issues between the other interested persons. Procedurally, a petition for formal closing may be made at any time after presentation of claims against the estate are barred. After notice to all interested persons is given and a hearing is held, the Court is authorized to issue orders that determine heirship, approve settlement and distribution and discharge the personal representative from further claims by interested persons. Discharge of the personal representative under this procedure would be complete.

Under the procedures described above, the question of whether decedent died leaving a valid will was not considered, therefore such a will could be probated within the three years from death limitation. [3–108]. In order to preclude this, or at least to finally determine the issue, the UPC again includes the necessary provisions. Without disturbing the informal characteristics of the administration, the heirs could file a petition for formal testacy seeking a judicial determination of whether the decedent left a will and of decedent's heirs. [3–401, 3–402(b)]. This petition can be made in conjunction with a request for informal appointment, [3–402(a)], or at any other time during administration. Naturally, as is characteristic of formal proceedings, prior notice of the hearing to interested persons is required. [3–403]. The order by the Court that there is no will and the determination of heirship is determinative and binding except as reversed on appeal or as modified or vacated by order of the Court. [3–412,

3–413]. The reasons for vacation are limited and are only available for a maximum of twelve months after the entry of the order.

One of the most imaginative possibilities under the UPC for dealing with the additional question of a will is the ability to combine a petition for formal settlement and closing with a petition for formal testacy. [3–1001(a)]. Under this procedure the estate would be informally administered by a full-powered personal representative without the necessity of court proceedings. When the estate is ready for closing, the interested parties, in essentially one proceeding, can have the protection of a court order on the issues of whether there was a valid will, heirship, distribution, settlement, and discharge of the personal representative for the conduct of the administration. Although the requirements for both formal closing and formal testacy proceedings must be followed, the advantages of combining these procedures with informal administration are obvious. Actually from both practical and interpretive standpoints, all formal closing proceedings instituted according to Section 3–1001 should include a determination of testacy so long as that issue has not previously been adjudicated and the limitation period for instituting formal testacy proceedings has not run.

b.   *Testacy*

The most obvious additional procedure that must be used if decedent dies testate is that the will must be probated. With only two exceptions, which are

not applicable at this point to this situation, the
UPC provides that title to property passing by will
cannot be proved unless the will is declared valid by
informal or formal probate. [3–102]. If universal
succession is sought, the application must include
the information necessary and a request for informal probate of the will. [3–313]. This would be the
only additional requirement under this procedure.
Similarly, if administration is desired, the named
executor or other person with priority should file an
application simultaneously for both informal probate and informal appointment. [3–301(a), 3–307].
Three beneficial consequences derive from approval
of such an application. Although subject to formal
proceedings within the later of three years from
death or one year from the date of informal probate,
informal probate provides the devisees with proof of
title so long as the contingency of a formal probate
does not occur. [3–108, 3–302]. In addition, as with
intestacy, informal appointment creates a personal
representative who upon appointment, acceptance
and issuance of letters can administer the estate
and can give marketable title to property sold during the administration of the estate. [3–701, 3–711,
3–714]. Furthermore, distributions by the personal
representative to persons who the personal representative believes are entitled thereto enable the
distributees to give good marketable title to purchasers even though the distributions subsequently
prove to be erroneous. [3–910]. Otherwise, the procedures used for opening and closing of the estate
would remain the same as those used in intestacy.

Combining formal testacy with formal closing is again a very useful procedure to follow. [3–1001(a)].

4. Protective Devices

Hypothetical: Decedent died leaving a substantial estate. The successors are not harmonious and show mutual distrust of each other. Suspicions of dishonesty, fraud and other wrongdoings are rampant.

The UPC possesses a large number of protective devices. Although interested persons have full discretion to select which protective device to use, they should be advised to use only those that are necessary to ensure the protection desired. The following discussion provides a brief outline of the most significant protective devices.

a. Demand for Notice

Any person who has a financial or property interest in the decedent's estate may file a written demand for notice with the Court anytime after death. [3–204]. This affirmative procedure provides the demandant with the protection of receiving notice of all other filings or orders concerned with the estate, including applications for universal succession, informal probate, or informal appointment, or combination thereof. Under the circumstances presented in this hypothetical, filing a demand for notice should be done as standard operating procedure by those interested in the estate.

b. *Formal Proceedings*

An interested person can terminate or foreclose universal succession or stay or suspend an informal appointment by petitioning for a formal appointment [3–414], and heirs or devisees under another will can force an informal probate into a formal testacy proceeding. [3–401.] In addition, one year from the date of appointment, and after the time limitation on presenting claims arising before death has expired, interested persons can petition for formal closing, which would include distribution. [3–1001(a), 3–1002]. Significantly, none of the above mentioned formal proceedings will entitle the Court to exercise a continuing supervisory position over the estate and its administration; however, any interested person may petition for supervised administration.

c. *Supervised Administration*

Supervised administration is a single continuous proceeding before the Court, concerned with the settling of one's estate. [3–501]. Its protective features include formal testacy, formal appointment and formal closing proceedings [3–502, 3–505]; distributions cannot be made without court order [3–504]; and the formal notice requirements must be fulfilled. [See 3–403, 3–414, 3–1001]. It also stays informal applications that are pending and restricts an earlier appointed personal representative from making distributions. [3–503]. Except for the restriction that distributions cannot be made without court order, the supervised personal representative has the same authority or powers as other personal representatives under the UPC. [3–504]. Interested persons may request, however, that other restrictions be endorsed on the letters, and when such restrictions are endorsed on these letters, they bind third parties dealing with the personal representative to any violation of the restriction by the latter. The protections afforded by endorsements on the personal representative's letters may represent the principal reason persons would elect to require a supervised administration because all of its other benefits may be employed as needed through individual formal proceedings.

The basic consequence of petitioning for supervised administration is to cause the estate to pass through a procedure similar to that existing in most non-UPC states presently. Some attorneys who are accustomed to such a cumbersome procedure may advise its use during the early years after the UPC's adoption. As they become more accustomed to the other procedures available under the UPC, it is clear that the use of supervised administration will diminish rapidly. In fact, the courts should precipitate such a change in approach by exercising their discretion to refuse such petitions for supervised administration. [3–502].

d.   *Other Protective Devices*

Less drastic protective devices provided to interested persons against acts of the personal representative include a petition for an order restraining actions that unreasonably jeopardize the applicant's

interests. [3–607]. An illustration of a useful purpose for such an order is one prohibiting the personal representative from selling a particular asset
in the estate. Another recourse, if circumstances
warrant, is a petition for removal for cause. [3–611].
Causes range from mismanagement and breach of
duty to incapacity and the best interest of the
estate.

A subtle protective device in the UPC is the
requirement that, before certain actions may be
taken or approved, 120 hours must have elapsed
since the decedent's death. This is applicable to
acceptance of informal probate, appointment of a
personal representative under informal appointment, and the granting of an application for universal succession. [3–302, 3–307(a), 3–315]. This five-
day rule permits the notice of death to permeate the
relevant communities and thus give most interested
persons informal notice that actions related to the
death may take place.

e. Bond

Under the UPC, bond is not required unless a
special administrator is appointed, the will requires
it, or an interested person petitions for it. [3–603].
Persons who have and retain an interest or a claim
valued in excess of 1,000 dollars may file with the
Registrar a demand that the personal representative give a bond. [3–605]. The personal representative must then give bond or other suitable security
in an amount specified by the Court or, if not
specified, in an amount not less than the estimated

value of the principal of the estate plus one year's income. [3–604]. This estimate must also be filed with the Registrar and must be under oath. Until the ordered bond is filed, the personal representative must refrain from administering the estate except to preserve it. [3–605; see § 19.01(A) for a discussion of trustee bonds].

f. Improper Distribution

Interested persons are well protected from improper distribution under an informal closing. Not only must the personal representative file a verified statement indicating that a closing statement and a full account have been sent to all distributees, the personal representative also remains liable for the administration for six months after the filing. [3–1003]. In addition, the distributees remain liable for one year after distribution or three years after death, whichever is later, to return the improperly distributed property and income or its date of distribution value whichever is less. [3–1004; see 3–104].

g. Fraud and Perjury

The UPC also includes broad protections against fraud, perjury and other wrongdoing. The limitation periods generally applicable to probate and administration do not apply when fraud has been involved. [1–106]. Instead, the perpetrator is liable for that fraud up to two years after its discovery. Except for bona fide purchasers, even innocent persons who have benefitted by the fraud are liable under the same limitation; however, the period of liability for these persons cannot exceed five years from the time of the commission of the fraud. This provision not only applies to acts by the personal representative but also to anyone else who participates in the administration of an estate.

The penalties of perjury are applicable to any deliberate falsification of any document filed with the Court. [1–310]. The mere filing of an application, petition or demand for notice is deemed to include a verification of its veracity. Consequently, the perjury prosecution threat has broad application.

h. Continuing Jurisdiction Over Personal Representatives and Applicants

Once the personal representative accepts appointment, the personal representative submits to the jurisdiction of the Court and remains subject to its jurisdiction until discharged, provided notice of any subsequent proceeding is adequately given. [3–602]. This provision gives interested persons protection from a personal representative who is bent upon being difficult to find or who attempts to leave the state.

In addition, the applicant of any application for informal probate or informal appointment submits personally to the continuing jurisdiction of the Court in any subsequent proceeding brought because of fraud or perjury related to the application. [3–301(b)]. This provision gives interested persons a long arm type basis of jurisdiction over the person who fraudulently or perjuriously files an informal application. Finally, the issuance of the statement of universal succession subjects the universal successors to the personal jurisdiction of the Court in any proceeding instituted relating to the estate or to any liability assumed by the successors. [3–318(a)].

5. Will Contests

Hypothetical: Decedent's will disinherits a natural child, X, and devises the entire estate equally to two other natural children, Y and Z. X is very displeased and will try to break the will. P Bank and Trust Co. is nominated as executor under the will.

As indicated, under the UPC any interested person may file a formal testacy petition to determine whether a decedent left a valid will. [3–401]. This petition must be filed within three years from death or within twelve months of an earlier informal probate, whichever is later. [3–108].

Many of the UPC's provisions concerned with will contests are similar to the non-UPC law in most states. Jury trials may be demanded by any party to the formal testacy proceeding. [1–306]. The burdens of proving lack of testamentary capacity, undue influence, fraud and duress are on the contestants. [3–407]. For ordinary wills, the UPC provides that at least one subscribing witness must testify, if competent and within the state, and that due execution may also be proved by other evidence. [3–406(a)]. The UPC has special presumptions applicable to self-proved wills. [2–504, 3–406(b)].

The primary differences between non-UPC law and the UPC appear in the mechanics of the procedure itself. First, formal testacy proceedings may be initiated by heirs as well as by executors and devisees under a will. [3–401]. In other words, even though no will has been probated or offered for probate, this proceeding may determine that the decedent died intestate. Second, subject to appeal [1–304, 3–414] and to limited reasons for vacation and modification [3–412(1)–(2)], the final order in a formal testacy proceeding is immediately conclusive as to all persons and all issues concerning decedent's testacy and heirs that were or might have been considered. [3–412]. Third, although a subsequently discovered will may give cause for vacating a formal testacy order [3–412(1)], no such will may affect the order after twelve months from its entry. [3–412(3)(iii)]. It may be a much shorter time. [3–412(3)(i)–(ii)]. Significantly, this provision is in direct conflict with the judicial decisions that the probate of a later discovered will is not a contest of a previously probated will and is not affected by expiration of the contest limitation period.

The strategies to follow when the existence or validity of a will is involved depend upon the desires of the interested persons. It would appear that administration and appointment of a personal representative should be initiated immediately. The devisees, for example, can begin by informally probating the will and informally appointing the named executor who has priority for appointment as personal representative. If a formal probate proceeding is not instituted, the will becomes conclusive three years from death. [3–108].

The devisees, however, may not wish to wait this long before their rights as devisees are secure. Another option would be to combine informal probate and informal appointment, followed immediately by a formal probate proceeding. This approach would start the administration processes and would quickly adjudicate the validity of the will thereby shortening the limitation period within which such issues can be litigated. If the question of validity is a serious problem, the formal probate proceeding litigates this issue at an early time thereby increasing the potential for early distribution.

Combining informal appointment and informal probate at the beginning, and then following it by petitioning for formal settlement at the time of petitioning for formal proceedings terminating administration is also a viable approach. This enables the interested parties to adjudicate all of the issues raised by probate and administration in one proceeding. [3–1001]. The principal questions of testacy, heirship, construction, accounting, settlement, and distribution can all be determined in this proceeding. The final order or orders rendered would fully protect the persons involved.

Significantly, the disinherited heir does not have to wait for the will beneficiaries to act. If formal proceedings are not instituted by the devisees, this interested person can force the issue either by immediately initiating formal appointment and formal probate proceedings or by bringing them anytime within the limitation period.

Another procedure available is to enter into a written compromise agreement if agreement can be reached between the opposing persons. [3–1101]. If approved by the court in formal proceedings, it is binding upon all parties including those (1) who signed it, (2) who are unascertained or unlocated, and (3) who are otherwise represented by parties and fiduciaries involved in the estate. [3–1102].

§ 10.02 General Provisions on Probate of Wills and Administration

A. DEVOLUTION OF DECEDENTS' ESTATES AND THE NECESSITY OF PROBATE AND ADMINISTRATION

The UPC provides that a decedent's estate, both real and personal property, devolves to decedent's heirs if intestate or to decedent's devisees if testate subject to the family protections, to the rights of creditors, to the elective share of the surviving spouse, and to administration of the estate. [3–101, 3–901]. The identification of the particular person to whom the property devolves is subject to alterations, however, because of lapse, disclaimer, or any other circumstance affecting devolution of the estate involved, depending upon whether it is a testate or an intestate estate. In addition, the scope of testation and the rights of creditors, devisees or heirs to a decedent's estate are subject to the UPC's restrictions and limitations that are designed to facilitate prompt settlement of the estate. The UPC includes an alternative section for community property estates that substantially applies the same rule to the decedent's half of community property and his separate property. [3–101A].

The rule providing that upon death a decedent's title devolves to heirs or devisees, requires further explanation and qualification. First, an heir or devisee will be treated as having predeceased the decedent if that person does not survive the decedent by 120 hours. [2–104, 2–601]. Second, title to property passing by will cannot be proved unless the will is declared valid by informal or formal probate proceedings. [3–102]. Third, except for the administration of ancillary estates, a personal representative must be appointed either formally or informally, accept appointment and be issued letters of that appointment in order to acquire the powers and to undertake the duties and liabilities of the fiduciary office. [3–103]. Fourth, the decedent's unsecured creditors may enforce their claims only after a personal representative is appointed. [3–104]. Even secured creditors are under the same rule as to any deficiency that they may seek above their security interest. After a personal representative has been appointed and has distributed the estate, however, the decedent's creditors may have rights against the distributees and the personal representative individually. [See 3–1004, 3–1005].

The UPC contains an exception regarding a devisee's title to property designed to eliminate the requirement that the will be declared valid in small estates and to provide a remedy in certain hardship cases. If proceedings are instituted under the affidavit procedure of Section 3–1201, title to property may be proved by the affidavit and therefore, probate of the will is not required. This exception, of course, applies only to the very small, $5,000 or less, estates. [See § 10.03(B)]. The clearly preferred and approved procedure to follow under the UPC is to informally or formally probate a will notwithstanding that administration of the estate may or may not be sought. [See 3–107].

B. TIME LIMITATIONS ON PROBATE AND ADMINISTRATION

One of the key provisions of the UPC concerns its time limitations on probate, testacy, and appointment of personal representatives. [3–108]. With five exceptions, this provision provides that no informal or formal proceeding may be commenced beyond three years after the decedent's death. The first exception concerns the request for the probate of a will in the UPC state where the will has previously been probated in the decedent's domicile. Under such circumstances the foreign will may be probated.

The next two exceptions concern the missing person. Under the second exception, if failure to prove the fact of decedent's death was the cause of a previous dismissal of a proceeding, appropriate proceedings for probate, appointment, or testacy may be maintained at any time thereafter so long as it is proved that decedent's death occurred before the date of the previous proceeding and that petitioner has not unduly delayed initiation of the new proceeding. The third exception provides that for all other persons whose death cannot be substantiated, a proceeding may be instituted within a three year period after the missing person's conservator is able to establish the death of the missing person. Under the second and third exceptions, the date of the commencement of the proper proceeding must be considered as the date of the decedent's death for purposes of other limitations under the UPC that refer to the decedent's date of death.

The fourth and fifth exceptions were added by the 1993 Technical Amendments. The fourth exception permits interested persons to commence informal appointment or formal testacy or appointment proceedings if no proceedings concerning succession or estate administration have occurred within the three year period after decedent's death. Any appointed personal representative under this exception is limited to possession of only the property necessary to confirm title in successors and only expenses of administration may be present against the estate.

The fifth exception permits formal testacy proceeding to commence after three years from decedent's death to establish an instrument necessary to control ownership of property. It is not limited to the situation where the testator's estate was not administered during the three year period. It does not provide for appointment of a personal representative, however. An example of its use includes the exercise of a power of appointment in testator's unprobated will that is not effective until another person's life ends. It may be helpful anytime title that is derived from an unprobated will needs to proved.

It is important to emphasize that these limitations apply only to the UPC's prescribed proceedings dealing with probate, testacy, and appointment. They specifically do not apply to proceedings to construe wills or to determine heirs of an intestate. [3–108]. In addition, inferentially they do not apply to any other proceeding that concerns controversies dealing with an estate currently being administered or with a will that has been properly probated.

The effect of the UPC's limitation periods is very important. First, unsecured creditor claims are barred after a maximum of one year after death. [3–803(a)(1)]. Second, when a decedent dies testate and the will is informally probated, if there are no formal testacy proceedings instituted within the later of three years of death or one year after the date of informal probate, devisees under the probated will are provided conclusive proof of their title regardless whether there is administration of the estate. Their titles are not only conclusive as against decedent's heirs, but also as against decedent's devisees under unprobated wills.

C. JURISDICTION, VENUE AND RE- LATED MATTERS FOR PROBATE AND ADMINISTRATION

1. Jurisdiction Over the Subject Matter

The subject matter jurisdiction of probate courts throughout this country is varied, complicated, and often perplexing. Generally, states confer probate jurisdiction on one of four types of courts: (1) on their chancery court; (2) on a separate probate court that has an equal status with courts of general jurisdiction; (3) on a probate court that definitely is inferior to the court of general jurisdiction; and, (4) on the court of general jurisdiction. [Model Probate Code, 420]. Inevitably, there are variations between those even in the same general category.

In light of this state of confusion, the UPC is extremely flexible and is designed to work within the framework of any state in which it is adopted. [See 3–105, 3–106, § 2.02]. Where the state separates probate jurisdiction from the jurisdiction of its other courts, the UPC gives the probate court exclusive jurisdiction over formal proceedings to determine how the decedents' estates over which it has territorial jurisdiction are to be administered, expended and distributed and concurrent jurisdiction over any actions or proceedings concerning succession or to which estates are made parties through their personal representatives. [3–105]. If the state does not divide subject matter jurisdiction between its probate courts and other courts, the distinction between exclusive and concurrent jurisdiction is inappropriate. [3–106, Comment]. In such a state, the Court is merely given plenary jurisdiction over all formal proceedings concerned with the administration and distribution of decedents' estates.

2. Jurisdiction Over the Person and Notice

When notice is required by the UPC or by rule of court, jurisdiction over the person in proceedings within the exclusive jurisdiction of the Court may be obtained by giving notice to interested persons in conformity with Section 1–401. [3–106; see § 2.03]. In addition, those properly notified are bound by the proceedings even though not all interested persons were appropriately notified. Methods of notice and service for obtaining jurisdiction over the person in proceedings within the concurrent jurisdiction of the Court may be governed by the State's general standard of civil practice and not by Section 1–401. [1 UPC Practice Manual (1977) 31–32]. Whether the general standards of civil practice for notice and jurisdiction or those established in Section 1–401 are applicable to a proceeding under the concurrent jurisdiction of the Court will apparently depend upon whether the proceeding is in personam, quasi in rem, or in rem. The latter two types of jurisdiction would probably be satisfied by Section 1–401. The former type might require the notice and service procedures for ordinary civil cases.

In special circumstances, the UPC provides a continuing type of jurisdiction over certain persons. First, once appointment is accepted, the personal representative submits personally to the jurisdiction of the Court and remains subject to its jurisdiction until discharged. [3–602; see 3–1003, Comment]. The only special requirement to sustain this jurisdiction is that adequate notice of any subsequent proceedings must be given to the personal representative. Adequate notice under this provision means that notice of each proceeding must either be delivered to the personal representative or mailed to the personal representative by ordinary first class mail both to the official address listed with the Court and to any other address known to the petitioner.

Second, the applicant of any verified application for informal probate or informal appointment also submits personally to the continuing jurisdiction of the Court in any subsequent proceeding brought because of fraud or perjury related to the application. [3–301(b)]. Presumably, the applicant must also be given adequate notice of any subsequent proceeding. This provision coincides with the UPC's provisions concerned with frauds perpetrated in connection with proceedings or filings made under this UPC [3–301, Comment; 1–106; see § 2.01(B)(1)], and with its reference to penalties for perjury for deliberate falsification of filings. [1–310; see § 2.01(B)(2)].

Third, the issuance of the statement of universal succession also subjects the universal successors to the personal jurisdiction of the Court in any proceeding instituted relating to the estate or to any liability assumed by the successors. [3–318(a)]. Notice of the proceeding, of course, must be given to the successor.

3. Venue

Venue is based upon certain factual contacts existing within the relevant judicial subdivision. The UPC lists only two contacts for satisfying venue requirements for informal and formal probate and for administration proceedings. The first and the preferred venue is, of course, the county of the decedent's domicile. [3–201(a)(1)]. Because venue based upon the decedent's domicile has great significance under the UPC [see, e.g., 3–203(g), 3–408, 4–201, 4–204], the UPC establishes a rule of priority for determining conflicting claims of domicile. This priority is placed in the first court in which the formal proceeding was commenced. [3–202; Collins v. Truman, 783 P.2d 813 (Ariz.App.1989)]. This court has the exclusive right to determine domicile, and its determination must be accepted in the other courts of the UPC state and in the courts of other UPC states. Significantly, a UPC court without this priority is required to stay or dismiss actions that are duplicative of actions previously filed. These principles should result in beneficially reducing the number of duplicative litigations over domicile. [3–202, Comment].

When the decedent is not domiciled within the state, the second appropriate venue is in any county where the decedent left property. [3–201(a)(2)]. Because the proper location for intangibles is sometimes difficult to determine, the UPC explicitly includes rules for this determination. [3–201(d)]. For debts other than those evidenced by investment or commercial paper or other instruments of title, the location of such an asset is where the debtor resides or if not an individual, where the debtor has its principal office. The situs of the instrument sets the location for commercial paper, investment paper and other instruments. Finally, interests in trust property are located wherever the trustee may be sued.

4. Independent Proceedings and Joinder

As previously discussed, with the exception of supervised administration, proceedings either before the Court or the Registrar are independent of each other in the same estate. [3–107]. On the other hand, if desirable and if undue delay will not occur, informal applications and formal petitions may combine various requests for relief in a single proceeding. Joining claims for relief, however, is optional and unless specifically required by proceedings described in the UPC, no petition is defective merely because it does not cover all matters that could have been contained in a final order. At the election of the interested persons, testacy, and appointment proceedings may be combined into one proceeding. For the purpose of emphasizing the nonsupervisory status of the Court, the UPC explicitly provides that a formal proceeding for appointment of a personal representative concludes when the Court issues its order either making or declining the appointment.

It might be helpful to emphasize again at this point that, whereas under non-UPC law the procedures for probate and for administration are inseparable, the UPC explicitly separates them. Probate, be it informal or formal, is solely concerned with the existence or nonexistence of a will. Administration is concerned with the personal representative, that representative's powers, duties and liabilities to creditors and successors and to those things between each other. Consequently, it may be common to find estates where only probate proceedings or where only administration proceedings are instituted. [See Art. III, General Comment].

The above rules need further clarification in one particular regard. Although each proceeding is independent, there necessarily is an interrelationship between informal proceedings and their corresponding formal proceeding. Consequently, informal probate either cannot be instituted or is superseded by formal testacy proceedings in the same state. [3–401]. The same interrelationship exists between informal appointment of a personal representative and its counterpart a formal appointment proceeding [3–414], and between a proceeding in the nature of informal proceedings for closing an estate and its counterpart a formal closing proceeding. [3–1001, 3–1002]. Although universal succession may be combined with informal probate if there is a will, it is foreclosed or terminated if either informal or formal appointment proceedings are filed. [3–314(b)]. Finally, supervised administration precludes any of the above informal proceedings because it generally requires formal appointment, formal probate, formal proceedings for interim distributions, and a formal closing proceeding.

5. Demand for Notice

Any person who has a financial or property interest in the decedent's estate, including creditors and successors, may file a demand for notice with the Court any time after death. [3–204]. Such an affirmative action provides the demandant with the protection of receiving notice of other filings or orders concerning the estate, including applications for universal succession, informal probate, or informal appointment or any combination thereof. Upon the termination of the demandant's interest in the estate, the requirement of notice under this provision ceases. In addition, if circumstances change, the demandant may waive the requirement in writing. Although failure to provide the necessary notice does not affect the validity of an order of Court or accepted filing, the person failing to provide the necessary notice may be liable to the demandant for any damages caused by the failure to notify.

Upon receipt of such a demand, the clerk is to mail a copy of it to any personal representative who has been appointed in the estate. In addition, petitioner must give notice to the demandant or the designated attorney according to the notice procedure prescribed in Section 1–401. [See § 2.03(A)].

6. Decedent's Causes of Action

The death of a person is a disrupting event to the successors of the estate. Consequently, delay commonly occurs between the time of death and the time when the interested persons have gathered sufficient facts and have instituted necessary procedures to settle the estate. With these disruption and delay factors in mind, the UPC extends any statute of limitations running against a claim belonging to the decedent before death for four months after the date of death. [3–109]. This extension applies, however, only if the statute of limitations ordinarily running against the cause of action was not barred on the date of death. Furthermore, the extension is from the date of death and not from the date of the expiration of the ordinary statute of limitations. [Compare 3–802].

§ 10.03 Procedures for Succession Without Administration

A. THE PASSIVE AND AFFIDAVIT PROCEDURES FOR SMALL ESTATES

The probate laws of every state include special procedures that simplify the administration processes for small estates. [See Scoles, Succession Without Administration, at 379 & n. 32]. Typically, the use of these procedures is dependent on the net value of the estate, e.g., $5,000, and the nature of the assets, e.g., no real property in estate. Although the UPC's ordinary procedures for settling an estate are efficient and uncomplicated without the inclusion of overlapping and potentially conflicting small estate procedures, for purposes of maximum flexibility the UPC includes one implied or inherent procedure and two special procedures for dealing with the small estate. [Art. III, Pt. 12, General Comment].

As previously explained, title to property passes to the heirs or devisee, subject only to administration. [§ 10.02]. If an estate consists solely of cash or other tangible personal property, and if the successors pay off all creditors against the estate, it may be inferred that successors may settle the estate without any administration at all. Because title passes automatically and administration is not a necessity, the appropriate successors may simply divide the property according to their desires. [3–102, 3–901]. Small, solvent, and liquid estates, which require no administration, are very common. [See § 10.03(C)].

When decedent's tangible personal property or instruments evidencing a debt, obligation, stock or chose in action are either owed or possessed by a third person, the nonadministration method for settlement is not satisfactory because the third person may refuse to deliver or to pay. When the net value of the decedent's entire probate estate does not exceed $5,000, however, the UPC provides that if the sole successor to these assets presents an affidavit to the debtor or possessor, the latter must make payment of the indebtedness or deliver the tangible personal property or other instrument of property to the successor. [3–1201]. The only requirement is that the affidavit must state that: (1) the property does not exceed the prescribed monetary amount; (2) thirty days have elapsed since the death of the decedent; (3) no application or petition for appointment is pending or has been granted in any jurisdiction; and (4) the successor claiming the property is entitled to payment or delivery of it. [3–1201(a)]. With a similar affidavit delivered to security transfer agents, title to securities can also be changed to the successor or successors. [3–1201(b)]. Significantly, the availability and effectiveness of this affidavit procedure does not depend upon the decedent dying domiciled in the UPC state where the affidavit is presented. [3–1202, Comment]. Furthermore, a proceeding may be brought by the rightful affiant to force a debtor to pay, possessor to deliver, or the transfer agent to transfer the property. [3–1202].

The effect of the affidavit is to discharge and release the person paying the debt or delivering the property, as if, and to the same extent, the person had dealt with the decedent's personal representative. [3–1202]. This person is further protected by not being required to see to the application of the personal property or to inquire into the truth of the content of the affidavit. The successor who receives payment, delivery or title is, of course, answerable and accountable to any personal representative of the decedent's estate or to any other person having a superior right.

The political popularity of this type of procedure has not waned even in UPC states. The trend has been to increase the threshold amount. For example, Arizona's comparable provision sets the amount at $50,000 [Ariz.Rev.Stat. § 14–3971], and New Mexico's provision is at $30,000. [N.M.Stat.Ann. 1978, 1995, § 45–3–1201].

B. THE SUMMARY PROCEDURE FOR SMALL ESTATES

Another alternative course of action deals with an estate which, after subtracting liens and encumbrances, is valued at less than the total of the relevant family protections, reasonable funeral and administration expenses and reasonable and necessary medical and hospital expenses of the last illness. If the decedent is survived by persons who are entitled to the relevant family protections, the UPC includes a summary administration procedure that substantially shortens the administration process. [3–1203, 3–1204].

Under this procedure, interested persons would begin the administration process in the ordinary manner. This would include having the person with priority file an application for informal appointment of a personal representative. [See § 12.03]. Informal appointment gives the personal representative full status. [See 3–307(b)]. If after inventory and appraisal it appears that the value of the entire estate less liens and encumbrances will not exceed the value of the family protections, costs of administration, reasonable funeral expenses, and the last illness' medical and hospital expenses, the personal representative may immediately disburse and distribute the estate to the appropriate persons without giving the normally mandatory notice to creditors. [3–1203]. Consequently, the personal representative may quickly pay the necessary bills and distribute the remainder to the appropriate persons in satisfaction of their family protection provisions. After the assets are distributed or disbursed, the personal representative can then close the estate by filing a sworn statement that to the best of the representative's knowledge the value of the entire estate did not exceed the family protections and the other deductible expenses, that the disbursement and distribution is complete and that a copy of this statement was sent to all distributees and known unpaid creditors. [3–1204(a)]. The consequences of this filing are: (1) successors and unbarred creditors have only six months from the date of that filing to assert a claim [3–1204(c), 3–1005]; and (2) the appointment terminates one year after the filing if no claims are pending. [3–1204(b)].

With the following two exceptions, the fact that the decedent died testate rather than intestate, would not change the above described procedure. First, the person nominated in the will as executor has priority for appointment. [See § 12.02]. Second, the person who has priority to be personal representative should simultaneously file an application for informal probate and informal appointment. [3–301]. So long as formal proceedings are not instituted within three years of death or one year of informal probate, devises under the will are provided proof of title. [3–108, 3–302]. Informally probating

the will, therefore, protects the devisees' titles and
rights if additional property is discovered.

C. UNIVERSAL SUCCESSION

1. Purpose and Effect of Universal Succession

Succession without administration, or Universal
Succession as it is titled in the UPC was added to
the UPC in 1982 with the addition of eleven sections to Article III, Part 3. [3–312 to–322]. Subsequently, these sections were made part of the
freestanding Uniform Succession Without Administration Act promulgated in 1983. Some commentators complained that the UPC's original version
did not go far enough to provide flexibility to successors. [See, e.g., Martin, Model of Estate Settle-
ment]. They urged the drafters of the UPC to
incorporate provisions that permit successors of a
decedent's estate to succeed to the properties
without the formalities of an administrative process. Although the UPC was extremely flexible
and offered convenient and efficient administration processes, a process without administration
was only accorded in the very small estates.

Universal succession provides the successors with
the opportunity to settle the estate without proceeding through any administrative process. [See Scoles,
Succession Without Administration, at 388–92]. By
following the requirements of these provisions, successors can pay creditor claims, distribute assets to
the proper successors, and prove title to those as-

sets upon subsequent transfer. Except for the requirement of an application to the Registrar, an informal probate if a will is involved, and a written statement of universal succession from the Registrar, no additional proceeding before the court is required. There is no requirement to notify creditors and, thus, there is no special nonclaim limitation. [See § 13.02]. Significantly, there is no monetary limitation on the availability of this procedure.

Although large and solvent estates may be propelled into some form of administrative processes because of tax complexities, estates in which (1) tax issues are not significant, (2) creditors do not exist or whose claims can be settled without difficulty, (3) assets and obligations owing the estate can be collected without administration processes, and (4) successors are easily identifiable and cooperative, are appropriate candidates for use of this extremely efficient and easy method of settling estates. Good candidates for this technique include estates that pass all their assets to a surviving spouse and in which the surviving spouse basically assumes all debts and is able to collect all obligations owing the decedent. This situation covers a large number of potential estates. Another common example is the surviving parent who dies leaving little property except personal effects, contractual obligations that pass upon death, and other assets in some form of joint ownership or living trust. These estates could be easily handled through universal succession.

Under universal succession, the heirs of an intestate or the residuary devisee under a will are per-

mitted at their option to become universal successors to the decedent's estate if they agree to assume
personal liability for the decedent's taxes, debts and
claims against the decedent or the estate and if
they agree to make proper distributions due other
heirs, devisee and other persons entitled to the
property of the decedent. [3–312]. In order to sustain universal succession, all heirs or residuary devisees must join in the application. [3–312, Com-
ment]. Consequently, this process is essentially a
consent procedure available when family members
are in agreement. Minors and incapacitated, protected, or unascertained persons cannot be universal successors under these provisions. The UPC
makes the competent heirs and residuary devisees
who seek universal succession responsible to the
incompetent heirs and legatees. Exclusion of incapacitated and unascertained persons is necessary in
order to permit the competent successors to deal
with the property of the decedent. [3–312, Com-
ment]. Incompetents and unascertained persons
may protect themselves by requesting bond or by
forcing the estate into administration.

2. Contents of Application for Universal Suc-
cession

An application for universal succession must conform to the UPC's specific requirements. [3–313].
This application must be directed to the Registrar,
signed by each applicant and verified to be accurate
and complete to the best of the applicant's knowledge and belief. [3–313(a)]. In addition, it must
contain the following statements:

(1)(a) If filed by the heirs of an intestate, the same information required for informal appointment under Section 3–301(a)(1) and (4)(I) and that the applicants constitute all the competent heirs;

(b) If filed by residuary devisees under a will, all statements required for informal appointment and informal probate under sections 3–301(a)(1) and (2) and that the applicants include all competent residuary devisees plus all heirs if the estate is partially intestate;

(2) Whether letters of administration are outstanding, whether a petition for appointment of a personal representative is pending in any court in the state, and whether the applicants waive their right to seek appointment as a personal representative of the decedent;

(3) The applicants accept responsibility for the estate and assume personal liability for the decedent's and decedent's estate's taxes, debts, claims, and distributions due to appropriate successors; and,

(4) An optional requirement of describing in general terms the assets of the estate. [3–313].

3. Registrar's Responsibilities and Findings in Universal Succession

The UPC grants very little discretion to the Registrar in regards to a universal succession application. The Registrar must grant the application if it finds the following matters satisfied:

(1) A complete application;

(2) All persons necessary have joined and properly verified the statement in the application;

(3) Venue is proper;

(4) Notice necessary under Section 3–204 has been given or waived;

(5) Time limitations for original probate or appointment proceedings have not expired;

(6) If informal probate is requested, the requirements admitting a will to probate have been satisfied; and,

(7) No applicant is a minor, an incapacitated, or a protected person.

[3–314(a)].

A Registrar cannot grant an application unless 120 hours or five days have lapsed since the decedent's death. [3–315]. The Registrar must deny the application under the following two situations:

(1) If letters of administration are outstanding; or

(2) If any creditor, heir or devisee who has an interest in the estate worth in excess of the monetary amount set out by Section 3–605 files an objection to the application.

[3–314(b) & (c)]. The Registrar does not have the same discretionary authority to reject universal succession as it has with regard to informal probate under Section 3–305. [3–314, Comment]. On the other hand, if the universal succession application includes an informal probate application as required in a testate situation, the Registrar's denial of informal probate under Section 3–305 would constitute a reason to deny universal succession.

The UPC takes the firm position that if letters of administration are outstanding or pending, universal succession cannot be approved. In addition, if an interested person, who has not waived a personal right to seek appointment as a personal representative, applies or petitions for appointment, universal succession should be foreclosed or terminated unless the application or petition is denied. [3–314, Comment]. Furthermore, devisees under a will that cannot be probated because the time limit for original probate has expired are precluded from requesting universal succession. [3–314(a)(5)].

When the Registrar grants an application, a written statement must be issued describing the estate as set out in the application, and stating that the applicants are the universal successors to the assets of the estate under Section 3–312, that the applicants have assumed liability for the obligations of the decedent, and that the applicants possess the powers and liabilities of universal successors. [3–315]. This statement is considered the evidence of the universal successors' title to the assets in the estate.

4. Powers and Liabilities of Universal Successors

A statement of universal succession accords the universal successors with full powers of ownership to deal with the assets of the estate in a manner consistent with the responsibilities set out by the UPC. [3–316(1)]. The universal successors are required to proceed expeditiously to settle and distribute the estate. No adjudication from a court is necessary unless invoked by the universal successor to resolve questions concerning the estate. In several regards, universal successors are treated the same as are distributees from a personal representative. [3–316(2); see § 10.03(C)]. They have the same powers as distributees. In addition, third persons, who deal with universal successors, are protected to the same extent as are persons who deal with the successors from personal representatives.

In an attempt to extend the universal succession concept beyond state lines, the UPC provides that universal successors have the same standing and power to collect assets in another state as personal representatives or distributees have in the UPC state. [3–316(3)]. It is not entirely clear whether other states would recognize this standing and power if litigation were to occur in another state not having the UPC's universal succession provisions.

5. Creditors' Rights Under Universal Succession

The universal successors assume all liabilities of the decedent that are not discharged because of the decedent's death and all claims that are incurred after death which would be valid claims against the decedent's estate. [3–317(a)]. This includes, for example, decedent's debts, taxes, and any charges incurred after death for the preservation of the estate. Liability is subject to any defense that would be available to the decedent or the decedent's estate. [3–321]. Generally, the universal successor's personal liability to any creditor, claimant or any other person entitled to the decedent's property may not exceed the proportion of the claim that the universal successor's share bears to the share of all the heirs and residuary devisee. The one notable exception is when the successor's liability arises from fraud, conversion or other wrongful conduct.

Payment to a creditor by a universal successor should be treated the same way as payment by the decedent during his or her lifetime. [3–321, Comment]. In addition, the universal successor is subject to all the rules of fraudulent transfer if insolvency is involved.

Universal succession should not be sought by heirs or devisees unless they are positive that claims and debts against the estate will not exceed the value of the estate's assets. Although liability is prorated among heirs and devises, it is equal in total among all the heirs and devisees to the full amount of the claims. In addition, because notice to creditors is not given, there is no nonclaim limitation cutting off creditor claims. The statute of limitations applicable to creditors under universal succession is limited to the shorter of one year from death provided by Section 2–803(a)(1) or the normal statute of limitations applicable to the claim involved plus the four-month extension provided by Section 3–802(b). [3–317, Comment; see § 13.02].

Because any heir or devisee, who voluntarily joins an application for universal succession, may not subsequently seek appointment of a personal representative and thus administration of the estate, the decision to seek universal succession must be made carefully. Thorough investigation of the value of the estate and its potential liability to creditors, debtors, etc. must be made. Otherwise, liability will not be limited to the value of the decedent's estate. It would seem justified and proper to provide a means by which the heirs and devisees who have sought universal succession may seek the protection of administration if the estate is insolvent due to no fault of their own.

Persons who have claims against the estate may exercise all remedies authorized by law against the universal successors. [3–322]. In addition, where qualified under Section 3–605, claimants may demand bond of the universal successors. Unless the demand for bond is withdrawn, or the claim is satisfied, or the universal successors post bond sufficient to protect the demand, a request for universal succession must be refused or if already granted, the demandant may seek administration of the estate. On the other hand, if the claim is paid, or a sufficient bond is posted, the demandant may not seek administration of the estate. Again, with the authority of the claimant to bring whatever actions permitted by law including suits to enforce a claim and specific performance, the authority to seek bond is more of a threat to force the successors to conform than an actual protective device. Forcing administration would hardly be a punishment to the universal successors if it in fact causes the potential liability to be reduced to the value of the estate less exemptions, homestead and administration costs.

If a personal representative is appointed after universal succession has been granted, the universal successors are personally liable for restitution of any property received from the estate but their liability is limited to that of a distributee. [3–320]. This amount is limited to the value of the property received and its income since receipt or the actual return of the property itself plus income since receipt. [3–320; see 3–909; § 14.02]. Even this liability is limited in time to the later of three years after the decedent's death or one year after receipt of the property. [3–1006]. The latter time limitation does not apply if the property was received as a result of fraud. Notwithstanding, if creditors and claimants become a problem to a universal successor, the best thing that can happen to the successor would be the initiation of administration processes and the appointment of a personal representative.

Issuance of a statement of universal succession confers personal jurisdiction of the court over all persons who join the application for universal succession. [3–318(a)]. This personal jurisdiction, of course, is limited only to proceedings relating to the estate or to any liability assumed by the universal successors.

6. Responsibility Among Universal Successors

After the first priority for creditors, the universal successors have the duty to distribute the estate among the appropriate heirs and devisees. [3–316(1)]. Distributions are subject to the normal rules of abatement and to private agreements. [3–902, 3–912]. Any successor who receives a disproportionate portion of the estate is liable to the other heirs or successors. [3–317(b)]. Attorneys' fees and preservation costs have priority only to the extent they are reasonable and properly incurred.

Heirs and devisees who sought universal succession must send information to the heirs and devisees who did not join in the application. [3–319]. The information must be delivered or sent by ordinary mail to the other heirs and devisees and must include the names and addresses of the universal successors, indicate that it is being sent to persons who may have some interest in the estate, and identify the court in which the application and statement of universal succession have been filed. Failure to provide this information is a breach of duty but is not jurisdictional and does not affect the validity of the universal succession processes or the powers or liabilities of the universal successors. [See § 12.04].

The information need only be sent to those for whom an address is reasonably available and may be sent to others if desired. [3–319]. Either delivery or ordinary first class mail may be used as a means of conveying this information. Other heirs, devisees and persons to whom assets are distributed are subjected to the same powers and liabilities as distributees are from a personal representative. [3–317(d); see 3–908, 3–909, and 3–910; § 14.02]. A fiduciary, such as a testamentary trustee, is liable only to the extent of the assets received by the fiduciary unless it has breached its fiduciary obligations or expressly undertaken a greater liability. [3–317(e)].

CHAPTER 11
APPOINTMENT AND TESTACY PROCEEDINGS

§ 11.01 Informal and Formal Appointment Proceedings

A. INTRODUCTION

Although not required by a substantial number of nations in the world, the administration of a decedent's estate by a so-called personal representative has become an integral part of the law of this country. The primary purpose of administration under the tutelage of a personal representative is to provide protection for the various rights of the decedent's creditors, debtors and successors. [Atkinson, Wills § 103]. This personal representative, consequently, is duty bound to protect the rights among interested persons within these classes and between different members within the same class. At common law, administration was limited to a decedent's personal property, and was not necessary for a decedent's real property because real property was not subject to the decedent's general obligations. Consequently, title descended directly to the decedent's heirs or devisees. In modern times, because real property is subject to the general obligations of the estate, it also is made subject to administration either by the power in the personal representative to sell the real property or by the requirement that the personal representative take possession of it.

With the exceptions previously discussed, the UPC adopts the position that the decedent's personal and real property is subject to administration by a personal representative. [3–101]. It is important to emphasize that except for administration of ancillary estates, a personal representative must be appointed in the UPC state, either formally or informally, and letters of that appointment must be issued in order for the personal representative to acquire the powers and to undertake the duties and liabilities of the fiduciary office. [3–103]. In fact, administration of an estate commences only upon the issuance of letters to a personal representative. The UPC includes two procedures by which a personal representative may obtain the letters. These are informal appointment and formal appointment.

B. INFORMAL APPOINTMENT

1. Initiation and Scope

Informal appointment is initiated merely by an applicant filing an application directed to the Registrar. [3–301]. This proceeding is truly non-adversary. The Registrar is only required to see that the application (1) satisfies the statutory requirements, (2) is not statutorily precluded from informal appointment, and (3) is in Registrar's opinion otherwise satisfactory. The informal appointment proceeding does not provide a procedure for persons, who are adversely affected by the appointment, to object. Concomitantly, applicants can not appeal a denial of informal appointment by the Registrar. All disappointed applicants and objectors must rely on the procedures and protections of formal appointment proceedings. [3–309]. If denial of informal appointment was due to an inadvertent failure to satisfy the application requirements, however, an amended application might be filed with the Registrar for review again.

When a person dies intestate, informal appointment will ordinarily be instituted alone. When a person dies testate, informal appointment may, and ordinarily will, be instituted in combination with informal probate proceedings. [See § 11.01].

2. Contents of Application

The UPC is very precise with respect to the requirements of an application for informal appointment. [3–301]. Substantively identical to an application for informal probate [see § 11.01(B)], the application must contain the following statements and information:

(1) The applicant's interest in the appointment of a personal representative;

(2) Decedent's vital statistics including decedent's name, date of death and age;

(3) The names and addresses of the decedent's spouse, children, heirs and devisees so far as the

applicant knows or with reasonable diligence can ascertain and the ages of any who are minors;

(4) The decedent's domicile and if not within the state, the basis of venue;

(5) The identity and address of any unterminated personal representative of the decedent appointed in the state or elsewhere;

(6) Whether the applicant has received a demand for notice or is aware of any demand for notice in any probate or appointment proceeding concerning the decedent which might have been filed in this state or elsewhere; and

(7) That more than three years have not passed since the decedent's death or if such time has elapsed, circumstances exist authorizing tardy informal appointment under Section 3–108.

[3–301(a)(1)(i)–(vi)].

Because appointment of a personal representative may be requested under a number of different situations, the UPC accordingly has special additional requirements for the application. When the application for informal appointment concerns an intestate estate, the application must also include the following statements:

(1)(a) The applicant is unaware of any unrevoked testamentary instrument that relates to property within the UPC state, or

(b) If such an instrument exists, the reason why it is not being probated;

(2) The priority of the person seeking appointment; and

(3) The name of all other persons who have an equal or prior right to appointment.

[3–301(a)(4)(i)–(ii)].

If the application for informal appointment is for a testate estate, the application must also include the following facts and statements:

(1) A description of the will by date of execution;

(2) The time and place of pending or completed probate proceedings;

(3) Adoption of the statements of the probate application or petition; and

(4) The priority, name and address of the person seeking appointment.

[3–301(a)(3)].

Other similar special requirements are established when the application for appointment concerns the appointment of a successor either due to a change in the estate's testacy status [3–301(a)(5)] or to resignation or termination by death or removal of a prior personal representative. [3–301(a)(6)].

On the application for informal appointment, the applicant must also verify to the best of that person's knowledge and belief that the information provided on the application is accurate and complete. [3–301(a)]. In addition, the applicant must show that notice of the application for informal appointment according to the procedures set out in

Section 1–401 was given to: (1) any person who filed a demand for notice under Section 3–204; and (2) any person who has an equal or prior right to appointment and who has not waived that priority in a writing filed with the Court. [3–308(a)(6), 3–310]. This is the only pre-application notice required, and it may be waived by the party to whom it must be given. [See 3–204].

3. Registrar's Responsibilities and Findings

The UPC requires the Registrar to make certain findings upon receipt of an application for informal appointment, and if they are in the affirmative, to appoint the applicant subject to qualification and acceptance. [3–307(a); see 3–601]. Such an appointment, however, may not be made until 120 hours have elapsed since the decedent's death. In addition, an order of appointment must be delayed thirty days when the decedent is a non-resident unless: (1) the decedent's will subjects decedent's estate to the laws of the UPC state; or (2) the applicant is the domiciliary personal representative. Issuance of letters under informal appointment gives the personal representative full powers and duties pertaining to the office. [3–307(b)]. Although an appointment and the office of personal representative may be terminated, it is not subject to retroactive vacation. [See § 12.04(D)].

The responsibilities of a Registrar, when considering an application for informal appointment, are not judicial in nature but are purely administrative in nature. Consequently, the Registrar makes no judg-

ment as to the veracity of any statement or facts
propounded by the applicant but merely makes a
determination whether the proper and necessary
statements and facts have been recited by the applicant. If the application meets the statutory requirements, the Registrar should appoint and issue letters to the applicant. [3–309]. Notwithstanding
these limitations on the Registrar's discretion, an
application for informal appointment may be denied
by the Registrar for "any other reason." This unreviewable power is given to the Registrar to provide
flexibility and a sort of efficient residual protection
for unnotified interested persons when the Registrar has knowledge or justified suspicions that the
application is inappropriate. [3–309, Comment]. Because of the extensive power given to an informally
appointed personal representative, this discretionary rejection power over informal appointment applications may be exercised liberally.

The UPC provides a check list for the necessary
findings to be made by the Registrar. If the application fails to contain the proper or necessary facts,
information or statements, the application must be
denied. Accordingly, the Registrar must determine
that:

   (1) The application—

     (a) Is complete,

     (b) Is verified by the applicant,

     (c) Is filed by an applicant who appears to be
an interested person as defined in Section 1–
201(24),

(d) Recites facts that indicate venue is proper,

(e) Indicates that the applicant has priority to the appointment (must be strictly enforced); [3–308(a)(1)–(4), and (7)], and presumably,

(f) Is filed within the time limits for original appointment;

(2) Except for appointment of a special administrator, the will, under which applicant seeks appointment, must have been probated; and,

(3) Necessary notices under Section 3–204 have been given.

[3–303(a)(5)–(6)].

The UPC also designates specific situations justifying denial of the application. These include an application which indicates:

(4) A personal representative, who has not resigned according to the requirements of Section 3–610(c) and whose appointment has not been terminated under Section 3–612, has been appointed in this or another county in the UPC state;

(5) An unterminated domiciliary personal representative has been appointed in another state unless the applicant is that domiciliary personal representative;

[3–308(b)], and

(6) An unrevoked testamentary instrument possibly exists that may relate to property subject

to the UPC state's laws and that has not been filed for probate in this Court.

[3–311].

C. FORMAL APPOINTMENT

Formal appointment proceedings are necessary anytime there is a question of the priority or qualification of an applicant for appointment, or of someone who had previously been appointed personal representative in informal proceedings. [3–414]. Formal appointment is also necessary when the Registrar in his or her discretion refuses to approve an informal appointment application. [3–309]. Although such a petition may be made by a person other than the one seeking appointment, the petitioner would have to be an interested person as defined in Section 1–201(24). The format of the petition will be the same as that required for an application for informal probate or for informal appointment.   [3–301(a)(1);   see   §§ 11.02(B), 11.03(B)]. If formal appointment is combined with formal testacy proceedings, the formal appointment petition must also satisfy the petition for formal testacy. [3–402; see § 11.02(B)].

The filing of a formal appointment petition has certain important consequences. First, after receipt of notice of the petition, any previously appointed personal representative must refrain from exercising any power of administration except such as is necessary to preserve the estate or such as the court otherwise orders. Second, when the filing of the formal appointment petition precedes the informal appointment of a personal representative, the filing has the effect of staying any pending informal appointment proceedings and precluding any such proceedings from commencing thereafter.

Notice must be given to all interested persons including, more specifically, all persons potentially interested in the administration of the estate as successors, any previously appointed personal representative and any person having or claiming priority for appointment. The Court, presumably after a hearing, is required to determine who is entitled to be appointed as personal representative. The priority procedures of Section 3–203 are to be used by the Court. [See § 12.02]. Upon making the selection, the Court must make the proper appointment and terminate any prior appointment if found to be improper. Termination of such an appointment must be made according to the procedures for removal under Section 3–611. [3–414(b); see § 12.09].

It is important to emphasize that although supervised administration may include a formal appointment proceeding, a formal appointment proceeding may be separate and apart from supervised administration. [3–414, Comment].

§ 11.02 Informal Probate and Formal Testacy Proceedings

A. INFORMAL PROBATE

1. Initiation and Scope

When a decedent dies with a will, the UPC ordinarily requires that that will must be probated in order to effectively pass title to the devisees. One method by which this will may become effective is by informal probate. As with informal appointment, informal probate is initiated merely by an applicant filing an application directed to the Registrar. This proceeding is also truly nonadversary. The Registrar is only required to see that the application (1) satisfies the statutory requirements, (2) is not statutorily precluded from informal probate, and (3) is of the opinion it is otherwise satisfactory. The informal probate proceeding does not provide a procedure for persons, who are adversely affected by the probate of the will, to object. Concomitantly, applicants cannot appeal a denial of informal probate by the Registrar. All disappointed applicants and objectors must rely on the procedures and protections of formal testacy. [3–305]. If denial of informal probate was due to an inadvertent failure to satisfy the application requirements, however, an amended application might be filed with the Registrar for review again.

Informal probate may, and usually will be, instituted in combination with informal appointment proceedings. [§ 11.02(A)]. Occasionally, it may even be combined with formal appointment proceedings. [3–107]. Informal probate may also be instituted separately, or even as the sole act taken in a particular estate. This latter type of action would be particularly applicable where devisees are not immediately aware of any property of the decedent but wish to establish their title thereto if any is subsequently discovered. In this situation, informal probate offers such devisees a convenient, efficient and inexpensive method for protecting their interests. Although nonadjudicative, the granting of informal probate becomes conclusive the later of either three years after death or one year after informal probate [3–108], unless it is superseded by formal proceedings. [3–302].

2. Contents of Application

The UPC is very precise with respect to the requirements of an application for informal probate. [3–301]. Substantively identical to an application for informal appointment [see § 11.02(B)], the application must contain the following statements and information:

(1) The applicant's interest in probating the will;

(2) Decedent's vital statistics including decedent's name, date of death and age;

(3) The names and addresses of the decedent's spouse, children, heirs and devisees so far as the applicant knows or with reasonable diligence can ascertain and the ages of any who are minors;

(4) The decedent's domicile and if not within the state, the basis of venue;

(5) The identity and address of any unterminated personal representative of the decedent appointed in the state or elsewhere;

(6) Whether the applicant has received a demand for notice or is aware of any demand for notice in any probate or appointment proceeding concerning the decedent filed in this state or elsewhere; and,

(7) That more than three years have not passed since the decedent's death or if such time has elapsed, circumstances exist authorizing tardy informal probate under Section 3–108.

[3–301(a)(1)(i)–(vi)].

In addition, an informal probate application must also include the following statements:

(8) The application includes either the original of the decedent's last will or an authenticated copy of such a will probated in another jurisdiction or that the original is in the possession of the Court;

(9) To the best of the applicant's knowledge, the applicant believes the will to have been validly executed;

(10) The applicant is unaware of any instrument revoking the will after a reasonably diligent search; and

(11) The applicant believes the offered instrument to be the decedent's last will.

[3–301(a)(2)(i)–(iii)].

On the application for informal probate, the applicant also must verify that to the best of the applicant's knowledge and belief the information provided on the application is accurate and complete. [3–301(a)]. In addition, the applicant must show that notice of the application for informal probate according to the procedures set out in Section 1–401 was given: (1) to any person who filed a demand for notice under Section 3–204 and (2) to any unterminated personal representative of the decedent. [3–306[*]]. This is the only pre-application notice required. Presumably, even it may be waived by the party to whom it must be given. [See 3–204].

3.   Registrar's Responsibilities and Findings

The UPC requires the Registrar to make certain findings upon receipt of an application for informal probate, and if they are in the affirmative, to issue a written statement of informal probate. [3–302; see § 2.02(B)]. Such a statement, however, may not be made until 120 hours have elapsed since the decedent's death. Issuance of the written statement of informal probate is in essence the approval of informal probate and is conclusive as to all persons until an order in a formal testacy proceeding supersedes it. In addition, an informal probate is not void merely because there is a defect in the application or in the procedure that led to its recognition.

When a Registrar considers an application for informal probate, his or her responsibilities are not judicial in nature but are purely administrative in nature. Consequently, the Registrar is not to make any judgment as to the veracity of any statement or facts propounded by the applicant. The Registrar merely makes a determination whether the proper and necessary statements and facts have been stated by the applicant. If the application meets the statutory requirements, the Registrar should issue a statement of informal probate. [3–305]. Notwithstanding these limitations on the Registrar's discretion, an application for informal probate may be denied by the Registrar for "any other reason." This unreviewable power is given to the Registrar to provide flexibility and a sort of residual protection for unnotified interested persons when the Registrar has knowledge or justified suspicions that the application is inappropriate. This power must be exercised very cautiously by the Registrar; otherwise, the usefulness of informal probate procedures, will be greatly diminished. [3–305, Comment].

The UPC provides a check list for the necessary findings to be made by the Registrar. If the application fails to contain the proper or necessary facts, information or statements, the application must be denied. Accordingly, the Registrar must determine that:

    (1) The application—

        (a) Is complete,

        (b) Is verified by the applicant,

(c) Is filed by an applicant who appears to be an interested person as defined in Section 1–201(24),

(d) Recites facts that indicate venue is proper,

(e) Is filed within the time limits for original probate,

[3–303(a)(1)–(4), and (7)],

(f) relates either to (I) a single will, (ii) a will and one or more of its codicils, or (iii) one or more of a known series of independent testamentary instruments the latest of which expressly revoke the earlier;

[3–304],

(2) The original or authenticated copy of a duly executed and apparently unrelated will is in the Registrar's possession; and,

(3) Necessary notices under Section 3–204 have been given.

[3–303(a)(5)–(6)].

The UPC also designates specific situations justifying denial of the application. These include an application that indicates:

(4) A personal representative has been appointed in another county in the UPC state; and

(5) This or another of decedent's wills has been the subject of a previous probate order in the UPC state.

[3–303(b)]. This last restriction does not apply to a will previously probated in another jurisdiction for

which probate is being requested in the UPC jurisdiction as an ancillary probate. [3–303(d)].

The UPC gives the Registrar three separate
methods by which to review the execution requirement of the will offered for informal probate. Under
these three tests, the will is considered proper and
informally probatable if: (1) it contains an attestation clause showing that the execution requirements of Sections 2–502 or 2–506 have been met; or
(2) the application includes a sworn statement or
affidavit by any person, whether a witness or not,
having knowledge of the circumstances surrounding
the wills execution; or (3) the Registrar believes the
will appears to have been properly executed. [3–
303(c)]. Clearly self-proved wills executed according
to 2–504 and international wills executed in compliance with Sections 2–1003 through –1005 satisfy
one or more of these requirements. Section 3–303(c)
includes a reference to wills executed according to
section 2–503. Before the 1990 changes to the UPC,
this section referred to the holographic will execution process. Holographic wills are now included in
Section 2–502 and Section 2–503 concerns the
Court's dispensing power over execution requirements. Wills offered for probate under Section 2–
503 should only be probatable under formal testacy
proceedings because they will require a Court determination of validity.

4. Special Notice Requirement

Because the pre-application notice for informal
probate was considered by many to be inadequate if

informal appointment was not also granted, the 1975 Technical Amendments inserted an optional provision. This provision provides that when no personal representative is appointed who would otherwise be required to give written information under Section 3–705, the applicant for informal probate must give written information of the probate to the heirs and the devisees. This writing must include the name and address of the applicant, the name and location of the court granting the informal probate and the date of probate. [3–306[(b)]]. It may either be delivered or sent by ordinary mail to each of the heirs and devisees whose addresses are reasonably available to the applicant. Failure to give this information does not affect the validity of the probate but constitutes merely a breach of duty to the heirs and devisees by the applicant.

B.   FORMAL TESTACY

1.   Purpose and Effect

In contrast to informal probate, formal testacy proceedings are characterizable as litigation. They are initiated only with a petition filed by an interested person, require pre-hearing notice of a hearing and terminate in a final order by the Court. [3–401]. The general purpose for such a proceeding is the determination of a decedent's testacy status. This may mean a finding that the decedent died with a valid will or wills or that the decedent died intestate.

The initiation of formal testacy proceedings may be desirable under several circumstances. The first, and most obvious, is the desire to obtain an order of Court probating a will. Second, such a proceeding may be used to set aside an informal probate. Third, it may be used to prevent a pending application from obtaining informal probate. And fourth, petitioners may seek an order of Court finding the decedent died intestate. Any one of the above specific purposes will also include a determination of heirship. Unless there is a thirty day waiting period because the decedent was a non-resident, it will be rare when formal proceedings are used to prevent informal probate, because the Registrar may ordinarily act immediately upon such an application.

The formal testacy petition may be the initial proceedings instituted concerning the testacy status of the decedent or it may follow informal probate of the same or other conflicting wills. At the petitioner's discretion, the petition may include a request for either informal or formal appointment. Once instituted, however, the pendency of a formal testacy proceeding prohibits the Registrar from acting upon any application for informal probate or for informal appointment.

Depending on the contents of the petition, a formal testacy proceeding has varying effects on a previous informal appointment. If the petition requests confirmation of the previous informal appointment, the appointed personal representative may exercise the powers and responsibilities of the office as if no petition had been filed. If confirmation is not requested and after receipt of notice of the initiation of the proceeding, a petition for formal testacy requires that the previously appointed personal representative refrain from exercising the power to make further distribution of the estate pending the outcome of the proceeding. If the petitioner requests the appointment of a different person to serve as personal representative, the petition may request a restraining order on the acting personal representative that prohibits the latter from exercising any of a normal personal representative's powers and that may request the appointment of a special administrator. When the latter request is absent or denied, the only effect upon a previously appointed personal representative caused by a petition of formal testacy is that the personal representative may not make further distributions until the proceeding is concluded.

2.   Contents of Petition

The UPC is very specific as to the content of a formal testacy petition. Two distinct types of petitions are recognized. One deals with the request for the probate of the will. The other deals with a request for an adjudication of intestacy. Both types must be directed to the Court, request an order of court after notice and hearing and satisfy the other requirements for the particular type of petition.

The petition for formal probate of a will must contain the following requests, information and statements:

(1) A request for an order probating the particular instrument offered in the petition;

(2) A request for determination of heirs;

(3) With the exception that it need not state that the original or authenticated copy of decedent's last will accompanies the application or is in the possession of the Court, it must contain the statement and information required in an application for informal probate; [see § 11.03(A)(2)].

(4) It must state whether the original of decedent's last will accompanies the petition or is in the possession of the Court; and

(5) If (4) is stated in the negative, it must also state the contents of the will and indicate that it is lost, destroyed, or otherwise unavailable.

[3–402(a)].

A petition for the adjudication of intestacy must include the following requests, statements and information:

(1) A request for a judicial finding and order that decedent died leaving no valid will;

(2) A determination of heirs;

(3) The same information and statements required in every application for informal probate or for informal appointment under Section 3–301(a)(1), and (4) [see § 11.02(B)(2)].

(4)(a) A statement that the applicant is unaware of any unrevoked testamentary instrument that relates to property within the UPC state, or

(b) If such an instrument exists, why it is not probated; and

(5) An indication whether supervised administration is requested.

[3–402(b)]. If an appointment of a personal representative is also requested, the petition must also contain the following statements:

(6) The priority of the person seeking appointment; and

(7) The name of all other persons who have an equal or prior right to appointment.

[See 3–301(a)(4)(ii)].

3. Pre–Hearing Notice

Being a formal proceeding, notice of a fixed time and place of hearing is essential. The manner of notice is that prescribed by Section 1–401. [See § 2.03(A)]. The UPC departs, however, from the normal requirement of giving notice to "interested persons" and specifically enumerates the persons to whom notice must be given. Accordingly, notice must be given to:

(1) Persons who have filed a demand for notice under Section 3–204;

(2) The surviving spouse, children and other heirs;

(3) The devisees and executors of any will that has been probated or offered for informal or formal probate in the UPC state or that the petition-

er knows has been probated or offered for informal or formal probate elsewhere; and

(4) Any unterminated personal representative appointed for the decedent.

[3–403(a)]. In addition, notice by publication must be given to persons who have an interest in the matters being litigated and who are either unknown or whose addresses are unknown. At the discretion of the petitioner, notice may also be given to other persons such as devisees and executors under known wills that have not been probated or offered for probate. [3–403, Comment].

4. Court Responsibilities and Content of Order

The Court's responsibilities are explicitly set out in the UPC. Before an order of formal probate can be issued, the Court must be satisfied that all of the following matters have been completed or proved:

(1) The time required for any notice has expired;

(2) Proof of notice was made;

(3) Any necessary hearing was held;

(4) Proof that decedent is dead;

(5) Venue is proper;

(6) The proceeding was commenced within the time limitations prescribed by Section 3–108.

[3–409]. In the order of formal testacy, the Court must determine the decedent's domicile, heirs and state of testacy.

If the petition requests the probate of a will and the will is found to be valid and unrevoked, the Court must order the will formally probated. When a formal testacy proceeding concerns the validity of two or more instruments that do not expressly or impliedly revoke one or the other, the Court may order the probate of more than one of these instruments. Although such an order must indicate what provisions control with respect to the nomination of an executor, it may but need not indicate how each provision of one instrument interrelates or is reconciled with each provision of the other instruments. [3–410]. If the Court does not reconcile the various instruments, subsequent proceedings for interpretation and construction may be necessary. [3–410, Comment]. A formal and final order that a will is formally probated, however, precludes any subsequent petition concerning the probate of any other instrument of the decedent except when a petition to vacate or modify is timely filed under Section 3–412. Even though one or more instruments may be ordered to formal probate, the decedent's estate may still be partially intestate. If this is the case, the Court is required to enter an order to that effect. [3–411].

5. The Uncontested Case

When a petition for formal testacy is uncontested, the Court is given discretion as to the procedure to follow to establish the allegations made in the petition. If the Court is satisfied that the prerequisites for an order of formal testacy have been met, it may make the appropriate order of probate or of intestacy merely on the strength of the pleadings. [3–405]. On the other hand, the Court may conduct an open hearing and require proof by the petitioner of the matters necessary to support the order requested. If the petition concerns a request to probate a will, an affidavit or the testimony of one of the attesting witnesses to the instrument is sufficient to establish due execution. If neither the affidavit nor the testimony of such person is available, other evidence or affidavit may be used to prove the due execution of the will. A special rule is set for a will that has been previously probated in another state in which at death decedent was domiciled. Such a will must be accepted as determinative by the Court if the following requirements are met: (1) there is a final order of the court of the state determining testacy, the validity or construction of a will; (2) notice to and an opportunity to contest the will was provided to all interested persons; and (3) the order includes or is based upon a finding that the decedent at death was domiciled in the rendition state. [3–408]. If the place where the foreign will has become effective does not provide for probate, the Court may accept as proof for probate a duly authenticated certificate from the place's legal custodian reciting that the copy of the will is a true copy. [3–409].

6. The Contested Case

The proof requirements for due execution in the contested case are more detailed. [3–406]. When the will offered for probate is neither notarized nor self-

proved, it is necessary in a contested case to introduce the testimony of at least one of the attesting
witnesses if that witness is within the state and is
competent and able to testify. [3–406(3)]. If such
testimony is not available, proof of due execution of
an attested or unattested will may be accomplished
by other relevant evidence including, for example,
affidavits of attesting witnesses and affidavits and
testimony of other persons having knowledge of the
execution. Attestation clauses signed by attesting
witnesses raise a rebuttable presumption of what
they state occurred. If a will is notarized, there is a
rebuttable presumption that the will satisfies the
execution requires. [3–403(2)]. The notarized will
was added in 2008 as a valid method of execution.
[See 2–502(a)(3)(B)].

When a self-proved will is involved, the signature
requirement for execution is conclusively presumed.
[3–406(1)]. In addition, all other requirements for
execution are presumed subject to rebuttal. This
means that except where proof of fraud or forgery
affecting the acknowledgment or affidavit on the
self-proved will is made by the contestants, support-
ive acknowledgment and affidavits need not be attached to the petition and the testimony of a witness is not necessary.

The UPC is very explicit with regard to the
burden of proof. Furthermore, when the UPC sets
the burden of proof on one of the parties, it means
that this party has the ultimate burden of persua-
sion as to the matter involved. The burden of establishing prima facie proof of death and venue falls on

the initiating petitioner. Proponents of a will have the same burden of proof for due execution and petitioners seeking to establish intestacy have the burden of proof of heirship. [3–407]. The order in which these issues must be handled is also set out in the UPC. If two wills have been petitioned for probate and one revokes the other, the petitioners for the revoking instrument must prove their will is entitled to probate first. When a will is opposed by a petition for a declaration of intestacy, the proponents of the will must establish that it is entitled to probate first. The burdens of proving lack of testamentary capacity, undue influence, fraud and duress are always on the contestants to the will. Evidentiary presumptions used to satisfy the burdens of proof remain unchanged by the UPC. [Youngs v. Hitz, 458 N.W.2d 221 (Neb.1990)].

Any interested person, who desires to contest the probate of a will, must state in pleadings the objections that the person has to the probate of the will. [3–404]. Presumably, if the initial petition for formal testacy is a request for a declaration of intestacy and subsequently the proponents petition for the probate of a will, the initiating petitioner should file a supplemental pleading stating the objections to the proponent's petition for probate. Sometimes the contestant's objection will be obvious such as when the contestant files a petition to probate a will that specifically revokes the initiating petitioner's will. [3–404, Comment]. If the heirs are not the initiating petitioners and wish to contest a will they, of course, will have to file a separate pleading which satisfies this rule.

It is important to note that unless a petition for formal testacy requests the probate or the determination of probate for several instruments, a request for the probate of each instrument must be made in a separate petition which includes the necessary requests, information and statements. The notice requirements for formal testacies must also be satisfied for each petition.

7. Effect of Order

The scope of finality of a formal testacy order is very broad under the UPC. [3–412]. Such an order is final as to all persons with respect to all issues concerning the decedent's estate that the Court actually considered or might have considered as a part of its decision making process relevant to the question whether the decedent left a valid will or to the determination of heirs or to both. Second, such an order is only subject to appeal and to vacation for a limited period of time and for limited reasons. The time and reasons concerned with an appeal are the same as in any civil case in the UPC state and would depend upon the rules of civil procedure in that jurisdiction. [1–304, 1–308].

The reasons and timing for a request for vacating an order in formal testacy are both limited in situation and in time. Proponents of a later discovered will may petition for modification or vacation of such an order and for probate of a will of the decedent when the proponents show they were unaware of the earlier proceeding and were given no notice except by publication. [3–412(1)]. Similarly, heirs may petition for a redetermination of heirship when they show that one or more persons were omitted from the determination and that these persons were: (1) unaware of their relationship to the decedent; (2) unaware of decedent's death; or (3) given no notice of the formal testacy proceeding except by publication. [3–412(2)].

Either of the above vacating petitions must be filed before the earliest of the following time limitations has expired:

(1) The time of entry of any order obtained by an appointed personal representative for the estate which approves final distribution of the estate;

(2) Six months after an appointed personal representative for the estate has filed a closing statement;

(3) No later than the time set for the possible initiation of an original proceeding to probate a will of the decedent; or

(4) Twelve months after the entry of the formal testacy order.

[3–412(3)]. If these requirements and limitations are met, the Court is empowered to order the appropriate modification or vacation as relevant under the circumstances. [3–412(4)].

In addition to the above vacation requirements, the Court, for good cause shown, may modify or vacate an order in formal testacy within the time for appeal. [3–413]. It has been held that this procedure is analogous to a motion to vacate a default judgment and that cases, which concern such motions, are relevant authority. [Craig v. Rider, 651 P.2d 397 (Colo.1982)]. "Good cause shown" is defined to require proof of at least excusable neglect. [Id.]. It has also been said to require a logical reason or legal ground, based on fact or law. [DeVries v. Rix, 279 N.W.2d 89 (Neb.1979)].

8. Formal Testacy and the Missing Person

The UPC attempts to protect the missing person from improper use of formal testacy proceedings. First, if the petition or other information indicates that the alleged decedent's death is in doubt, petitioners must send a copy of the notice of the hearing on the formal testacy petition by registered mail to the alleged decedent's last known address. [3–403(b)]. Any interested person may also cause such notice to be required upon the filing of a written demand with the Court. When such a notice to the decedent is necessary, the Court is also required to direct the petitioner to make and to report back the results of a reasonably diligent search for the decedent. This search may take the form of any or all of the following approaches:

(1) A general public periodical notice or advertisement requesting information concerning the decedent and decedent's whereabouts;

(2) Notification of the alleged decedent's disappearance to enforcement officials and public welfare agencies in appropriate locales; or

(3) Employment of an investigator to make a search for the alleged decedent.

The cost of any such directed search must be borne by the petitioner when there is to be no administration or by the alleged decedent's estate when there is administration.

The second level of protection occurs at the time when the Court makes its findings. If the Court is not satisfied that petitioners have shown the alleged decedent to be dead, the petition must be dismissed or ordered to be appropriately amended. [3–409]. An appropriate amendment would include a request for a proceeding to protect the estate of a missing person. [3–409, Comment].

Finally, protection is provided with regard to the effect of a final order of testacy. Ordinarily, when notice of the hearing of the petition has been given and the required search has been made as required above, the finding of fact of death is made conclusive on the alleged decedent. This finality is not complete, however, as to the decedent's assets in certain circumstances. [3–412(5)]. If the alleged decedent proves to be alive and not dead as assumed, and notwithstanding any notice sent or search made, the alleged decedent may recover the estate assets possessed by the personal representative. This person may also recover any of the estate or its proceeds that distributees presently possess or their value if equitable in view of all the circumstances. Naturally, the alleged decedent would also have all of the remedies available by reason of fraud or intentional wrongdoing. The finality of a finding of fact of death as far as the alleged decedent is concerned, therefore, is only generally applicable for the protection of creditors of the estate and the good faith actions on the part of the personal representative. [Model Probate Code, at 105].

§ 11.03   Supervised Administration

Supervised administration is the most formalistic proceeding included in the UPC for the administration of a decedent's estate. It inserts the power and supervision of the Court more directly and more often into the settlement of a decedent's estate. [3–501]. The general philosophy under the UPC that self-help is better than continual court involvement is somewhat abandoned under a supervised administration proceeding. The supervised personal representative is not only responsible to the interested parties but also to the Court and is subject to the directions of the Court made either on its own motion or on the motion of any interested persons. Furthermore, the power of the Court to supervise extends from the granting of a petition for supervised administration until the entry of a final distribution and termination order.

Although under the control of the Court and subject to certain other restrictions, a personal representative under supervised administration generally has the same duties and powers as any counterpart who is not supervised. Consequently, supervised administration does not so much subject the personal representative to continuing supervision as much as it subjects the personal representative to potential supervision.

Under the UPC, supervised administration is characterized both as an in rem proceeding and as a single proceeding which extends throughout the entire course of administration. [3–501]. The in rem characterization means that it is not necessary to personally serve interested persons in order for the Court to obtain jurisdiction. [Model Probate Code, 91–92]. In addition, the single proceeding concept means that subsequent notices are not necessary throughout the administration. The elimination of personal service and subsequent notices does not apply when the adverse interests of third persons concerning the estate are being litigated. In addition, distribution and closing orders must include the notices required under Section 3–1001. [3–505]. The notice requirements for interim orders including those directing partial distributions or granting other relief are left up to the Court to determine and set. [See, 1 UPC Practice Manual, at 265].

A supervised administration petition may be filed by any interested person or by an appointed personal representative. [3–502]. If the petition constitutes the initial proceeding in the estate, it must be commenced within three years of death. [3–108]. If filed after informal proceedings have been commenced, however, it may be filed anytime before final settlement and distribution. [3–502]. It is permissible to join a petition for supervised administration with a petition for formal testacy and formal appointment proceedings. Actually, if such formal proceedings have not been adjudicated, the supervised administration petition must request that these issues be litigated. When this is the case, the proceeding must satisfy the requirements of formal testacy and formal appointment proceedings including the content of the petition, notice and hearing requirements and other applicable procedures. [See 3–402, 3–403, 3–414; §§ 11.01(C), 11.03(B)]. Even if formal proceedings have been adjudicated and are no longer necessary, notice must be given to interested persons presumably in the manner provided in Section 1–401. [3–502]. Presumably, a supervised administration proceeding cannot include a formal testacy or formal appointment proceeding if the time limitation for instituting either or both of the latter proceedings has expired. [3–108; see § 10.02(B)].

The UPC gives the Court guidelines in determining whether to grant or to deny a petition for supervised administration. [3–502]. In applying these guidelines, however, the Court is given a great amount of discretion. First, in the ordinary case where the decedent's will states nothing with regard to supervised administration, the Court must order supervised administration only if it finds it "necessary under the circumstances." Second, where the decedent's will expressly directs unsupervised administration, the Court must not order supervised administration unless it finds that persons interested in the estate need its protection. Finally although the Court must ordinarily order supervised administration when the decedent's will directs that the estate proceed in that manner, it is even given discretion to deny such a supervised administration petition if it finds that since the execution of the will circumstances bearing on the need for it have changed and its necessity no longer exists. Significantly, even when a petition for supervised administration is denied, the Court must conduct formal testacy and formal appointment proceedings if such proceedings have not previously been adjudicated or barred.

Because of the direct relationship between the two proceedings, the effect of supervised administration on other proceedings is substantially the same as the effect of a formal testacy proceeding on other proceedings. [3–503; see § 11.03(B)]. First, the pendency of a supervised administration proceeding stays all pending or subsequently filed applications. [3–503(a)]. Second, unless the time limitation has expired, any informally probated will must proceed through a formal testacy proceeding. [3–503(b)]. Finally, an appointed personal representative upon receipt of notice the filing of a supervised administration petition must refrain from exercising the power of distribution of the estate. [3–503(c)]. There is no other effect on a personal representative's powers and duties, however, unless the Court so restricts by direction following a full hearing on petition. [3–607].

The restriction on the power of a personal representative to distribute continues throughout the supervised administration. [3–504]. Consequently, distributions cannot be made without an interim or final order approving the exercise of the distribution power. If a "distribution" is concomitant with "distributee," it means that no distribution of any of the decedent's property may be made other than to a creditor or purchaser. [See 1–201(13)]. This would apparently be a prohibition on payment of even the family protections. [1 UPC Practice Manual, at 262–64].

During the pendency of a supervised administration petition an appointed personal representative is not otherwise restricted in the exercise of the office's powers and duties. If any other restriction on the power of a personal representative is desired, it becomes effective against third parties dealing in good faith with the personal representative only upon petition, order of court and endorsement of the restriction on the personal representative's letters of appointment. [3–504]. This third party effect of an endorsement of a restriction on the letters of appointment is probably the most typical reason for supervised administration.

Termination of a supervised administration proceeding will be made according to the rules, notices and procedures established for formal closing proceeding under Section 3–1001. [3–505; see § 14.04(C)]. On application of the personal representative and at any time during the pendency of a supervised administration proceeding, the Court may issue interim orders which approve or direct partial distribution or which grant other relief. The only explicitly provided pre-notice requirement in the UPC for such interim orders would be the notice to those persons who demanded notice under Section 3–204. Any other notice requirements for such orders must be developed and set by the Court. [1 UPC Practice Manual, at 265].

CHAPTER 12
THE PERSONAL REPRESENTATIVE

§ 12.01 Introduction to the Personal Representative

If a decedent's estate is made subject to some form of an official administration, it is essential that a personal representative or multiple personal representatives be appointed. [Atkinson, Wills § 103]. The office of personal representative, therefore, has significant responsibilities and status in the administration of a decedent's estate. Generally and briefly, these responsibilities include collection of assets, settling of claims, and final distribution of the estate. Similarly, the attributes of a personal representative's status include recognition as the estate's legal entity, as officer of the court, as a fiduciary and as title holder of the decedent's personal property. [Atkinson, Wills § 104]. The office, itself, is considered of such extreme importance that the selection of a specific person or entity to serve as personal representative is one of the most important reasons for having a will.

Personal representatives have generally been referred to by specific names depending upon the condition of the estate. [Atkinson, Wills § 104]. A personal representative named in the will is called

409

an "executor." If appointed under an intestate estate, the name is "administrator." Several Latin
phrases are added after the term "administrator"
to describe the personal representative who is appointed under other circumstances. An administrator cum testamento annexo (c.t.a.) is a personal
representative appointed when an executor fails to
qualify or is not named in the will. An administrator de bonis non (d.b.n.) is the personal representative who succeeds an administrator. An administrator c.t.a. d.b.n. is the successor to the executor or an
administrator c.t.a.

The primary importance of these titles concerns
questions of the personal representative's qualification and authority. Many present laws make
distinctions between whether the personal representative is an executor or an administrator. For
example, persons named in the will as executor
may have priority of appointment, less grounds
for disqualification, bond waived and additional
powers during administration. Except for priority
of appointment, the UPC has abolished these distinctions between a person named in a will as executor and one appointed as an administrator. In
fact even the titles have been abolished because
all such persons are referred to merely as the
"personal representative." [1–201(36)]. This term
is used in the UPC to refer to all persons who
perform substantially the same function including
executors, administrators, successor personal representatives and even special administrators.

§ 12.02   Priority and Disqualification for Appointment

Every state has legislation dealing with the qualification and disqualification of executors and administrators. [Atkinson, Wills §§ 108, 109]. Qualification is typically phrased in the form of a priority list and disqualification is phrased with respect to a candidate's particular prohibited status. The UPC includes a provision dealing with both issues. [3–203].

CHART 12–1

PRIORITY ORDER FOR APPOINTMENT OF A DOMICILIARY
PERSONAL REPRESENTATIVE

Priority Rank	Description of Candidates
1	Persons named in will (including named successors and nominated selectees under a power in the will).
2	Surviving spouse who is a devisee (or the surviving spouse's selectee).
3	Other devisees (or the devisees' selectee).
4	Surviving spouse (or the surviving spouse's selectee).
5	Other heirs (or the heirs' selectee).
6	Any creditor forty-five days after death.

Chart 12–1 describes the priorities set for appointment in both informal and formal proceedings except for the appointment of a special administrator. [3–203(a), and (h)].

Several features of Chart 12–1 deserve additional explanation. The first three priorities concern the estate of a decedent who died testate. The next two priorities concern the decedent who died intestate. Under the last priority, creditors have priority rights only when there are no persons fitting the priority categories or persons with priorities refuse or do not apply for appointment.

Many non-UPC states are also very specific as to when a person is disqualified or incompetent to serve either as an administrator or as an executor or both. [Atkinson, Wills §§ 108, 110]. Persons who might be disqualified or barred from appointment, for example, include minors, persons convicted of infamous crimes, or persons adjudged incompetent because of drunkenness, improvidence, mental incapacity or integrity. The additional status of being a non-resident commonly disqualifies a person from becoming an administrator unless a resident agent for service of process is appointed.

The UPC eliminates in its disqualification provision any distinction between administrators and executors and most of the specificity. It simply provides that persons under the age of twenty-one and those found unsuitable by a Court in a formal proceeding are disqualified. [3–203(f)]. The UPC's suggested age requirement is a legislative option and the term "unsuitable" will have to be defined by the courts. Persons disqualified for either reason do not retain any priority status which they may have otherwise had. One additional temporary disqualification rule worthy of noting is that a nonresident may not be appointed as personal representative in the initial informal appointment proceeding until thirty days have elapsed from the date of the decedent's death. [3–307(a)].

The UPC's provision on priority for appointment is applicable to both informal and formal appointment proceedings. In an informal appointment proceeding, the Registrar must strictly comply with the prescribed order of priority. [3–308(a)(7)]. Although the Registrar must rely upon the statements made in the application, the residual rejection authority under Section 3–309 "for any other reason," gives the office an authority to reject an application if the Registrar believes that the person seeking appointment does not possess priority. Persons who object to an appointment, however, can only do so by filing a formal proceeding for appointment. [3–203(b)]. This latter rule permits informal appointment proceedings to always remain nonadjudicative and administrative in nature.

The priority schedule raises no problems when only one person can be classified within the rank having priority. In other words a person named as sole executor in a probated will who is not otherwise disqualified clearly has priority and should be appointed in either informal or formal proceedings. The same can be said for the decedent's surviving spouse who is not otherwise disqualified when decedent has died intestate. When two or more persons share priority, however, an informal appointment can only be made if all with priority who are not otherwise disqualified apply for appointment, or all, except the applicant or applicants, renounce their priority, or all concur in a nominee. [3–203(c)]. Priority can clearly be established by renunciation of all who have priority except those who are applying and by nomination of a selectee by all of those who have priority. [3–203(e)].

When priority of the applicants is not set by the UPC's ranking, renunciation or nomination, formal proceedings must be instituted. Significantly, formal proceedings may only be instituted by persons having a substantial interest in the estate, including creditors in insolvent cases. [3–203(b)(1)–(2)]. In any properly instituted formal proceeding, the Court is given guidelines for purposes of making an appointment. First, the Court is to appoint according to the statutory priority order. [3–203(b)]. This means, for example, that when several devisees have equal priority, the Court may merely appoint all such devisees who are not otherwise disqualified as co-personal representatives. Second, the Court must appoint the person specifically given priority by a decedent's will even though heirs and devisees object unless that person is otherwise disqualified. [3–203(b)(2)]. This preference for the person named or nominated in the will is recognition of the maxim "whom the testator will trust, so will the law." Third, when heirs and devisees object to the appointment of a person in any other situation, the Court may appoint the person nominated and acceptable to the heirs and devisees who have in the aggregate interests in the estate apparently equal to more than one half of the probable distributable value of the estate. [3–203(b)(2)]. Fourth, when none of the above rules are applicable, the Court may appoint any suitable person. "Suitable person" is not defined and is left to the discretion of the Court. Fifth, when the value of the estate is worth more than the family protections and the cost of administration, but insufficient to meet all unsecured claims, the Court may appoint any qualified person on petition of the creditors. [3–203(b)(1)]. Finally, before the Court can appoint one without priority, it must determine that those who have priority have been given notice of the proceeding and have failed to request or to nominate another for appointment and that administration is necessary. [3–203(e)].

The UPC gives to specific persons the authority to nominate, renounce or agree to appointment even where they would ordinarily be disqualified to serve as a personal representative. First, although persons must normally be twenty-one years of age or older to serve as a personal representative, a person who is otherwise qualified, who is eighteen years of age or over, and who except for the age would have priority, may nominate a qualified person to act as personal representative or may renounce that right to nominate such a person in a writing filed with the Court. [3–203(c)]. Second, conservators of protected persons and guardians other than guardians ad litem for minors and incapacitated persons may exercise their ward's right to nominate, to object to another's appointment or to agree to a selectee when determining the preference of a majority of those who have an interest in the estate. [3–203(d)].

The above discussion of priority is relevant only to the estate of a person who dies domiciled in the UPC state or whose estate has not been administered in the state of decedent's domicile. When a personal representative has been appointed in the decedent's domicile, that domiciliary foreign personal representative has priority over all other persons unless the decedent's will nominates different persons for different jurisdictions. [3–203(g)]. In addition, any domiciliary foreign personal representative may nominate another person who immediately assumes first priority for appointment. [See § 12.11(B)].

§ 12.03   Appointment, Bonding and Control

A.   APPOINTMENT

Upon determining the identity of the proper person who is to serve as personal representative, the Court or Registrar must appoint that person by order or statement. Letters of the appointment may be issued to the appointed personal representative, however, only after that person has filed with the appointing Court any bond required and a statement of acceptance of the duties of the office of personal representative. [3–601]. Furthermore, once a person accepts the appointment, the person submits personally to the jurisdiction of the Court for any proceeding instituted by interested persons concerned with the estate. [3–602; see § 10.02(C)(2)].

Generally, a person must be appropriately appointed, qualified and issued letters in order to possess and to undertake the duties and liabilities of the fiduciary office of personal representative of a decedent. [3–103]. Consequently, administration of an estate does not begin until the letters are issued to the personal representative.

Four exceptions to this rule merit mention. First, it does not apply to a domiciliary foreign personal representative's power given in Article IV. [See § 12.11(B)]. Second, the UPC explicitly empowers the named executor in a will to carry out written instructions concerning the decedent's body, funeral and burial even though prior to appointment. [3–701]. Third and probably most importantly, the powers given to a personal representative after appointment can relate back to actions that are beneficial to the estate but that were taken by the person actually appointed prior to the appointment. Fourth, actions by third persons, which a personal representative might have taken, can be ratified by the subsequently appointed personal representative.

The UPC also has a special provision dealing with the unusual situation where two or more persons receive general letters of administration. [3–702]. The first person to whom letters are issued is given exclusive authority and is empowered to recover any property of the estate held in the possession of other representatives. Any acts by those subsequently issued letters, however, that are taken in good faith and before notice of the first letters are not void merely because of the lack of validity of the appointment.

B. BONDING

Under the UPC, bond is not required in informal proceedings unless a special administrator is appointed, the will requires it, or an interested person petitions for it. [3–603]. Bond is not required in formal proceedings if the will waives the bonding requirement, unless interested parties have requested a bond and the Court agrees that it is desirable. In all other formal proceedings, bond may be required at the discretion of the Court at the time of appointment. Even if bond is required by the will, the Court may dispense with the bond in formal proceedings if it determines it is not necessary. Finally, professional fiduciaries who have deposited cash or collateral with a state agency according to statutory mandate in order to secure performance of their duties are not required to offer a bond. The Court, upon petition of the personal representative or of any other interested person, is given broad discretion concerning the bonding requirement including the power to excuse such a requirement, increase or reduce the bond's amount, release sureties or permit the substitution by the same or different sureties of another bond. [3–604].

Persons, who have and retain an interest or a claim valued in excess of $1,000, however, may file with the Registrar a demand that the personal representative give bond. [3–605]. If the personal representative has previously been appointed and qualified, a copy of the demand must be mailed to the personal representative. Unless the demandant ceases to have an interest in the estate or the bond is excused under Sections 3–603 or 3–604, the Court must require under such a demand that the personal representative provide bond. Until the ordered bond is filed, the personal representative must also refrain from administering the estate except to preserve it. Failure of the personal representative to give suitable bond within thirty days after receipt of notice of the requirement to do so is cause for removal and for the appointment of a successor.

When bond is required, the amount of the bond may be set in any of the following manners: (1) by the terms of the will; (2) by order of the Court; or (3) in an amount not less than the estimated value of the principal of the estate plus one year's income. [3–604]. The latter estimated value is set by the person seeking to satisfy the bonding requirement by filing a verified statement with the Registrar indicating that person's best estimate of the appropriate values of the estate. The Registrar then has the responsibility of determining whether the bond is properly executed by a corporate security or by one or more individual sureties who have guaranteed their performance by pledging personal property, mortgages on real property or other adequate security with the Court. At the Registrar's discretion, the amount of bond may be reduced or satisfied by the value of estate assets included in accounts that have restrictions placed upon them preventing their unauthorized disposition and that are deposited with domestic financial institutions.

When bond is satisfied by sureties, the UPC sets the following terms and conditions:

(1) It must be conditioned upon the faithful discharge of the personal representative's fiduciary duties as set by law;

(2) The state must be named as obligee for the benefit of persons interested in the estate including distributees and creditors;

(3) All sureties must be jointly and severally liable with the personal representative and with each other;

(4) All sureties must state their addresses on the bond;

(5) Each surety by executing an approved bond, consents to the jurisdiction of the Court when named party defendant to proceedings pertaining to the personal representative's fiduciary duties (each surety is entitled to notice of such proceeding by personal delivery or by mail to its filed address and any other known address);

(6) Proceedings for the breach of the bond may be brought against the sureties on petition of a successor personal representative, any other co-personal representative or any interested person; and

(7) Each surety is liable on its bond until the penalty is exhausted regardless of how many proceedings it takes to exhaust it.

[3–606(a)(1)–(5)]. When applicable, sureties are accorded the defenses of res judicata and of any statute of limitations which might be raised by the primary obligor. [3–606(b)].

See § 19.01(A) for a discussion of trustees' bonds.

C. CONTROL PROCEDURES

Although not subject to constant supervision by the Court, a personal representative may be put under the control of the Court upon a filing, at anytime, of a petition by a person who has an interest in the estate. [3–607]. A similar request can also be combined with a timely petition for formal testacy. [3–607, Comment; see 3–401]. Under this procedure, if the Court determines that the personal representative may take some action that would unreasonably jeopardize the applicant's interest or the interest of some other interested person, it may issue a temporary restraining order against the personal representative from performing specific acts. [3–607(a)]. The scope of these restraining orders may relate to all matters of the administration including acts of administration, disbursements, distribution, the exercise of any power, or the discharge of any duties of his office. Under similar circumstances, the petition may request orders that affirmatively require the personal representative to perform a proper function of the personal representative's duties.

Notice as directed by the Court must be given to the personal representative, the attorney of record, if any, and any other party defendants. [3–607(b)]. Unless all parties otherwise consent, the hearing must be set within ten days after the date of the petition. Third persons who may transact business with the personal representative may be made party defendants. It is only by making such third persons party defendants that it can be guaranteed that they will be made bound by the orders on the personal representative.

§ 12.04   Duties, Powers and Liabilities

A.   INTRODUCTION TO DUTIES, POWERS AND LIABILITIES

Generally, the law in non-UPC states and the provisions in the UPC substantially differ with respect to how the personal representative is to carry out the functions of the office. Non–UPC law concerned with the administration of decedents' estates frequently includes several unmeritorious characteristics. First, nearly every action taken by a personal representative requires an order by the appropriate Court either when initiating the action or when obtaining approval for it or at both times. Second, and even of a greater hindrance to efficient administration, the personal representative lacks any degree of broad powers necessary to administer the estate. Finally, the restrictiveness of the law places a burden of severe potential liability on the personal representative if one attempts to act on one's own without Court order. The consequence of these characteristics is that the prudent, cautious personal representative is forced to obtain Court approval for every action taken thereby substantially increasing the time and cost involved in the administration of an estate. Significantly, provisions limiting Court involvement, broadening the personal representative's powers and exculpating the personal representative from certain liabilities typically constitute a substantial and significant portion of a well drafted will in these states.

The UPC incorporates these good estate planning techniques into all administered estates unless specifically restricted by the terms of the will, supervised administration or other formal proceedings brought by interested persons. [3–704; see 3–715]. Except as so restricted, the personal representative is to administer the estate as rapidly as possible without Court supervision or intervention. [3–704]. When the assistance of the Court is desired to resolve a question, however, the personal representative has authority to invoke its jurisdiction.

The UPC subjects the personal representative to a pervasive standard of care and performance which is the same as that set for a trustee. [See § 19.02]. It provides that one must act as a prudent person dealing with the property of another. [3–703(a), 7–302]. The general duty in the use of the authority conferred by the UPC is properly to distribute and settle the estate in an expeditious and efficient manner that is consistent with the best interests of the estate. [3–703(a)].

B. DUTIES

Upon appointment under the UPC, the personal representative, other than a special administrator, has two particular and important notice requirements that must be satisfied. First, and as soon as possible, notice to creditors should be published in order to get the nonclaim period of limitation running. [3–801; see § 13.02]. Second, also within thirty days of appointment, information about the appointment must be delivered or mailed to the heirs and devisees. [3–705]. This information must include the following:

(1) the personal representative's name and address;

(2) whether bond has been filed;

(3) a description of the appointing court;

(4) an indication that the recipient has or may have an interest in the estate;

(5) administration in the particular state court is without court supervision;

(6) recipients are entitled to information regarding administration from the personal representative; and,

(7) recipients may petition the court in any matter relating to the estate including distributions and administration expenses.

Only those heirs and devisees whose addresses are reasonably available need receive or be sent this information. At the personal representative's discretion, however, the information may be delivered or sent by first class mail to other persons. It need not be sent to persons who have been held in prior formal testacy proceedings to have no interest in the estate. A failure to publish notice to creditors or to give the appropriate information to the heirs and devisees is a breach of duty on the part of the personal representative but does not affect the validity of the appointment, powers or other duties. [3–801, Comment; 3–705].

Although the UPC contains an inventory and appraisal requirement, as compared to typical non-UPC states, it materially alters how it is to be accomplished and what is to be done with it when completed. In a traditional manner, the UPC provides that the personal representative must prepare an inventory within three months after the appointment. [3–706]. In fact, the personal representative is subject to removal for failure to complete the inventory responsibilities. [3–706, Comment; see 3–611(b)]. This inventory must list the decedent's assets with reasonable detail indicating the fair market value and the amount of any encumbrance existing as to each asset. [3–706]. Once the inventory is prepared, however, the personal representative is only required to mail a copy of it to interested parties who request it. A request may take the form of a demand for notice under Section 3–204 or in any other manner that reasonably informs the personal representative that a proper request has been made. [1 UPC Practice Manual, 315]. In addition to this mailing, the personal representative has discretion whether to file the original of the inventory with the Court. Filing with the Court does not extend its role but merely makes it a public depository.

The Court is also not involved in the appraising process. Actually, there is no procedure established for Court appointed appraisers. The UPC provides that the personal representative may personally value the assets at fair market value or may employ other qualified and disinterested appraisers as is required under the circumstances. [3–707]. The UPC grants specific authority to hire different appraisers for different types of assets. If outside appraisers are employed, their names and addresses must be included and the item they appraised must be indicated on the inventory.

If subsequent property is discovered or the value or description of property on the original inventory is erroneous or misleading, the personal representative must prepare a supplementary inventory and appraisement which provides the same information necessary on the original item for the subsequently discovered property or for the property revalued or redescribed. [3–708]. In addition, this supplementary inventory must be sent or filed or both as the original inventory had been.

Several exceptions deserve mention. Special administrators do not have a duty concerning inventory and appraisement. [3–706]. Successor personal representatives also do not have such a duty unless the duty was not previously discharged, was improperly discharged or property which was not listed on the original inventory is discovered. [3–706; see 3–708].

Ordinarily, the personal representative has a duty and a right to take control and possession of the decedent's property. [3–709; see also § 19.02(I) for a discussion of this duty as it relates to trustees]. The personal representative does not, however, hold title to the property because title immediately vests in the heirs or devisees or both subject to administration. [3–101]. If necessary, however, the personal representative may institute proceedings to recover possession of property or to determine its title. Once in possession, the personal representative must pay taxes and take all actions reasonably necessary for its management, protection, and preservation.

The UPC makes two exceptions to the personal representative's duty to take possession or control of the decedent's property. [3–709]. First, a valid and probated will of the decedent may provide otherwise. It is not unusual in wills to provide that survivors are entitled to remain in possession of decedent's personal effects and residence. Second, the personal representative has discretion to leave or surrender any real property or tangible personal property with or to the person presumptively entitled to the property. Such action by the personal representative is in no way a "distribution" of the property to the recipient. [1 UPC Practice Manual, 317]. It merely constitutes revocable possession in the recipient. In fact, any request by the personal representative for return of the surrendered property is conclusive evidence in a Court proceeding that the personal representative needs possession of the property for purposes of administration. This power in the personal representative to regain possession of the property continues until termination of the appointment. [See 3–608].

The discretion to surrender property to heirs and devisees will be exercised most often when personal effects and residences are left in the control and possession of related and resident survivors and where property otherwise not needed for administration is specifically devised to identifiable beneficiaries. [See 1 UPC Practice Manual, 316–17]. Property, which may have to be sold and property not specifically devised that earns income, should be possessed or controlled by the personal representative.

C. POWERS

In order to permit administration without continual or frequent Court involvement, the UPC confers upon a personal representative significant administrative powers. To begin with, the personal representative is given the same power over the title to decedent's property that an absolute owner would have except that it is in a trust-like relationship for the benefit of all interested in the estate including creditors and successors. [3–711; see also § 19.02(O) for discussion of a similar provision relating to trustees]. When exercising this power, the personal representative is not required to give notice, have a hearing, or obtain an order of Court. In addition, for the protection of unsecured creditors, the personal representative has exclusive authority to recover void or voidable transfers made by the decedent during his lifetime. [3–710]. Finally and in a manner similar to proper draftsmanship of testamentary instruments, the UPC authorizes the personal representative and any successors to perform twenty-seven specified transactions. [3–715; see also § 19.02(O) for discussion of a similar enumerated set of powers for trustees]. The following are examples of powers included within this provision: (1) to make extraordinary repairs or alterations on the estate's structural assets [3–715(7)]; (2) to borrow money [3–715(16)]; (3) to hold securities in the name of a nominee [3–715(14)]; (4) to set reasonable compensation for the personal representative's own services [3–715(18)]; (5) to employ agents who may perform acts of administration whether or not discretionary [3–715(21)]; and (6) to incorporate any of decedent's businesses or ventures engaged in at the time of his death. [3–715(25)]. All of these powers must be exercised "reasonably for the benefit of interested persons." [3–715]. In other words, the power is given, but it may only be exercised if the latter standard is satisfied.

D. LIABILITIES AND THE EXCULPATORY PROVISION

The UPC generally provides that a personal representative is liable to interested persons for any damage or loss that results from a breach of a fiduciary duty in the improper exercise of a power. [3–712]. This liability is characterized as the same as that of a trustee of an express trust. Consequently, prior law concerning the liability of trustees as developed by the statutes and courts is relevant. [See § 19.04 for a discussion of the liability of trustees.]

In addition to potential liability for loss and damages due to breach of a fiduciary duty, sales or encumbrances of estate property by the personal representative to the personal representative, personally, or to the personal representative's spouse, agent, attorney, or any corporation or trust in which the fiduciary has a substantial beneficial interest are voidable by any person interested in the estate. [3–713]. Similarly, any other transaction that is affected by a substantial conflict of interest on the part of the personal representative is voidable. Only the following three situations are specifically recognized as exceptions to these rules: (1) the person who objects has consented after fair disclosure; (2) the decedent's will or pre-death contract expressly authorizes the transaction; or, (3) the Court approves the transaction after notice to interested persons. [See § 19.04 for a discussion of similar provisions as they relate to trustees.]

The UPC also relieves the personal representative of potential liability under certain special circumstances. If authorized at the time to exercise a power, a personal representative will not be surcharged for the exercise of that power although the power is later determined to have been nonexistent. [3–703(b)]. This has special relevance to distributions made by the personal representative to devisees or heirs in situations when subsequent to the distribution decedent's testacy status changes either because of new informal probate or formal testacy proceedings. Under this situation, the protection only applies if the distribution was made prior to the personal representative's knowledge of a pending proceeding concerned with testacy, vacation, formal appointment or supervised administration. On the other hand, the personal representative is not protected from wrongful distributions because of improper construction of the will or inadequate determination of heirship. [1 UPC Practice Manual, 311–12].

§ 12.05 Liability of Third Persons

As previously discussed, the UPC confers upon the personal representative the authority to perform numerous transactions without Court supervision. Under the present law of most non-UPC states, any third person who deals with a personal representative faces the possibility of being liable for having participated in the personal representative's breach of the fiduciary responsibilities. [See 4 Scott, Trusts § 279A]. The principal problem for third persons is not the rule but its application. Consequently, third persons have become very cautious and conservative in dealing with fiduciaries such as personal representatives. Without changing or abandoning the basic rule, and for purposes of encouraging third persons to deal with a personal representative, the UPC reduces the potential liability of third persons in their dealings with the personal representative. If a person dealt with or assisted a personal representative in good faith and for value, that person is protected as if the personal representative properly exercised a power. [3–714]. In addition, a third person is not required to inquire into the existence of a power or the propriety of its exercise because one knows one is dealing with a personal representative. A third person who pays or delivers assets to the personal representative is also not required to see to its proper application. Finally, unless the person had actual knowledge of a restriction on the personal representative's powers, of restrictive provisions in a will or even of court orders restricting the personal representative's power, restrictions of this nature are ineffective to cause the third person to be liable. The only exception to this rule provides that third persons are bound by restrictions on the powers of a personal representative that have been endorsed on letters of a supervised personal representative under Section 3–504. [See § 11.04]. [See § 19.04(I) for similar provisions as they relate to third parties who deal with trustees.].

The reason why the exercised power is improper makes no difference in the application of these protective rules. The impropriety of the action may be because of procedural irregularities, jurisdictional defects occurring in proceedings leading to the issuance of the letters, and even due to the fact decedent is found to be alive. Although this very comprehensive protection for third persons dealing with fiduciaries is much broader than that which generally exists under the law of most non-UPC states, it is not intended to replace comparable statutes relating to commercial transactions and security transfers by fiduciaries such as the Uniform Commercial Code and the Uniform Act for the Simplification of Fiduciary Security Transfers.

§ 12.06   Successor and Co-personal Representatives

The UPC adopts the rule that successor personal representatives have all of the same powers and duties as their original predecessors. [3–716]. The only exception concerns the decedent's will that specifically makes the power personal to a named executor or person. Successor personal representatives also may be substituted in all actions and proceedings to which the former personal representative was a party. [3–613]. If the former personal representative properly received notice, process or a claim, no further action need be made upon the successor.

When two or more persons serve as co-representatives, generally all must concur on all actions taken during the administration and distribution of the estate. [3–717]. Several exceptions, however, are specifically mentioned. First, the will may provide that unanimous concurrence is not necessary and may set the basis upon which actions other than by unanimous consent can be taken. Second, concurrence is not necessary when it cannot be readily obtained in time to preserve the estate due to an emergency. Third, any co-representative may receive and give receipts for property due the estate. Fourth, co-representatives may delegate the responsibilities for certain acts to a single representative. Finally, third persons dealing with less than all of the co-representatives are protected as if they had dealt with all of the co-representatives if these persons are actually unaware that another co-representative has been appointed or if they have been advised by the personal representative with whom they deal that that person has authority to act alone under any of the above exceptions.

When there are two or more co-representatives and when one or more of their appointments terminate for any reason leaving one or more personal representatives surviving, the survivors may exercise all the powers incident to the office. [3–718]. This applies as well in the situation in which less than the number nominated as co-executors is appointed. A validly probated will, however, may restrict or alter the application of these two rules. [See § 19.01 for similar provisions relating to successor trustees and cotrustees.]

§ 12.07 Compensation and Expenses of the Personal Representative and Other Agents

With respect to the determination of compensation to the personal representative and for other agents employed for the estate, the UPC follows a less structured approach than generally found under non-UPC law. The personal representative is simply entitled to reasonable compensation [3–719] and is permitted to personally determine the amount. [3–715(18)]. Unless there is an underlying contract, a personal representative may even renounce a provision in the decedent's will that sets compensation for the personal representative and thereby become entitled to reasonable compensation. [3–719]. Naturally, the personal representative may in a writing filed with the Court renounce all right to all or any part of the compensation.

A personal representative is also given the authority to set the compensation for all agents, including attorneys, employed for purposes of administering the estate. [3–715(18), (21)]. Furthermore, a personal representative is entitled to reimbursement for necessary expenses and disbursements, including reasonable attorney's fees, for any good faith, successful or unsuccessful, defense or prosecution of any proceeding concerning the estate. [3–720].

Protection is provided for interested persons by a provision that permits them to bring a special proceeding solely for the purpose of reviewing the reasonableness of all fees paid the personal representative and other agents, including attorneys. [3–721]. Upon petition and after notice to all interested persons, the Court is empowered to review all disbursements from the estate as payment for services rendered. The Court may order any person who has received excessive compensation from the estate to make appropriate refunds. Because the Court probably has jurisdiction over these matters under Section 3–105, this provision represents more of a psychological restriction on over-charges rather than an additional remedy for interested persons. [3–721, Comment].

The courts are beginning to develop definitions for "reasonable compensation." It is said to require the consideration of several factors including, for example:

(1) Time and labor required, novelty and difficulty of questions involved, and skill needed to resolve issues;

(2) The likelihood that other employment will be precluded by acceptance of this employment;

(3) The fee customarily charged in the locality;

(4) The amount involved and the results obtained;

(5) The time limitations upon such services; and

(6) The experience, reputation and ability of the worker.

[Colorado State Board of Agriculture v. First Nat'l Bank, 567 P.2d 820 (Colo.App.1977)].

See § 19.01(G), (H) for similar provisions as they relate to trustees.

§ 12.08   The Personal Representative's Liability to Third Persons

The UPC deals directly with the difficult problem of a personal representative's personal liability to third persons on contracts, from ownership or control of the estate's property and from torts arising out of the administration of the estate. Under the UPC the estate is made into a "quasi-corporation" for purposes of such liability. [3–808, Comment]. Accordingly, the personal representative becomes an agent of this entity and is liable not individually but only as an agent would be liable. [3–808]. More specifically, a personal representative is personally liable under the following circumstances: (1) on contracts properly made in the course of the estate's administration only when expressly provided in the contract or when the representative capacity of the personal representative is not revealed in the contract. [3–808(a)]; and, (2) for torts or for obligations arising from property ownership or control only when the personal representative is personally at fault. [3–808(b)]. Third persons may sue the estate for such claims in the name of the personal representative in a representative capacity regardless of the personal representative's personal liability. [3–808(c)]. The personal representative's personal liability to the estate may be litigated during the third person's initial action against the estate or in any other appropriate proceeding such as a proceeding for an accounting. [3–808(d)].

See § 19.04(I) for similar provisions as they relate to trustees.

§ 12.09   Termination and Removal

The UPC provides for termination of the appointment of a personal representative for various reasons including death or disability, voluntary action and involuntary removal. Termination of an appointment has a special and important meaning under the UPC. With one exception, termination means that the personal representative's rights and powers, which pertain to the office and which are conferred on the office by the UPC or in the decedent's will, end. [3–608]. Termination, in other words, refers to the occurrence of events that end a personal representative's authority. [3–1003, Comment]. The exception provides that unless distribution has occurred or a Court has restrained or enjoined the personal representative, a personal representative may exercise all power necessary to protect the estate and to deliver the assets to the successor. [3–608]. Notwithstanding termination, a personal representative may continue to be liable for transactions or omissions occurring prior to termination. A personal representative still must preserve, account for and deliver the assets subject to control, and still is subject to the jurisdiction of the Court.

When a personal representative dies or becomes subject to a conservatorship, the appointment terminates and a qualified successor or special administrator must be appointed. [3–609]. Until such latter appointment, the representative of the deceased or protected person has the duty to protect the estate and is conferred the power to perform all necessary acts to do so. Upon the appointment and qualification of a successor or special administrator, the deceased or protected person's representative must account for and deliver the assets of the estate to the newly appointed representative.

The UPC includes three specific methods by which a person may voluntarily terminate an appointment. First, a personal representative's appointment terminates one year after the filing of a closing statement under Section 3–1003. [3–610(a); see § 14.04(A)]. Second, a personal representative's appointment terminates upon a court order closing the estate under the formal closing proceeding of Sections 3–1001 or 3–1002. [3–610(b); see § 14.04(C)]. The third procedure constitutes a sort of informal voluntary termination procedure. This procedure permits a personal representative to file a written statement of resignation with the Registrar. [3–610(c)]. Persons known to be interested in the estate must be given at least fifteen days notice. Termination occurs if, and only if, a successor personal representative is appointed and qualifies and the assets are delivered to the successor. If within the time indicated in the notice no one applies or petitions for appointment, the filed resignation statement is ineffective.

The UPC also provides a formal proceeding for the involuntary removal of a personal representative. [3–611]. Any person interested in the estate may institute such an action at any time by filing with the Court a petition requesting removal. [3–611(a)]. Being a formal proceeding, notice of the time and place for the required hearing must be given to the personal representative and to other persons as the Court directs. Upon receipt of notice of the removal proceeding, the personal representative must not act except to account, to correct maladministration, to preserve the estate or as ordered by Court under Section 3–607. If the Court orders the personal representative removed, it must also direct in its order the disposition of the assets remaining in the name or control of the removed personal representative.

A personal representative will only be removed by the Court for cause. Cause is both generally and specifically defined in the UPC. [3–611(b)]. Generally, the Court should remove a personal representative for cause when removal would be in the best interest of the estate. The UPC then recites the following more specific reasons when a personal representative can be removed for cause:

(1) The appointment was obtained by intentionally misrepresented material facts;

(2) The personal representative—

    (a) Disregarded a Court order,

    (b) Has become incapable of discharging the responsibilities of the position,

    (c) Has mismanaged the estate,

(d) Has failed to perform any duty pertaining to the fiduciary office; or,

(3) A domiciliary personal representative appointed in another state requests removal incident to seeking appointment as ancillary personal representative. [See § 12.11(B)].

[3–611(b)].

Although, during the administration of an estate, a will is discovered that appoints a person as executor who is not serving currently as personal representative, the current personal representative is not immediately removed or replaced but retains the office until another appointment procedure is instituted. [3–612]. If this procedure is not instituted within thirty days after the expiration of time for appeal from the order that changes the nature of the administration, the original personal representative may be appointed again to serve in that capacity. Naturally, termination does occur if the person entitled to appointment under the new testacy proceedings is appointed.

See §§ 19.01(D), (E) for provisions relating to the removal and resignation of trustees.

§ 12.10   The Special Administrator

In the vast number of cases, the UPC has eliminated the need for special administrators. The ease and speed by which persons can obtain informal appointment, for example, eliminates the typical reason for having a special administrator appointed. Under the law of many non-UPC states, it is often necessary to have a special administrator appointed between the time of filing the petition for probate of a will and the time of decision due to the notice requirements. [Atkinson, Wills § 104]. Another example of a substitute for the special administrator in the UPC is the power of a general personal representative to delegate responsibility in order to take care of the situation where the personal representative is temporarily absent or incapacitated. [3–715(21), 3–614, Comment].

Notwithstanding the UPC's substitutes for special administrators, there continue to exist situations in which a special administrator is essential or significantly helpful. The following situations are examples:

(1) When informal appointment is not feasible because of a petition for formal appointment or a formal testacy proceeding requests that a special administrator be appointed;

(2) To perform a function that the general personal representative believes will cause undue friction or hostility between successors and the personal representative;

(3) To perform a function that, if the general personal representative performed or accomplished, would constitute a conflict of interest, e.g., the general personal representative may desire to purchase an asset from the estate; and

(4) To perform the function of a personal representative during an extended time of incapacity or absence where the delegation of authority pro-

vision will not satisfy or adequately handle the problem.

[1 UPC Practice Manual, 308–09]. Consequently, the UPC contains provisions specifically dealing with the appointment, administration and termination of special administrators. Both informal procedures and formal proceedings are included for their appointment. Significantly, the fiduciary relationship of special administrators is specifically distinguished from the related but broader relationships of general personal representative and successor personal representative. [See 1–201(36), (45) and (47)]. One example of the importance of this difference is that bond is ordinarily required for special administrators in all situations whereas it ordinarily is not required for general and successor personal representatives. [3–603; see § 12.03(B)].

The informal appointment of a special administrator procedure provides that when it is necessary to protect the estate of a decedent prior to the appointment of a general personal representative, or when a prior appointment has terminated because of death or disability under Section 3–609, the Registrar may appoint a special administrator upon the application of any interested person. [3–614(1)]. When the delay in appointing a general personal representative is due to a pending application or petition for probate, the Registrar may appoint the person named executor in the will if that person is available and qualified. [3–615(a)]. Otherwise, any proper person may be appointed by the Registrar.

[3–615(b)]. The duties of an informally appointed special administrator are limited to the collection, management and preservation of the assets of the estate, to account for them and to deliver them to an appointed general personal representative when qualified. [3–616]. Necessarily, the UPC gives the special administrator all powers necessary to perform the above duties.

When informal appointment is not available, a special administrator must be appointed by order of the Court. Ordinarily, a formal proceeding to appoint a personal representative begins with the petition of an interested person. [3–614(2)]. After notice and hearing, the petition results in an order appointing a special administrator if the Court finds that the appointment is necessary to preserve the estate or to secure its proper administration. Included within the latter standard are situations in which a general personal representative cannot or should not perform the acts desired. When the appearance of an emergency exists, the Court may order an appointment of a special administrator without notice. Unless the Court's appointment order imposes limits on duties, a formally appointed special administrator has all of the powers of a general personal representative. [3–617]. Significantly, the Court may make an appointment limited in time, to the performance of particular acts or on any other terms.

The termination of the appointment of a special administrator occurs (1) on the appointment of a general personal representative, (2) according to the provisions of the order of appointment, or (3) according to the reasons and procedures set for terminating a general personal representative. [3–618].

§ 12.11   Foreign Personal Representative and Ancillary Administration

A.   THE MULTI–STATE ESTATE

With the mobility of our society today, it is not an uncommon situation for an individual to own property located in two or more states. Although the principal administration will be in the state of the decedent's domicile, ancillary administrations may still be necessary wherever property is situated. Under the law of many non-UPC states, this ancillary administration requires a completely separate administration causing undue costs and complexities. The UPC includes multiple, less formalistic and more efficient procedures.

Although the UPC recognizes the territorial concept of the state's jurisdiction and control over title to its real property [1–301], a primary goal of the UPC is a unified administration for a decedent's estate that has multi-state contacts. [1 UPC Practice Manual, 432]. The UPC seeks to accomplish this unification by coordinating the laws, actions and decisions of the various states that assume jurisdiction over a decedent's estate. Another technique by which this is accomplished is through the significant powers given to the domiciliary personal representative. Significantly, these rules and techniques which are applicable to ancillary administration control within the UPC state regardless of whether the domiciliary state has reciprocal rules and techniques. An inherent limitation in the UPC's provisions concerned with multi-state estates is that, with a few exceptions, the UPC's provisions only apply to administration, domiciliary or ancillary, in jurisdictions in which it has been enacted. The new and convenient devices included in the UPC for ancillary administration, therefore, are available ordinarily only in a UPC jurisdiction.

Several exceptions to this limitation deserving mention concern the UPC's efforts to give a domiciliary personal representative appointed under its provisions authority and responsibility in other ancillary jurisdictions, whether or not the latter jurisdictions have the UPC or similar concepts. First, such a domiciliary personal representative is given the power to prosecute and defend claims of any nature concerning the protection of the estate or of the personal representative's fiduciary responsibilities in any jurisdiction. [3–715(22)]. This provision is contrary to the common holding that a personal representative has no legal status or standing outside the state of appointment. [Atkinson, Wills § 106]. Second, the domiciliary personal representative has the same standing to sue or be sued in any jurisdiction as the decedent would have had immediately before death for claims which survive the decedent's death. [3–703(c)]. This provision not only includes the common case where decedent was in an automobile accident in another state, but also all other types of claims over which the other state can obtain jurisdiction under its long-arm provisions.

B. THE DOMICILIARY FOREIGN PERSONAL REPRESENTATIVE

Through the exercise of the powers of the office, the domiciliary personal representative has several options in settling a decedent's estate in a UPC ancillary jurisdiction. First, sixty days after the decedent's death and with nothing more than an affidavit, a domiciliary foreign personal representative may solicit or receive payments of debts and deliveries of property held by persons in the UPC jurisdiction. [4–201]. This affidavit must recite the date of death, that no local administration is pending and that the domiciliary personal representative is entitled to the payment or delivery. The debtors or possessors, who act in good faith, are released to the same extent as if their payments or deliveries had been made to a local personal representative. [4–202]. Resident creditors may prevent such payments or deliveries, however, by notifying the debtors or possessors that they should not be made. [4–203]. The term "resident creditor" means any claimant against the estate who is domiciled or doing business in the UPC ancillary jurisdiction. [4–101(3)].

A concurrent or alternative procedure under the UPC provides that by filing in a court in the UPC ancillary state authenticated copies of the domiciliary appointment and the official bond, if any, a

domiciliary foreign personal representative is entitled to exercise all powers that a local personal
representative could exercise. [4–204, 4–205; see
§ 12.04(C)]. These powers specifically include the
power to bring legal proceedings that any nonresident could bring in courts of the UPC ancillary
jurisdiction. [4–205; see also 3–916(h), § 14.03].
This filing has the above effect only if neither a
local administration is pending nor a local personal
representative is functioning pursuant to appointment proceedings under Article III. [4–206; see 4–
101(1)–(2)]. Actually, the institution by interested
persons of informal or formal appointment terminates the domiciliary foreign personal representative's power under this provision except as allowed
by the Court. [4–206]. Persons who dealt with the
domiciliary foreign personal representative before
they received actual notice of a pending local administration proceeding, however, are not to be
prejudiced as far as any change of position is concerned. If a local personal representative is appointed, this personal representative assumes all duties
and obligations that arose during the exercise of the
domiciliary foreign personal representative's powers
and may be substituted for the domiciliary foreign
personal representative in all actions or proceedings
pending in the UPC ancillary state.

In an estate where the will has been probated in
the testator's domicile, the domiciliary foreign personal representative may also exercise the authority
to file for informal probate. [3–303(b)]. Because the
UPC requires devisees to probate a will in order to

prove title, informal probate in the UPC ancillary state would at least be necessary if the devolution of real estate is involved. [3–102; see § 10.02(A)]. There is no three year after death limitation on such informal probates. [3–108].

If an interested person petitions for local appointment, the domiciliary foreign personal representative or the representative's nominee is given priority of appointment in the ancillary state. [3–203(g)]. Unless the decedent's will appoints a different person to serve as personal representative in the ancillary jurisdiction, the domiciliary foreign personal representative may obtain removal of anyone else appointed. [3–611(b)]. In addition, the domiciliary foreign personal representative is the only person who may file for an informal appointment in the UPC ancillary jurisdiction when an appointment has previously been made in the state of domicile. [3–308(b)].

Locally interested persons are not without protection. Within the UPC's rules on statute of limitations and res judicata, interested persons have all of the affirmative action protections accorded interested persons in the domiciliary jurisdiction. [4–207]. These protections would include the possibility of petitioning for formal probate, appointment, or closing, for supervised administration or for any other proceeding or order permissible under Article III. [See § 10.01(B)(4)(d)].

C. JURISDICTION OVER THE FOREIGN PERSONAL REPRESENTATIVE

Significantly, the UPC also includes comprehensive provisions dealing with jurisdiction over the foreign personal representative. The foreign personal representative submits himself to personal jurisdiction under the following four situations: (1) when he accepts appointment in a UPC jurisdiction [3–602]; (2) when he obtains his powers through the filing of authenticated copies of his domiciliary appointment; (3) although limited to the value of the property collected, when he receives voluntary payments or deliveries; or (4) when he does any other act within the state which would permit that state to assume jurisdiction over him as an individual. [4–301]. A foreign personal representative is also subject to the jurisdiction of any state in which the decedent would have been subject to jurisdiction prior to death. [4–302]. Service of process upon the foreign personal representative may be made in any of three methods: (1) by registered or certified mail addressed to the last reasonably ascertainable address requesting the return receipt be signed only by the addressee; (2) by ordinary mail if method (1) is unavailable; or (3) by a manner permitted by other service of process provisions in the UPC state on either the foreign personal representative or the decedent immediately prior to death. [4–303(a)]. Upon proper service, the foreign personal representative must be allowed thirty days to appear or respond. [4–303(b)].

See § 17.02(E) for a discussion of foreign trustees.

D. COORDINATION OF DOMICILIARY AND ANCILLARY PROCEEDINGS

The UPC contains numerous provisions that attempt to coordinate laws, actions and decisions between the various states which assume jurisdiction over a decedent's estate. Under the UPC, adjudications and actions taken in the domiciliary and other relevant jurisdictions are to be given recognition in local administration and probate proceedings initiated in the ancillary jurisdiction. After proper notice and an opportunity for contest by all interested persons, domiciliary adjudications concerned with testacy, will validity and its construction must also be considered res judicata in a UPC, nondomiciliary jurisdiction. [3–408; see § 11.03(B)(5)]. Although a finding of a domicile is required, it may be satisfied through a formal closing proceeding. [3–1001, 3–1002]. Furthermore, adjudications for or against a personal representative either in a domiciliary or ancillary jurisdiction are binding on the local personal representative as if she were a party to the adjudication. [4–401]. Adjudications obtained by fraud or collusion are impliedly excepted. [See 1–106, § 2.01(B)(1)]. Conflicting claims as to the location of the decedent's domicile are also avoided by the UPC because the first court in which formal proceedings are commenced has the exclusive right to determine domicile and its determination is binding on all UPC courts. [3–202; see § 10.02(C)(3)].

Unsecured creditor's claims that are barred by the domiciliary nonclaim statute are also barred in a UPC, nondomiciliary jurisdiction. [3–803(b)]. The nonclaim period may be extended in the ancillary jurisdiction, however, if the first publication for claims in that state occurs before the period has run in the domiciliary state.

The UPC also deals with the problems surrounding the settlement and distribution of an estate that is administered in two or more states. First, decedent's assets, wherever their situs and administration, are subject to the properly filed claims of any administration of which the personal representative is aware. [3–815(a)]. Second, in insolvent estates, distributions in UPC ancillary administrations are to be coordinated with distributions made in other jurisdictions, including administration in the decedent's domicile. [3–815(b)–(c)]. This coordination includes: (1) satisfying the domicile's family protections if assets in the domicile are insufficient; (2) paying claims and charges in all jurisdictions on a pro rata basis; (3) adjusting claims and charges between creditors who have received a preference payment in other jurisdictions with those creditors who have not received a preference; and (4) transferring any balance remaining after the above payments to the domiciliary personal representative.

With three specific exceptions, the UPC provides that in solvent estates the nondomiciliary personal representative must distribute the assets in her possession to the domiciliary personal representative for distribution to the appropriate beneficiaries.

[3–816]. The first exception recognizes that either the provisions of a decedent's will or choice of law rules may identify successors according to the local law of the ancillary jurisdiction and to the exclusion of the law of the decedent's domicile. This exception may have significant application where decedent dies with real estate in the ancillary jurisdiction. The second exception anticipates the situation where, after reasonable inquiry, the local personal representative cannot discover the existence or identity of a domiciliary personal representative. This exception may have importance where the decedent died domiciled in a state in which she left no administrable assets. The third exception accords the Court authority in a formal closing proceeding under Section 3–1001 to order distribution other than to the domiciliary personal representative.

CHAPTER 13
CREDITORS' CLAIMS

§ 13.01   Introduction to Creditors' Claims

Two of the principal reasons for having administration of a decedent's estate are the protection of creditors and the settlement of their claims. [See 3–101, 3–711]. The UPC not only includes provisions concerning the determination and settlement of claims, but it also contains many provisions previously discussed which provide the creditor with protection from misuse of the UPC's administration procedures. For example, the creditor may request and use any of the following protective devices:

(1) Demand for notice under Section 3–204;

(2) Demand that a personal representative post bond and be removed for failure to do so under Section 3–605;

(3) Initiate formal appointment proceedings under Sections 3–401 and 3–414;

(4) Initiate supervised administration proceedings under Section 3–502;

(5) Initiate proceedings to obtain further restrictive orders from the Court under Section 3–607; and

(6) Initiate proceedings against distributees for improper distribution under Sections 3–909 and 3–1004.

[See 1 UPC Practice Manual, 335–40].

As indicated, the UPC includes a set of provisions dealing with the determination and settlement of creditors' claims. The primary issues considered in the following discussion include notice and the time limitations on presenting claims, the procedures for presentation, allowance and rejection of claims, the payment of claims and special issues related to these matters.

See § 18.02 for a discussion of the claims of creditors against property that is held in trust.

§ 13.02   Notice and Nonclaim Limitations

The UPC's provision for notice to creditors is one of the special notice procedures in which it departs from using Section 1–401. [3–801, 1–401; see § 2.03(A)]. The Supreme Court decision in Tulsa Professional Collection Services v. Pope, 485 U.S. 478 (1988) held that a nonclaim statute, which barred creditors' claims not filed within two months after notice by publication only, is unconstitutional as applied to known or reasonably ascertainable creditors. In 1989, the UPC was amended to respond to this decision despite a belief that the decision did not affect the UPC's notice procedure. [Code, App. IV, Background Comment].

The UPC makes a proactive response to the *Tulsa* challenge in adopting three interrelated limitation periods to deal with creditors' claims. First, the

UPC adopts a one year period in gross after which all claims arising before decedent's death are barred regardless whether any notice was given. [3–803(a)(1)]. This one year period is shorter than the UPC's original three year from death period. [3–108; § 10.02(B)]. Mere nonaction by successors for a year after death cuts off creditors if none of the latter seek to force administration.

Second, the UPC adopts two special interrelated notice procedures that may be used to reduce the nonclaim period. [3–803(a)(2), 3–801(a), 3–801(b)]. The UPC leaves to each enacting state the decision whether to make these procedures mandatory or optional for an appointed personal representative. One procedure sets out a four month nonclaim period following the date of first publication of notice. The other procedure sets out a sixty day nonclaim period following the date of the mailing of a notice to a known creditor. When the two procedures are exercised simultaneously, the mailed notice may refer to the four month nonclaim period used in the notice by publication. If the two notice procedures are not coordinated and exercised concurrently, creditors' claims are barred only after the later of the limitation periods. In other words, if a creditor is given actual notice less than sixty days from the expiration of the four month notice by publication procedure, the creditor that received actual notice has no less than the sixty day period to file the claim. [3–803, Comment]. On the other hand, if the four month period is a date later than the sixty day notice period, a creditor has until the four month period expires to file the claim. Because the one year period requires no action to cut off claims, one would not want to give actual notice or notice by publication any time within sixty days or four months of the expiration of the one year period. Actual mailed and published notice should be used, when appropriate, to shorten the limitation period.

If notice by publication is used, notice must be published once a week for three successive weeks in a newspaper with general circulation and located in the proper governmental subdivision in which appointment has been made. [3–801]. The notice must announce the personal representative's appointment and address and indicate to the estate's creditors that their claims must be presented within four months after the date of first publication or they will be forever barred.

Written notice may be given by the personal representative by mail or other delivery. [3–801(b)]. The notice must provide the same information as the published notice requires. The time limit may state that claims must be presented the later of 60 days after mailing or delivery or four months after the date of the first publication of notice if relevant.

In summary, creditors with claims that arose before death must properly present their claims within the earlier of:

   1.   One year after decedent's death if no notice has been made [3–803(a)(1)]; or,

2. The later of four months after the date of first notice by publication, or sixty days after mailing or delivery of actual notice [3–803(a)(2)]; or,

3. The nonclaim limitation in the decedent's domiciliary jurisdiction if that time period expires before the procedures for notice to creditors are initiated in the ancillary UPC jurisdiction. [3–803(b); see § 12.11(D)].

If a state mandates a personal representative to give proper notice to creditors, failure to give the notice is considered a breach of duty and the personal representative will be liable for any damages due to the breach. [3–801, Comment]. If a state gives the personal representative discretion to give proper notice to creditors, failure to give the notice does not subject the personal representative to liability either to creditors or successors. If effective notice is not given, there is no effective way for the personal representative to close the estate, terminate the appointment or obtain a discharge unless a year has passed from decedent's death. [See 3–1001, 3–1002, 3–1003; §§ 14.04(A)–(C)].

Creditors with claims that arose at or after death must present their claims (1) within four months after the personal representative's performance is due on contract claims, or (2) within the later of four months or one year after decedent's death after the claim arises on any other type of claim. [3–803(c)].

All claims against the estate, the personal representative, and the heirs, devisees, and nonprobate transferees of the decedent that arose before death are barred "whether due or to become due, absolute or contingent, liquidated or unliquidated, founded on contract, tort, or other legal bases" including claims of the UPC state and its subdivisions are covered within these nonclaim period limitations. [3–803(a)–(b)]. Claims do not include estate or inheritance taxes or title questions between third persons and the decedent on assets alleged to be included in the estate. [1–201(6)]. Similarly, the nonclaim limitation does not apply to actions for specific performance of pre-death contract claims. [Bradshaw v. McBride, 649 P.2d 74 (Utah 1982)].

The nonclaim limitation period has broad application and overrides other normally relevant statutes of limitation. Unlike a statute of limitations, the nonclaim statute may not be waived or tolled. "The nonclaim statute imposes a condition precedent to the enforcement of a right of action; by contrast, a statute of limitations does not bar the right of action, but only the remedy." Estate of Hall v. Hartley, 948 P.2d 539 (Colo.1997). For example, claims are not tolled by reason of a claimant's minority whereas they would be under the usual rule for statutes of limitation. [Estate of Daigle, 634 P.2d 71 (Colo.1981)].

The UPC includes the following explicit and limited exceptions from these limitations:

(1) The enforcement of mortgages, pledges, or liens on property [3–803(d)(1); see 3–104, 3–809];

(2) Claims protected by liability insurance up to policy limits [3–803(d)(2)];

(3) The collection of fees and reimbursements for the estate's personal representative, attorney and accountant [3–803(d)(3)];

(4) Actions pending at decedent's death [3–804(2)]; and,

(5) Claims against the personal representative concerning any personal liability. [3–803, Comment; but see 3–808].

The strength of the public policy underlying the nonclaim limitation that claims against a decedent's estate should be identified and resolved quickly is evident from the strict enforcement of the time limitation. For example, it has been held that the court has no authority to extend the time for presentment despite possible injustice to the creditor. [Oney v. Odom, 624 P.2d 1037 (N.M.App.1981)].

§ 13.03 Presentation, Allowance and Rejection of Claims

Presentation of a claim by a creditor is made by a written statement of the claim delivered or mailed to the personal representative or filed with the clerk of court. [3–804(1)]. This statement must include the amount claimed and the name and address of the claimant. When presented to the personal representative, an itemized bill containing this information should be sufficient. [Art. III, Pt. 8, General

Comment]. The form necessary for a written statement should be liberally construed in favor of the creditor. [See Strong Brothers Enterprises, Inc. v. Estate of Strong, 666 P.2d 1109 (Colo.App.1983)]. A claim not due must also state when it is due and a contingent or unliquidated claim must also state the nature of the uncertainty. [3–804(1)]. Although these two rules are stated as a prerequisite, a failure to contain the required information in the claim does not invalidate an otherwise proper presentation. Claims are deemed effectively presented upon written receipt received from the personal representative or upon filing with the Court, whichever first occurs. When a claim is filed with the Court, the Court performs mere depository and proof of the filing date functions. [3–804, Comment]. Commencement within the nonclaim period of a Court proceeding against the personal representative is also a means of presentation. [3–804(2)].

The personal representative may mail notice to the claimant of either allowance or disallowance. [3–806(a)]. Failure to mail such notice constitutes an allowance sixty days after the expiration of time for original presentation of the claim. Ordinarily, a personal representative can change, in whole or in part, an allowance to a disallowance, or vice versa. [3–806(b); Swett v. Estate of Wakem, 490 A.2d 679 (Me.1985)]. An allowance cannot be changed to a disallowance, however, after court action directs that it be paid. Also, a disallowance of a claim cannot be changed to an allowance if any limitation period has run against it. A judgment against the personal representative on a claim against the estate, however, constitutes an automatic allowance of it. [3–806(d)].

Proceedings by creditors on rejected claims must be commenced sixty days after notice of disallowance. [3–804(3), 3–806(a); see Estate of Hall v. Hartley, 948 P.2d 539 (Colo.1997)]. The personal representative or the Court on petition may extend this period for an additional sixty days when the claim is not presently due or is contingent or unliquidated although the extension cannot extend beyond the applicable statute of limitations. [3–804(3)].

Claims barred by any statute of limitations must be disallowed by the personal representative when the estate is insolvent or unless waived by all successors whose interests are affected, when the estate is solvent. [3–802]. This rule has broad application to any claim that arose before decedent's death. Such a claim may be barred because of any of the following periods of limitation: (1) the ordinary limitation period for such claims as extended for four months after death [3–802(b)]; (2) the non-claim periods [3–803(a)]; (3) the sixty day period in which to initiate a proceeding to contest a disallowance [3–804(3), 3–806(a)]; or (4) the one-year-after-death limitation when notice to creditors has not been given. [3–803(a)(1); 3–802, Comment].

§ 13.04 Payment of Claims

The personal representative must pay all claims allowed upon expiration of the earliest relevant

non-claim limitation; however, provisions must also
be made for the family protections, claims not yet
allowed and other unbarred claims. [3–807(a)].
Claimants may obtain court orders directing a personal representative to pay their allowed claims
after the above period has run by filing a petition to
the court or by motion if the estate is under supervised administration. No execution under a judgment may issue or be levied against property of the
estate, however, after death except for the appropriate enforcement of mortgages, pledges or liens. [3–
812]. Allowed claims not paid within sixty days
after the time for original presentation of claim has
expired bear interest at the legal rate or at the rate
set in the contract which represents the claim. [3–
806(e)].

At any time and for convenience sake, the personal representative may also pay any just claim that
has not been barred regardless of presentation. The
personal representative, however, is subject to personal liability to other claimants whose claims are
allowed and who suffered loss due to the improper
payment, if payment is made, without proper security, before the nonclaim period expires or negligently or willfully deprives an injured claimant of a
valid priority. [3–807(b)]. So long as the personal
representative does not make such a payment in a
manner that negligently or willfully deprives other
claimants of their priority, the personal representative can confidently make such payments if the
nonclaim period has expired and if security for
refund from the payee is obtained.

If the estate is not sufficient to pay all claims, the UPC sets the following order or priority: (1) costs and expenses of administration; (2) reasonable funeral expenses; (3) federal preferred debts and taxes; (4) reasonable and necessary medical expenses of the last illness including compensation for services rendered; (5) state preferred debts and taxes; (6) all other claims. [3–805(a)]. Claims within the same class share proportionately whether or not due. [3–805(b)].

Allowed or established claims that were not due or were contingent or unliquidated when presented must be paid by the personal representative in the same manner as any other presently due or absolute claim would be paid if they become due or certain before distribution of the estate. [3–810(a)]. When certainty or dueness will not occur before distribution, the personal representative or the claimant may petition the Court to determine the claim in a special proceeding for that purpose. [3–810(b)]. The Court may determine the value of the claim in one of two methods: (1) with the claimant's consent, the claim's present or agreed value may be set taking into account all uncertainties; or (2) an arrangement for future or contingent payment may be made, which for this purpose creates a trust fund, gives the claimant a mortgage, bond or security from the distributee, or sets payment in any other agreed manner.

When it appears to be in the best interests of the estate, the personal representative may compromise any presented claim including claims due or not due, absolute or contingent, liquidated or unliquidated. [3–813]. In addition, the personal representative may deduct from a presented claim any counterclaim that the estate has against the claimant regardless whether the counterclaim is liquidated or unliquidated, arises from a transaction other than one upon which the claim is based or exceeds, or is different from the kind sought in the claim. [3–811]. The Court is given the power to determine the amount of the deduction due to the counterclaim and even to issue a judgment against the claimant in any amount by which the counterclaim exceeds the claim.

§ 13.05   Secured Claims and Encumbered Assets

Secured claims including those entitled mortgages, pledges, or other liens, raise special problems for the personal representative in the administration of the decedent's estate. First, as previously mentioned, the nonclaim period does not apply to proceedings that attempt to enforce a mortgage, pledge or other lien upon the property of the estate. [3–803(d)(1); see 3–104, 3–809]. This means that as to the value of the security interest, the personal representative does not have control over the time or manner of enforcement of the claim against the estate. Consequently, the UPC gives the personal representative significant authority in how to deal with such encumbered assets. According to this authority, the personal representative may take any of the following courses of action: (1) pay all or any part of the encumbrance; (2) renew or extend the security obligation; or (3) satisfy the security interest in whole or in part by transferring the asset to the creditor. [3–814]. The personal representative may take any of these actions whether or not the secured creditor presented a claim but in all cases the action taken must be for the best interest of the estate. The share of any distributee of the encumbered property is not increased by payments of the security interest unless the distributee is entitled to exoneration under Section 2–607. [See § 7.06(B)].

If the secured creditor seeks payment of the allowed secured claim, the UPC provides three methods by which such claim may be paid. First, if the creditor surrenders the security, the personal representative may base payment upon the amount allowed. Second, when the creditor has exhausted the security before receiving payment, the personal representative may pay the amount allowed less the fair value of the security unless, of course, the creditor is precluded by law from collecting the excess of the claim above the security. [3–809(1)]. Third, when the creditor has not or cannot exhaust the security, the personal representative may also pay the amount of the allowed claim less the value of the security. [3–809(2)]. The value of the security under the latter method must be determined either by converting it into a money value according to the terms of the agreement or by the agreement, arbitration, compromise or litigation between the creditor and personal representative.

CHAPTER 14

DISTRIBUTION AND CLOSING PROVISIONS

§ 14.01 General Distribution Rules

The ultimate objective in the administration of a solvent estate is final and complete distribution of the assets to the successors. Because many special problems arise in making distribution determinations, the UPC gives the personal representative a set of guidelines to follow.

The personal representative may begin making distributions of property to successors and releases of title to property in the hands of successors as soon as the determination of the probable charges against the estate and its solvency has been made. Distributions are, of course, subject to the fiduciary's responsibility and liability to creditors and taxing authorities. If the personal representative determines that the plan for distribution needs to be reviewed by all of the recipients, the proposal for such distribution may be mailed or delivered to all persons who have a right to object to it. If no written objection is received from any distributee within thirty days of mailing or delivery, the proposal is binding on them as to the kinds or values of the assets in the proposed distribution. [3–906(b)]. This proposal procedure may be very useful where the releases or agreement of all the distributees may be impossible or difficult to obtain.

A problem that arises in some estates is that the estate does not have sufficient funds to satisfy all devises in a will. The cause for this problem of abatement may be due to creditors' claims, an election by the spouse or pretermitted children, expenses of administration, taxes or a general insufficiency of funds. Under the common law, in the absence of a specific order indicated in the testator's will, the order of abatement for personal property was as follows: (1) intestate property; (2) residuary legacies; (3) general legacies; and (4) specific and demonstrative legacies. [Atkinson, Wills § 136; see § 7.01]. Within each of the classes of testamentary gifts, the assets would contribute and abate ratably. Although subject to specific statutory or judicial exceptions today, real property was not subject to debts. Some states abate, however, according to the status of the devisee, e.g., spouse, descendant, etc. [20 Pa.Con.Stat.Ann. § 3541].

Except for the rule that there is no preference between real and personal property, the UPC's general rules follow the common law approach. [3–902(a)]. Because the UPC does not contain definitions of the various types of testamentary gifts, the common law definitions remain applicable. [See § 7.01]. The UPC also continues the rule that a testator may expressly control the order and manner by which devises shall abate. [3–902(b)]. In addition, several exceptions to the general rule must be mentioned. First, if the abatement problem is caused by a surviving spouse taking under the elective share provisions, the UPC provides that all beneficiaries under the will are to suffer the reduction pro rata and not according to the UPC's general order of abatement. [3–902(a), 2–210]. Second, if the personal representative determines that an express or implied purpose of the testamentary plan would be defeated by following the general order of abatement, the abatement must be made in a manner necessary to carry out the testator's intent. [3–902(b)]. Third, the UPC contains a special provision dealing with the apportionment of estate taxes which does not follow the general order of abatement. [3–916; see § 14.03; see also 2–302(a)(2)(iv); § 5.01(B) (pretermitted children)].

From the personal representative's viewpoint, the second exception is the most important and may cause the most difficulty. A situation in which the exception may be applicable would be in the case when the residuary devisees of a will are the testator's primary beneficiaries. Under these facts, a personal representative could determine that it was the testator's implied purpose to favor the residuary beneficiaries to the detriment of the other general and specific devisees. Although the exception clearly gives an escape device from the rigidity of the general order of abatement, it will just as clearly subject personal representative to the wrath and objection of those who believe the general rule should be applied. When this exception is applied, the personal representative would be wise to seek court approval for such a decision. An efficient way to obtain this approval would be in conjunction with a formal closing proceeding. [See 3–1001, 3–1002; 1 UPC Practice Manual, 380].

If it becomes necessary for the personal representative to sell a devise which is preferred over other interests in the estate, the other interests must be abated in favor of the preferred devisee according to the general rule. [3–902(c)]. The UPC also includes a special provision with regard to community property states. This provision provides that in an estate which consists of both separate and community property, debts and expenses of administration must be apportioned or charged against these different kinds of property in proportion to their relative value of the estate. [[3–902A(c)]].

The UPC contains several other miscellaneous provisions concerned with distribution. Under its right of retainer provision, a debtor-successor's debt must be offset against her interest in the estate. [3–903]. The successor, however, may take advantage of any defense that could have been raised in a direct proceeding against the successor to collect the debt such as the expiration of any relevant statute of limitations. With regard to interest on the general pecuniary devises, the UPC provides that unless the will indicates otherwise such devises bear the legal rate of interest beginning one year after the initial appointment of a personal representative. [3–904]. This differs from the law of most non-UPC states which provide that such devises bear interest from the date of death. [3–904, Comment].

The UPC also codifies the rule in many states that an anti-contest or anti-claim clause in a will is unenforceable against an interested person if that person had probable cause to institute the proceeding. [3–905; replicated in 2–517]. Under its probable cause test, this clause protects the devisee and other direct or indirect beneficiaries under the will who would receive more if the will were denied probate or, who is also a creditor of the estate and wishes to collect on his claim.

The UPC has special provisions dealing with distributions to trustees, distributions to persons under disability and dispositions of unclaimed assets. Under the UPC the trustee is treated as a distributee under Section 1–201(13) and therefore has all the privileges and protections accorded distributees in the administration of a decedent's estate. [3–913]. Before distributing assets to the trustee, however, the personal representative may require the trustee to perform certain acts. [See § 17.04(A)]. The UPC's provision concerned with unclaimed assets is optional due to the possible existence of and preference for comprehensive legislation on the subject matter. [3–914, Comment]. It requires a personal representative to distribute the share of any missing distributee or claimant to the conservator appointed for that person, if any, or to the appropriate state entity. [3–914(a)]. The state entity must pay the appropriate share to any person who shows proof of entitlement. If it refuses, the Court, on petition of the person entitled to the property and upon notice to the state entity, may make a determination as to the person's right in the property and order payment to that person if such right is established. The petitioner must pay all cost and expenses incident to the proceeding and is not entitled to interest on the assets held by the state entity. No petition and, therefore, no right of recovery is possible after eight years from the date of payment to the state entity. [3–914(b)].

The UPC contains a special facility of payment provision for persons under disability. [3–915]. First, if a distributee is a person under disability, the personal representative may discharge the distribution obligations by making distributions to such a person according to the expressed terms of the will. [3–915(b)]. In addition, and unless the will expressly prohibits, distributions to persons under disability according to any statutory facility of payment procedures discharge the personal representative. [See 3–501; § 15.05]. Distribution to an appointed conservator discharges the personal representative, also.

Finally, the UPC includes a special facility of payment provision for person under disability other than minors. [3–915(c)]. This provision permits a personal representative to make a distribution for a disabled devisee or heir either to:

(1) an attorney in fact under a valid power of attorney authorizing the receipt of property for the principal; or

(2) a spouse, parent or other close relative with whom the distributee resides if the distribution

does not exceed $10,000 per year or $10,000 in a lump sum.

The Court may authorize amounts greater than $10,000 on petition of the personal representative.

If any of the facility of payment conditions are met, the personal representative is discharged from liability for misappropriation by the recipient. Persons to whom the property is delivered or paid must apply the money or property to the disabled person's present needs for support and education. These same recipients are also empowered to reimburse themselves for out of pocket expenses for goods and services necessary for the disabled person's support although they may not pay themselves for their own services. The recipient must preserve excess sums for future support. The personal representative is not responsible for supervising the recipient's application of the payments made. If the personal representative knows that an appointed conservator exists or that a proceeding for the appointment of one is pending, payments must be made to the conservator. [3–915(c); see also § 15.05].

§ 14.02 Distribution in Kind

The UPC sets a definite preference for distribution in kind notwithstanding the type of gift involved. [3–906]. Obviously, the thing devised to the specific devisee should be distributed to that devisee. [3–906(a)(1)]. Persons entitled to exempt property under Section 2–402 are also entitled to receive the items selected to satisfy this requirement. In addition and with three provisos, the homestead, the family allowance, and all cash devises may be satisfied in kind at their fair market value on the date of distribution. [3–906(a)(2)]. The preference for in kind distribution in these situations can be rebutted if the following two situations exist: (1) the recipient of the distribution demands cash [3–906(a)(2)(i)]; or (2) a residuary devisee requests that the asset to be distributed in kind remain a part of the residue of the estate. [3–906(a)(2)(iii)]. Finally, the residuary estate must be distributed in any manner determined equitable under the particular circumstances. [3–906(a)(4)]. The personal representative possesses wide discretion in this regard. From a practical standpoint, agreement of the residuary devisees is suggested as a recommended, first approach to residuary distribution.

When property is distributed in kind to satisfy the homestead, the family allowance, or cash devises, it is necessary to determine the fair market value of the property distributed as of the date of distribution. [3–906(a)(2)(ii)]. If a security is the type of asset distributed in kind, its value is determined by the price of its last sale on the business day prior to the distribution or the median between the bid and asked prices if no sale was made on that day. [3–906(a)(3)]. A collectible obligation due the estate is valued at its sum due with accrued interest or at its discounted value on the date of distribution. When an asset distributed in kind does not have a readily ascertainable value, a reasonable appraised value set not more than thirty days prior to the date of distribution controls. The personal representative is given the discretionary authority to ascertain valuation in any reasonable way. Appraisers may be hired even if the assets had been previously appraised.

When distribution in kind is made, the personal representative must execute the appropriate instrument which assigns, transfers or releases the assets to the distributee. [3–907]. Proof of receipt of the instrument or of payment in distribution gives the distributee conclusive evidence that the latter has succeeded to that interest in the assets distributed. [3–908]. As these two provisions indicate, the executed instrument or other distribution does not constitute a transfer of title but constitutes evidence of the distributee's title in the property.

Except for the personal representative, no other person interested in the estate may directly attack or set aside the distribution. The personal representative is, therefore, the only person who is entitled to recover the assets or their value for an improper distribution. Even that recovery is barred if the distribution or payment has been adjudicated, the doctrine of estoppel is applicable or any relevant period of the limitations has expired. [3–909; see 3–1006, § 14.04(B)]. When these restrictions do not apply, however, the personal representative may recover from the distributee or from a claimant any improper distribution or payment. [3–909]. The distributee or claimant must either return the property received and its income since distribution, or if not possible, pay the value of the property at the date of distribution and its income and gain received from that date. Under the UPC, both trustee and beneficiaries of a testamentary trust are included within the definition of "distributee." [1–201(13)]. Impliedly, the personal representative would be able to obtain the same remedy from donees or other non bona fide purchasers who have received the property from a distributee. [1 UPC Practice Manual, 386–87].

Notwithstanding the potential liability of a distributee, third persons who purchase from or lend to the distributee or the distributee's transferee for value are broadly protected from potential liability. As bona fide purchasers and lenders, they take title free of all rights of any interested person and are not subject to personal liability to the estate or to any interested persons. [3–910]. Even bona fide transactions made with the personal representative who is also a distributee are covered by this restriction. Furthermore, the bona fide party need not inquire into the propriety of the personal representative's distribution in kind even if the personal representative has made the distribution to herself or even when the personal representative's authority has terminated before distribution. If the UPC state provides for a state documentary fee on its recorded instruments, the appearance of such documented fee on the recorded instrument constitutes prima facie evidence that the third party dealt with the distributee for value.

If partition of undivided interests in property distributed in kind is necessary, either the personal representative or one or more of the distributees may petition the Court for an order of partition. [3–911]. A petition for partition, however, must be made before formal or informal closing of the estate has been completed. In addition, notice must be made to the distributees and to the personal representative. The Court may order partition or sale if partition cannot be conveniently made.

§ 14.03 Apportionment of Estate Taxes

The UPC has a special section dealing with abatement caused by the payment of estate taxes, both federal and state. [3–916]. The UPC basically copies the Uniform Estate Tax Apportionment Act except that it tailors the Act to UPC terminology and philosophy and packages the Act in one multi-subparagraphed section. [3–916, Comment; see Uniform Estate Tax Apportionment Act]. As with other abatement provisions, the UPC's apportionment rule does not apply if decedent's will directs that a different method be applied. [3–916(b)]. Under such a circumstance, the decedent's will controls. Directions in the will, however, must be specific, clear and not susceptible to reasonable contrary interpretation if they are to override this section's tax apportionment scheme. [Estate of Huffaker, 641 P.2d 120 (Utah 1982)]. If the UPC's apportionment rule is determined to be inequitable, the Court is given discretion to direct apportionment in any equitable manner it determines appropriate. [3–916(c)(2)]. On petition of the personal representative or other interested persons, the Court in which venue lies for the administration of the decedent's estate may make an apportionment determination. [3–916(c)(1)].

Basically, when the UPC's apportionment rule is to be applied, the rule provides that each interest of a person interested in the estate must bear a portion of the tax equal to the proportion of the value of each person's interest as it bears to the total value of all interests in the estate. [3–916(b)]. Values for purposes of the apportionment are the values used for determining the estate tax or taxes. In calculating the apportionment, all allowances, deductions and credits are to be taken into account. [3–916(e)(1)]. Most significantly, interests entitled to deductions such as the marital deduction and the charitable deduction are not subject to apportionment. [3–916(e)(2), (5)]. An exception to the latter rule is that a life or other temporary interest is not subject to apportionment and the tax on both the temporary and remainder interest is to be paid out of the corpus of the property involved. [3–916(e)(2), 3–916(f)]. This exception is a rule of convenience rather than the rule of equity because it may make a charitable remainder subject to tax even though the property passing to the charity constitutes a legitimate deduction from the tax and is otherwise not taxable. If, because of negligent delay of the fiduciary, penalties or interest or both are assessed by the taxing authorities on the tax, the Court may determine that no apportionment of these additional amounts be charged against the persons with interests in the estate and that the fiduciary be personally responsible for these amounts. [3–916(c)(3)].

The person obligated to pay the tax, including a personal representative, has a variety of remedies available to insure that all obligated persons will pay their fair share of it. First, the person obligated to pay the tax may withhold the amount of tax attributable to an interest from any distribution of property to persons interested in the estate. [3–916(d)(1)]. If the amount possessed by the person obligated to pay the tax is not sufficient to pay the apportioned amount of tax, that person may recover the deficiency from persons interested in the estate. The same recovery possibilities exist even if no property is in the possession of the person obligated to pay the tax. When an action is necessary to recover the apportioned tax from persons interested in the estate, a Court's prior determination of apportionment is considered prima facie correct. [3–916(c)(4)].

The person obligated to pay the taxes is not under a duty to institute an action to recover the apportioned tax from a person interested in an estate during the three month period after the final determination of the tax. [3–916(g)]. After that time, however, that person must bring an action within a reasonable time or be subject to potential liability or surcharge if, because of the unreasonable delay, the apportioned tax was uncollectible. When the uncollectibility is not considered the fault of the person obligated to pay the tax, the additional tax due is equitably apportioned among all remaining who are still subject to apportionment.

Persons obligated to pay the tax who are domiciled or appointed in other jurisdictions are given the authority to institute actions to recover the apportioned tax due from persons who are either domiciled in the UPC state or whose property is subject to attachment or execution in the UPC state. [3–916(h); see § 12.11(B)]. Again, the prior determinations by the Court having jurisdiction over the administration of the decedent's estate are considered prima facie correct.

§ 14.04 Closing Estates

A. INFORMAL CLOSING PROCEDURE

The UPC establishes a procedure by which a personal representative may close an estate without the necessity of obtaining an adjudication from the Court. This informal closing procedure is accomplished only when a general personal representative for the estate files a sworn statement no earlier than six months after the date of the original appointment. [3–1003]. An estate being administered under supervised administration may not be closed in this manner.

The UPC is very explicit about the content of the sworn statement. It requires that the verified statement recite that the general personal representative or any predecessors in that position have satisfied the following prerequisites:

(1) The time for presenting claims has expired as proscribed by Section 3–803(a);

(2) Decedent's estate has been fully administered and distributed except as specified;

(3) If some claims remain undischarged, a detailed explanation of how they will be accommodated;

(4) A copy of the statement has been sent to all distributees of the estate;

(5) A copy of the statement has been sent to all creditors whose claims are neither paid nor barred; and

(6) A written full accounting of the administration has been sent to all distributees whose interests are affected.

[3–1003(a)(1)–(3)]. An explicitly approved solution to the problem of undischarged claims is to have the distributees agree to assume liability for their payment. [3–1003(a)(2)].

After the passage of varying periods of time, the filing of the sworn statement has the effect of both terminating the administration and, unless wrongdoing is involved, discharging the personal representative from liability to distributees and creditors. Discharge from liability occurs if successors or unbarred creditors or both have not instituted proceedings against the personal representative for breach of a fiduciary duty within six months after the date the sworn statement was filed. [3–1005]. Necessarily, this limitation period does not apply to actions brought by successors or creditors for the personal representative's fraud, misrepresentation or inadequate disclosure related to the settlement of the decedent's estate.

Termination of the personal representative's authority concerning the estate occurs one year after the date on which the closing statement was filed if no proceedings involving the personal representative are pending in the Court. [3–610(a), 3–1003(b); see § 12.09]. The UPC does not terminate the personal representative's authority upon the filing of the sworn statement because it was determined to be necessary to provide the personal representative with continuing authority for a period of time just in case there was a need to adjust or correct distributions made to distributees or creditors or both. [1 UPC Practice Manual, 304]. Obviously, it would be more convenient and efficient for a personal representative who continued to have authority to make the adjustments or corrections necessary rather than to rely upon individual actions brought by the aggrieved persons or upon a new proceeding and appointment of a personal representative under subsequent administration.

B. DISTRIBUTEE LIABILITY

When there has not been an appropriate adjudication concerning distribution of a decedent's estate, distributees have potential pass-through liability. They remain potentially liable to a personal representative acting on behalf of the rights of creditors, heirs or devisees. [3–1006]. The time limitations set on this liability provide that a distributee is not liable (1) to a creditor of the decedent beyond one year from the decedent's death or (2) to any other claimant beyond three years after the decedent's death or one year after the date of distribution, whichever is later in time. Naturally, in accord with Section 1–106, the limitation period will not bar the liability of a distributee who received the property as the result of fraud. [See § 2.01(B)(1)]. In addition, this limitation will not bar proceedings by an alleged decedent who proved to be alive. [3–1006, Comment; see § 11.03(B)(8)]. Rights of devisees and heirs can also be barred by a previous formal testacy proceeding [3–412; see § 11.03(B)(7)] and all types of claimants including creditors can be cut off by a formal closing proceeding. [See 3–1001, 3–1002; see § 14.04(C)].

A distributee's liability to undischarged and unbarred creditors is further limited. [3–1004]. First, a distributee is not liable to creditors for amounts received as part of the family protections. Second, total liability cannot exceed the value of the distribution at the time of distribution. Third, distributees are entitled to contribution from other distributees as each would have suffered abatement had the claim been paid during administration. A distributee, however, who fails to notify the other distributees of the demand made by a creditor in sufficient time to permit these distributees to join in the proceeding, can lose this right to contribution from other distributees. In addition, the fact that one or more distributees are insolvent or otherwise unable to make contribution does not constitute a justifiable deduction from devisees who are able to pay. [3–1004, Comment].

C. FORMAL CLOSING PROCEEDINGS

The UPC provides two related but different procedures for formally closing a decedent's estate. One procedure deals with the estate wholly testate but in which formal testacy proceedings have not been brought and the devisees do not desire to bring such proceedings. [3–1002]. The other procedure deals with all other estates in which a formal closing proceeding is desired by the interested persons. [3–1001].

Formal proceedings terminating testate administration concern the estate wherein a will has been informally probated. [3–1002]. The proceeding must be instituted by petition by the personal representative or any devisee under such will. The petition must not request an adjudication of decedent's testacy status. In addition, no proceeding may be entertained by the Court until the time for presenting creditors' claims which arose before the death of the decedent has expired. Beyond that limitation period, the personal representative may bring the proceeding at any time and devisees may bring it any time after one year from the date of the appointment of the original personal representative.

Although a request for formal testacy may not be made under this proceeding, the petition may request any other determination concerned with the settlement and distribution of the estate including a request for a final accounting, construction of the will and final settlement of the estate. A hearing is to be held only after notice has been given to all devisees and the personal representative. The Court is empowered to issue a broad range of orders including determination of distribution under the will, approval of settlement, approval and direction of distribution and the discharge of the personal representative from creditors, devisees made party to the proceeding and those represented by the personal representative.

If at any time a part of the estate appears to be intestate, the proceeding must be dismissed or amended to conform with the provisions of Section 3–1001. The lack of an adjudication of testacy and the limitation on the scope of the proceeding means that this particular procedure will not be used by interested persons very often. Its principal use arises where it is desired to totally distribute, terminate and discharge the personal representative before the ordinary statute of limitations on initiating proceedings has run, i.e., the later of three years from death or one year after informal probate, and where the petitioners do not want to rouse the interest and curiosity of heirs by providing them notice of a formal closing proceeding. [1 UPC Practice Manual, 392]. Since the passage of time will finalize testacy questions under informal probate, it would appear that letting the time run would be the most practical solution to this problem rather than bringing this type of closing proceeding. [3–108]. After the time has run, there would be no danger in initiating the following comprehensive formal proceeding which includes the determination of testacy.

The UPC includes an alternative and unrestricted formal proceeding for terminating and settling administration of decedents' estates. [3–1001]. Many of the requirements are very similar to the above described closing proceedings. The format is for the personal representative or any interested person to petition for an order of complete settlement of the estate. This petition may not be entertained until the time within which creditors may present claims has expired. Upon the expiration of this limitation, the proceeding may be instituted by the personal representative at any time and by any other interested person at any time after the passage of one year from the appointment of the original personal representative. As indicated, the range of requests to the Court is broader than the previously discussed proceedings. Not only may it include a request for final accounting, distribution, construction of the will, and final settlement of the estate, it should also request a determination of formal testacy or of heirs. [1 UPC Practice Manual, 391]. Formal testacy, however, may only be instituted if it has not previously been adjudicated and if the time limit for its institution has not passed. The determination of heirs may be requested at anytime, however, unless previously adjudicated because there is no time limitation, itself, on such a proceeding. [3–108].

Petitioners are required to give notice to all inter-ested persons. If formal testacy proceedings were not previously instituted and adjudicated, notice by publication to unknown and unascertained heirs and devisees will be necessary. In all other cases, notice should be given to all applicable interested persons as defined in Section 1–201(24) and to all unpaid and unbarred creditors. [1 UPC Practice Manual, 391]. After notice and hearing, the Court has the power to issue an order or orders on a broad range of matters concerned with the estate and its settlement depending on what is appropriate under the circumstances and what is requested in the petition. These matters may include an order of formal testacy, a determination of the persons enti-tled to distribution, approval of settlement, approv-al and direction of distribution and the discharge of the personal representative.

This formal closing proceeding may also be used as a curative device in situations where notice was not given to one or more heirs or devisees in previ-ous formal proceedings. [3–1001(b)]. Under this de-vice, it is necessary to give notice to the omitted or unnotified persons and to other interested parties. The list of interested parties should be shorter than it was in the prior formal proceeding because it is to be presumed that the prior proceeding was conclu-sive as to all persons given notice of the earlier proceeding. The Court may determine, confirm or alter its previous order of testacy as it affects all interested persons in light of the new situation. If the omitted or unnotified persons do not object, the evidence received in the original formal testacy proceeding constitutes prima facie proof of its findings as to the due execution of a will admitted to probate or as to the fact that decedent died leaving no valid will. The existence of this curative device will be extremely useful when persons are inadvertently omitted in prior formal proceedings.

The order of the Court under either proceeding is a final adjudication and constitutes both a termination of the administration of the estate and a discharge of the personal representative. Such a judgment is subject only to reversal by appeal and to attack for the perpetration of fraud under Section 1–106. Except for questions of testacy under the former proceeding, distributees under such an order are similarly protected. The final order presumably carries with it all of the protections of res judicata and collateral estoppel.

D. DISCHARGE OF SECURITY FOR FIDUCIARY PERFORMANCE

When a personal representative's appointment has terminated under the UPC [see § 12.09], the personal representative, sureties for the personal representative, or any successor of either, may apply to the Registrar for a certificate that will discharge any lien upon any property given to secure the personal representative's performance. [3–1007]. The filed verified application must show that as far as the applicant knows there are no actions concerning the estate pending in any court. Significantly, the discharging certificate does not affect the liability of the personal representative or the surety, if any, but merely constitutes a release of the security itself. [3–1007, Comment].

E. SUBSEQUENT ADMINISTRATION

A personal representative, who has been discharged under a formal closing proceeding or whose appointment terminated because a year passed since the filing of a closing statement, has no authority to deal with after-discovered property which requires further administration. [3–1008, 3–608]. Consequently, in order to deal with this property, a successor personal representative must be appointed. This appointment can be accomplished either through informal appointment proceedings [3–401; see § 11.01(B)] or through a special formal appointment proceeding. [3–1008]. Under the latter proceeding upon the petition of an interested person, the Court, after notice that it directs, is empowered to appoint the same or a successor personal representative. Unless the Court orders otherwise, the new formally appointed personal representative is subject to the ordinary and appropriate provisions of the UPC in the administration of the subsequently discovered property. A creditor's claim, however, which was previously barred may not be asserted in the subsequent administration.

§ 14.05 Settlement Agreements

The UPC contains what might be called both formal and informal private settlement procedures.

Under the informal procedure, a written private agreement that alters the normal intestate or testate distribution pattern between all of the successors who are affected by the agreement must be followed by the personal representative subject, of course, to any fiduciary obligation. [3–912]. An agreement of this nature is necessarily subject to the rights of creditors and taxing agencies. Because trustees under such an agreement are merely treated as devisees, the personal representative is not responsible for seeing to the performance of any testamentary trust. The trustee, of course, is not relieved of the duties owed to the trust beneficiaries.

The UPC also contains a formal procedure for compromising and settling controversies between persons holding the beneficial interests in a decedent's estate. [3–1101, 3–1102]. The types of controversies that may be compromised under this procedure are very broad in scope. They include controversies as to the admissibility of a will to formal probate, to disputes concerning other governing instruments covering gratuitous transfers, to construction, validity or effect of wills or other instruments, to the rights or interests of any successor in the estate and to issues arising during the administration of the estate. A compromise under this procedure is binding on all persons made parties to the procedure so long as it is approved in a formal proceeding before the Court. [3–1101]. Unborn, unascertained, or otherwise unlocatable persons may be bound by the court order if they are virtually represented by other parties with substantially identical interests in the proceeding. [1–403(2)(iii); § 2.03(B)]. This binding effect of an approved compromise is also applicable as against trusts or other inalienable interests. Necessarily, creditors or taxing authorities who are not parties to the compromise cannot have their rights impaired. The comprehensive binding effect of a formal settlement makes it a desirable settlement method where some of the successors are not competent or are unknown.

The UPC outlines the procedure to follow in order to get court approval of a compromise. [3–1102]. A petition may be submitted to the Court with the written compromise agreement attached by any interested person including the personal representative or a trustee. [3–1102(2)]. The written agreement must set forth the terms of the compromise and must have been executed by all competent persons and the parents acting for minor children who have a beneficial interest or claim affected by the compromise. [3–1102(1)]. Only those persons affected by the compromise need to execute the compromise. Concomitantly, those persons not executing the compromise or not represented under Section 1–403 by persons executing the compromise are not bound by its terms. [See 3–1102, Comment]. Minor children can be bound by their parents executing the compromise only if other competent persons with similar interests also execute the compromise. [3–1102(3)]. If no other competent person executes the compromise, minor children would have to be represented by guardians ad litem in order to be bound by the approved compromise.

Several prerequisites must be satisfied before the Court can approve a compromise. First, notice must be given to all interested persons or their representatives, including any appointed personal representative of the estate and all trustees of trusts affected by the compromise. Actual notice of the settlement proceedings to all interested parties is essential. [In re Estate of Girod, 645 P.2d 871 (Hawai'i 1982)]. If all are not notified, problems of the finality of the settlement may arise. For example, an heir, who did not receive notice of the settlement, was not barred, in the absence of a showing of prejudice to the other parties by reason of the heir's delay after gaining actual knowledge of the settlement, from challenging the settlement anytime prior to the close of the probate estate. [Id.]. Only those affected by the settlement agreement, however, are interested persons within the notice requirement. [Columbia Union Nat'l Bank & Trust Co. v. Bundschu, 641 S.W.2d 864 (Mo.App. W.D.1982)].

The second prerequisite is that the Court may approve the compromise only if the underlying controversy is in good faith and the effect of the agreement upon the interests of persons represented by fiduciaries or other representatives is just and reasonable. If satisfied in this regard, the Court then must make an order approving the compromise and directing all fiduciaries subject to its jurisdiction to execute it. [3–1102(3)]. The terms of any approved and executed compromise must be followed by these fiduciaries when making further dispositions of the estate. An advantage of the court approved formal compromise procedure, as compared to the informal compromise procedure, is that it provides the compromising parties a procedure for forcing fiduciaries concerned with the estate to execute the compromise even though the latters' approval might be against their own personal or financial interests, as employees entitled to compensation from the estate or trust. [3–1102, Comment].

PART FOUR

THE PROTECTION OF PERSONS UNDER DISABILITY AND THEIR PROPERTY

CHAPTER 15

GUARDIANSHIP AND CONSERVATORSHIP

§ 15.01 Introduction to Guardianship and Conservatorship

The concept and necessity of guardianship derive from the circumstance when a person is under some type of disability which causes that person to be unable to manage his or her own personal or business affairs or both. [Woerner, Law of Guardianship § 1]. Through the guardianship device, the disabled person's rights and interests can be protected. Generally, the person who suffers from such disabilities is either a minor, mental incompetent or other incompetent. The disability of a minor is presumed by legislative determination depending upon the person's age. [Id.]. The other forms of disability require voluntary action by the person or some form of legal proceeding to determine the incompetency status.

An important feature of guardianship is that it serves two distinct functions. The first and most apparent is guardianship of property. Under such a guardianship, the guardian manages (receives and expends) the ward's property or estate for the purposes of the guardianship. The second, which is particularly important in the case of minors, is the guardianship of the person. Here the guardian has custody and, therefore, physical control over the ward. The same person may be permitted to serve in both capacities.

Guardianship laws, with a few exceptions, remained unchanged for many years. [2 UPC Practice Manual, 495]. Consequently, many of the procedures and substantive regulations suffer unreasonably from excessive formality or administrative restrictions or both. In addition, they frequently were antiquated, poorly organized, fragmented and insufficient in coverage. Despite these inadequacies, legislatures have been slow to act and when revisions have occurred the resultant legislation has often been unsatisfactory.

Although in the 1946 Model Probate Code attempted to improve and modernize guardianship laws, it did not stir reform in the states. [Model Probate Code, at 189–234]. In order to remedy this unfortunate state of affairs, the UPC includes a comprehensive and modernized article on the law dealing with the protection of persons under a disability and their property.

§ 15.02   Overview and Policies of the UPC

In 1982, the National Conference of Commissioners on Uniform State Laws promulgated the Uniform Guardianship and Protective Proceedings Act as a freestanding act. The provisions in this Act were simultaneously integrated into the Uniform Probate Code as a revision to Article V, Parts 1, 2, 3, and 4. Although many of the UPC's provisions in the 1969 version of Article V were merely renumbered or altered in minor ways, a significant number were substantively changed and new concepts were incorporated into the Article. This Nutshell will be concerned with the 1982 Act as it was integrated into the UPC.[1]

1. In 1997, the National Conference of Commissioners on Uniform State Laws adopted a new Uniform Guardianship and Protective Proceedings Act. The Act initially is a freestanding Act and now integrated into the UPC. Although the new Act follows the basic outline of the prior version, major changes were made. The emphasis of the 1997 provisions is to encourage limited guardianships and conservatorships. The court should create a guardianship or conservatorship only when no alternative to one is available. Courts must tailor the guardianship or conservatorship to fit the needs of the incapacitated person and may remove only those rights that the incapacitated person can no longer exercise or manage.

The "incapacitated person" is defined as "an individual who, for reasons other than being a minor, is unable to receive and evaluate information or make or communicate decisions to such an extent that the individual lacks the ability to meet essential requirements for physical health, safety, or self-care, even with appropriate technological assistance." UNIFORM GUARDIANSHIP AND PROTECTIVE PROCEEDINGS ACT OF 1997 § 102(5). Noncourt standby guardianship provisions are available in a wide variety of situa-

The UPC's approach to these matters is significantly different from prior law. [Effland, Caring for the Elderly, at 376]. For overview purposes, it is helpful to outline the UPC's underlying policies. The UPC's procedures and rules are designed to:

(1) Allow persons to anticipate incapacity problems and to create their own solutions to them;

(2) Improve and intensify Court involvement when appropriate and necessary;

(3) Limit the invasion into the person's lifetime activities to the least intrusive device or technique;

(4) Protect persons from improper and unnecessary guardianships and conservatorships (require due process and prohibit undue encroachment upon the control of one's lifetime activities);

(5) Provide extensive procedural flexibility and numerous alternatives;

(6) Recognize distinctions between guardianship (custody) and conservatorship (estate man-

tions where there is a need for a guardian to step in immediately upon the occurrence of an event.

Although counsel is not mandated, a visitor must be appointed. The court may order professional evaluation if requested by the ward or it is found appropriate. Petitioner and respondent must be at the hearing unless excused by the court. The burden of proof is the clear and convincing evidence standard.

Changes in how a guardianship and conservatorship operates are also made. The ward's views must be taken into account when decisions are made by the fiduciary. Court monitoring is enhanced. Annual reports must be filed. Continuation of the guardianship or conservatorship must be considered. A visitor may be appointed during the monitoring processes.

agement) and minors versus other persons under a disability;

(7) Reduce the stigmatization and embarrassment for those who are subjected to incapacity procedures;

(8) Resolve conflicts between concurrent judicial and quasi judicial proceedings;

(9) Streamline procedures to reduce costs (eliminate redundant and superfluous procedures and remove overpaternalistic court involvement); and

(10) Treat the conservator as a trustee with broad powers to manage the protected person's estate.

It is no small task to offer provisions that will satisfy all of those policies. In fact, some of them are conflicting and require consistent resolution only by individualization of the procedures and remedies.

The comprehensiveness and the number of alternatives and procedural safeguards against misuse or over-use of procedures add a degree of complexity to the UPC. Thus, the UPC does not provide users with a single and inflexible trail to follow but requires each to cut one's own trail. This attribute does not detract from the UPC's merits and benefits; however, it does cause some resistance to its enactment. Chart 15–1 outlines the procedures, techniques, and protections that would be available in a UPC state to deal with persons under a disability.

CHART 15–1

OUTLINE OF PROCEDURES AND TECHNIQUES TO DEAL WITH PERSONS UNDER A DISABILITY

A.	Guardianship	Citation
1	None created except when necessary	5–204(a), 5–306(a)
2	Testamentary/lifetime appointment	5–202, 5–301
3	Limited guardianship	5–204(b), 5–306(a), (c)
4	Full guardianship	5–207, 5–306(b)
B.	Conservatorships	Citation
1	Facility of payment or delivery	5–101
2	Multiple-party accounts	Art. 6
3	Durable powers	Art. 5, Pt. 5
4	Inter vivos trusts	General law of trusts in Code state
5	Single transaction and protective arrangement authorization	5–408
6	Limited conservatorship	5–407(a)
7	Full conservatorship	5–407(b)
C.	Protection Devices and Concept	Citation
1	Full notice and hearing	5–206(b), 5–304, 5–405, 5–406
2	Representation by counsel	5–406(a)
3	Impartial visitor procedure	5–103(21), 5–406(b), (c)
4	Standard of proof	5–207, 5–103(10) 5–306(b), 5–103(7) 5–401
5	Selection of best person for fiduciary position	5–207, 5–305, 5–409
6	Informal objection procedure by ward	5–203, 5–311(b)
7	Bond	5–410
8	Accounting	5–418

The discussion of Article V of the UPC in this Nutshell will not include an analysis of every section or concept. Instead, some of it will be only summarized or generalized.

§ 15.03   Organization, Interrelationships and Definitions

Article V of the UPC organizes the many different issues concerning persons under a disability into logical and relevant categories. Part 1 includes general provisions and definitions dealing with the alternative device of facility of payment or delivery, delegation of powers by a parent or guardian, general definitions, and a request for notice by interested persons. All of these provisions are either self-contained or are applicable to all of the other parts of the Article. This makes it convenient to make reference to a single part of the UPC.

Parts 2, 3, and 4 are the heart of Article V. They include the provisions concerning guardians of minors, guardians of incapacitated persons other than minors, and conservatorships or the protection of property of persons under disability and minors.

Although Parts 2 and 3 are somewhat duplicative in that each contains provisions for the appointment, removal, termination, venue, court procedures, notice requirements and powers and duties of a guardian and of a guardianship, the drafters of the UPC felt that the significant distinctions between the issues relating to minors versus the same issues relating to other incapacitated persons demanded separate treatment. [Compare 5–201 to 5–212 *with* 5–301 to 5–312]. Although separate treatment may increase the size of the UPC a small amount, it actually decreases its complexity. By separating the provisions related to minors from the provisions related to other incapacitated persons, the UPC clearly indicates what provisions are applicable to each situation. There is no confusion whether a particular provision applies to one case or the other. It has been held that the guardianship of minors and of incapacitated persons are mutually exclusive procedures under the UPC. [Guardianship of Evans, 587 P.2d 372 (Mont.1978)]. Part 2 of Article V must be used for the guardianship of minors notwithstanding a minor's other incapacities. Part 3 must be used for the guardianships of all other types of incapacitated persons.

The separation of Part 4, dealing with conservatorships or what are called "protective proceedings," from Parts 2 and 3, dealing with guardianships, is also meritorious. [See 5–401 to 5–431]. This separation clearly defines the range of each of the fiduciary relationships. The guardian is responsible for care and custody of the ward; the guardian is not responsible for money management. [5–103(6), 5–209, 5–309]. The existence of a guardianship indicates the ward is incapacitated from a contractual standpoint. This means that consent of the guardian is necessary for a wide range of activities in which the ward may participate. On the other hand, the conservator is responsible for the ward's financial management. [5–103(3), 5–423]. With limited exception, the conservator is not responsible for the care and custody of the ward. In addition, the existence of a conservatorship does not automatically affect the normal capacity of the protected person. [See Effland, Caring for the Elderly, at 398–400]. If that is a problem, the conservator should seek the appointment of a guardian. Similarly if financial management is necessary, the guardian should seek appointment of a conservator.

It is also important to emphasize that under the UPC, just because a guardian of the person is necessary, it does not mean that protective proceedings are required, or vice versa. Situations may arise in which a person may need a guardian but has no property or assets requiring a conservator. On the other hand, a person may require a conservator but not require a guardian. For example, a missing person whose assets require management certainly does not need a guardian appointed to take care and custody of his absent person.

As with other parts of the UPC, a large number of definitions are included that are applicable throughout Parts 1–4 of Article V. [5–103(1)–(22); see § 2.01(B)(4)]. For informational and overview purposes, Chart 15–2 lists them in alphabetical order.

CHART 15–2

Terms Defined for Provisions on Disabled Persons

Claims	Lease	Proceeding
Conservator	Letters	Property
Court	Minor	Protected person
Disability	Mortgage	Protective
Estate	Organization	proceeding
Guardian	Parent	Security
Incapacitated	Person	Visitor
person	Petition	Ward

§ 15.04 Jurisdiction and Venue for Guardianship and Protective Proceedings

A. JURISDICTION OVER THE SUBJECT MATTER

The UPC Court is expressly given jurisdiction over the subject matter for guardianship and protective proceedings. [1–302(c); see § 2.02]. For emphasis and clarity, however, the UPC includes several special provisions that are exclusively related to proceedings concerned with persons under disability. First, guardianship and protective proceedings for the same person may be consolidated if they are commenced or pending in the same court. [5–102(b)]. Because the requirements for the above two proceedings are not identical, however, it is necessary that the parties involved take care to satisfy the requirements of both proceedings even though consolidated. [2 UPC Practice Manual, 503–04]. Second, the UPC recognizes that in a proceeding subsequent to appointment concerned with a guardian of a minor or a guardian of an incapacitated person, the ward may not reside any more in the judicial subdivision wherein the initial proceeding for appointment was instituted or in which acceptance of a testamentary appointment was filed. Under this circumstance, the Court where the ward presently resides has concurrent jurisdiction over resignation, removal, accounting and other proceedings relating to the guardianship with the court in which the guardian was appointed or the acceptance was filed. [5–211, 5–312]. Generally, the decision whether to retain or to transfer should be based upon concepts similar to those employed under the doctrine of forum non conveniens.

Third, for formal protective proceedings the UPC recognizes a distinction between exclusive and concurrent jurisdiction. The Court in which the protective proceeding petition has been filed has, until termination, exclusive jurisdiction over the following issues:

(1) The determination of the need for a protective order or the appointment of a conservator [5–402(1)];

(2) The determination of the manner in which the protected person's estate that is subject to the laws of the UPC state must be managed, expended or distributed to or for the use of the protected person or any of his or her dependents [5–402(2)];

(3) The determination of matters subsequent to appointment such as bonding, accounting, distribution or any other appropriate relief [5–415(a)];

(4) The determination of instructions requested by the conservator [5–415(b)]; and

(5) The determination of termination of the protective proceeding. [5–429].

The Court also has concurrent jurisdiction with any other court that also may obtain jurisdiction over issues concerned with the determination of the validity of third persons' claims against the protected person individually or against his or her estate and for the determination of his title to any property or claim. [5–402(3); see 5–427].

B. JURISDICTION OVER THE PERSON

Similar to the rule applicable to personal representatives [see § 10.02(C)(2)], the UPC provides a continuing type of personal jurisdiction power in the Court of appointment or acceptance over the fiduciaries serving persons under disability. This continuing jurisdiction power is applicable to guardians of minors [5–208], guardians of incapacitated persons [5–307] and conservators of their estates. [5–412]. It subjects these fiduciaries to any proceeding relating to their fiduciary office that may be instituted by any interested person. The only special requirement to sustain this jurisdiction is that a specific notice requirement must be satisfied for each proceeding.

C. VENUE

For proceedings dealing with the guardianship of a minor, venue is in the place where the minor resides or is present. [5–205]. Venue for proceedings dealing with the guardianship of an incapacitated person is also generally in the place where the incapacitated person resides or is present. [5–302]. Venue in such latter proceedings, however, may also be in the Court of competent jurisdiction that had ordered the incapacitated person admitted to an institution. Venue for protective proceedings may be either in the place where the person to be protected resides or if that person does not reside in the UPC state, in any place where she has property. [5–403(1)–(2)]. Venue for protective proceedings based upon the person's residence is not affected by a guardian having been appointed in another place. [5–403(1)]. It is important to note that the one appropriate venue recognized for all three types of proceedings concerned with a person under a disability is based upon the disabled person's residence and not her domicile. Reconciliation of identical proceedings in two or more appropriate venues must be made according to Section 1–303. [See § 2.02].

D. REQUEST FOR NOTICE

Using a procedure similar to the demand for notice procedure in Article III, the UPC provides that any interested person may file a request for notice with the Registrar. [5–104; see 3–204,

§ 10.02(C)(5)]. Governmental agencies paying or planning to pay benefits to the protected person are considered interested persons under this procedure. The request must include the following information and statements: (1) the interest of the person making the request; (2) the demandant's address or that of the attorney; and (3) that the request is effective only to matters occurring after the date of its filing. Upon the payment of any required fee, the clerk must mail a copy of the request to any appointed conservator.

§ 15.05   Miscellaneous Avoidance Devices

One of the goals of the UPC's provisions concerned with persons under disabilities is to minimize the necessity for employing the devices and procedures and to simplify these procedures and devices when it is essential to employ them. Several collateral but related devices incorporated within the UPC which support this goal deserve discussion at this point.

In the case of a minor, the UPC includes a facility of payment provision. Under it, any person who owes the minor $5,000 or less of cash or personal property per year may pay or deliver it either to the minor, if eighteen or married, to the minor's custodian, to the minor's guardian or into a federally insured financial institution savings account in the minor's name and with notice to the minor of the deposit. [5–101]. If these conditions are met, the person making the payment or delivery is discharged from liability for misappropriation by the recipient. Any person to whom the property is delivered or paid, other than the minor and the financial institution, is obligated to apply the money or property (1) to the minor's present needs for support and education, (2) to preserve any excess for future payment for support, and (3) to preserve any excess above the first two purposes for delivery to the minor upon attaining majority. These same recipients are also empowered to reimburse themselves for out of pocket expenses for the minor's support although they may not pay themselves for their own services. Payments or deliveries may not be made under this section if the person who owes the minor has actual notice that an appointed conservator exists or that a proceeding for the appointment of one is pending. This facility of payment provision will provide a convenient alternative to a conservatorship and other protective proceedings, for example, where contractual obligors such as insurance companies have small and annual payments due to a minor. [5–101, Comment]. The UPC also has a special facility of payment provision for distributions from estates by personal representatives. [3–915; § 14.01].

The UPC includes another provision which, under its limited circumstances, may also avoid the necessity of the appointment of a guardian for both a minor and an incapacitated person. Except for the power to consent to a minor's marriage or adoption, a parent or guardian may temporarily delegate to another person any of the care, custody and property powers exercisable for the benefit of the ward.

[5–102]. The only two requirements for such a delegation are that the form of the delegation must be made by a properly executed power of attorney and its term cannot exceed six months in duration. This provision provides a parent or a guardian with a convenient and simple method to provide continual guardianship protection in case an emergency would arise while the parent or appointed guardian was absent. For example, the delegatee could give consent to an emergency operation. [5–102, Comment]. The delegation of parental powers, however, does not necessarily change the child's legal residence or custody. [Chapp v. High School District No. 1 of Pima County, 574 P.2d 493 (Ariz.App. 1978)].

§ 15.06   Durable Powers of Attorney

Durable power statutes exist in all state and equivalent jurisdictions in this country. [See Collin, Moses, & Lombard, Drafting the Durable Power of Attorney]. They have become a significant alternative for conservatorships. They permit persons to anticipate the problem of diminished or full incapacity without the need for court involvement. For many estate planners, the durable power is as an essential document for their clients as is the will.

The UPC incorporates the Uniform Durable Power of Attorney Act, as amended, into Part 5 of Article V. [5–501 to 5–505; see Uniform Durable Power of Attorney Act]. Two principles are adopted that make powers of attorney more durable than under the common law. First, the civil law rule with regard to the effect of the principal's death, disability or incompetence applies to all written powers of attorney. [5–504]. It provides that actions by the attorney in fact in good faith and according to the written power of attorney are valid even though such actions take place after the principal's death, disability or incompetence so long as the attorney in fact did not have actual knowledge of the happening of such an event. Any such valid action taken binds the principal and the principal's heirs, devisees and personal representative. For the protection of third parties dealing with the attorney in fact and in the absence of fraud, an affidavit executed by the attorney in fact stating that the attorney in fact did not have knowledge at the time of his action of a revocation or termination caused by death, disability or incompetence is conclusive proof of nonrevocation or nontermination of the power to act at that time. [5–505]. If the action taken requires the execution and delivery of a recordable instrument, the affidavit is also recordable when authenticated. Significantly, this provision does not alter or effect any inconsistent provision in the power of attorney dealing with revocation or termination.

Second, the UPC permits the creation of a true durable power of attorney in the instrument creating the power merely by the inclusion of specific provisions. [5–501 to 5–503]. Under the relevant sections, a written power of attorney may specifically provide that the disability of the principal does not affect the power of the appointed attorney in fact to act. [5–502]. The UPC offers suggestions for the necessary phrases to create such a power. [5–501]. For a power of attorney that is immediately effective, the phrase suggested is "This power of attorney shall not be affected by disability or incapacity of the principal or lapse of time." For a power which will become effective in the future due to disability, called a "springing power," the suggested phrase is "This power of attorney shall become effective upon the disability or incapacity of the principal." Neither phrase constitutes words of art and the substance of their purpose and effect may be stated with other similar words.

Under a true durable power, all actions taken according to the power by the attorney in fact during a period of disability or incompetence of the principal have the same binding and beneficial effect as if the principal was not disabled. [5–502]. In addition, the same effect applies to actions taken under circumstances where it is uncertain whether the principal is dead or alive. These durable powers remain effective until a time explicitly expressed in the instrument, if any is expressed, or until terminated by the death of the principal, whichever first occurs.

If due to the disability or disappearance a conservator is appointed for the principal, the attorney in fact must account to the conservator as well as the principal. [5–503(a)]. The conservator now has the same power over the attorney in fact as the principal would have had if incapacity or disappearance had not occurred, including the power to revoke, suspend or terminate any part or all of the power.

This power over the attorney in fact does not apply to a guardian of the person for the principal.

Significantly, the principal may include in the durable power a nomination of the person whom the principal desires to serve as conservator if protective proceedings are commenced. [5–503(b)]. Usually, a principal names the attorney in fact as the nominee in order to prevent any conflict that might arise between two persons serving in different fiduciary roles. The principal may also nominate in the durable power the person to serve as guardian of the person. The Court must appoint the nominee unless good cause for disqualification is shown.

§ 15.07   The Guardian of a Minor

Guardianship of a minor is treated in the UPC as a separate relationship. A full set of provisions are provided specifically dealing with the guardian's necessity, selection, appointment, powers, duties, liabilities, duration and termination. [5–201 to 5–212]. Because incapacity due to minority is assumed by law, the procedures provided for the establishment of a guardianship for a minor are not as comprehensive and protective as they are for the creation of guardianships for other persons under a disability.

Under the UPC, no guardianship by any method may be created for a person who is incapacitated solely because of minority unless the minor is unmarried and all parental rights of custody have been terminated or suspended. [5–202(b), 5–204(a)].

Consequently, a natural or adoptive parent is automatically the guardian of the person of his or her minor natural and adopted children. There need be no official acceptance or court action taken in these situations. Presumably, any parent would have to be removed according to removal proceedings before any other person could be appointed guardian of that parent's minor children. [5–204(a); see 5–212].

The UPC creates a nearly unique procedure for the appointment of a guardian for a minor. This is called parental appointment and is analogous to informal appointment under Article III of the UPC. [5–202; see § 11.01(B)]. Under this procedure the parent of an unmarried minor may appoint a guardian for the minor by will or by any other writing which is signed by the parent and attested by at least two witnesses. [5–202(a)]. Under circumstances where a guardian of a minor may be appointed, the mere filing of the parental appointment or the probate of the appointing will in the proper court, constitutes an effective creation of the guardianship. [5–202(b), and (c)]. Upon acceptance, the guardian must give notice to the minor and to any person having the minor's care or the minor's nearest adult relative. [5–202(d)]. A parental appointment may be prevented or terminated by a minor ward who is fourteen or more years of age. [5–203]. The ward must object before the appointment is accepted or within 30 days after receiving notice of its acceptance. If the objection is proper and timely, a guardian may only be appointed by the court.

The court appointment of a guardian of a minor is analogous to formal appointment under Article III of the UPC. [5–204; see § 11.01(C)]. It requires the filing of a petition, notice, hearing, and order of appointment. [See 5–204 to 5–206]. The court is duty bound to appoint the person whose appointment would be in the best interest of the minor. [5–207]. The nominee of the minor fourteen or more years of age may but need not necessarily be appointed. Temporary guardians, with full powers of general guardians, may be appointed but their terms may not run more than 6 months. [5–204(b)].

Under the UPC, a guardian of a minor has the powers and duties of a parent who properly has custody and whose child is unemancipated. [5–209(a), (b), and (c)]. The guardian is specifically required to become and continue to be personally acquainted with the ward. [5–209(b)(1)]. Although the guardian must protect the ward's assets and use available monies for the benefit of ward's support, care and education, the guardian is not the conservator and is primarily responsible for controlling the minor's personal activities and relationships. This includes, for example, the authority to establish a residence, consent to medical or other professional care, and consent to marriage or adoption of the ward. [5–209(c)]. The guardian has a duty to seek the appointment of a conservator or other protective proceeding, if necessary, and to turn excess monies over to a conservator. Any compensation for services or reimbursement for room, board or clothing, or both, for the guardian must be approved by a court or an independent conservator appointed for the estate of the ward. [5–209(d)].

The UPC includes a provision for limited guardianships for minors. [5–209(e)]. This permits the court to restrict the guardian's control over the ward's personal conduct in certain ways. It might, for example, restrict the guardian as to a particular place of abode or residence. [5–209, Comment]. Any limitation placed on the guardian's statutory powers, however, must be endorsed on the letters of guardianship.

The guardian does not have a duty to provide bond or to file periodic or final accountings. Presumably, the Court with its inherent power over these matters could order both to be given. [See 2 UPC Practice Manual, 509–10]. In addition, it is very significant to emphasize that a guardian's duties and powers do not terminate even though she moves herself and ward from the state of appointment. [5–201; 5–209(c)(2)]. The guardian, of course, is liable to ward for injury caused by any breach of duty or improper exercise of a power or both.

A guardianship of a minor continues until the minor dies, is adopted, marries or attains majority and it terminates upon the guardian's death, removal or approved resignation. [5–210]. A testamentary appointment is also terminated if the will which makes the appointment is denied probate in formal testacy proceedings. Although a guardian may resign fiduciary office, the resignation does not terminate the guardianship until it is approved by the Court. Termination means the guardian's authority and responsibility end, but does not affect the guardian's liability for prior acts or her duty to account for the ward's funds and assets.

Removal proceedings may be instituted by any person interested in the ward's welfare or by the ward personally if fourteen years of age or more. [5–212(a)]. The ground for removal is that it would be in the best interest of the ward. Notice of the proceeding must be given to the ward, the guardian and others as court ordered. [5–212(b)]. After notice and a hearing, the Court may order termination by removal and may make any other appropriate orders. [5–212(c)]. If the Court determines that the ward's interests are or may be inadequately represented, it can appoint a guardian ad litem for the minor at anytime during the proceeding. [5–212(d)]. When the minor is fourteen or more years of age, the Court is to give preference to the attorney selected by the minor.

§ 15.08   The Guardian of an Incapacitated Person

The UPC defines an incapacitated person as one who for any reason except minority is "lacking sufficient understanding or capacity to make or communicate responsible decisions." [5–103(7)]. Although any cause which meets the standard is covered, specifically mentioned examples of the cause of such a condition include mental illness, mental deficiency, physical illness or disability, chronic use of drugs and chronic intoxication. It must be emphasized that this guardian is not the guardian of the incapacitated person's property but is the caretaker of the incapacitated person's person. [See 5–309]. Consequently, the definition of incapacity makes questions concerning the alleged incapacitated person's ability to manage the person's estate irrelevant. [2 UPC Practice Manual, 520].

Similar to the parental appointment procedure for the appointment of a guardian for a minor, the UPC includes an appointment procedure for parents or spouses of other incapacitated persons. [5–301; see § 15.07]. Under this procedure the spouse or parent of an incapacitated person may appoint a guardian for the person by will or by any other writing which is signed by the spouse or parent and attested by at least two witnesses. [5–301(a), and (b)]. A spouse's appointment takes priority over a parent's appointment if they conflict. [5–301(b)]. In addition, the appointment in the will of the last parent to die has priority over the first to die unless the surviving parent has been adjudged incapacitated or the will of the last parent to die is denied probate in formal testacy proceedings. [5–301(a)]. Apparently any person can be appointed. [See 5–301(d); 5–301, Comment]. A testamentary guardian who has accepted appointment under a will probated in another state which is the testator's domicile must also be recognized in the UPC state. [5–301(c)].

An appointment under this procedure becomes effective upon the nominee's filing of an acceptance of appointment in the Court in which the will has been, either informally or formally probated, or in which the instrument is filed at the place where the incapacitated person resides or is present. [5–301(a), and (b)]. The appointed guardian must give seven days advance notice to the incapacitated person and to the person's caretaker or to the person's nearest adult relative. The notice must state that the appointment may be terminated by the incapacitated person filing a written objection with the Court. Concomitantly, the incapacitated person can prevent the appointment from taking effect or terminate a previous testamentary appointment by filing a written objection with the appropriate Court. [5–301(d)]. This objection would not necessarily foreclose the person from eventually being appointed but would restrict that person's appointment solely to the result of a court appointment procedure.

When testamentary appointment is not available or desired, a guardian for an incapacitated person must be appointed by the Court. The UPC's court appointment procedures are meritoriously rigorous and designed to prevent unwanted appointments of such guardians. The procedure is initiated by the incapacitated person, or by any person interested in the person's welfare, filing a petition for a finding of incapacity and for the appointment of a guardian. [5–303(a)]. Although the UPC does not state what the contents of the petition must have, it is very explicit with regard to the requirements for notice

520 DISABLED PERSONS Ch. 15

of the date and time of the hearing on such a petition. [5–304]. The person alleged to be incapacitated must be personally served with notice and waiver of such notice is ineffective unless that person is present at the hearing or a visitor confirms the waiver after an interview with the person. [5–304(c)]. The person's spouse, parents and adult children must also be personally served if they can be found within the state. [5–304(a)(1), (c)]. Finally, any guardian, conservator, caretaker, or custodian, parents and spouse of the person, if not found within the state, must be given notice as provided in Section 1–401. [5–304(a)(2), (c)]. If the alleged incapacitated person's spouse, parents, and adult children are not notified, then one of the person's closest adult relatives must be notified if one can be found. [5–304(a)(3)].

Protection is also provided to the alleged incapacitated person throughout the proceeding. First, the person must be represented by personally selected or appointed counsel. [5–303(b)]. Counsel has the duties and powers of a guardian ad litem. Second, the person must be examined by a court appointed physician or other qualified person who must submit a written report on the examination to the Court. Third, the person must be visited before appointment by a "visitor" who has no personal interest in the proceeding and who is either trained in law, nursing or social work. [5–303(b), 5–103(21)]. Finally, the alleged incapacitated person is entitled to be present at the hearing and to have counsel present evidence and cross-examine all relevant witnesses. [5–303(c)].

The scope and necessity of a jury trial in a hearing concerned with the incapacity of a person is left to the option of the enacting jurisdiction. [5–303(c)]. The bracketed phrases grant the alleged incapacitated person an election to have a jury trial or not.

Although any qualified person may be appointed guardian of an incapacitated person, the UPC provides a nonmandatory priority list of suggested candidates that will be followed unless a lack of qualification, good cause or the best interest of the incapacitated person dictates otherwise. [5–305(a), and (b)]. The suggested order for consideration is as follows:

(1) Person nominated in the most recent durable power of attorney executed by the incapacitated person;

(2) Incapacitated person's spouse;

(3) Spouse's nominee under 5–301;

(4) An adult child of the incapacitated person;

(5) Incapacitated person's parent;

(6) Parent's nominee under 5–301;

(7) Any relative with whom the incapacitated person resided for more than 6 months;

(8) Person nominated by incapacitated person's caretaker.

[5–305(b), and (c)]. The Court must select the best qualified among candidates of equal priority. [5–306(d)].

Before a guardian for an incapacitated person is appointed, the Court must be satisfied that the person for whom a guardian is sought is actually incapacitated and that the appointment is necessary or at least desirable for the purpose of providing continuing care and supervision of the incapacitated person. [5–306(b)]. If the circumstances do not satisfy these criteria, the Court may dismiss or make any other appropriate order which presumably must be in the incapacitated person's best interest.

The Court is instructed "to encourage the development of maximum self-reliance and independence of the incapacitated person" and thus should tailor the appointments and orders to the specific needs of the incapacitated person. [5–306(a)]. To aid the Court in carrying out these policies, the UPC includes a provision for limited guardianships. [5–306(c)]. This permits the court to restrict the guardian's control over the ward's personal conduct in certain ways. It might, for example, limit the guardian to authorization of medical treatment. [See 5–306, Comment]. Any limitation placed on the guardian's statutory powers, however, must be endorsed on the letters of guardianship.

The UPC also includes provisions concerning the Court's power to appoint temporary guardians. [5–308]. When an emergency exists for an incapacitated person who has neither a guardian nor any other person with authority to act, the Court may appoint a temporary guardian who may exercise powers granted by the Court. [5–308(a)]. These powers are limited by a specific time period as determined by the enacting state. The Court is empowered to suspend the authority of a court-appointed permanent guardian and to appoint a temporary guardian for a period not to exceed six months, if the Court finds that the appointed guardian is not effectively performing the duties of the office and the welfare of the incapacitated ward requires immediate action. [5–308(b)]. Such an appointment may be made with or without notice.

Except for restrictions imposed on the limited guardian, the guardian of an incapacitated person must take care, custody and control of the ward. [5–309]. The guardian is not liable to third persons, however, merely by reason of those responsibilities. The guardian of an incapacitated person has the same duties, powers and responsibilities as a guardian for a minor. [See § 15.07].

A guardian of an incapacitated person does not have a duty to provide bond or when no conservator is appointed, to file periodic or final accountings. Presumably, the Court with its inherent powers over these matters could order both to be given. As with a guardian of a minor, the duties and powers of a guardian of an incapacitated person do not terminate even though the guardian and ward move from the state of appointment. [5–309, 5–209(c)(2)]. The guardian of an incapacitated person, of course, is liable to the ward for injury caused by a breach of duty or improper exercise of a power or both.

Termination of a guardianship for an incapacitated person occurs when either the guardian or the ward dies, when the guardian is determined to be incapacitated or when the guardian is removed or resigns according to proper procedures and proceedings. [5–310]. A testamentary appointment is also terminated if the will that makes the appointment is denied probate in formal testacy proceedings. Such a termination means the guardian's authority and responsibility end but does not affect the guardian's liability for prior acts or duty to account for the ward's funds and assets.

Removal proceedings may be instituted by the ward or by any other person interested in the ward's welfare. [5–311(a)]. The ward may request a removal order merely by sending an informal letter to the Court or judge and any intentional interference by any person with such a communication may constitute contempt of court. [5–311(b)]. So that a ward who is displeased about being judicially found to be incapacitated does not continually bring new removal proceedings, the order adjudicating incapacity can specify a discretionary restriction on review. This discretionary restriction on review is phrased in terms of time and cannot exceed six months. [See 5–311, Comment]. The procedures for removing a guardian, for accepting the resignation of a guardian and for ordering that the ward is no longer incapacitated contain the same safeguards as the proceedings to appoint a guardian. [5–311(c)].

§ 15.09   Protective Proceedings and the Conservator

A.   GENERALLY

As previously emphasized, the UPC separates its provisions concerned with the custody and care of the ward's person from its provisions concerned with the management of the protected person's estate. Under the heading "Protective Proceedings," disabled persons who are in need of having their assets and property managed or protected may have a conservator appointed or obtain some other protective court order for such a purpose. [5–401]. The term "disabled person" is not separately defined but means a person who is either a minor or an incapacitated person or a person who is confined, detained or missing.

Although the provisions dealing with the management of property for minors and for all other disabled persons are combined into a single part of the UPC, there are several important differences in treatment. Most important of these is that the standards upon which the Court is to base its decision to act are different. Thus a conservator may be appointed or other protective orders issued by the Court for a minor only when the minor (1) has property needing otherwise unobtainable management or protection, (2) has business affairs which minority may jeopardize or prevent, or (3) has a need for support and education funds better obtainable through a protective proceeding. [5–

401(b)]. Whereas for all other disabled persons, similar court action may be taken only when a person for any reason is unable to manage her property and affairs and either (1) the person's property may be wasted or dissipated without proper management, or (2) support, care and welfare funds for that person are necessary and better obtainable through a protective proceeding. [5–401(c)].

The only method by which protective action may be obtained, including the appointment of a conservator, is by formal proceedings before Court. [5–401(a)]. These proceedings are initiated by a petition requesting a protective order or appointment. They may be filed by any of the following persons: (1) the prospective protected person; (2) any person interested in the protected person's estate, affairs or welfare; or (3) any person adversely affected by the lack of effective management. [5–404(a)].

The notice requirements for the date and time of the hearing on such a petition depend on whether a minor or other incapacitated person is involved. [5–405(a)]. The notice is the same as it is for a hearing to appoint a guardian. [5–206 (minors); 5–304 (incapacitated persons)]. If notice by personal service on the proposed protected person is impracticable because of disappearance or other reason, notice must be given by publication as provided in Section 1–401.

The UPC attempts to protect a person from misuse of its protective proceedings by requiring representation for the person or review of his condition by independent third persons. In the case of minors, if the Court determines that it would be in the best interest of the minor to have an attorney appointed, it may appoint an attorney who can represent the minor as a guardian ad litem. [5–406(a)]. For other disabled persons, the person to be protected must have his own counsel or the Court must appoint an attorney to represent him as a guardian ad litem. [5–406(b)]. In addition, if the person to be protected is an incapacitated person, the Court may direct that the alleged incapacitated person be examined by a physician or send a visitor to interview him, or both. The physician selected must not be affiliated with any institution in which the person is a patient or is committed. The visitor may either be a guardian ad litem or a court officer or employee. For evaluation purposes, a public or charitable agency may be used as an additional visitor at the Court's discretion. [5–406(c)]. The person to be protected has a right to be at the hearing, be represented by counsel, present evidence, and cross-examine witnesses including those used by the court to evaluate the person. [5–406(d)]. On the Court's determination that it would be in the best interest of the person and according to its conditions, others may be allowed to participate in the proceeding. [5–406(e)]. If requested by the person to be protected or his counsel, the proceeding may be closed or before a jury (if a jury is allowed by the enacting state). [5–406(d)].

The Court may appoint a conservator or make some other protective order only after a hearing and after it is convinced that a need is established. [5–406(f)]. It is important to emphasize that the Court is instructed to order the least intrusive protective device possible under the circumstances. [5–407(a)]. The scope of these orders include what are called both protective arrangements and single transaction authorization. [5–408]. Actually, it is difficult to make a clear distinction between the two devices. Basically, protective arrangements deal with court orders which are designed to set up stable and continuing arrangements for purposes of handling the ward's foreseeable needs with respect to security, service or care. [5–408(a)]. In a non-exclusive list of permissible arrangements, the UPC permits the Court under this device to issue orders dealing with payment arrangements concerned with the ward's cash or personal effects, real estate or contractual rights. In addition, the Court is given the authority to establish a suitable trust for the ward. These protective arrangements may be particularly beneficial to third persons including, for example, life insurance or annuity companies that owe the person to be protected sums of money but that do not know to whom or how properly to pay. A protective order is available under these protective arrangements to direct such third persons on these matters and to protect them from potential liability for improper payment.

Basically the single transaction power permits the Court to make any authorization, ratification or other direction which would be in the best interest of the protected person with respect to any transaction relating to the person's financial affairs or estate. [5–408(b)]. Such court orders would include single transactions such as the sale of an asset or may be a series of independent but related transactions. As its name indicates, this power is related to isolated or related transactions and not to a continuing type of an arrangement.

Under the terms of both of these devices, the Court is specifically given the authority to exercise them without appointing a conservator. [5–408(a)–(b)]. Consequently, they have obvious usefulness any time a conservatorship is not necessary. Notwithstanding this usefulness, the Court must give consideration to the interests of the protected person's creditors and dependents as to whether the continuing protection of a conservator is required. [5–408(c)]. In addition, in order to be able to carry out the protective arrangement or authorized single transaction, the Court is given the authority to appoint a special conservator for these purposes. Such a conservator has the authority conferred by the Court, must report to the Court all matters pursuant to the appointment and is discharged only by court order.

B. SELECTION AND BONDING OF THE CONSERVATOR

Because of the authority and power given by the UPC to an appointed conservator and the potential for misuse of this device, the UPC establishes several guidelines by which one must be appointed. A pervasive requirement is that the conservator must be an individual or a corporation possessing trustee powers. [5–409(a)]. As with other appointment procedures in the UPC, it also lists specific priorities for the Court's consideration in making an appointment. [5–409(a)(1)–(7)]. Chart 15–3 describes these priorities for appointment.

CHART 15–3
PRIORITY ORDER FOR
APPOINTMENT OF A CONSERVATOR

Priority Rank	Description of Candidates
1	Similar kind of fiduciary appointed by an appropriate court in any jurisdiction in which the protected person resides
2	Nominee of the protected person if the latter is at least fourteen years of age and the Court determines he has sufficient mental capacity to make an intelligent choice
3	The spouse of the protected person
4	Any adult child of the protected person
5	A parent of the protected person including a deceased parent's testamentary nominee
6	Any relative with whom the protected person resided for more than six months prior to the petition
7	Any person nominated by the person caring for or paying benefits to the protected person

Chart 15–3 requires additional explanation. The first priority would apparently include an appropri-

ate fiduciary appointed in a foreign country. Including the nominee of the protected person, persons holding priority through the first six ranks may nominate in writing another person to serve in the nominator's stead. [5–409(b)]. The seventh priority would include public or governmental agencies such as the Veterans' Administration. [2 UPC Practice Manual, 533]. Between persons of equal priority, the Court has discretion to select the one best qualified if more than one is willing to serve. In addition, for good cause shown, the Court has discretion to ignore these priorities and to appoint anyone, including a person with less or without any priority. [5–409(b)].

If a conservator is appointed, the obligation to furnish a bond is left to the discretion of the Court. [5–410]. If required, the bond must be conditioned upon the faithful discharge of a conservator's fiduciary duties. Unless the Court directs otherwise, the bond must equal in value the aggregate capital value of the property of the estate plus one year's estimated income reduced by the value of court controlled securities deposited under special arrangements and by the value of real estate held by the conservator but which the conservator cannot sell without court authorization. The Court is also given discretion to accept other means of security for the performance of the fiduciary duties. Terms and conditions for bonds required are similar to those required for personal representatives. [5–411; see 3–606; § 12.03(B)]. A conservator is entitled to reasonable compensation. [5–413].

C. POWERS OF THE COURT

In dealing with the estate of a protected person, the Court is given paramount control and authority. [5–407]. During the pendency of a protective proceeding, the Court is given the power to preserve and to apply the property of the person to be protected in any manner necessary for the benefit both of that person or her dependents. [5–407(a)(1)]. Although the Court must have a preliminary hearing, there need not be any notice to other persons of this hearing.

After proper formal proceedings have been completed, the Court has extensive powers over the estates of both minors and other disabled persons. With respect to a minor without other disability, the Court has all powers over the minor's estate and affairs which are or might be necessary to the best interest of the minor, the minor's family and members of the minor's household. [5–407(a)(2)]. Much broader powers are given to the Court with respect to the estate of a person needing protection for a reason other than minority. Here, the Court has all powers over the protected person's estate and affairs which that person could exercise if present and not under the disability. [5–407(b)(3)]. The Court, however, explicitly does not have the power to make a will for the disabled person. Among the specifically mentioned powers which the Court has are the power to make gifts, release property interests, create revocable or irrevocable trusts, exercise the elective share for a surviving spouse and change beneficiaries under insurance or other contractual programs. Any such change of beneficiary, release, disclaimer or gift exceeding twenty per cent of any year's income of the estate may be ordered by the Court only after notice and hearing and after it is determined to be in the best interest of the ward. [5–407(c)]. Significantly, any court order made under this provision must follow and consider any estate plan of the protected person of which the Court has knowledge. [5–426].

Court orders under this provision have no effect upon the capacity of the protected person. [5–407(d)]. Consequently, the protected person is, in spite of any court order, still able to bind herself by contract and transfer her property at least as effectively as any equitable owner of property is able. [2 UPC Practice Manual, 537].

When a conservator is appointed, there is a direct relationship between the powers given to the Court and those given to the conservator. First, the Court is given the authority to exercise its powers either directly or indirectly through a conservator. [5–407]. Second, the Court may in its discretion and subject to the restrictions put upon its own powers, confer upon the conservator any of its own powers or it may give the conservator none of its powers and even limit the powers which a conservator normally possesses. [5–425]. Any such limitation on a conservator's ordinary powers, however, would have to be endorsed upon the conservator's letters of appointment in order to bind third parties.

D. POWERS, DUTIES AND
LIABILITIES OF THE
CONSERVATOR

The powers, duties and liabilities of a conservator are extensively detailed in the UPC. Of the three kinds of fiduciaries provided for persons under disability dealt with in the UPC, the conservator is clearly made the most important and is necessarily given the broadest authority as well as being the most supervised by the Court. Generally, the UPC treats the conservator's authority over the property of the protected person in a manner very similar to the authority that a trustee has in dealing with the trust estate. [2 UPC Practice Manual, 535]. Because a conservator both is given extensive powers and is dealing with the property of a person by definition unable to effectively manage or apply one's own estate, the UPC includes protective devices against overreaching or other abuses by such a fiduciary.

Although the Court has paramount authority over a conservator's powers, in the ordinary case such powers are not exercised by the Court. The conservator is given, therefore, a broad and explicit array of fiduciary powers. [5–423]. Generally, in addition to specifically conferred powers, the conservator is given all powers that a trustee would have under the law of the UPC state. [5–423(a)]. Thus, the conservator is specifically accorded the power to invest and reinvest funds of the estate without court authorization or confirmation according to the law applicable to trustees investing trust assets. [5–423(b)]. Finally, when reasonably necessary to carry out the purposes of the conservatorship, a conservator is empowered to take any of a long list of specified actions and transactions without court authorization or confirmation. [5–423(c)]. These enumerated powers accorded a conservator are nearly identical to those given to a personal representative of a decedent's estate under the UPC. [Compare 5–423(c)(1)–(26) with 3–715(1)– (27); see § 12.04(C); see also § 19.02(O) for a discussion of trustee powers].

In addition to the above administrative powers, the conservator is accorded substantial and significant distributive powers. Again, without court authorization or confirmation, the conservator is empowered to expend and distribute the estate's income or principal or both for the protected person's support, education, care or benefit. [5–424(a)]. In making such expenditures and distributions, the conservator is given several guidelines. First, the recommendations made by the protected person's parent or guardian must be considered. [5–424(a)(1)]. By acting pursuant to such recommendations, the conservator will be liable only if the conservator knows that a parent or guardian is deriving personal financial benefit from the payment either directly or indirectly as relief from a legal duty of support, or if the recommendations are clearly not in the protected person's best interest. Second, when expending or distributing the protected person's assets, the conservator must consider the size of the estate, the anticipated duration of the conservatorship, the potential for future termination of the conservatorship, the protected person's accustomed standard of living and the latter's other funds or sources of funds. [5–424(a)(2)]. Third, the conservator may also consider the protected person's legal dependents or other members of the relevant household who are in need and are unable to support themselves. [5–424(a)(3)]. Finally, payments may be made to reimburse any person, including the protected person, for proper expenditures or may be made in advance of services when the conservator reasonably expects them to be performed and when advance payment is customary or reasonably necessary. [5–424(a)(4)].

Except for the requirement of court approval for amounts exceeding twenty per cent of the income of the estate for any year, a conservator is permitted to make gifts to charities and to other objects in the same manner as the protected person would be expected to make if the estate is otherwise sufficient for the purposes of the conservatorship. [5–424(b)]. Significantly, this gift-making power does not apply to the conservator of a person who is disabled solely because of minority.

Upon majority for a minor and upon the ceasing of the disability for other protected persons, the conservator is required to pay over all of the unprotected person's funds and properties to him as soon as possible. [5–424(c)–(d)]. Before making payment, however, the conservator must pay all prior claims and expenses of the administration.

A conservator's power may even extend beyond the protected person's death. If the protected person dies and no personal representative is appointed or no application for such appointment is made within forty days from the date of death, the conservator may be authorized by the Court to act as personal representative. [5–424(e)]. Notice must be given to persons demanding notice under Section 3–204 and to any person nominated executor in any known will of the deceased. Under this section there need not be an actual transfer of title from the conservator to the conservator as personal representative.

If a guardian has not been appointed for a minor who is unmarried, under eighteen years of age, and without parents, a conservator has no duty to commence guardianship proceedings and may, if willing, perform the functions of a guardian until the minor becomes eighteen or married. [5–423(a)]. This discretionary power in a conservator may in the appropriate case eliminate the need for the appointment of a guardian of a minor. The same power does not exist in a conservator for a person who is disabled for reasons other than minority.

The conservator's duties are commensurate with the conservator's powers. A conservator's pervasive duty is to exercise the power of the office as a fiduciary according to the standard of care set out in the UPC for trustees. [5–416; see §§ 19.02(D) and 19.03(A) for a discussion of the standard of care for trustees]. In addition, every conservator is required to prepare and to file with the appointing court within ninety days of the appointment a complete inventory of the protected person's estate. [5–417]. Copies of this inventory must be provided to the protected person if the person is fourteen years of age or more and has sufficient mental capacity to understand these matters. A copy of the inventory must also be provided to the parent or guardian with whom the protected person resides.

A conservator also has a record keeping and accounting requirement. Under the UPC, the conservator is required to keep suitable records of the administration for the inspection and perusal of any interested person. [5–417]. Not less often than annual and on termination, a conservator is required to account either to the Court or to the protected person or the latter's personal representative. [5–418]. The conservator may voluntarily or involuntarily proceed through formal intermediate and final accountings before the Court. [See § 15.09(I)]. In such an accounting proceeding, the Court may require, in any manner it specifies, the conservator to submit to a physical check of the estate under conservator's control.

In the overall administration of a protected person's estate, including the investment and distribution of assets, the conservator, as is the Court in the exercise of its extensive power, is required to take into account any known estate plan of the protected person. [5–426]. The UPC includes the protected person's will, trust and any other will substitutes within the term estate plan. Naturally, the conservator is given the authority to examine the protected person's will. This is a beneficial provision with the goal of reducing unfair and unintentional hardship or loss to the eventual beneficiaries of the protected person's estate.

At any time during the administration of a conservatorship, the UPC provides that any person interested in the welfare of the protected person is permitted to file a petition requesting special protection from the conservator's misconduct or for any other appropriate relief. [5–415(a)]. Notice and hearing are necessary for such proceedings. [5–415(c)]. The scope of the petition and of the resultant order is very broad. The conservator may also seek instructions concerning the fiduciary relationship. [5–415(b)].

Although not specifically stated in the UPC, a conservator is liable to interested persons for any damage or loss that results from a breach of any fiduciary duty in the improper exercise of a power. This liability should be characterized as the same as a trustee of an express trust. [See 3–712; see also § 19.04 for a discussion of the liability of trustees].

In addition to potential liability for loss and damages due to breach of a fiduciary duty, sales or encumbrances of estate property by the conservator to the conservator, personally, or the conservator's spouse, agent, attorney or any corporation or trust in which the conservator has a substantial beneficial interest are voidable unless the Court approves the transaction after notice to interested persons and to others as the Court directs. [5–421]. Similar-

540 DISABLED PERSONS Ch. 15

ly, any other transaction involving the estate which is affected by a substantial conflict of interest on the part of the conservator is voidable.

E. THE CONSERVATOR'S TITLE

Contrary to the common law and to the law of most non-UPC states today, the UPC vests in a conservator a trustee's title to all of the protected person's property. [5–419; see 2 UPC Practice Manual, 537]. This title vests upon appointment and covers not only the property presently held by the protected person but any property thereafter acquired and any property held by custodians or attorneys in fact for the benefit of the protected person. In order that this transfer of title by operation of law does not have unexpected and undesired consequences, the UPC specifically provides that the vesting of title in the conservator upon appointment is not a transfer or alienation for purposes of general provisions in statutes, regulations, contracts or other estate planning devices that restrict or penalize the transfer or alienation by the protected person. A specific provision in a contract or other dispositive instrument concerning the effect of the appointment of a conservator will be given effect, however. [See 2 UPC Practice Manual, 537–38]. A spendthrift effect is included with regard to voluntary and involuntary transfers by the protected person. [5–419(b), and (c)].

Proof of the transfer of title between the protected person and the conservator, and vice versa, is handled in an extremely efficient manner in the UPC. [5–420(a)]. For the transfer from the protected person to the conservator, the letters of conservatorship represent evidence of the transfer. For the transfer between the conservator and the protected person or the latter's successors, an order of the Court terminating the conservatorship is evidence of the transfer.

For the purpose of being able to give record notice of title as between the conservator and the protected person, the UPC permits the letters of conservatorship and the court order terminating a conservatorship to be filed or recorded. [5–420(b)]. The requirements of the filing and recording statutes must be satisfied. This procedure is essential to protect the conservator from third persons claiming title to real estate purchased directly from the protected person. [See 2 UPC Practice Manual, 538]. This conflict of titles is a possibility because conservatorship, alone does not affect the legal capacity of the protected person. [5–407(d)].

F. LIABILITY OF THIRD PERSONS

As previously discussed, the UPC confers upon the conservator the authority to perform numerous transactions with third persons without court supervision. Under the present law of most non-UPC states, any third person who deals with a conservator faces the possibility of being liable for having participated in the conservator's breach of the fiduciary responsibilities. [See § 12.05]. Under the

UPC, a third person, who has dealt with or assisted a conservator in good faith and for value, is protected as if the conservator properly exercised a power unless the transaction is of the type that requires a court order under Section 5–407. [5–422; see § 15.09(C)]. In addition, the third person is not required to inquire into the existence of a power or into the propriety of its exercise merely because ones knows the other is a conservator. An exception to this rule provides that third persons are bound by restrictions on the powers of a conservator which have been endorsed on the letters of conservatorship under Section 5–425. [See § 19.04(I) for a discussion of the rights and protections of third parties who deal with trustees.]

G. CREDITORS' CLAIMS

As with a fiduciary who manages any kind of an estate, one of a conservator's responsibilities is the payment and settlement of claims against the estate. The UPC has a provision dealing with this problem which is in some respects similar to its provisions concerned with creditor's claims against a decedent's estate. [5–427; see §§ 13.03, 13.04].

A conservator upon presentation and allowance is required to pay all just claims against the estate and the protected person. [5–427(a)]. This rule applies whether the claim arose before or after the date on which the conservator was appointed. The conservator may either allow or disallow the claim. [5–427(b)]. Failure to mail notice of disallowance constitutes an allowance sixty days after the claim's presentation. Any applicable statute of limitations against a properly presented claim is tolled until thirty days after its disallowance. Consequently, actions on disallowed claims must be instituted by the claimant within the applicable statute of limitations and the tolled period.

If claimants desire, they may forego the presentation procedure and directly petition the Court for determination of the claims. [5–427(c)]. Upon due proof of the claim the creditor may obtain an order for its allowance and payment from the estate. In order for a judgment against a protected person to constitute a claim against the protected person's estate, however, the successful litigant must give notice of the proceeding to the conservator. This notice is necessary both for proceedings pending against the protected person at the time of the conservator's appointment and for those initiated against the protected person after the appointment.

If the estate of the protected person is insolvent, the conservator must follow an abatement procedure similar to that required for estates. [5–427(c), and (d); see § 13.04].

H. THE CONSERVATOR'S LIABILITY TO THIRD PERSONS

The UPC deals directly with the difficult problem of a conservator's personal liability to third persons on contracts, from ownership or control of the estate's property and from torts arising out of the administration of the estate. [5–428]. The content of the provision is identical to the provision included for personal representatives in Article III. [3–808; see § 12.08].

See § 19.04(I) for a discussion of the rights and protections of third parties who deal with trustees.

I. DURATION, TERMINATION AND REMOVAL OF THE CONSERVATOR

When a minor attains majority or when the conservator is satisfied that the protected person's disability no longer exists, the conservator is empowered and required to terminate the conservatorship and to pay over and distribute all funds and assets to the protected person as soon as possible after the payment of claims and expenses of administration. [5–424(c)–(d)]. On such a termination, a conservator is required to account either to the Court or to the protected person or, if deceased, the personal representative. [5–418].

Upon a petition by the protected person, the personal representative if the person is dead, any person interested in the protected person's welfare or the conservator, the Court in its discretion may terminate the conservatorship. [5–429]. Throughout the steps of the termination proceeding, the protected person has the same rights and procedural protections as if it were a proceeding to initiate a protective order. If the Court determines that minority or disability has ceased, it may terminate the conservatorship. Upon termination by Court order, title to the protected person's property passes either to the protected person or to his successors. The order of court may make the title, however, subject to expenses of administration, or for evidence purposes to a conservator's conveyance, or to both conditions.

Removal proceedings may be instituted by any person interested in the welfare of the protected person. [5–415(a)(4)]. The conservator can be removed by the Court for good cause upon notice and a hearing. [5–414]. Although a conservator may resign the fiduciary office, the resignation does not terminate the conservatorship until it is approved by the Court. The Court is empowered to appoint another conservator if a vacancy occurs because of resignation, removal or death. If a new conservator is appointed, the successor conservator assumes the title and the powers of the prior conservator. A conservator who has resigned or has been removed must account to the Court. [5–418].

A conservator may end potential liability by petitioning the Court for a reviewed and approved intermediate or final accounting. [5–418]. After notice and hearing, the Court's order concerning such an accounting adjudicates up to the time of the accounting all of the conservator's unsettled liabilities to the protected person and to all the latter's successors subject of course to the ordinary time limitations for appeal or vacation.

§ 15.10 The Foreign Conservator

Similar to the administration of a decedent's estate, the administration of a protected person's estate may require the conservator to administer property in two or more states. [See § 12.11(A)]. Consistent with its general purposes, the UPC strives to ease and unify the administration of a protected person's multi-state estate. First, a foreign conservator or similar fiduciary appointed by a court in the state where the protected person resides may collect debts or property from persons within the UPC state by presenting to the debtors or possessors proof of the appointment and an affidavit. [5–430; compare 4–201; see § 12.11(B)]. This procedure is available, however, only when there has been no local appointment.

Second, concurrently or alternately, a domiciliary foreign conservator is entitled to exercise all powers which a local conservator could exercise merely by filing in a court in the UPC state authenticated copies of the domiciliary appointment and the official bond, if any. [5–431; see § 15.09(D); compare § 12.11(B)]. These powers specifically include the power to bring legal proceedings which any nonresident could bring in the courts of the UPC nondomiciliary jurisdiction. Similarly, this filing has the above effect only if no local protective proceeding is pending and no local conservator has been appointed.

Unlike its comparable provisions in Article IV, there are no supplemental provisions dealing with the protection of locally interested persons [see 4–207, § 12.11(B)] or providing for personal jurisdiction over the foreign conservator. [See 4–301; § 12.11(C)]. Presumably, these deficiencies can be cured by the inherent power of the Court over protective proceeding matters together with the UPC state's long-arm statute.

Several other provisions concerned with foreign conservators deserve mention. First, as previously discussed, any foreign conservator or similar fiduciary appointed in the jurisdiction where the protected person resides has priority over all other persons to be appointed conservator in the local UPC state. [5–409(a)(1)]. This provision greatly protects the foreign conservator in the administration of the protected person's property in the local jurisdiction. The UPC also attempts to give extraterritorial authority to a conservator appointed under its provisions. Such a conservator is given the power to prosecute and defend claims of any nature concerning the protection of the estate or of the conservator's fiduciary responsibilities in any jurisdiction. [5–423(c)(25)]. Although some states may refuse to recognize this power, it should aid conservators greatly in administering the protected person's assets in most jurisdictions.

PART FIVE
NONPROBATE TRANSFERS

CHAPTER 16
NONPROBATE TRANSFERS

§ 16.01 Nontestamentary Contractual Arrangements

It is not unusual for persons to insert in various contractual arrangements provisions concerning the consequences of the death of the parties or the primary party to the contract. For example, in a partnership between two persons it may be desirable for each of the partners to provide in the partnership agreement that the partnership will automatically transfer to the surviving partner whomever it may be. Another arrangement that is found particularly in family dealings concerns a parent who has loaned money to a child and received back a promissory note which has in that note a provision that the obligation of the note ceases upon the death of the promisor or promisee or that the obligation on the debt to the promisor is to be paid to another person.

Provisions of this nature have often been held by courts to be invalid because they are characterized as testamentary and unless the instruments were executed with the same formalities as a will including testamentary intent, they are ineffective to pass the interest conveyed upon death. [Atkinson, Wills § 44]. In modern transactions, similar type provisions are often found in life insurance and retirement benefit instruments. They constitute a very convenient way to pass the interest in property outside the probate process and because they are ordinarily represented by a written instrument they carry with them many of the same protections that the statute of wills demands by its execution formalities for wills. It is desirable, therefore, to validate these instruments.

In a broadly phrased provision, the UPC accords nontestamentary status to three types of provisions sometimes found in inter vivos transactions. [6–101]. These provisions have often been held by courts to be invalid because they were characterized as testamentary. [Atkinson, Wills § 44]. The three provisions that the UPC recognizes as nontestamentary are provisions which in substance provide as follows: (1) to pay money or other benefits due to, controlled, or owned by an obligee to a designated person on the death of the obligee; (2) to waive a debt on the event of the death of the obligee; and (3) to permit the obligee to designate the beneficiary of contractual or property rights which are the subject of an instrument. [6–101(a)(1)–(3)]. The first and third provisions above may be included within either the instrument of creation of the transaction or a separate writing, including a will, executed at the same time or subsequently.

This section will not only establish the validity of many common provisions found in insurance policies, pension plans, annuity contracts, trust agreements and other family arrangements, but it will also validate the use of these provisions in a wide range of commercial transactions including bonds, mortgages, promissory notes, and conveyances. With their guaranteed validity and because the effect of the provision is to avoid the process of the administration of the estate, the use of these provisions in all forms of written instruments may become extremely popular. Although the assets passing by the terms of the provisions are valid and avoid the burden of administration, they do not infringe upon the rights of a creditor established under other laws of the UPC state. [6–101(b)].

The UPC provision does not intend to bootstrap the validity of the underlying document, financial arrangement, or instrument. [See 6–101, Comment]. For example, it is not intended to validate an ineffective inter vivos gift such as an undelivered deed to real property. The deed transfer is ineffective for lack of delivery and thus the property does not pass or is not transferred to the donee. This provision is not designed to convert the lifetime transfer attempt into a transfer on death. The 1969 version of the UPC which made reference to "or any other written instrument effective as a contract, gift, conveyance or trust" was interpreted by the Supreme Court of Washington to eliminate the need for delivery of lifetime gifts of deeds. [Estate of O'Brien v. Robinson, 749 P.2d 154 (Wash.1988)]. The North Dakota court correctly held that this section did not eliminate the necessity of the delivery of deed to effectuate a lifetime gift of an asset. [First National Bank in Minot v. Bloom, 264 N.W.2d 208 (N.D.1978)]. In 1989 the offending language was removed and replaced with the phrase "or other written instrument of a similar nature." The comment clearly indicates that this provision is not to validate otherwise invalid transfers or contractual arrangements.

§ 16.02   Multiple–Party Accounts

A.   INTRODUCTION TO MULTIPLE–PARTY ACCOUNTS

A very common and popular method of holding accounts and deposits with financial institutions is in some form of two or more names. These arrangements are called multiple-party accounts and typically have taken one of the following forms:

(1) Joint accounts, e.g., an account payable to "A or B";

(2) Trust accounts, e.g., an account held as "A in trust for B"; and,

(3) Accounts payable on death or POD accounts, e.g., an account held as "A payable on death to B."

[2 UPC Practice Manual, 564].

Unfortunately, accounts in these forms generate an inordinate amount of litigation concerning various legal problems. [See Scott, Trusts, §§ 58–58.6]. Much of the litigation deals with the determination of the legal foundations for the creation of the multiple accounts. The pervasive issue is whether they are effective to pass property to the non-contributing party at the death of the donor or whether they are testamentary and therefore must satisfy the execution requirements of a Statute of Wills. [1 Page, § 6.18].

All three of the above types of multiple-party accounts generate litigation over other issues as well. These issues relate to problems arising before the donor's death or after donor's death or at both times. Pre-death problems include the rights in the account between the donor and the donee and the rights of the donor's and the donee's creditors in the account. Post-death problems include, in addition to the validity question, the rights of the decedent's creditors and the rights of the donor's surviving spouse or other persons protected from disinheritance. Excluding the many tax issues raised by multiple-party accounts, the other pervasive issues include the manner and time of revocation, the sufficiency of evidence to rebut survivorship and the relationship of the fiduciary institution which holds the account of the persons named on the account and their successors.

The UPC addresses the question of the validity of multiple-party, POD, and trust accounts as well as their pre-and post-death problems, including the protection of financial institutions. [Art. VI, Part 2]. The UPC's technique (1) eliminates references to the "joint" account and substitutes the more generic term "multiple-party account" and (2) consolidates treatment of the POD account and the trust account so that the same rules apply to both. [Prefatory Note, Art. 6]. Its provisions are divisible into three categories:

(1) General and clarifying definitions of terms;

(2) Ownership issues as between the parties of the multiple-party accounts and other persons including creditors and successors; and

(3) Issues concerning the liability of the financial institutions.

The latter two categories are intentionally separated so that differing intentions of the parties may affect arrangements in the second category without endangering the element of definiteness needed for the third category to induce financial institutions to offer such accounts to their customers. [6–206; see 2 UPC Practice Manual, 565].

B. DEFINITIONS AND GENERAL PROVISIONS FOR MULTIPLE– PARTY ACCOUNTS

Article VI contains twelve special definitions of terms which are applicable to its provisions on multiple-party accounts. [6–201]. A knowledge of these definitions is essential to an understanding of

Article VI. For informational and overview purposes
Chart 16–1 lists them in alphabetical order.

CHART 16–1
TERMS DEFINED FOR MULTIPLE PARTY ACCOUNTS

Account	Payment
Agent	POD designation
Beneficiary	Receive
Financial institution	Request
Multiple-party account	Sums on deposit
Party	Terms of the account

With the following noted exceptions, the meaning
of each term will be provided only when the definition is necessary and relevant to the discussion in
the text. Several terms require separate explanation
here because of their pervasive importance to an
understanding of the following discussion of Article
VI.

First, it is necessary to understand the type of
account with which Article VI is concerned. An
"account" is defined as any type of contractual
arrangement for the deposit of funds between a
depositor and a financial institution and includes
the ordinary checking account, savings account, certificate of deposit and the share account. The definition of "multiple-party account" is broadly phrased
to include any account having more than one owner
with a present interest in the account. [6–201, Com-
ment]. Technical distinctions in the wording of the
terms of the account are eliminated. Use of terms
such as "joint tenancy," "tenancy in common,"
"or," "and," "right of survivorship," "JTWROS,"

or "JT TEN," are unnecessary to qualify as a multiple-party account and are covered by the terms of the UPC's multiple-party account provisions. Although this broad definition encompasses any account that has two or more names, partnership, joint venture, corporation, charitable organization, or other fiduciary or trust accounts, in which the relationship is established by separate instrument or arrangement, are expressly excluded from coverage of these provisions. [6–202].

An understanding of the terms "party," "POD designation," and "beneficiary" is also essential. A "party" is a person, other than a beneficiary or agent, who has a present right to payment from the multiple-party account, subject to making a proper request for payment. [6–201(6)]. This right to payment must be set forth by the terms of the multiple-party account. A "request" constitutes the prescribed method set by the financial institution for obtaining payment from the account. [6–201(10)].

Although the definition of the word "party" is the same for multiple-party accounts, POD accounts and trust accounts, its application to each of them is different. In a multiple-party account, all of the persons named on the account are parties. [6–201, Comment]. For a POD account and a trust account it means the original payee and the trustee, respectively, who make deposits during their lifetimes. Upon the death of the original payee and trustee, the surviving POD payee and the beneficiary of a trust account, respectively, become parties to the accounts.

A "POD designation" is the designation of a beneficiary in one of two types of accounts. [6–201(8)]. First, it refers to the designation of a beneficiary in an account payable on request (1) to one party during the party's lifetime and upon the party's death to one or more beneficiaries or (2) to multiple parties during their lifetimes and upon the death of all of them to one or more beneficiaries. Second, it refers to the designation of a beneficiary in an account in the name of one or more parties as trustee for the benefit of one or more beneficiaries if the terms of the account state such a relationship and the corpus of the trust is only the sums on deposit in the account. A "beneficiary" is the name of the person to whom sums on deposit in an account are payable on request after the death of all the parties or for whom a party is named as trustee. [6–201(3)].

An agency designation is the designation of an agent who is authorized to make account transactions but who holds no beneficial right to sums in the account. [6–201(2); 6–205(a); 6–211(d)].

Any account may be for a single party or multiple parties. Both types may have a POD designation, an agency designation, or both. [6–203]. Any account with multiple parties may be with or without right of survivorship. On the other hand, a POD designation in a multiple-party account must include a right of survivorship. [6–212(c)].

C. MULTIPLE–PARTY ACCOUNT FORMS FOR FINANCIAL INSTITUTIONS

In order to provide more uniformity to accounts issued by various financial institutions, the UPC includes a suggested form that can be used by financial institutions for their depositors. [6–204(a)]. If an institution uses the suggested form, its actions in accordance to the terms of the form are protected. [6–204, Comment; 6–226]. If an institution uses forms that contain different provisions, the account is governed by the UPC's provisions that most closely conforms to the depositor's intent. [6–204(b)].

The form is cast in the nature of a checklist with options provided to the depositor as to how the latter wants the account to be established. By initialing the appropriate options on the checklist, the depositor incorporates the UPC's law of multiple-party accounts into the contract of deposit. Proper use of the form will require a full explanation to the depositor by the financial institution personnel of the meaning and effect of the options.

D. OWNERSHIP DURING LIFETIME OF MULTIPLE–PARTY ACCOUNTS

An account is presumed to belong to the parties, during their lifetimes, in proportion to the net contribution of each. [6–211(b)]. This presumption is rebuttable by clear and convincing evidence of a different intent such as an intent to make a gift to the non-contributing party. [6–211, Comment]. A beneficiary in an account with a POD designation has no right to the sums on deposit during the lifetime of any party. [6–211(c)]. Similarly, an agent in an account with an agency designation has no beneficial right to sums on deposit. [6–211(d)].

When, under the above rules, ownership belongs to more than one party, the division of this ownership during the lifetime of the parties is in proportion to the net contribution of each. [6–206(b)]. "Net contribution" of any party at any given time is an amount equal to the sum of all deposits made by or for that party and a pro rata share of any interest or dividends remaining in the account, less any withdrawals from the account made by or for the party that have not been paid to or applied to the use of any other party. [6–211(a)]. Although the drafters deliberately included no provision for the situation where the parties are unable to prove their net contributions, they included a clear rule concerning the amount of "net contribution" as between spouses that cannot estimate the actual amount. [6–211, Comment]. For spouses, the "net contribution" for each is presumed to be an equal amount, subject to contrary proof. [6–211(b)].

E. RIGHTS AT DEATH FOR MULTIPLE–PARTY ACCOUNTS

The UPC deals with the consequences of the death of one or more of the persons named on the account. Basically, it creates a right of survivorship for interests in the account. On the death of a party to a multiple-party account, ownership to the sums on deposit belong to the surviving party or parties. [6–212(a)]. Ownership of the account's balance in the survivors is presumed unless a nonsurvivorship arrangement is specified by the terms of the account. [6–212, Comment]. "Sums on deposit" means the remaining balance in the account at the death of a party and includes interest and dividends earned up to that date and deposit life insurance added to the account due to the death. [6–201(11)].

When two or more parties survive and one is the surviving spouse of the decedent, the surviving spouse owns the amount to which the decedent spouse held beneficially immediately before death. [6–212(a); 6–211]. When two or more parties survive and none is the surviving spouse of the decedent, their ownership in the account is the sum of the value of their proportion that they owned in the account before the decedent's death plus an equal share of the interest that the decedent owned immediately before death. In other words, if in a multiple-party account among three persons, A had contributed 50 per cent, B 25 per cent and C 25 per cent and if C died, A's ownership would equal 50 per cent of the account plus one-half of 25 per cent (12½) and B's ownership would equal 25 per cent plus one-half of 25 per cent (12½). After C's death, A owns 62½ per cent and B owns 37½ per cent of the account. This presumption of, and calculation for, survivorship continues until only one party survives.

The UPC's survivorship rule with regard to accounts with a POD designation is very similar. Upon the death of one of two or more parties, the ownership rights in the sums on deposit are governed by the same provision of the UPC described above. [6–212(b)(1)]. When the last survivor of two or more parties dies, ownership belongs to the surviving beneficiary or beneficiaries. [6–212(b)(2)]. If there are two or more beneficiaries, ownership belongs to them in equal and undivided shares, and there is no right of survivorship if a beneficiary later dies. If there is no surviving beneficiary, ownership belongs to the estate of the last surviving party.

Any interest of a decedent, who is a named party in a single-party or multiple-party account that has no effective POD designation or right of survivorship, passes through the decedent's estate. [6–212(c)]. A tenancy in common designation on an account establishes that the account is without right of survivorship. In addition, a party's proper requests prior to death for payment from the financial institution, e.g., a check written to a named payee, are payable even if not paid at the time of the death. [6–212(d)]. Surviving parties, beneficiaries or the decedent's estate are proportionately liable to the payee to discharge the request if it was not paid by the institution upon proper request for payment by the payee.

Rights of survivorship are determined by the form of the account as it exists at the death of a party. Alteration to this form may be made only by a party who gives written notice of the alteration and this notice must be received by the financial institution during the party's lifetime. [6–213(a)]. Any proper written notice may stop or vary the payment under the terms of the account. Significantly, the right of survivorship cannot be changed by the will of a party or of any other person. [6–213(b)].

Except as the surviving spouse is protected by a spouse's elective share [2–201 to 2–214], and creditors and others are protected in insolvent estates [6–215], transfers resulting from these rules are nontestamentary. [6–214]. This provision means that for purposes of passing an interest to survivors at death, the accounts need not satisfy the execution requirements for wills and are not subject to administration procedures required for assets passing through the decedent's estate. [6–214, Comment].

F. RIGHTS OF CREDITORS IN MULTIPLE–PARTY ACCOUNTS

When a party to a multiple-party account dies, the account is not subject to the claims of creditors or other claimants unless the estate is insufficient. [6–215(a)]. The account is subject to payment of the estate's debts, taxes, expenses of administration, and the family protections only to the extent of the proportionate share of the amount received necessary to discharge the claims and allowances remaining unpaid after application of the decedent's estate. [6–215(b)]. Consequently, the account is subject to these claims only to the extent of the lesser of (1) the estate's insufficiency of funds or (2) the amount that the decedent owned beneficially immediately before death or (3) the proportionate share necessary to discharge the claims.

Before a proceeding may be instituted to collect from the account, the proper claimants must make a written demand to the personal representative. [6–215(b)]. Thereafter, only the personal representative may bring the proceedings and, in turn, must commence the proceeding within one year from the date of the decedent's death. Significantly, sums recovered by the personal representative become part of the decedent's estate. [6–215(d)]. This provision means that the claim of the initiating claimant gets no priority for the payment. Finally, a financial institution is discharged by payments made according to the terms of the account if made before it is served with process in a proceeding instituted by the personal representative.

Under the multiple-party account provisions, the surviving spouse is not protected from disinheritance above the value of the family protections. A surviving spouse, however, is protected from such disinheritance by the augmented estate concept of the UPC's elective share procedure. [2–203; see also § 4.01(C)]. Multiple-party accounts to which the decedent was a party and which pass the decedent's interests to third persons are includable within Segment 2 of the augmented estate. [2–205(1)(iii); see § 4.01]. Multiple party accounts that pass interests of the decedent to the surviving spouse are includable in Segments 3 or 4 of the augmented estate. [2–206 and 2–207; see § 4.01(C)].

G. PROTECTION FOR FINANCIAL INSTITUTION USING MULTIPLE–PARTY ACCOUNTS

As previously mentioned, the UPC contains separate provisions dealing with the protection of financial institutions. A "financial institution" is very broadly defined to include any organization dealing with financial affairs, including, for example, banks, savings and loan companies, trust companies and credit unions. [6–201(4)]. The basic philosophy of these provisions is that if the financial institution follows the rules set out in making payments, it will not be subsequently liable to other persons even though the payments as between persons named on the account is improper.

First, on proper request, a financial institution may pay funds out of a multiple-party account to any one or more of the parties. [6–221; see also § 16.02(D)]. A proper "request" is simply the manner by which the financial institution permits withdrawals. [6–201(10)]. Second, in spite of the actual net contribution between the parties, the financial institution has no duty to inquire into the source of the deposit or to the application of withdrawals. [6–221].

The UPC also segregates its financial institution protection provisions depending on which type of account is involved. As far as the financial institution protection is concerned, payment under a multiple-party account may be made to any one or more of the parties. [6–222(1)]. Payment may not be made, however, to the personal representative or to the heirs of a deceased party unless their proof of death shows the decedent to be the last survivor or that there is no right of survivorship. [6–222(2)].

According to the terms of the account with a POD designation, a financial institution may make payment to (1) one or more of the parties, (2) the beneficiary or beneficiaries if proof of death of all the parties is presented to the financial institution, or (3) the personal representative or heirs upon their proof of death showing that the decedent survived all parties or beneficiaries. [6–223].

Protection is also given to financial institutions for payment to an agent upon request of an agent under an agency designation account [6–224], and to a minor designated as a beneficiary pursuant to the Uniform Transfers to Minors Act. [6–225].

Payments made pursuant to the above rules discharge the financial institution from all claims for amounts paid. [6–226]. This is true although the payment may not be consistent with the beneficial ownership between all persons named on the account or their successors. The above payment rules do not protect a financial institution, however, if it has received written notice from a party altering or limiting the rules for withdrawal set by the terms of the account. The protection of the payment rules can be reacquired if the party making the notice withdraws the notice or concurs in a withdrawal. No other notice or form of information will cause the financial institution to lose the benefit of the protection of the payment rules unless a financial institution has been served with process in an action or proceeding. [6–226(b)].

When a party to a multiple-party account is indebted to the financial institution, the institution may set-off against the account, money owed to it up to the amount of the party's beneficial interest immediately before death. [6–227]. When a party's net contributions are not provable, an equal share with all other parties to the account may be set-off. This set-off provision does not qualify or limit any other statutory right to set-off or lien and is itself subject to any contractual agreement between the party and the institution.

§ 16.03   Uniform TOD Security Registration Act

A.   INTRODUCTION TO SECURITIES REGISTERED IN BENEFICIARY FORM

The UPC incorporates the Uniform TOD Security Registration Act into Part 3 of Article VI. Concurrent ownership principles are different for securi-

ties held in joint names than they are for other
financial multiple-party accounts. [Art. 6, Pt. 3,
Prefatory Note]. While multiple-party accounts permit a cotenant to control the asset, cotenants of
securities must act together, thus sharing control of
the asset. Many people use the joint titled security,
however, as a means to avoid the probate process,
despite the troublesome issues attendant with jointly titled securities. The TOD Security Registration
Act, now incorporated into the UPC, allows owners
of securities to make a nontestamentary transfer of
securities directly to a designated transferee on the
owner's death. [6–309]. Significantly, creditors of
security owners do not lose any rights against beneficiaries and other transferees.

B. DEFINITIONS FOR SECURITIES
REGISTERED IN BENEFICIARY
FORM

Five special definitions of terms are applicable to
the TOD Security Registration Act's provisions. [6–
301]. For informational and overview purposes
Chart 16–2 lists them in alphabetical order.

CHART 16–2
TOD DEFINITION OF TERMS

Beneficiary form	Security
Register	Security account
Registering entity	

First, it is necessary to understand what the Act
means when it uses the terms "security" and "se-

curity account." The Act adopts the definition of security provided in Section 8–102 of the Uniform Commercial Code. [6–301, Comment]. This definition means any share, participation, or other interest in property, business or in an obligation of an enterprise or other issuer and includes certificated and uncertificated securities and security accounts as well as mutual funds and other investment companies. [6–301(4)]. Because individuals commonly own securities and related interests in security accounts set up by brokers, the Act permits beneficiary form ownership for these accounts. "Security account" is broadly defined to include (1) security operated reinvestment accounts; (2) accounts of securities with a broker; (3) cash balances in brokerage accounts; (4) cash, interest, earnings and dividends earned or declared on a security in security accounts; (5) brokerage reinvestment accounts; (6) all other brokerage accounts; and, (7) all earnings or proceeds from trading transactions due the owner. [6–301(5)]. All payments due an account at the time of the owner's death are also included notwithstanding that the amounts due are unpaid at that time. It does not include securities held in the name of the trust institution for the benefit of a trust. [6–301, Comment].

Under the Act, an individual is allowed to obtain registration of securities in "beneficiary form." Beneficiary form is defined as a registration that shows the present owner of the security and indicates the owner's intent regarding who becomes the security's owner upon the owner's death. [6–

301(1)]. The owner's intent may be shown by the words "transfer on death," the abbreviation "TOD," "pay on death," or the abbreviation "POD," after the name of the registered owner and before the beneficiary's name. [6–305]. A security is deemed registered in beneficiary form when the registration includes a designation of a beneficiary to take ownership at the death of the owner or at the death of all multiple owners. [6–304]. A certificated security is registered when a certificate is issued showing ownership of the security, while an uncertificated security is registered when an account showing ownership is initiated or transferred. [6–301(2)].

C. OWNERSHIP DURING LIFETIME OF THE OWNER OF SECURITIES REGISTERED IN BENEFICIARY FORM

Although the purpose of the TOD Act is to permit owners of securities to obtain registration of securities in beneficiary form, there are restrictions as to what type of owner may obtain this registration. The Act specifically limits registration in beneficiary form to individuals. Thus, only natural persons may register as an owner or co-owner of a security. The Act does not restrict the owner's choice of beneficiary, however. Any person, including all legal entities, may be a beneficiary. [6–301; 1–201(35) and (32)].

The individual must have either sole ownership of the security or multiple ownership with right of survivorship. [6–302]. If co-owners fail to specify a survivorship form of ownership, the Act holds them as joint tenants with right of survivorship, tenants by the entireties, or as owners of community property. [6–302, Comment]. Furthermore, registration in beneficiary form negates ownership as tenants in common. The rationale for this is that co-owners who desire to name individual beneficiaries for each individual fractional interest will normally split their holdings into separate registrations. Once divided each co-owner would name a personal choice of beneficiary.

In order to encourage registering entities to permit registration in beneficiary form, the Act adopts an expansive choice of law rule regarding the validity of the beneficiary form transfer technique. [6–303 and Comment]. If any of the listed contacts take place on a state that has enacted the Act or some other similar statute, the forum is to apply that law. The purposes of this provision are twofold. First, it instructs the forum court in a state with the Act to apply forum law when one or more of the listed contacts occurred in the forum. Second, it attempts to attach contractual validity to beneficiary form registration if any of the listed contacts occurred in a state that has the Act or similar law. Accordingly, a forum in a non-Act state is encouraged to apply the law of an Act state so long as any of the listed contacts occurred in the latter state. The specific choice of law contacts are as follows:

(1) the issuer's state of organization;

(2) the registering entity's state of organization;

(3) the registering entity's principal place of business;

(4) the registering entity's office making the registration;

(5) the office of the registering entity's transfer agent; or,

(6) the owner's address listed as of the time of registration.

The range of potentially relevant contacts expands further when considering that a "registering entity" may, as relevant, include the issuer, the issuer's transfer agent or anyone acting for or as the issuer of securities and the broker who maintains security accounts. [6–301(3)]. Even if the proper choice of law for a registration in beneficiary form is to the law of a jurisdiction that has not enacted the TOD Act or similar statute, there is a statutory presumption that the registration is valid and authorized as a matter of contract law. [6–303].

Prior to death of the sole or last surviving owner, the beneficiary holds no ownership interest in a security registered in beneficiary form and the designation of a beneficiary may be canceled or changed at any time by the sole owner or by all surviving owners. [6–306]. Concomitantly, the owner or owners do not need to get the consent of the beneficiary. The Act does not address, however, how a TOD beneficiary designation may be canceled.

The terms and conditions of the registering entity for cancellation or alteration are the relevant procedures to observe. If the terms and conditions are silent, cancellation might be effected by reregistration showing a different beneficiary or omitting reference to the beneficiary altogether. [6–306, Comment].

D. OWNERSHIP ON THE DEATH OF THE OWNER OF SECURITIES REGISTERED IN BENEFICIARY FORM

When the sole owner or the last surviving owner of securities registered in beneficiary form dies, ownership of these securities passes to the beneficiary or beneficiaries who survive all owners. [6–307]. If no beneficiary survives all the owners, the securities held in beneficiary form become the property of the estate of the deceased sole owner or the estate of the last surviving owner. If the beneficiary does survive, however, the security may be reregistered in the beneficiary's name upon proof of the death of all owners and compliance with any transfer requirements of the registering entity. If there are multiple beneficiaries who survive the death of all owners, they hold their interests as tenants in common. Unless the beneficiary designation indicates otherwise, the surviving beneficiaries take an equal share. As amended by the 1993 Technical Amendments, the survival requirement is the UPC's pervasive 120 hour survival requirement. [1–201(50); see 2–104, 2–702; §§ 3.04, 8.02].

E. PROTECTION FOR REGISTERING ENTITIES USING SECURITY REGISTRATION IN BENEFICIARY FORM

The TOD Act makes it clear that the registration of securities in beneficiary form, while valid and authorized, is a privilege and not a right. The owner of securities may only "request" to register securities in beneficiary form. This "request" may be in any form chosen by the registering entity and may include any terms and conditions established by the entity. [6–308, Comment; See also 6–310]. The registering entity is not required to offer or to accept a request, but if the registering entity does offer registration, the owner is deemed to assent to the protections given to the registering entity in the Act. [6–308(a)]. Upon acceptance of a request for registration, the registering entity agrees to implement registration in accordance with the procedures in the TOD Act. So long as the registering entity performs in accordance with certain requirements, the registering entity is discharged from all claims to the security by the deceased owners' estate, creditors, heirs, or devisees. [6–308(c)]. On the other hand, the registering entity should not reregister or make payment under the beneficiary form after it has received written notice from a claimant to an interest in the security. In addition, the protection afforded the registering entity has no affect on rights of the beneficiaries in ownership disputes with others. [6–308(d)].

PART SIX

TRUSTS: THE UNIFORM TRUST CODE AND TRUST PROVISIONS OF THE UNIFORM PROBATE CODE

CHAPTER 17

GENERAL PROVISIONS RELATING TO TRUSTS

§ 17.01 UTC Article 1: General Provisions and Definition

A. INTRODUCTION

As noted above [see § 1.03], the UPC is now complimented by the UTC which was promulgated in 2000, over 30 years after the UPC. Conscious of the growing use of trusts in both personal and business transactions, and of the fact that few states had codified their trust law, the National Conference drafted the first national comprehensive trust code. The UTC was intended, among other

things, to supersede the provisions in Article VII of
the UPC that relate to trust administration. However, while some states that adopted the UTC expressly repealed the trust provisions of the UPC, others
did not. Some states make the UTC applicable only
to trusts created after the date of enactment, so the
UPC provisions may still be relevant for older
trusts. Also, there are some states that have
adopted the UPC but not the UTC, so the trust
provisions of the UPC remain viable in those states.
Part Six of this Nutshell is devoted primarily to an
explanation of the provisions of the UTC and the
structure of this Part mirrors that of the UTC.
However, this Part also describes the UPC provisions relating to trusts in the context of the discussion of comparable provisions of the UTC.

Article 1 of the UTC contains definitions that
apply throughout the UTC and a number of general
provisions that do not fit into any of the other
articles of the Code. UTC Section 101 states that
the Code may be cited as the ''Uniform Trust
Code.'' [UTC 101]. Many states entitle their enactments as the {State} Trust Code.

UTC Section 102 limits the application of the
UTC to express trusts, whether charitable or noncharitable, and to any trust that is created by a
statute, judgment or decree that is meant to be
administered in the same way as an express trust.
[UTC 102]. The Comment points out that the trusts
to which the UTC will most likely be applicable are
those that are created in the estate planning or gift
planning context. However, express trusts may also

be created in the context of a divorce or in a
number of commercial contexts. For example, under
UPC Section 5–411(a)(4), a court can order the
creation of a trust to manage the property of a
protected person. [See § 15.09(C)]. The UTC does
not cover implied trusts (resulting and constructive
trusts), which are not created by an express agreement between a settlor and a trustee but rather
either arise by operation of law or are imposed by a
court to remedy an inequitable situation.

The UPC includes an extensive definition of
trusts that covers the same types of trusts that are
included under UTC Section 102. This definition
expressly excludes anything that is not an express
trust or in the nature of an express trust. Included
among the enumerated exclusions in the UPC are
"other constructive trusts," resulting trusts, conservatorships, the administration of a decedent's
estate, trust accounts, custodial devices, business
trusts, common trust funds, voting trusts, security
arrangements, employee benefit trusts and nominee
arrangements." [1–201]. Basically, everything is excluded that is not an express trust or truly in the
nature of an express trust. [1–201, Comment].

Although these terms are not defined, some UPC
provisions and UTC comments refer to trusts that
are "inter vivos" or "testamentary." An inter vivos
trust is one that is set up while the settlor is alive.
A testamentary trust is one the terms of which are
laid out in the settlor's will and which does not
come into being until sometime after the settlor has
died. The UTC sometimes refers to a testamentary

trust as a trust that is "created by will." [See, e.g., UTC 204].

B. DEFINITIONS

1. In General

Like the UPC [see § 2.02], the UTC contains a number of definitions that are applicable throughout the Code. In addition to the general discussion of certain key terms that is contained in this subsection, the meaning of each word will be provided in this Part Six of the Nutshell only when the definition is relevant to the discussion of other sections of the UTC. The terms that are defined in UTC Section 103 are listed alphabetically in Chart 17–1.

CHART 17–1
UTC DEFINITIONS § 103

Action	Power of Withdrawal
Ascertainable Standard	Property
Beneficiary	Qualified beneficiary
Charitable Trust	Revocable
Conservator	Settlor
Environmental Law	Spendthrift Provision
Guardian	State
Interests of the Beneficiaries	Terms of a Trust
Jurisdiction	Trust Instrument
Person	Trustee

The UTC does not contain a definition of the word "trust." The definition that appears in UPC Section 1–201(54) is subsumed into UTC Section

102, which is described in the preceding section. [See § 17.01(A)]. Both Codes contain definitions of the term "trustee" that clarify that the term includes an original trustee as well as additional and successor trustees and cotrustees. [1–201(55), UTC 103(20)].

The UPC defines five other terms that are also defined terms in the UTC:

(a) The term "beneficiary" is defined extensively in UPC Section 1–201(3) as it relates to trusts, charitable trusts, and non-probate designations (such as life insurance policies and payable on death accounts) because the UPC covers all of these forms of transfer. The UTC restricts the definition to persons who have a vested or contingent present or future interest in a trust or who hold a power of appointment over trust property. [UTC 103(3)]. As discussed immediately below, the UTC also introduces the term "qualified beneficiary."

(b) The terms "conservator" and "guardian" are defined in the UPC by reference to those portions of the UPC that cover these fiduciaries. [1–201(7), (19), see Ch. 15]. The UTC defines these terms more substantively, with the term "conservator" referring to a person appointed by a court to administer the estate of a minor or incapacitated adult and the term "guardian" to refer to a person appointed by a court or parent or spouse to make decisions regarding the personal welfare of a minor or incapacitated adult. [103(5), (7)]. The terms themselves are bracketed in the UTC, which signals to adopting states that the states may substitute for these terms the terms that are used in that particular state to refer to these fiduciaries. For example, in some states a conservator is referred to as a "guardian of the property" while a guardian is referred to as a "guardian of the person."

(c) The UPC defines the term "person" briefly as an individual or organization. [1–201(34)]. The UTC defines the term by adding a non-exclusive list of organizations which includes a "corporation, business trust, estate, trust, partnership, limited liability company, association, joint venture, government; governmental subdivision, agency, or instrumentality; public corporation, or any other legal or commercial entity." [103(10)].

(d) The UPC defines a "state" as a "state of the United States, the District of Columbia, the Commonwealth of Puerto Rico, or any territory or insular possession subject to the jurisdiction of the United States." [1–201(47)]. The UTC includes in this definition any Indian tribe formally recognized by federal law or by a state. [103(17)].

2. Qualified Beneficiary

The UTC introduces the term "qualified beneficiary" [UTC 103(13)] which has not appeared in previous uniform acts. An understanding of this term is crucial because these are at times the only beneficiaries to whom notice must be given or from whom consents must be received. [See, e.g., UTC 107, 417, 704, 705, 813]. A "beneficiary" is a person who "(A) has a present or future beneficial interest in a trust, vested or contingent; or (B) in a capacity other than that of trustee, holds a power of appointment over trust property." [UTC 103(3)]. A "qualified beneficiary" is a beneficiary who "(A) is a distributee or permissible distributee of trust income or principal; (B) would be a distributee or permissible distributee of trust income or principal if the interests of the distributees described in subparagraph (A) terminated on that date without causing the trust to terminate; or (C) would be a distributee or permissible distributee of trust income or principal if the trust terminated on that date." [UTC 103(13)]. Thus, the definition does not include beneficiaries who are remote or contingent. As noted throughout this Part, qualified beneficiaries are given special rights that are not granted to contingent beneficiaries. [See §§ 17.01(D), 18.01(B)(3), 19.01(C), 19.01(D), 19.02(M)]. Qualified beneficiaries are determined by taking a "snapshot" of the beneficiaries on the date of determination and seeing which beneficiaries fall into the categories set out in UTC Section 103(13).

UTC Section 110 expands the definition of qualified beneficiary by providing that certain other persons are treated as qualified beneficiaries for certain purposes. These expansions fall into two categories. The first category relates to which beneficiaries are required to be given notice. UTC Sections 108(d), 417, 705(a)(1) and 813(c), for example, require notice be given to qualified beneficiaries of various transactions and reports. Under UTC Section 110(a), this notice must also be given to any other beneficiary who has requested notice, thus giving that beneficiary the same rights as a qualified beneficiary. [See § 19.02(M)]. The second category relates to charitable trusts. Often charitable trusts do not have specific beneficiaries as they are usually established for the good of the public at large. [See § 18.01(A)(4)]. However, a charitable trust may name a specific organization as the recipient of trust income or principal. If the organization is one that is a permissible distributee under the circumstances set forth in the definition of "qualified beneficiary," the charitable organization is entitled to the same notice as a qualified beneficiary. Charitable organizations that are excluded from this definition are those that are not named in the trust or that hold remote or contingent interests. UTC 110(d), which is an optional provision, gives the state attorney general the identical notice rights for a charitable trust because in many states the attorney general is the state officer who is responsible for enforcing these trusts. UTC Section 110(c) gives notice rights to a person who has been appointed to enforce the provision of a trust created for an animal or for another noncharitable, beneficial purpose. [See § 18.01(A)(4)].

CHART 17–2
QUALIFIED BENEFICIARIES

Settlor sets up an irrevocable trust on May 1, 2010 with the following provisions:

(a)   Income to be paid to the Settlor's spouse, Sarah, for Sarah's life;

(b)   When Sarah dies, the income is to be paid in equal shares to Settlor's child Anna until she reaches age 30.

(c)   When Anna reaches age 30, the remainder is to be paid outright to her.

(d)   If Anna dies before reaching age 30, the remainder is to be paid to her then living lineal descendants.

(e)   If Anna dies before reaching age 30 and has no living lineal descendants, the remainder is to be paid to the American Fund for the Prevention of Lymphoma or its successor in interest.

On May 16, 2010, two weeks after the trust is created: Sarah and Anna are alive. Anna is age 19 and has one child, Candace. The American Fund for the Prevention of Lymphoma is an existing charitable organization

Question: Using the definition in UTC 103(13), who are the qualified beneficiaries of this trust?

Answer: Take a "snapshot" of the beneficiaries who are alive and ascertainable on May 16, 2010:

"(A) A distributee or permissible distributee of trust income or principal"
SARAH meets this definition as she is the current income beneficiary of the trust on May 16, 2010.

"(B) A distributee or permissible distributee of trust income or principal if the interests of the distributees described in subparagraph (A) terminated on that date without causing the trust to terminate."

ANNA is a qualified beneficiary under this category because she would take the income interest were her mother to die on May 16, 2010. Sarah's death would cause Sarah's interest to terminate but the trust would not terminate on that date.

"(C) A distributee or permissible distributee of trust income or principal if the trust terminated on that date."

CANDACE is a qualified beneficiary under this category because she would be the living lineal descendant of Anna should Anna die on May 16, 2010, which event would cause the trust to terminate.

The American Fund for the Prevention of Lymphoma is not a qualified beneficiary because, although it is a named beneficiary, under these facts, it would not take anything if Anna died on May 16, 2010 due to the fact that Anna has a living lineal descendant.

However, if the facts were changed slightly so that Anna had no living lineal descendants on May 16, 2010, the fund would be treated as a qualified beneficiary because it would be the distibutee of the remainder interest were Anna to die on that date.

3. Knowledge

The UTC drafters devote an entire Code section, UTC Section 104, to defining when a person is deemed to have knowledge of a fact. A number of provisions in the UTC are dependent upon whether and when persons (beneficiaries, trustees, third parties) "know" a fact. [See, e.g., UTC 109, 305, 604(b), 812, 1009, 1012]. A person has knowledge of a fact if the person has actual knowledge; has received notice of the fact; or has reason to know the fact due to all the other facts and circumstances known to the person. Because, as noted above, "person" is defined broadly in UTC Section 103(10) to be an individual or an organization, subsection (b) of UTC Section 104 explains how an organization or entity has notice or knowledge of a fact. As noted in the Comment, notice to an organization does not occur when a notice is delivered to the organization's mail room. Notice or knowledge of a fact is achieved by an organization only when an employee who has responsibility for acting for the trust learns the fact or receives the notice or would have received such notice had the organization exercised reasonable diligence. "Reasonable diligence" means that the organization "maintains reasonable routines for communicating significant information to the employee having responsibility to act for the trust and there is reasonable compliance with the routines." The communication of such information must be part of the employee's regular duties or, alternatively, the employee is one who has knowledge that the fact would materially affect the trust. UTC 104 is modeled after Uniform Commercial Code Section 1–202. [Schmidt v. Killmer, 201 P.3d 1121 (Wyo.2009)].

C. DEFAULT AND MANDATORY RULES AND COMMON LAW

The UTC is "primarily a default statute." [UTC Art. 1, General Comment]. This means that most of the provisions in the UTC can be overridden or modified by the settlor in the trust instrument. If the settlor does not so do, or fails to address a certain matter, the provisions of the UTC will apply. UTC Section 105 lists thirteen provisions of the UTC that cannot be overridden or changed by the settlor. These provisions and their accompanying UTC sections are listed below. The provisions are discussed in depth in the remaining portion of Part Six of this Nutshell. These provisions and the sections in which they are discussed are as follows:

1. the requirements for creating a trust [UTC 401–409, § 18.01(A)];

2. the duty of a trustee to act in good faith and in accordance with the terms and purposes of the trust and the interests of the beneficiaries [UTC 801, 814(a), §§ 19.02(A), (N)];

3. the requirement that a trust and its terms be for the benefit of its beneficiaries and that the trust have a purpose that is lawful, not contrary to public policy, and possible

to achieve [UTC 404, 801, 802(a), 814, 1008, §§ 18.01(A), 19.02(A), (B), (N), 17.10(G)];

4. the power of the court to modify or terminate a trust [UTC 410–416, § 18.01(B)];

5. the effect of a spendthrift provision and the rights of certain creditors and assignees to reach a trust [UTC Art. 5, § 18.02];

6. the power of the court to require, dispense with, or modify or terminate a bond [UTC 702, § 19.01(A)]

7. the power of the court to adjust a trustee's compensation specified in the terms of the trust which is unreasonably low or high [UTC 708(b), § 19.01(G)];

8. the duty to notify qualified beneficiaries of an irrevocable trust who have attained 25 years of age of the existence of the trust, of the identity of the trustee, and of their right to request trustee's reports [UTC 813(b)(2), (3), § 19.02(M)];

9. the duty to respond to the request of a qualified beneficiary of an irrevocable trust for trustee's reports and other information reasonably related to the administration of a trust [UTC 813(a), § 19.02(M)];

10. the effect of an exculpatory term [UTC 1008, § 19.04(G)];

11. the rights of a person other than a trustee or beneficiary [UTC 1010–1013; § 19.04(I)];

12. periods of limitation for commencing a judicial proceeding [UTC 604, 1005, §§ 18.03(D), 19.04(D)];

13. the power of the court to take such action and exercise such jurisdiction as may be necessary in the interests of justice; and

14. the subject-matter jurisdiction of the court and venue for commencing a proceeding [UTC 203, 204, § 17.02].

As is discussed in § 19.02(M), subsections (b)(8) and (b)(9) of UTC Section 105 are highly controversial and thus appear in brackets in the UTC, which is the drafters' method of indicating that adoption of those provisions is optional.

UTC Section 106 provides that, unless modified by the UTC or another state statute, the common law, including principles of equity, continues to govern trusts. [UTC 106; see 1–103, § 2.01, for discussion of a similar provision in the UPC].

D. GOVERNING LAW AND PRINCIPAL PLACE OF ADMINISTRATION

UTC Section 107 contains provisions that explain which state's laws will be used to determine the meaning and effect of the terms of a trust. [See UTC 401, § 18.01(A) for a description of the law that governs whether a trust has been validly created.] Generally, a settlor is allowed to designate in the trust instrument which state's laws will govern. This designation will be respected unless the designation is contrary to a strong public policy of the jurisdiction that has the most significant relationship to the matter at issue. If no designation is made, the court will look to the law of the jurisdiction that has the most significant relationship to the matter at issue. Borrowing from the Restatement (Second) of Conflict of Laws Sections, 270 Comment. c and 272 Comment. d (1971), the UTC Comment lists a variety of factors that should be considered when determining which jurisdiction has the most significant relationship. These include: "the place of the trust's creation, the location of the trust property, the domicile of the settlor, the trustee, and the beneficiaries" as well as general factors such as "the relevant policies of the forum, the relevant policies of other interested jurisdictions and degree of their interest, the protection of justified expectations and certainty, and predictability and uniformity of result." The Comment states that this UTC provision was modeled after the Hague Convention on the Law Applicable to Trusts and on their Recognition, signed on July 1, 1985.

The Comment to UTC Section 107 notes that the law of the trust's principal place of administration will usually govern the trust's administrative matters. UTC Section 108 defines the trust's principal place of administration. As in UTC Section 107, the settlor is allowed to designate a principal place of administration in the trust instrument. This designation is important because it will determine where the trustee and beneficiaries have consented to suit [UTC 202] and venue [UTC 204]. A settlor's desig-

nation will be respected as valid and controlling if
the jurisdiction is one in which the trustee is a
resident, the trustee's principal place of business is
located, or all or part of the trust administration
actually occurs in that jurisdiction. The trustee has
a continuing duty to administer the trust in a place
that is appropriate to the purposes and administration of the trust and the interests of the beneficiaries. [See UTC 103(8) for the definition of the
"interests of the beneficiaries."]. In furtherance of
this duty, a trustee may move a trust to another
jurisdiction inside or outside the United States.
Before doing so, however, the trustee must give the
qualified beneficiaries notice of the proposed transfer that gives the particulars of the move, an explanation of why the move is appropriate, and the date
by which a qualified beneficiary must file any objection to the move. If a qualified beneficiary objects,
the trustee may not move the trust unilaterally but
must instead seek court permission to do so. Sometimes a transfer to a new place of administration
will involve the appointment of a successor trustee,
which is governed by UTC Section 704. [See
§ 19.01(C)].

The UPC defines the principal place of administration as the place that is designated in the trust
instrument or, if none is designated, the place that
is the trustee's usual place of business where the
trust records are kept. When cotrustees from more
than one place are involved and when the trust
instrument fails to designate, the UPC provides an
order of priority for determining the principal place

of administration: (1) the usual place of business of a sole corporate trustee, if any; (2) if no corporate trustee is involved, the usual place of business or residence of a sole professional individual fiduciary, if any; and (3) under all other circumstances, the usual place of business or residence of any of the co-trustees as they agree among themselves. [7–101]. The UPC makes it a trustee's affirmative duty to administer the trust in the most appropriate location considering the purposes of the trust and its sound, efficient management. [7–305]. If according to this standard a trust should be administered in another more appropriate location, the trustee must request a change in the place of administration. Upon such a request the Court is given the authority to release registration, remove a trustee and appoint a trustee in another place in the UPC state or even in another state. If contrary to efficient administration or the purposes of the trust, the Court may order a deviation from clauses in the trust instrument that expressly set the place of administration or explain changes in such places. The Court is to give "weight" to the opinions of adult beneficiaries in making any decision as far as the suitability of the trustee or the place of administration or both are concerned.

E. NOTICE

Several provisions of the UTC require that beneficiaries or others receive notice before certain actions can take place. [See, e.g., UTC 107, 411, 417,

701, 704, 705]. UTC Section 109 provides that methods by which such notice may be given. Subsection (a) provides that the following are acceptable methods of giving notice: "first-class mail, personal delivery, delivery to the person's last known place of residence or place of business, or a properly directed electronic message," but that any other form of notice is valid if it is accomplished in a reasonably suitable manner and is likely to result in receipt of the notice. Subsection (b) relieves the trustee from giving notice to a party whose identity and location are unknown to the trustee and not reasonably ascertainable by the trustee. Subsection (c) allows a person to waive notice. Subsection (d) clarifies that notice of judicial proceedings must be made in accordance with the court's rules. [See 1–401, § 2.03(A) for the UPC treatment of notice.]

F. NON–JUDICIAL SETTLEMENTS

The UTC recognizes that courts may be called upon to resolve disputes relating to trusts [UTC Art. 2, § 17.02] but also encourages alternative forms of dispute resolution and gives appropriate non-judicial settlements the same binding effect as judicial orders. UTC Section 111 describes the procedure by which "interested persons" may enter into such a binding agreement. "Interested persons" are "persons whose consent would be required in order to achieve a binding settlement were the settlement to be approved by the court." [UTC 111(a)]. They may enter into non-judicial settlements on a variety of trust matters, including but not limited to: "(1) the interpretation or construction of the terms of the trust; (2) the approval of a trustee's report or accounting; (3) direction to a trustee to refrain from performing a particular act or the grant to a trustee of any necessary or desirable power; (4) the resignation or appointment of a trustee and the determination of a trustee's compensation; (5) transfer of a trust's principal place of administration; and (6) liability of a trustee for an action relating to the trust." [UTC 111(d)]. The settlement must not violate a material purpose of the trust and must only include terms and conditions that could validly be approved by a court. [UTC 111(c)]. Even though the settlement is nonjudicial, UTC Section 111(e) allows any interested person to request court approval of the settlement itself, of whether the interested persons were properly represented, and of whether the agreement is one that could have been properly approved by a court. [UTC 111(e)].

G. RULES OF CONSTRUCTION OF TRUST TERMS

The final provision in UTC Article 1, UTC Section 112, is an optional one relating to the rules of construction of trust terms. The suggested provision states simply that the rules of construction that apply in the enacting state to the construction of wills should also apply to the construction of trusts. The Comment to UTC Section 112 suggests that instead of enacting this provision, some states may wish to enumerate the rules of construction that will apply to trusts. The Comment notes also that the rules of construction for a particular state may be found in cases or state statutes. The UPC contains an extensive array of rules of construction for wills and other governing instruments. [See §§ 7.01 through 8.05]. Some states that have adopted both the UPC and the UTC have included in their equivalent of UTC Section 112 an express reference to the UPC construction provisions. [See, e.g., Ala. Code 1975, § 19–3B–112].

§ 17.02 UTC Article 2: Judicial Proceedings

Although it encourages the use of non-judicial forms of dispute resolution [111, § 17.01(F)], the UTC recognizes that court intervention in trust matters must be available. UTC Article 2 does not contain extensive rules regarding litigation of trust matters, as those rules will typically be a matter of state civil procedure laws. UTC Section 201 allows a court to intervene in matters relating to a trust, including a request for instructions or an action to declare rights. The section makes it clear that the continuing supervision of a trust by the court is not the norm. Such supervision occurs only if the court so orders. As discussed in this section, the UPC contains a variety of provisions relating to jurisdiction and venue, many of which revolve around trust registration, a concept that was not carried forward to the UTC. The UPC also includes provisions for foreign trusts and foreign trustees that are not found in the UTC. This section discusses these UPC

provisions in the event that a state has adopted the
UPC and not the UTC or has adopted the UTC but
not repealed Article VII of the UPC.

A. PERSONAL JURISDICTION AND TRUST REGISTRATION

UTC Section 202 provides non-exclusive rules for
establishing jurisdiction over the parties to a trust
matter. A trustee who accepts a trusteeship submits
personally to the jurisdiction of the courts of the
state in which the trust has its principal place of
administration. [See 108, § 17.01(D) for the discussion of the principal place of administration.] If the
trustee moves the trust's principal place of administration, the trustee then consents to the personal
jurisdiction of the state to which the trust is moved.
A beneficiary who receives distributions from a
trust consents to the personal jurisdiction of the
court of the state in which the trust has its principal place of administration.

The UPC treats personal jurisdiction differently.
As a preliminary matter, it is important to note that
the UPC established a concept known as "trust
registration" which was not carried forward to the
UTC. The primary effect of registration is to establish a court where, after appropriate notice, the
trustee and the beneficiaries are subject to the
jurisdiction of the court with respect to their affairs
and interests in the trust. [7–103]. Basically then,
registration establishes a single jurisdictional forum
for determining litigable issues dealing with the

internal affairs of the trust. [See 7–201]. The registration court is not authorized to maintain continuing supervision over the trust or to require periodic accounting from the trustee. [7–201(b); see also UPC Art. VII, Pt. 1, General Comment].

Under the UPC, registration is accomplished merely by filing with the proper court a statement that includes the following information: (1) The name and address of the trustee; (2) An acknowledgment of trusteeship by the trustee; (3) A statement whether the trust has been registered elsewhere; and (4) A brief identification of the trust. [7–102]. Identification specifications differ depending upon whether the trust is inter vivos or testamentary. If the trust is inter vivos, the statement must give the name of each settlor, the name of the original trustee and the date of the instrument. If the trust is testamentary, the statement must give the name of the settlor-testator and the date and location of the domiciliary probate. With the exception of oral inter vivos trusts, the registration statement does not require revelation of the beneficiaries or of the terms of the trusts. The registration statement must be filed in the court where the principal place of administration is located. [7–101].

The registration statement for oral inter vivos trusts, however, not only must include information identifying the settlor, or any other source of the trust's corpus, but also must include information describing the time and manner of the trust's creation and its terms including a description of its subject matter, beneficiaries and time of performance. This additional information greatly assists all of the parties, i.e., settlor, trustee and beneficiaries, in identifying and establishing their rights and duties as far as these trusts are concerned.

Generally, a registration statement must be filed for any trust that has its principal place of administration in the Code state. [7–101; see § 17.01(D) for a discussion of principal place of administration]. Registration may be waived only when a person or several persons hold a presently exercisable general power of appointment over the trust, and when the holder or all co-holders direct or agree with the trustee to refrain from registration. [1–108]. A common example when the above waiver will be available to the trustee will be when the settlor of the trust retains the power of amendment or revocation. [7–104, Comment]. Any attempt by the settlor to merely waive the registration requirement, even by the express terms of the trust instrument, is void. [7–104]. Furthermore, a trustee is subject to removal, denial of compensation or surcharge for failure to register a trust within thirty days after receipt of a written demand to register made by the trust's settlor or beneficiary. Notwithstanding a failure to register, the trustee is still subject to the personal jurisdiction of any court in which the trust could have been registered.

The UPC provides a continuing type of personal jurisdiction power over the trustee in the court in which a trustee registered a trust or accepted a trusteeship of a previously registered trust. [7–103(a)]. The beneficiaries are similarly under the continuing jurisdiction of this court. [7–103(b)]. These rules of personal jurisdiction subject the trustee and the beneficiaries to any proceeding brought under the court's exclusive subject matter jurisdiction. [See 7–201]. The only special requirement to sustain this personal jurisdiction is that specific notice requirements be satisfied for each proceeding. For a trustee, notice of each proceeding must either be delivered to the trustee or mailed to the trustee by ordinary mail both to the official address listed with the Court and to any other address known to the petitioner. [7–103(a)]. The beneficiaries must be notified of any proceeding brought against them by notice given pursuant to UPC Section 1–401. [7–103(b); see § 2.03(A) for a discussion of notice].

B. SUBJECT MATTER JURISDICTION

UTC Section 203 provides an optional provision relating to subject matter jurisdiction. This provision allows the enacting states to designate which court (probate court, chancery court, superior court) has exclusive jurisdiction over trust matters and which courts have concurrent jurisdiction over trust matters.

The UPC approaches subject matter jurisdiction differently. The court with the proper venue has exclusive jurisdiction over the "internal" affairs of the trust. [7–201(a)]. Generally, the internal affairs of a trust include issues dealing with the administration and distribution of the trust and with determination of rights, responsibilities, and other matters between the trustee and the trust beneficiaries. Proceedings brought under the exclusive jurisdiction of the court are instituted by petition after notice to interested parties. [7–206]. Additional persons may be notified at the discretion of the court, but any decree is valid against those who were given notice even though fewer than all the interested persons had been notified. The UPC provides separately that interested persons may also petition this court for review of the propriety of any employment of any person by the trustee and the reasonableness of compensation for any person so employed, including the reasonableness of the trustee's own compensation. [7–205]. The court, under this proceeding, may order refunds for any excessive compensation paid from the trust. Significantly, exclusive jurisdiction proceedings do not result in court proceedings of a continuing supervisory nature. [7–201(b)].

C. VENUE

UTC Section 204 contains optional provisions for states that do not have procedural rules that cover the venue of matters relating to trusts. Generally, the proper venue is the county of the state in which the trust's principal place of administration is or will be located. [See § 17.01(D) for a discussion of the principal place of administration.] If the trust is created in a will, the venue is the county in which the estate is being administered. If the pending matter is the appointment of a trustee, venue can be in the county in which a beneficiary resides, the county in which any trust property is located, or in the case of a testamentary trust, the county in which the estate is being administered. [UTC 204].

Under the UPC, venue for exclusive jurisdiction proceedings is set in the court wherein the trust is registered. [7–202; see § 17.02(A) for a discussion of trust registration]. If a trust is not registered, venue is in the court where the trust could have been registered properly or otherwise by the rules of civil procedure. This court is also given concurrent jurisdiction with other courts in the state to deal with litigation between third parties and the trust. [7–204]. Such litigation would include actions to determine the existence of inter vivos trusts, by or against debtors and creditors of the trust and any other actions between the trustee and nonbeneficiary third parties.

D. FORUM NON CONVENIENS FOR FOREIGN TRUSTS

The UPC contains provisions for foreign trusts and trustees that were not included in the UTC. A "foreign trust" under the UPC is a trust that is registered or has its principal place of administration in another state. The UPC includes a special statutory forum non conveniens rule applicable to foreign trust that applies to exclusive jurisdiction proceedings concerned with trusts that are registered or have their principal place of administration in another state. [7–203]. If the rule applies, the court must refuse to entertain the proceeding when a party objects to the jurisdiction. The only two mentioned situations that would cause the court not to employ this rule are: (1) when the state of registration or principal place of administration is unable to bind by litigation in its court all appropriate parties; or (2) when the interests of justice are potentially seriously impaired. Frequent use of the rule is encouraged by the power of the court to suspend proceedings or to make conditional dismissals subject to jurisdiction being obtained in the court in the other state.

E. FOREIGN TRUSTEES

The UTC does not contain a separate provision for foreign trustees. However, the UPC covers several important and related problems of trust administration concerning the registration, qualification and powers of a nonresident or foreign trustee. Several different fact situations are involved and for clarity need to be distinguished from each other. The first situation involves the nonresident who serves as trustee of a trust that has its principal place of administration within the UPC state. The second involves the foreign trustee of a foreign trust who has to administer assets or to bring legal proceedings within the UPC state. The third situation involves the locally domiciled testator whose will creates a foreign trust and appoints a foreign trustee. When analyzing the above situations, it is also often important under non-UPC law to determine whether the foreign trustee is an individual or a corporation. The UPC addresses itself in some manner to all three situations and to the importance of the type of trustee involved. Generally, the UPC eliminates restrictions frequently imposed on foreign trustees and removes discriminations frequently applied against foreign corporate trustees. [7–105, Comment].

Because any trust that has its principal place of administration within a UPC state must be registered in the proper court, any individual or corporate foreign trustee who maintains the principal place of administration of the trust within the state must register that trust. [7–101]. Under such a situation, a foreign corporate trustee must also qualify as a foreign corporation doing business within the state. [7–105]. This foreign corporate qualification requirement, however, does not apply to a foreign corporate co-trustee solely because a co-trustee of the trust maintains the principal place of administration of the trust in the UPC state. When a trust is registered in the UPC state, however, it has the effect of submitting all of its foreign trustees to the personal jurisdiction of the registration Court. [7–103(a)].

With respect to the first situation, some states have statutes that bar a foreign corporate trustee from acting as a local trustee unless the law of the jurisdiction in which the foreign corporation is organized or has its principal office permits local corporate fiduciaries to perform in a similar manner.

These are called reciprocity statutes and have been enacted in several states. [See 5 Scott, Trusts § 588]. These statutes do not apply to a foreign trustee who is an individual. The UPC does not have such a reciprocity requirement with respect to either a nonresident individual or a foreign corporate trustee.

With reference to the second situation, the UPC gives both the nonresident individual and the foreign corporate trustee of a foreign trust broad authority to deal with trust matters within the UPC state. These powers include the authority to hold, invest in, manage or acquire property located, and to maintain litigation, in the UPC state. [7–105]. Significantly, unless otherwise required by law, a foreign corporate trustee is not required to qualify as a foreign corporation doing business in the state merely to perform one or more of the above acts.

Finally, the UPC also permits a nonresident individual or foreign corporate trustee to receive distributions of assets under a will from a domiciliary estate and to remove these assets to the foreign jurisdiction. [7–105]. Fear that such a trustee-devisee [1–201(11)] may take its distributive share and never be heard from again motivated the inclusion of some protection for the trust's beneficiary. Before making distribution to a nonresident or foreign trustee named as a devisee under a will, the personal representative of an estate, in the personal representative's exonerated discretion, may either (1) require the trustee to register if registration is possible in the state of administration; (2) require the trustee to give notice and information to the beneficiary concerning the trust; or, (3) require the trustee to post bond if it would appear necessary for the protection of persons and beneficiaries unable to protect themselves. [3–913]. If appropriate, all three actions by the trustee may be required before any distribution.

§ 17.03 UTC Article 3: Representation

In matters relating to trusts and estates, it is not uncommon for the trust or estate to have numerous beneficiaries with interests of varying nature (e.g., vested vs. contingent, income vs. remainder). Some of these beneficiaries may be unknown, unborn, or unascertainable, thus hampering a fiduciary's ability to give notice or to obtain needed consents. UTC Article 3 addresses ways in which these beneficiaries may be represented either by fiduciaries (trustees, personal representatives, guardians) or by others who are similarly situated. (See Bart & Welch, for a survey of state variations on UTC Art. 3). Representation is also addressed to a lesser extent in UPC Section 1–403. [See § 2.03(B) for the UPC's coverage of virtual representation].

A. REPRESENTATION GENERALLY

UTC Section 301 sets out the general rule that notice to a person who is authorized to represent and bind a beneficiary under UTC Article 3 will be given the same effect as if the notice had been given directly to the beneficiary. Likewise, consent given by such a representative is binding upon any benefi-

ciary who does not object before the consent would
becomes binding. Subsection (c) of UTC Section 301
authorizes a person who represents a settlor who
lacks capacity (e.g., guardian, conservator, agent
under a power of attorney) to receive notice and
give consent for that settlor, except as otherwise
provided in UTC Section 411 [modification or termination of a noncharitable trust, § 18.01(B)(1)] and
UTC Section 602 [revocation of a revocable trust,
§ 18.03(B)]. These UTC code sections limit this
authorization to those situations in which the authority is expressly set out in the power of attorney
or a court approves the authority. The 2004 amendments to the UTC added optional subsection (d)
which provides that a settlor may not represent and
bind a beneficiary with respect to a modification or
termination under UTC Section 411(a). [This reflects the 2004 amendments to UTC 411, which are
discussed at § 18.01(B)(1)].

UTC Section 302 allows the holder of a general
power of appointment to represent and bind persons, such as permissible distributes and takers in
default, whose interests may be affected by the
power. [A similar provision, discussed below, appears at 1–403(2) of the UPC]. However, the holder
of the power of appointment may not bind these
persons if there is a conflict of interest between the
holder and the person whose interest is affected.
The Comment gives the example of a holder of a
power of appointment who is also the income beneficiary of a trust and points out that that person
could act in a way that would enhance her interests

to the detriment of the permissible appointees or takers in default. Thus, the holder of the general power of appointment in this situation would not be able to bind those persons. [See Brams Trust #2 v. Haydon, 266 S.W.3d 307 (Mo.App. W.D.2008)].

UTC Section 303 addresses the degree to which fiduciaries may bind persons and parents may bind their children. [A similar provision appears in UPC 1–403(2), discussed below.] The section applies only if there is no conflict of interest between the representative and the person represented. Specifically under this section a conservator may represent and bind a ward and a guardian may represent and bind the ward if there is no conservator. The Comment points out that a provision in the order granting the guardianship may override the need to have a conservator appointed and that such authority may already be present in states that have adopted UPC Section 1–403, which is discussed at § 2.03. An agent may represent and bind the principal but only to the extent the agent is authorized to do so. The Comment points out that certain UTC sections, specifically UTC Section 411 [modification or termination of a noncharitable trust, § 18.01(B)(1)] and UTC Section 602 [revocation of a revocable trust, § 18.03(B)] require that authority to appear in either the trust or the power of attorney, but that for other situations, a broad grant of powers in the power of attorney may suffice. Under UTC Section 303(4), a trustee may bind the beneficiaries of the trust. UTC Section 303(5) authorizes a personal representative (executor or administrator) of a decedent's estate to bind persons who are interested in the estate. Finally, UTC Section 303(6) allows a parent to represent and bind the parent's minor or unborn child if a conservator or guardian has not been appointed for that child.

B. VIRTUAL REPRESENTATION UNDER THE UTC

UTC Section 304 codifies the concept of virtual representation, whereby a person who has an interest that is substantially identical to other persons can represent and bind those persons. Such a doctrine is necessary to facilitate trust management and transactions when there are some beneficiaries who are unavailable or legally incapable to binding themselves. The Comment points out, for example, that if a trust benefits the settlor's children as a class, the minor and unborn children of the settlor may be represented, even if the children's interests are not exactly identical. [UTC 304, Comment.]. This UTC section, which is an expansion of UPC Section 1–403(2)(iii) [which is discussed at §§ 2.03 and 9.05(C)], applies only to persons who are otherwise unrepresented. These could include a minor, an incapacitated individual, an unborn individual, or a person whose identity or location is unknown and not reasonably ascertainable. [The UPC did not include minors or incapacitated individuals.] If there is no conflict of interest, these persons may be bound by another who has a substantially identical interest with respect to the particular question or dispute. The UPC allows these persons to be bound if their interests are "adequately" represented by the other. [1–403(2)(iii)]. The UTC drafters preferred to leave the question of adequate or sufficient representation to the courts. [UTC 304, Comment]. The UTC Comment points to sources for determining whether the representation was adequate, including the (First) of Property, §§ 181 and 185 (1936).

UTC Section 305, which is derived from UPC Section 1–403, allows a court that determines that an interest is not represented or that the representation is inadequate to appoint a "representative" to receive notice, give consent, and otherwise represent, bind, and act on behalf of a minor, incapacitated, or unborn individual, or a person whose identity or location is unknown. This representative may represent more than one person. The term "representative" is bracketed in case adopting states have another more appropriate term. The drafters deliberately chose not to use the UPC term "guardian ad litem" because, among other reasons, the representative can represent persons in nonjudicial settlements. [UTC 305, Comment]. Subsection (c) of UTC Section 305, which has no explanation in the Comment, states that the representative may consider a general benefit that would accrue to members of the represented family. This subsection may apply, for example, if a representative is asked to consent to a proceeding that would redirect trust property from a minor child to a surviving parent. Such a redirection may result in reduced estate taxes, which could eventually redound to the benefit of the entire family, including the represented child.

See § 2.03(B) for a discussion of the UPC's provision on virtual representation. [1–403].

CHAPTER 18
CREATION AND MODIFICATION OF TRUSTS

§ 18.01 UTC Article 4: Creation, Validity, Modification, and Termination of Express Trusts

A. CREATION OF A VALID TRUST

The first nine sections of Article 4 of the UTC, sections 401–409, set forth the requirements for creating a valid trust and the methods by which such a trust may be created.

1. Requirements for the Creation of a Valid Trust

The UTC provides that a trust must meet the following requirements: 1) the settlor must have the capacity to create the trust [see § 18.03(A)]; 2) the settlor must have the intent to create the trust [see Restatement (Third) of Trusts, §§ 13, Comment b]; 3) there must be at least one definite beneficiary (with some exceptions, as described below in § 18.01(A)(4) there must be duties for the trustee to perform [see § 19.02]; and 5) if there is only one trustee and one beneficiary, the trustee and beneficiary cannot be the same person. [UTC 402(a)].

There is no requirement in the UTC that the trust terms be in writing, although such a requirement may apply under some other statutes, such as traditional state statutes of frauds that require a transfer of real property to be evidenced by a writing. If the trust is oral, its creation and terms must be established by clear and convincing evidence. [UTC 407; see Restatement (Third) of Trusts, § 20; Restatement (Second) of Trusts, §§ 43–45.]

A trust can only be created for purposes that are lawful, not contrary to public policy, and possible to achieve. [UTC 404; see Restatement (Third) of Trusts, §§ 27–30]. Examples of trusts that would not meet this requirement are trusts that reward or encourage tortuous or criminal acts, trusts that are intentionally used to defraud creditors, or trusts that interfere with fundamental freedoms such as the freedom of religion or the freedom to marry. [UTC 404, Comment; see Restatement (Third) of Trusts, § 28–29; Restatement (Second) of Trusts, §§ 60–62].

The UTC provides that a trust is not valid if its creation was induced by fraud, duress, or undue influence. [UTC 406]. In so doing, the UTC incorporates into trust law the traditional grounds by which a will can be set aside as invalid. [See Restatement (Third) of Trusts, § 12; Restatement (Second) of Trusts, § 333.]

The UTC recognizes the validity of trusts that are created pursuant to the laws of a variety of jurisdictions. A trust is valid if it is created in accordance with the laws of the jurisdiction in which the trust was established or the laws of the jurisdiction in which: a) the settlor was domiciled or had a place of abode or was a national; b) the trustee was domiciled or had a place of business; or c) any of the trust property is located. [UTC 403; see also, UTC 107, § 17.01(D) on laws that govern the meaning and effect of the terms of a trust]. Traditionally, in order to be valid, a trust had to meet the requirements of the jurisdiction that had the most significant contacts with the trust. [UTC 403, Comment]. These UTC rules do not apply to trusts created by wills. The validity of a will was typically tied to the law of the place in which the decedent was domiciled at the date of death. [UTC 403, Comment]. However, the UPC contains a more expansive choice of law for determining the validity of a will. [See § 6.02(D)].

2. Methods of Creation

At common law, an express trust typically was created when the settlor transferred property owned by the settlor to another person to act as trustee. This transfer could take place during the settlor's life (in which case the trust is referred to as a "living" or "inter vivos" trust) or at the settlor's death pursuant to a direction in the settlor's will (in which case the trust is called a "testamentary trust"). The UTC codifies three methods for creating an express trust: 1) a transfer of property to another party to serve as trustee, which transfer is made either by the settlor during life or by way of the settlor's will after the settlor has died

[Manning v. Snyder, 2009 WL 792821 (Tenn.Ct. App.2009)]; 2) a declaration by the settlor that the settlor himself or herself holds the property as trustee in trust; or 3) the exercise of a power of appointment that results in the appointive property being appointed to a trustee. [UTC 401]. These methods of trust creation reflect those described in § 10 of the Restatement (Third) of Trusts and § 17 of the Restatement (Second) of Trusts. The procedures on this list are not the only means by which a trust may be created. The UTC makes reference to trusts that may be created by statute, judgment or decree, but these types of trusts are not covered by the UTC. [UTC 102]. Also, under limited circumstances, a trust may be created sheerly by an enforceable promise to place into trust the promisor's rights or interest in property. [UTC 401, Comment; Restatement (Third) of Trusts, § 10(e); Restatement (Second) of Trusts, § 14 Comment. h, § 26 Comment n.].

As noted above, a settlor may create a trust simply by declaring that she no longer holds her own property absolutely but that she now holds it as trustee. This is typically accomplished through a written "declaration of trust" (e.g., "I hereby declare myself trustee of the property listed in Schedule A") but may also be accomplished by the settlor deeding property to herself "as trustee." [See Restatement (Third) of Trusts, § 10, Comment e]. A declaration of trust may place property in the trust merely by attaching a schedule that lists the property that is to be held in trust, but the better practice is to transfer or re-register title to the property from the settlor's individual name to the named settlor "as trustee." [UTC 401, Comment]. Absent such re-registration, confusion may arise after the death of the settlor as to what property was intended to be trust property and what property was intended to be retained as the settlor's individually-owned property. [See, e.g., In re Trust of Rosenberg, 727 N.W.2d 430 (Neb.2007)].

A trust can be created by the exercise of a power of appointment when an individual who holds such a power directs that the property subject to the power should be transferred to a trustee. The UTC does not cover in detail the exercise of a power of appointment but rather directs the reader to the Restatement (Second) of Property: Donative Transfers, § 11.1–24.4 (1986) and the Restatement (Third) of Property: Wills and Other Donative Transfers. [UTC 401, Comment]. [See § 9.06].

3. The Requirement of Trust Property

Despite the fact that there is no express statement to this effect in the UTC, inherent in each of the three methods of trust creation outlined above is the common law requirement that a trust be funded with some type of property in order to come into existence. The term "property" is defined broadly in the UTC to include "anything that may be the subject of ownership" and includes property interests whether real or personal, legal or equitable. [UTC 103(12)]. Consequently, the Comments confirm the approach taken almost universally throughout the United States that the mere naming of a trust as the beneficiary of a life insurance policy or retirement plan constitutes a property interest that is sufficient to support the creation of a trust. [UTC 103(12), Comment; 401, Comment].

4.   Requirements Relating to Trust Beneficiaries

A basic tenet of common law is that a trust must have at least one beneficiary and must be created and administered for the benefit of its beneficiaries. [UTC 402(a)(3); 404; Restatement (Third) of Trusts, § 27(2)]. A trust must have beneficiaries because there must be someone who can enforce the trust or on whose behalf the trust can be enforced. [See Restatement (Third) of Trusts, § 44, comment a]. From this it follows that a trust is not valid if the sole beneficiary is also the sole trustee. [UTC 402(a)(5)]. The identity of the sole beneficiary and the sole trustee causes the trust to be invalid because there is no separate person to whom the trustee's duties will flow. Instead, the trustee-beneficiary becomes the absolute owner of the property. [See Bogert, §§ 129, 168; Atkins v. Marks, 288 S.W.3d 356 (Tenn.Ct.App.2008)].

In its prohibition against the sole beneficiary being the same person as the sole trustee, the UTC adopts the common law "merger" doctrine which provides that a trust terminates if the legal title and all of the equitable interests under the trust become united in the same person. [See Restatement (Third) of Trusts, § 69; Restatement (Second) of

Trusts, § 341]. The UTC Section 402 Comment indicates an expansive definition of the term "same person." The Comment provides as an example of a trust to which the doctrine of merger would apply "a trust of which the settlor is sole trustee, sole beneficiary for life, and with the remainder payable to the settlor's probate estate." [UTC 402, Comment]. Thus, the Comment equates the settlor's estate with the settlor herself. The Comment warns also that some state courts have inappropriately applied the merger doctrine to invalidate a trust in which the settlor is the sole trustee and the sole life beneficiary. Such a trust is not invalid if other persons are designated as the remainder beneficiaries. [See Welch v. Crow, 206 P.3d 599 (Okla.2009)].

The UTC recognizes three categories of trusts that are defined by the nature and ascertainability of the trust beneficiaries. The first type of trust is a trust that has one or more definite, ascertainable, non-charitable beneficiaries. [UTC 402(a)(3)]. This traditionally has been referred to as a "private" trust although the UTC does not incorporate that term. [See English, UTC Significant Provisions p. 164]. The second is a trust that is created for charitable purposes. This is referred to in the UTC as a "charitable trust." [UTC 402(a)(3)(A)]. The third type of trust, which was at common law referred to as an "honorary trust" (a term that is used in the Comment but not the text of the UTC [UTC 408, Comment]), was not always recognized at common law as a valid trust due to the lack of definiteness or ascertainability of the beneficiaries.

The UTC recognizes as valid two types of honorary trusts: trusts for animals [402(a)(3)(B), 408] and certain trusts of limited duration for noncharitable, unascertainable beneficiaries. [402(a)(3)(C)].

a. *The Definite Beneficiary Requirement*

As noted above, with some exceptions, an essential element of a trust is that the trust have at least one definite beneficiary. [UTC 402(a)(3)]. A beneficiary is definite if the beneficiary can be ascertained when the trust is created or at any time in the future that does not violate the applicable rule against perpetuities. [UTC 402(b); see Restatement (Third) of Trusts, § 44; Restatement (Second) of Trusts, § 112]. The requirement for a definite beneficiary is met under the UTC if the trust does not name a beneficiary but instead allows the trustee to select a beneficiary from a class of persons (e.g., "my children"), even if the class is indefinite—that is, a class of persons who are not easily ascertainable (e.g., "my favorite students."). [UTC 402(c); Restatement (Third) of Trusts, § 46, Comment a]. The UTC provision that validates a trust even if the beneficiaries are members of an unascertainable or indefinite class reverses traditional doctrine, under which such a trust would be invalid and the trustee would not have been permitted to exercise such a power. [See Restatement (Third) of Trusts, § 46, Comment a.]

b. *Charitable Trusts*

UTC Section 405 lists the purposes for which a charitable trust may be created. These are: "the relief of poverty, the advancement of education or religion, the promotion of health, governmental or municipal purposes, or other purposes the achievement of which is beneficial to the community." [UTC 405]. These purposes, which appear at Restatement (Third) of Trusts, § 28 and Restatement (Second) of Trusts, § 368, date back to the English Elizabethan era and have stood the test of time for both their flexibility and their broad applicability. [UTC 405, Comment]. The trust may name a specific charitable purpose or may express only a general charitable intent. In the latter case, the trustee or, if the trustee does not do so, the court may select charitable purposes or beneficiaries that are consistent with the expressed intent. [UTC 405(b), Comment]. UTC Section 405(c) reverses common law by allowing the settlor to bring an action to enforce the trust. Also under the UTC, the charitable organization, if any, to which trust distributions are being directed has standing to bring suit. [UTC 110(b), § 17.01(B)]. In most states, the state attorney general is authorized to play a role in the enforcement of the terms of a charitable trust. [UTC 110(d), Comment, § 17.01(B); see Hicks v. Dowd, 157 P.3d 914 (Wyo.2007)]. [See § 18.01(B)(2)(e) for a discussion of the modification of charitable trusts using the doctrine of *cy pres.*]

c. *Trusts for Animals*

Both the UPC and the UTC gives pet-owners the option to create a valid trust for the care of an animal. Traditionally, such "honorary trusts" were not recognized in many states due to the lack of a human beneficiary to enforce the trust. [Bogert, § 165]. But as more and more pet-owners have expressed the desire to provide for their care of their pets after death, creative estate planners have devised a means for this to occur. [See Beyer & Wilkerson, Pet Trusts, p. 1220].

UTC Section 408 validates a trust that is set up during the life of the settlor for the care of one or more animals. The trust lasts through the lifetime of the animal or animals. [UTC 408(a)]. Because the animal "beneficiary" itself cannot enforce the trust, the UTC allows the settlor or the court to appoint a person to enforce the trust. Anyone who has an interest in the animal may request the court to appoint such a person and also may request removal of the appointed person. [UTC 408(b)]. The property in the trust is to be used only for the care of the animal. However, a court may decide that the amount that is in the trust exceeds the amount needed for this use. The settlor can provide in the trust for the disposition of such excess funds and also for the disposition of funds that are left over after the last animal beneficiary dies. If the trust does not specify to whom such excess funds should go, the funds will be paid to the settlor, if the settlor is living and, if not, to the settlor's successors in interest. [UTC 408(c)]. This disposition reflects the manner in which excess funds would be distributed at common law using the fiction of a "resulting trust." [See Restatement (Third) of

Trusts, § 47; Restatement (Second) of Trusts, § 124].

The UPC's 1990 revisions to Article II, as modified by the 1993 Technical Amendments, include an alternative section dealing with honorary trusts, including trusts for pets. The UPC specifically permits assets to be transferred in trust for the care of designated domestic or pet animals. [2–907(b)]. Although validity is guaranteed under the provision, it limits the duration of the trust to the lives of the covered animals living when the trust is created. Instruments are to be liberally construed and extrinsic evidence freely admitted to determine transferor's intent. The UPC contains provisions similar to those in UTC Section 408 that deal with the use of the trust property, the transfer of unexpended funds, and court reduction of the amount held in trust. [2–907(c)].

d. *Trusts of Limited Duration for Noncharitable Purposes*

In addition to the recognition of trusts for animals, both the UPC and the UTC recognize two other types of noncharitable trusts that would have been treated at common law as honorary trusts. These are trusts for noncharitable purposes that do not have a definite or ascertainable beneficiary and trusts for noncharitable but otherwise valid purposes that will be selected by the trustee. [2–907(a); [UTC 409(1)]. As noted above, such trusts would not be enforceable at common law because there was no ascertainable beneficiary to enforce them.

[See Hirsch, Bequests for Purposes, pp. 33–42; Levy, Idaho's Noncharitable Purpose Trust Statute, pp. 810–13; Restatement (Third) of Trusts, § 47; Restatement (Second) of Trusts, § 124]. The Comment to UTC Section 409 notes that the most common form of trust in the first category is one that is set up for the purpose of maintaining a cemetery plot. [UTC 409, Comment]. In the second category would fall trusts in which the settlor directs the trustee to use the trust property for such benevolent purposes as the trustee might select. Although trusts covered by this UTC section are limited in duration (21 years is the optional time suggested in the UTC Section 409(1)), these trusts are also subject to other statutes. The Comment points out, for example, that state statutes pertaining to cemetery plots may allow for perpetual care, as opposed to limiting the maintenance to 21 years. The purposes of these trusts are subject to the limitations set forth in UTC Section 404. [See § 18.01(a)(1)]. Because these trusts have no definite beneficiary, UTC Section 409(2) allows the settlor to name in the trust a person who will be responsible for enforcement. If no person is named, the court may appoint a person to enforce the trust.

The property in this type of trust can be applied only for its intended use. As with trusts for animals, a court may decide that the amount that is in the trust exceeds the amount needed for this use. The settlor can provide in the trust for the disposition of such excess funds. If the trust does not specify to whom such excess funds should go, the funds will be paid to the settlor, if the settlor is living and, if not, to the settlor's successors in interest. [2–907(c); UTC 409(3)].

B. MODIFICATION, TERMINATION, REFORMATION, CONSOLIDATION AND DIVISION OF TRUSTS

The remaining provisions of Article 4 of the UTC (Sections 410–17) provide alternative ways in which a trust may be terminated or modified. The Comment to Article 4 explains that "[t]he overall objective of these sections is to enhance flexibility consistent with the principle that preserving the settlor's intent is paramount." Some of the modifications or terminations described in these sections may be accomplished by the beneficiaries themselves or by the beneficiaries in conjunction with the settlor; some may be accomplished by court order; and some may be accomplished by the trustee without the consent of the beneficiaries or the court.

UTC Section 410(a) lists the typical circumstances under which a trust may terminate without action by a beneficiary, the trustee or a court. A revocable trust will terminate upon revocation. [See § 18.03 on revocable trusts]. A trust may terminate in accordance with the terms of the trust instrument. Additionally, a trust will terminate if "no purpose of the trust remains to be achieved, or the purposes of the trust have become unlawful, contrary to public policy, or impossible to achieve." [UTC 410(a)]

UTC Section 410(b) describes who may bring an action or proceeding under UTC Sections 411–17. An action to gain court approval of a proposed modification or termination of a trust may be commenced by a trustee or beneficiary. The settlor of a charitable trust may commence an action to modify the trust. An optional section would allow the settlor to commence an action for termination or modification pursuant to UTC Section 411.

1. Modification or Termination by Beneficiaries

a. Joint Action by the Beneficiaries and the Settlor

UTC Section 411, which applies only to noncharitable trusts that are irrevocable, describes the circumstances under which a trust may be modified by the beneficiaries, with or without the consent of the settlor. As originally promulgated, UTC Section 411(a) would allow the settlor and beneficiaries to come together to modify or terminate the trust, without court approval, even if such action was inconsistent with a material purpose of the trust. This approach, which was already allowed by statute in some states before the promulgation of the UTC, was based on the theory that the settlor had changed her mind about the terms or even the existence of the trust and thus had joined the beneficiaries in consenting to a termination or modification. [See Bogert § 1005]. This approach was also endorsed in Restatement (Third) of Trusts, § 65(2) and Restatement (Second) of Trusts, § 338(2) (1959). In other states, the settlor and beneficiaries could not modify or terminate the trust on their own, but were rather required to gain court approval of such action, which approval would presumably be granted if the court found unanimous consent by all the parties. [See Bogert § 1005]. In neither situation is the trustee required to consent to the proposed action, although the trustee does have standing to object if the proposed termination or modification is the subject of a court proceeding. [UTC 410, 411, Comment].

In the years following its original promulgation, UTC Section 411(a) became the subject of much debate among the tax experts who comprised the Estate & Gift Tax Committee of the American College of Trust & Estate Counsel (ACTEC). The UTC drafters responded to this debate with the 2004 amendments to UTC Section 411. The concern of some of these experts was that allowing a settlor to join with the beneficiaries in consenting to the modification or termination of an "irrevocable" trust would result in so much control by the settlor that the trust property would be treated as the settlor's own property for tax purposes, which often would result in undesirable and unanticipated tax consequences. [See Bogert § 1005].

Under the 2004 amended version, states that enact UTC Section 411 are offered four options: 1) not adopt subsection (a) at all and thus leave whatever state law is already in place to control; b) adopt the original (now bracketed) version of subsection (a) that allows modification or termination upon the unanimous consent of the settlor and beneficiaries without court approval; c) adopt the bracketed second version, that requires court approval; or d) make the new provision applicable only to irrevocable trusts created after or that became irrevocable after the effective date of the enactment of the trust code. In May, 2009, the Internal Revenue Service issued three Private Letter Rulings (PLRs 200919008, 200919009, 200919010) in which the settlor had used a state law provision similar to that of the original version of UTC Section 411 to amend the administrative provisions of the trusts. The Internal Revenue Service stated that these amendments would not cause the adverse tax consequences feared by the critics. However, these PLRs (which cannot be relied upon as precedent by anyone other than the parties to whom they are issued) all noted that the amendments sought by the settlor were to administrative provisions only, while the UTC seems to apply to any amendment made by a settlor, whether to the administrative or dispositive provisions of the trust.

If a state enacts one of the provisions that allow the settlor to join the beneficiaries in the consent for a modification or termination of the trust, UTC Section 411(a) also describes the circumstances under which three persons other than the settlor may consent on behalf of the settlor. First in priority is an agent under the settlor's power of attorney. However, the agent may consent only to the extent the power of attorney or the terms of the trust authorize the agent to do so. [See § 18.03(B) for a discussion of UTC 602(e), which describes an agent's power to revoke a revocable trust.] If there is no agent who is authorized to do so, consent may be given by the settlor's conservator with the consent of the court that is supervising the conservatorship. (The term "conservator," which is defined in UTC 103(5), is bracketed to allow the states to substitute whatever term they use to describe the person who is appointed by a court to manage the property of a minor or an incapacitated individual.) [See § 15.09 for a description of conservators' powers under the UPC.]

If there is no authorized agent and no conservator, the power may be exercised by the settlor's guardian, with the approval of the court that supervises the guardianship. (The term "guardian," which is defined in UTC 103(7), is also bracketed to allow the states to substitute whatever term they use to describe the person who is appointed to make decisions regarding the support, care, education, health, and welfare of a minor or incapacitated adult).

b. *Action by the Beneficiaries Only*

UTC Section 411 also describes the circumstances under which the beneficiaries may consent to the modification or termination of a trust, without the consent of the settlor. Under UTC Section 411(b), the beneficiaries may terminate or modify the trust by unanimous consent if the appropriate court concludes that continuance of the trust is not required to achieve a material purpose of the trust and the proposed modification is not inconsistent with any material purpose of the trust. [See § 17.03 for a discussion of who may consent on behalf of a beneficiary.] This provision codifies the common law doctrine that was first set down in *Claflin v. Claflin*, 20 N.E. 454 (Mass.1889). The ability of the beneficiaries to modify or revoke the trust without participation by the settlor appears in the Third Restatement of Trusts but not in the Second Restatement. [Compare Restatement (Third) of Trusts, §, 65 (2003) with Restatement (Second) of Trusts, §, 338(1) (1959).] Under subsection (d) of UTC Section 411, if the trust is terminated, the remaining trust property will be distributed in the manner agreed to by the beneficiaries. [UTC 411(d)].

The Comment offers some guidance for courts as to whether the proposed termination or modification is inconsistent with the material purposes of the trust. The Comment states that "[m]aterial purposes are not readily to be inferred" but instead require "some showing of a particular concern or objective on the part of the settlor, such as a concern with regard to the beneficiary's management skills, judgment, or level of maturity." [UTC 411, Comment; see Vaughn v. Huntington National Bank Trust Div., 2009 WL 342697 (Ohio 2009)].

Subsection (c) of UTC Section 411, as originally enacted, provided that a spendthrift provision in a trust was not presumed to be a "material purpose" of the trust that would preclude modification or termination under subsection (b). However, in 2004, subsection (c) of UTC Section 411 was made optional because several of the states that were enacting the UTC already had state law in place to the contrary. The result was that these states either refused to enact subsection (c) or rewrote it to reverse the presumption. [UTC 411, Comment; see, e.g., K.S.A. Supp. 2003, § 58a–411, discussed in In re Estate of Somers, 89 P.3d 898 (Kan.2004)].

Subsection (e) of UTC Section 411 addresses the situation in which the unanimous consent of the beneficiaries is not obtained, either because one or more beneficiaries object or cannot consent (for example, if there are unborn beneficiaries). This subsection allows the court to approve a modification or termination that is requested by fewer than all of the beneficiaries. In doing so, the court must ensure that the interests of any non-consenting beneficiary are adequately protected. The Comment suggests the following mechanisms as possible methods of protecting these interests: ''partial continuation of the trust, the purchase of an annuity, or the valuation and cashout of the interest.'' [UTC 411, Comment].

2. Modification or Termination by Court Order

UTC Sections 412–16 describe a variety of circumstances under which a court may modify, terminate, or reform a trust without the consent of the beneficiaries. While most of these provisions apply to both charitable and noncharitable trusts, UTC Section 413 (which is discussed at the end of this section) contains special provisions that apply only to charitable trusts. The power of a court to modify or terminate a trust under these UTC sections prevails over any trust terms to the contrary. [UTC 105(b)(4)].

a. *Modification or Termination Due to Unanticipated Circumstances*

UTC Section 412(a) allows the court to modify the administrative or the dispositive terms of a trust or even terminate the trust if the court determines that circumstances that were not anticipated by the settlor are somehow impairing the purposes of the trust. The modification must adhere to the extent practicable to the settlor's "probable intention." This section codifies and broadens a doctrine known in common law as "equitable deviation." [See Restatement (Third) of Trusts, § 66 (2003)]. While at common law the doctrine applied only to the administrative provisions of a trust [see Restatement (Second) of Trusts, § 167 (1959)], the language of subsection (a) of UTC Section 412 indicates that the court's power applies both to the provisions relating to the trust's management and the provisions covering distributions of benefits from the trust. [See White v. Kansas Health Policy Authority, 198 P.3d 172 (Kan.App.2008)]. An example given in the Comment of the application of this section is the increase of distributions for support of a beneficiary who has become unable to support himself. The comments accompanying § 66 of the Restatement (Third) of Trusts contain many other illustrations of the application of equitable deviation. This section was cited in *In re Estate of Som-*

ers, 89 P.3d 898 (Kan.2004) to justify a distribution of part of the trust corpus to the charitable remainder beneficiary after an unanticipated growth in the value of the principal of the trust.

Subsection (b) of UTC Section 412, which does not require a finding of unanticipated circumstances, allows a court to modify the administrative (but not the dispositive) provisions of a trust "if continuation of the trust on its existing terms would be impracticable or wasteful or impair the trust's administration." The Comment points out that this subsection is not grounded in common law, but had previously been introduced in some states by statute. [UTC 412, Comment]. Subsection (c) of UTC Section 412 provides that, if the trust is terminated, distribution of the trust proceeds shall be consistent with the trust purposes. The Comment observes that "[t]ypically, such terminating distributions will be made to the qualified beneficiaries, often in proportion to the actuarial value of their interests, although the section does not so prescribe." [UTC 412, Comment; see § 17.01(B) on qualified beneficiaries.]

b.   *Modification or Termination of Uneconomic   Trusts*

As discussed below, UTC Section 414(a) permits a trustee to terminate certain small trusts. Subsection (b) of UTC Section 414 allows the court to modify or terminate a trust or remove and replace the trustee, regardless of the size of the trust, if the court determines that the costs of administration are not justified by the value of the trust property. The Comment cautions that modification or termination should be ordered only after careful consideration of the trust purposes. For example, a court may conclude that it is better to pay for the trust administration than to run the risk involved were the beneficiary to be given the funds outright. The Comment suggests that in some situations the costs of administration may be lowered by replacing the trustee. [UTC 414, Comment.] As with UTC Section 412, if a trust is terminated under UTC Section 414, the distribution of the remaining trust property should be consistent with the trust purposes. [UTC 414(c)]. The Comment points out that UTC Section 816(21) provides an array of alternate methods of payment if it would not be advisable to pay the trust property directly to one or more of the beneficiaries. [UTC 414, Comment]. Included among these are payments to the beneficiary's conservator or guardian or custodian under a Uniform Transfers to Minors account. [UTC 816(21); see § 19.02(O)].

UTC Section 414 expressly does not apply to conservation or preservation easements. [UTC 414(d)]. A conservation easement is "a nonpossessory interest of a holder in real property imposing limitations or affirmative obligations the purposes of which include retaining or protecting natural, scenic, or open-space values of real property, assuring its availability for agricultural, forest, recreational, or open-space use, protecting natural resources, maintaining or enhancing air or water quality, or preserving the historical, architectural, archaeological, or cultural aspects of real property." [Uniform Conservation Easement Act, § 1(1)]. The drafters of the UTC noted that these easements often take the form of charitable trusts and thus would potentially be susceptible to the application of UTC Section 414. The drafters concluded that the settlor of a conservation easement would prefer the easement to continue even if the value of the underlying land, and thus the trust, was diminished. [UTC 414, Comment].

c. *Reformation to Correct Mistakes*

Reformation is the process by which a trust is reworded for the purpose of correcting a mistake of fact or law made either by the settlor or the scrivener. The purpose of a reformation is to effectuate the settlor's intent at the time the trust was drafted. [UTC 415, Comment; see In re Harris Testamentary Trust, 69 P.3d 1109 (Kan.2003); Manning v. Snyder, 2009 WL 792821 (Tenn.Ct.App.2009)]. UTC Section 415 allows a court to reform a trust to conform to the settlor's original intent. This Code section applies whether the mistake was one of "expression" ("when the terms of the trust misstate the settlor's intention, fail to include a term that was intended to be included, or include a term that was not intended to be included") or "inducement" ("when the terms of the trust accurately reflect what the settlor intended to be included or excluded but this intention was based on a mistake of fact or law"). [UTC 415, Comment, citing Restatement (Third) of Property: Donative Transfers Section 12.1 Comment II (2003]. Mistakes of expression (e.g., drafting errors) may be made by the settlor or by the scrivener, while mistakes of inducement are typically mistakes of the settlor. [UTC 415, Comment]. UTC Section 415 applies even if the terms of the trust are unambiguous. As noted in the Comment, "reliance on extrinsic evidence is essential." [UTC 415, Comment; see In re Estate of Shults, 2008 WL 490643 (Tenn.Ct.App. 2008)]. Because a reformation involves changing, deleting or adding terms to a trust that may be otherwise clear on its face based on evidence that is potentially fraudulent or contrived, a reformation can occur only if it can be proved by clear and convincing evidence that both the settlor's intent and the terms of the trust were affected by a mistake of fact or law. [UTC 415, Comment; see In re Trust Created by Isvik, 741 N.W.2d 638 (Neb. 2007), in which the court reformed a letter purporting to revoke a trust under the theory that the letter was part of the "terms of the trust."; see also Manning v. Snyder, 2009 WL 792821 (Tenn.Ct.App. 2009)]. The 2008 amendments to the UPC include new UPC 2–805, which applies the rule of UTC 415 to all instruments governing donative transfers. [See § 8.06].

d.   *Modification to Achieve Tax Objectives*

Restatement (Third) of Property: Donative Transfers Section 12.2 (2003) and some state statutes expressly allow a court to modify a trust to achieve the tax objectives of the settlor. UTC Section 416 codifies this provision. The Comment likens this type of modification to that allowed for unanticipated circumstances (see description of UTC Section 412 above) and clarifies that this action is a modification as opposed to a reformation (see description above of UTC Section 415) because it is designed to meet the settlor's ongoing objective rather than to effectuate the settlor's original intent. [UTC 416, Comment].

Practically speaking, it is often difficult to distinguish between cases that involve reformation to achieve tax objectives and those that involve modification. [See Bogert, § 994]. A modification under UTC Section 416 may be made retroactive by the court. The Comment notes, however, that whether the modification will be respected by the Internal Revenue Service and the tax courts is a matter of federal law (see, e.g., Internal Revenue Code § 2055(e)(3)), not state law, and that modifications most likely to be given binding effect are those made before the actual taxing event to which they pertain. The Comment enumerates as examples of modifications that the IRS has authorized or respected "the revision of split-interest trusts to qualify for the charitable deduction, modification of a trust for a noncitizen spouse to become eligible as a qualified domestic trust, and the splitting of a trust to utilize better the exemption from generation-skipping tax." [UTC 416, Comment; see In Re Harris Testamentary Trust, 69 P.3d 1109 (Kan.2003)]. The 2008 amendments to the UPC include new

UPC 2–806, which applies the rule of UTC 416 to all instruments governing donative transfers. [See § 8.06].

e. Modification or Termination of Charitable Trusts

Common law has long recognized the power of equity to "save" a charitable gift that has become impossible to fulfill by engaging in a modification that allows the donor's original charitable intent to be realized. This power has been known as "cy pres," from the Norman French phrase "cy pres comme possible" or "as near as possible." At common law, the court would substitute a new charitable object or otherwise modify the provisions of the gift so as to carry out the donor's intent as closely as possible. [See Bogert § 431]. The doctrine of cy pres applies to all manner of charitable gifts. UTC Section 413 codifies and expands that doctrine for charitable trusts. Subsection (a) of UTC Section 413 provides that cy pres is available if the charitable purpose "becomes unlawful, impracticable, impossible to achieve or wasteful" whereas common law allowed cy pres only if the purpose became "impossible, impracticable or illegal." [See Restatement (Second) of Trusts, § 399]. UTC Section 413 also expands the doctrine because, unlike at common law, there is no requirement of a finding of a general charitable intent on the part of the settlor. [See Restatement (Second) of Trusts, § 399]. Rather, under the UTC, such intent is presumed. [UTC 413, Comment]. Subsection (a) of UTC Section 413 prevents the charitable trust from failing and the trust property from reverting to the settlor or the settlor's successors in interest by allowing the court to redirect the application or distribution of the trust property in a manner that is consistent with the presumed charitable purpose of the settlor. This could involve simply modifying the trust or terminating it altogether. For example, if a trust was created to fund research for a cure for a particular debilitating disease and such a cure is eventually found, the court may redirect the funds toward research on another debilitating disease. If a trust is created to fund the construction of a hospital and there are funds left over after the construction is completed, the court may direct that the surplus be used to purchase laboratory equipment for the hospital.

As noted above, under UTC Section 410(b), the settlor of a charitable trust may commence an action to modify the trust. This was not allowed at common law. [See Restatement (Second) of Trusts, § 391 (1959)].

Subsection (b) of UTC Section 413 adds another provision that did not appear at common law. This provision not only expands a court's ability to use cy pres but also is designed to cure the "severe administrative inefficiency" that may occur when the settlor designates a noncharitable beneficiary as the recipient of the trust property upon the failure of the specific charitable purpose. [English, UTC Significant Provisions, p. 179]. In some cases, this "gift over" to a noncharitable beneficiary has been used to negate the application of cy pres by showing that the settlor's intent was not "entirely" charitable. [See Chester, Failed Charitable Trusts, pp. 47–48.] As noted immediately above, that problem has been cured in UTC Section 413 by presuming charitable intent. But even if such intent is presumed, a gift over to a noncharitable beneficiary often will not occur until many decades after the creation of the trust and will thus raise numerous administrative difficulties, such as the clogging of title or the need to search for the descendants of the settlor's heirs. [UTC 413, Comment; English, UTC Significant Provisions, p. 179]. Subsection (b) of UTC Section 413 provides that the gift over to a noncharitable beneficiary may override the court's power to apply cy pres only in two narrow circumstances: 1) if the recipient is the settlor and the settlor is still living or 2) if fewer than 21 years have passed since the trust was created. The Comment notes that this provision does not apply to a "charitable lead trust," which is a tax-oriented mechanism by which the trust pays income to a charity for a certain period and then the remainder to a noncharitable beneficiary because in this situation the gift to the charity does not fail. [UTC 413, Comment].

3.   Modification or Termination by the Trustee

UTC Sections 414(a) and 417 allow the trustee, without court order or the consent of the beneficiaries, to engage in the modification or termination of trusts, including the consolidation of two or more trusts into a single trust and the division of a trust into separate trusts.

a. Modification or Termination of Uneconomic Trusts

UTC Section 414(a) allows a trustee, without court permission, to terminate a trust if the trustee determines that the value of the trust does not justify the cost of administering the trust. The suggested value of a trust for which the costs are presumed to outweigh the value is $50,000, although this value may be changed by the enacting states. Because this termination does not involve court action, this subsection is not covered by UTC Section 105(b)(4) (which is discussed in § 17.01(C)). This means that a settlor may choose to state expressly in the trust instrument a specified value that would trigger the application of this subsection or provide that this subsection could never be used by the trustee. [UTC 414, Comment]. Before terminating a trust of $50,000 or less, the trustee must give notice to the qualified beneficiaries. [See § 18.01(B)(2)(b) for a discussion of the modification or termination of an uneconomic trust by court order.]

b. Consolidation or Division of Trusts

UTC Section 417 authorizes a trustee to consolidate one or more trusts or to divide a trust into one or more separate trusts provided "the result does not impair rights of any beneficiary or adversely affect achievement of the purposes of the trust."

This authority is consistent with that found in many state statutes and is also often granted in the express terms of trusts. [UTC 417, Comment]. The trustee must notify the qualified beneficiaries before engaging in a consolidation or division, but need not get court permission. Because this action is not subjected to a court for approval, a trustee proceeds at its own risk when deciding to consolidate or divide trusts. The Comment suggests that a trustee may want to seek court approval of the consolidation or division under UTC Section 410. [UTC 417, Comment].

UTC Section 417 contemplates that trusts that will be the subject of consolidation will be a number of trusts created by different family members that may differ only in small respects. [UTC 417, Comment]. There is no requirement that the terms of the trusts be identical; however, as noted in the Comment, "[t]he more the dispositive provisions of the trusts to be combined differ from each other the more likely it is that a combination would impair some beneficiary's interest. . . . " [UTC 417, Comment]. The Comment suggests that a consolidation may be one way of dealing with the problem of an uneconomic trust. [UTC 417, Comment; see discussion above of UTC 414, § 18.01(B)(3)(a)]. In fact, the Comment goes further to opine that the trustee may have the responsibility to pursue consolidation under UTC Section 805 (duty to incur only reasonable costs, discussed at § 19.02(E)) if the economies of the trusts so dictate.

The Comment describes the division of trusts as being "beneficial" in many cases "and, in certain circumstances, almost routine." Divisions may occur for both tax purposes and non-tax purposes. The division of a trust may result in the maximization of the exemption for the federal generation-skipping tax and the Comment notes that the failure to pursue this tax advantage may constitute a breach of fiduciary duty. [UTC 417, Comment]. The division of a trust into separate trusts may allow the new trusts to receive favorable income tax treatment as qualified Subchapter S trusts. [See In Re Harris Testamentary Trust, 69 P.3d 1109 (Kan. 2003)]. From a non-tax standpoint, the division of a trust into separate trusts may be a way to deal with disputes among the various beneficiaries as to investment objectives. [UTC 417, Comment]. The Comment cautions, however, that a breach of fiduciary duty may occur if the trustee divides a trust into separate trusts solely for the purpose of increasing trustee fees or terminating the trusts as uneconomic trusts. [UTC 417, Comment; see UTC 414, § 18.01(B)(2)(b) on uneconomic trusts]. As with UTC Section 414(a), the settlor is free to expand, narrow or even prohibit the trustee's powers to act under UTC Section 417 by so stating in the trust instrument.

§ 18.02 UTC Article 5: Creditors' Claims: Spendthrift and Discretionary Trusts

Article 5 deals with the ability of a creditor to reach property that is held in trust. The article covers separately the claims of a creditor of a beneficiary of the trust [UTC 501–04, 506], the claims of a creditor of the settlor of the trust [UTC 505], and the claims of a creditor of the trustee of the trust [UTC 507]. The rules in Article 5 are mandatory rules that may not be modified by the settlor in the trust instrument. [UTC 105(b)(5), see § 17.01(C)]. These rules purposely do not detail the means by which a beneficiary's or settlor's interest in the trust can be reached by creditors because such means will be the subject of widely-diverse state and federal laws. These include but are not limited to state laws relating to garnishment and attachment and fraudulent conveyances as well as federal bankruptcy laws. The provisions of Article 5 have been the subject of heated debate among practitioners, lawmakers and academics and, as noted herein, the criticisms leveled against Article 5 have caused some states either to modify the provisions of Article 5 or to retain their own state law relating to creditors' rights. [Millard, Trust Beneficiary's Creditors, pp. 67–79].

A. CLAIMS BY CREDITORS
OF A BENEFICIARY

When property is held in trust for a beneficiary, it is not unusual for the creditors of that beneficiary to attempt to reach that property to satisfy their claims, even though the property is not immediately available to the beneficiary. These creditors also would prefer to go directly to the trustee rather than run the risk of trying to collect after trust property has been paid out to the beneficiary. Every section of Article 5 except UTC Sections 505 and 507 applies to claims made by a creditor of a beneficiary.

1. General Rule

UTC Section 501 provides the general rule that applies if the beneficiary's interest in the trust is not subject to a spendthrift provision. [Spendthrift trusts are covered in UTC 502 and 503.] This section, which is consistent with common law, allows a court to authorize a creditor or assignee of a beneficiary to reach the beneficiary's interest in the trust by attaching distributions to the beneficiary or by other means. [UTC 501; Restatement (Third) of Trusts, § 58; Restatement (Second) of Trusts, § 152]. The process of attachment allows the creditor to receive payment directly from the trustee rather than to have to wait until trust property reaches the hands of the beneficiary. The term "other means" refers to other mechanisms relating to creditors' rights that may appear in the enacting state's laws. [UTC 501, Comment]. This UTC section allows a creditor to attach both present and future distributions from the trust, thus minimizing the need for a creditor to re-apply for court authorization every time a trust distribution is due. [UTC 501, Comment]. The Comment points out that even with this provision a creditor may not always be able to reach a beneficiary's interest as the interest may be too indefinite or contingent or it may be protected by some other state law. [UTC 501, Comment]. The second sentence of UTC Section 501 recognizes the equitable nature of this type of relief by allowing the court to limit the relief to that which would be appropriate under the circumstances. The Comment notes, for example, that the court "may appropriately consider the circumstances of a beneficiary and the beneficiary's family."

2. Spendthrift Trusts

American law has long respected the ability of a settlor to protect a beneficiary's interest in a trust by including language in the trust (a "spendthrift clause") that prohibits the creditors of the beneficiary from attaching that beneficiary's interest. [See Restatement (Third) of Trusts, § 57, Restatement (Second) of Trusts, §§ 150. 159]. UTC Sections 502–03 contain the requirements for creating a valid spendthrift trust and describe certain creditors ("exception creditors") who can reach the beneficiary's interest despite the spendthrift provisions.

UTC Section 502 requires the settlor to include spendthrift language in the trust in order for the protection to apply. In other words, trusts that are silent on the issue of creditors' rights are not presumed to be spendthrift trusts. This reflects the common law and that of most state statutes. [English, UTC Significant Provisions, p. 181]. UTC Section 502(b) takes an expansive approach to the type of language that is required, providing that a statement in the trust instrument that the beneficiary's interest is subject to a "spendthrift trust, or words of similar import" is sufficient to create a spendthrift trust.

The term "spendthrift provision" is defined in UTC Section 103(16) as a trust term that restrains both voluntary and involuntary transfer of a beneficiary's interest. [See In re Marcato, 2009 WL 1856578 (Bkrtcy.M.D.Ala.2009)]. UTC Section 502(a) reflects this definition by requiring that, in order to be valid, a spendthrift provision must prohibit both voluntary and involuntary transfers of the beneficiary's interest. The drafters of the UTC concluded that it would be unfair to prohibit a beneficiary's creditors from reaching the interest while at the same time allowing the beneficiary to assign that interest to a third party. [English, UTC Significant Provisions, p. 181.] However, some enacting states chose to allow the settlor to restrain either voluntary or involuntary transfers and do not require that both be prohibited. [Millard, Trust Beneficiary's Creditors, p. 60]. Even if both types of transfers are prohibited by the spendthrift provision, the beneficiary may effectively have the right to make a voluntary transfer if the trust provides the beneficiary with a power of appointment. [English, UTC Significant Provisions, p. 181].

Unlike the Restatement and many state statutes, UTC Section 502 does not provide explicitly that a settlor may not protect her own interests with a spendthrift clause. [See, e.g., Restatement (Second) of Trusts, § 156]. The Comment to UTC Section 502 states that this concept is inherent in the

provisions of UTC Section 505(a)(2) (discussed below) that allow a creditor of the settlor to reach any
interest that can be distributed to the settlor or
used for her benefit. [UTC 502, Comment]. Some
states now allow settlors to protect their own assets
through the use of a spendthrift trust. [English,
UTC Significant Provisions, p. 181].

UTC Section 503 lists certain creditors (''exception creditors'') to whom a spendthrift provision
will not apply. In other words, these creditors of a
beneficiary can reach a beneficiary's interest in the
same manner as is described in UTC Section 501,
the language of which is repeated in UTC Section
503(c). UTC Section 503 was reworded by a 2005
amendment but the substance was not changed.
This section recognizes three types of exception
creditors: 1) spouse and children; 2) certain judgment creditors; and 3) the state and federal govern-
ments. Despite critics' claims that this list is not
exclusive and thus could be expanded by the courts,
UTC Section 502(c) makes it clear that these are
the only creditors who can reach a beneficiary's
interest in a spendthrift trust. Other creditors who
have been recognized at common law or in state
statutes as exception creditors but were not included in UTC Section 503 are creditors who provided
necessaries to the beneficiary and tort judgment
creditors. [See Restatement (Third) of Trusts,
§ 59(b) and Comment a(2)]. The drafters of the
UTC believed that most of the creditors in the
former category are government agencies and thus

would be included as exception creditors under the third exception of UTC Section 503.

Under the first exception, a "child" (defined as "any person for whom an order or judgment for child support has been entered in this or another State" [UTC 503(a)]), spouse or former spouse can reach the beneficiary's interest, but only to satisfy a judgment or court order for support or maintenance. Although some species of such an exception has long been recognized as good public policy, most of the enacting states either did not include or modified this exception. The variations are many. Some states retained children but not spouses, others retained spouses but not former spouses, while still others narrowed the type of judgment that could be satisfied. [Millard, Trust Beneficiary's Creditors, pp. 61–62]. The Utah version of this statute, which includes only a child as an exception creditor, has been applied to allow the beneficiary's ex-spouse to garnish the beneficiary's interest in the spendthrift trust for unpaid child support payments. [Booth (2006)].

The second exception creditor is defined narrowly as a "judgment creditor who has provided services for the protection of a beneficiary's interest in the trust." [UTC 503(b)(2)]. This exception, which is recognized in Restatement (Third) of Trusts, § 59 and Restatement (Second) of Trusts, § 157, is desirable for two reasons. First, it could constitute unjust enrichment to allow a beneficiary to use the services of someone, such as a lawyer, to protect the beneficiary's interest in the trust but then restrain payment to that service provider. Second, if the beneficiary does not otherwise have the ability to pay for the service, exception of this type of creditor would give the beneficiary the means to pay for the protection of the beneficiary's interest. [See Restatement (Third) of Trusts, § 59, Comment d].

The third exception creditor is the state or federal government "to the extent a statute of this State or federal law so provides." [UTC 503(b)(3)]. As recognized by the drafters, the federal preemption doctrine overrides any attempt by the states to prohibit collection of certain debts owed the United States. [UTC 503, Comment]. Similarly, enacting states may have a variety of statutes relating to the collection of their claims.

3. Discretionary Trusts

A spendthrift provision is not the only bar to a creditor attaching a beneficiary's interest in a trust. Some settlors give the trustee the discretion to determine the timing and amount of distributions to the beneficiary, as opposed to, for example, mandating that the trust income be paid to a named beneficiary on a quarterly basis. This discretion may be very broad (some trusts use the term "in the trustee's sole discretion") or may be tied to some sort of standard (i.e., "those amounts that my trustee determines are needed to support the beneficiary in the beneficiary's accustomed standard of living"). If the discretion is broad, the beneficiary cannot compel the trustee to make a distribution and, concomitantly, the beneficiary's creditor cannot force a distribution. [See Restatement (Second) of Trusts, § 155; Pohlmann (2006)]. Common law recognized another type of trust on the spectrum between mandatory and discretionary trusts that is referred to as a "support trust." A support trust typically would direct the trustee to use the trust property to support the beneficiary. Even though the language of such a trust would appear to be mandatory, the trustee is inherently granted the discretion to decide what amounts would be needed to fulfill this "support" responsibility. [Millard, Trust Beneficiary's Creditors, p. 69]. At common law, certain exception creditors who could not reach the beneficiary's interest in a purely discretionary trust could reach the interest in a support trust. [Restatement (Second) of Trusts, § 157]. It was not always easy to determine whether a trust was a discretionary trust or a support trust so the drafters of the UTC abandoned this "evasive distinction" and subsumed support trusts under the same rules that apply to all other discretionary trusts. [English, UTC Significant Provisions, p. 183].

Under UTC Section 504, whether or not the trust contains a spendthrift provision, a creditor cannot attach a beneficiary's interest in a discretionary trust. This rule applies whether the trustee's discretion is unlimited or tied to a standard of distribution and regardless of whether the trustee has abused this discretion. [UTC 504(b)]. However, if there is a standard with which the trustee has not complied or the trustee has otherwise abused the trustee's discretion, UTC Section 504(c) provides the same exception for children, spouses and former spouses that appears in UTC Section 503(b)(2). This exception is further restricted in UTC Section 504(c)(2) by a provision that allows the court to allow the creditor access only to that amount of the beneficiary's interest that is "equitable under the circumstances" and that does not exceed the amount that would have been distributed to the beneficiary if the trustee had complied with the standard or not abused its discretion. As occurred with UTC Section 503(b)(2), almost all of the enacting states either omitted or modified this exception. [Millard, Trust Beneficiary's Creditors, p. 63].

Subsection (d) of UTC Section 504 clarifies that the provisions of UTC Section 504 apply only to the creditors and do not in any way restrict the beneficiary's right to bring an action to compel the trustee to perform.

Subsection (e) of UTC Section 504 was added in 2004 to address a tax-related issue that had not been originally contemplated by the drafters. In many trusts, the trustee is also a beneficiary of the trust. The trustee/beneficiary is allowed to make distributions to herself, but those distributions are limited by "ascertainable standards," such as health, education, maintenance and support. These ascertainable standards are common in trusts because, under Internal Revenue Code § 2041(b)(1)(A), the power of a trustee/beneficiary to appoint trust property to herself could cause the value of that property to be included in the trustee/beneficiary's gross estate unless the power to appoint is limited by such ascertainable standards. Thus, it is a standard estate planning practice to include a power of appointment that is limited by these standards. A comment to the Restatement (Third) of Trusts, § 60 (Comment g) indicated that having such a power would allow the creditors of such a trustee/beneficiary to reach that person's interest in the trust. New subsection (e) of UTC Section 504 contradicts the Restatement comment and provides that a creditor may not reach or compel a distribution of such trustee/beneficiary if the power to make a distribution is limited by an ascertainable standard. The Comment indicates that the term "ascertainable standard" has the same meaning as that found in federal tax law. [UTC 504, Comment].

UTC Section 504 has been the target of much criticism by those who believe that the UTC has weakened the protection of a beneficiary's interest in a discretionary trust. These criticisms and the responses to them, which are too complex for treatment in this treatise, are summarized in a clear and balanced manner in Millard, Trust Beneficiary's Creditors, pp. 67–79.

4. Overdue Distributions

In contrast to UTC Section 504, which deals with creditors' access to discretionary distributions from a trust, UTC Section 506 deals with creditors' access to mandatory distributions. As was noted above, the beneficiary's creditors cannot reach amounts subject to the trustee's discretion for the simple reason that they, like the beneficiary, cannot compel the trustee to make such a distribution. Some trusts, however, contain provisions that require the trustee to make distributions. A "mandatory distribution" is defined in UTC Section 506(a) as "a distribution of income or principal which the trustee is required to make to a beneficiary under the terms of the trust, including a distribution upon termination of the trust." [See Hilgers (2008)]. The definition explicitly excludes any discretionary distributions, even if the discretion is tied to some standard of distribution or the language that allows the discretionary distribution "couple[s] language of discretion with language of direction." The Comment gives the following example of the latter type of provision: "my trustees shall, in their absolute discretion, distribute such amounts as are necessary for the beneficiary's support." (This language and the accompanying Comment were added in 2005 and were based on the modifications made by the state of Ohio when it enacted its version of the UTC. [UTC 506, Comment].)

The problem addressed by UTC Section 506 is that which would arise when a trustee delays making a mandatory distribution from the trust. The delay may be due sheerly to an administrative glitch or it may be a deliberate attempt on the part of the trustee to avoid allowing the distribution to reach the hands of the creditors of the beneficiary. The drafters view UTC Section 506 as a "compromise" in that it allows the creditors of the beneficiary to reach an overdue distribution but only if the trustee has been allowed a "reasonable time after the designated distribution date" to make the distribution. This approach reflects that of Restatement (Third) of Trusts, § 58, Comment g.

B. CLAIMS BY CREDITORS OF THE SETTLOR

UTC Section 505 addresses the ability of creditors of the settlor to reach the trust property. That ability varies dependent upon whether the trust is revocable or irrevocable and upon whether the creditor is attempting to reach the trust property while the settlor is alive or after the settlor's death. This section also covers persons who have a power of withdrawal from a trust, essentially treating these persons as settlors of the property over which they have the power of withdrawal. ["Power of withdrawal" is defined in UTC 103(11)].

1. Rights of Creditors if Trust Is Revocable and Settlor Is Still Alive

UTC Section 505(a)(1) allows the creditors of the settlor of a revocable trust to reach the trust property during the settlor's lifetime. [See § 18.03 on revocable trusts]. This approach is reflected in Restatement (Third) of Trusts, § 25, Comment e, despite the fact that the Restatement (Second) of Trusts contained conflicting language on this issue. [Compare Restatement (Second) of Trusts, § 156(1) (which allowed the settlor's creditors to reach the settlor's beneficial interest in the trust) with Restatement (Second) of Trusts, § 330, Comment o (which provided that the settlor's creditors could not reach a power of revocation)]. This rule applies regardless of whether the trust contains spendthrift language. The rule, which the drafters of the UTC referred to as a "well-accepted conclusion" [UTC 505, Comment] and the drafters of the Restatement (Third) of Trusts characterized as "sound public policy" [Restatement (Third) of Trusts, § 25, Comment e], is based on the theory that a settlor should not be able to insulate her property from her creditors merely by placing that property in a trust to which the settlor has ready access.

2.   Rights of Creditors if Trust Is Irrevocable and Settlor Is Still Alive

UTC Section 505(a)(2) provides that the creditor or assignee of a settlor of an irrevocable trust in which the settlor has retained a beneficial interest may reach the maximum amount that could be distributed to the settlor or for the settlor's benefit. If there are two or more settlors, the creditor or assignee can only reach that amount attributable to the contribution made by the particular settlor against whom the settlor is pursuing a claim. This provision, which the drafters felt reflected the "traditional doctrine" and was "sound policy" prevents "a settlor who is also a beneficiary [from using] the trust as a shield against the settlor's creditors." [UTC 505, Comment]. In choosing to retain the traditional doctrine, the drafters chose not to follow the trend in some states to allow self-settled asset protection trusts. [See, e.g., Utah Code Ann. § 25–

6–14(a)(ii) (2004)]. Utah has adopted the UTC. [See Utah Code Ann. § 75–7–505(1)(b), which contains an exception for asset protection trusts that meet the requirements of Utah § 25–6–14(a)(ii) (2004)].

One important aspect of UTC Section 505(a)(2) is that it limits the creditor to reaching only that amount that is available to the settlor. Thus, if distributions to the settlor are completely discretionary, the creditor could not compel payment because the settlor/beneficiary could not compel payment. [UTC 504; UTC 505, Comment]. Although the UTC does not so provide, presumably this protection would be available only if the settlor is not also the trustee.

This subsection does not address the issues that could arise if the settlor's transfer to the trust is made while the settlor is insolvent or otherwise would fall under the state's fraudulent conveyance laws. The Comment indicates that such issues would be decided under the state or federal bankruptcy laws relating to fraudulent conveyances. [See Sowers (2008)].

3. Rights of Creditors if Trust Was Revocable and Settlor Has Died

UTC Section 505(a)(3) addresses the ability of the creditors of the settlor to reach the assets in a trust that was revocable during the settlor's death after the settlor has died. To a limited extent, this section treats the trust property as if it had been owned outright by the settlor during life, thus making it available to the creditors as if it were part of the settlor's probate estate. [See § 13.04]. The Comment indicates that this subsection reflects the fact that many settlors use revocable trusts as will substitutes. [See § 18.03 on revocable trusts]. Specifically, this subsection makes the trust property subject to "claims of the settlor's creditors, costs of administration of the settlor's estate, the expenses of the settlor's funeral and disposal of remains, and statutory allowances to a surviving spouse and children." The subsection does not attempt to prioritize these claims or address any procedure for the collection of them, leaving such matters to the enacting state's probate laws. The subsection does specifically allow the settlor to direct the source from which the liabilities will be paid (e.g., from the trust property or from the residue of the estate). If no such direction is given by the settlor, the trust property can be used only to the extent the property in the probate estate is insufficient to pay the enumerated claims, costs, and expenses.

4. Rights of Creditors if the Trust Was Irrevocable and the Settlor Has Died

UTC Section 505(a) does not address the rights of creditors of the settlor to reach the assets of an irrevocable trust once the settlor has died. Theoretically, this property will not be subject to the settlor's creditors as any ownership interest the settlor had in the property is extinguished at the settlor's death. However, claims against non-probate property of this sort may be covered by other state laws. [See, e.g., 6–102, Ch. 16].

5. Property Over Which an Individual Has a Power of Withdrawal

UTC Section 103(11) defines a "power of withdrawal" as "a presently exercisable general power of appointment other than a power: (A) exercisable by a trustee and limited by an ascertainable standard; or (B) exercisable by another person only upon consent of the trustee or a person holding an adverse interest." A general power of appointment is basically the power of an individual to appoint some or all of the trust property, without limitation, to anyone he chooses, including himself, his estate, his creditors or the creditors of his estate. If an individual has the power to withdraw property from a trust, UTC Section 505(b), with one exception, treats that property as if the individual were the settlor of a revocable trust as to that property, thus bringing into play the provisions of UTC Section 505(a). This is the same approach as that taken in Restatement (Third) of Trusts, § 56 Comment b. If the power to withdraw is unlimited, during the time that the power is exercisable (which presumably will be during the individual's lifetime), the property is available to the creditors to the same extent as set forth in UTC Section 505(a)(1). Although the UTC does not so state, if the power is limited, the creditors would logically only have access to the property to the extent the individual has the power to withdraw it. If the power is still retained by the individual at the time of the individual's death, the provisions of UTC Section 505(a)(3) would be applicable.

Often trusts will contain withdrawal powers that lapse or otherwise become unexercisable after a certain period of time. The most common of these is the *Crummey* power, named for the case in which this power was recognized. [Crummey (1968)]. *Crummey* powers are important for donors who wish to exclude as a countable gift for gift tax purposes property that is transferred to a trust. Under Internal Revenue Code § 2503(b), a gift of a present interest that equals or exceeds a certain amount (currently $13,000) is not deemed to be a taxable gift. This exclusion is available on an annual basis and applies separately to each donee. Consequently, a donor can give $13,000 to a number of donees in one year and repeat that process for years to come and never have these amounts treated as potentially taxable gifts. As noted, however, a key ingredient to this exclusion is that the gift be one of a "present interest." If a gift is given to a beneficiary through a trust, arguably, because the beneficiary does not have immediate access to the trust, the gift is not one of a "present interest." The *Crummey* case allows a donor to give a gift to a trust in which the beneficiary has an immediate, but time-limited (often 30–60 days) right to withdraw the gift. Even if the beneficiary does not withdraw the gift, the annual exclusion is available for the gift, thus taking it out of the ambit of the gift tax. The Internal Revenue Code also provides that if such a power of withdrawal "lapses" (that is, the beneficiary does not exercise the power), the property that was subject to the power of withdrawal will still be included in the gross taxable estate of the beneficiary if the value of the property over which the lapsed power could have been exercisable exceeds the greater of $5000 or 5% of the value of the total trust assets. [I.R.C. § 2041(b)(2)]. Additionally, if there are other beneficiaries of the trust, the beneficiary's refusal to withdraw the *Crummey* contribution will be deemed to be a gift to the other beneficiaries under Internal Revenue Code § 2514(e) unless the amount is less than or equal to the $5000/5% amount described above. Consequently, *Crummey* trusts will typically limit the beneficiary's power to the greater of both the annual exclusion amount and the $5000/5% amount. UTC Section 505(b)(2) recognizes this common estate planning technique and reflects it by providing that a lapsed, released, or disclaimed power of withdrawal will not be treated as a settlor's revocable trust property except to the extent it exceeds the amounts in the Internal Code Sections described above. The UTC drafters added brackets at the end of this subsection that allow enacting states to choose between the amounts set forth in these Internal Revenue Code sections on the date this UTC provision is adopted by the state, or on the amounts set forth in these Internal Revenue Code sections as later amended. Many of the states that have enacted UTC Section 505(b) have modified this Code section. [Millard, Trust Beneficiary's Creditors, pp. 65–66.]

See § 9.05 for a discussion of the UPC's extensive treatment of powers of appointment.

C. CLAIMS BY CREDITORS
OF THE TRUSTEE

The last provision of Article 5 is a simple provision that addresses any attempt by a creditor of the trustee to reach trust property to satisfy that creditor's claims. UTC Section 507 states that trust property is not subject to any personal obligations of the trustee, regardless of whether the trustee is insolvent or bankrupt. This provision reflects federal bankruptcy law. [UTC 507, Comment]. The drafters of the UTC state in the Comment that "[t]he exemption of the trust property from the personal obligations of the trustee is the most significant feature of Anglo–American trust law" and note that a principal motivation of the Hague Convention on the Law Applicable to Trusts and on their Recognition is to extend this protection to Anglo–American trusts that are engaging in transactions in civil law countries.

§ 18.03   UTC Article 6: Revocable Trusts

The drafters refer to Article 6 of the UTC as "one of the most important of the Code." [Art. 6, General Comment]. The provisions in this section are grounded in the theory that a revocable trust is the functional equivalent of a will. The drafters cite the "widespread use in recent years of the revocable trust as an alternative to a will." Because this is a relatively new phenomenon, traditional trust law has left unanswered many questions relating to the use of a revocable trust as a will substitute. [English, UTC Significant Provisions, pp. 186–87.] This estate planning mechanism involves the settlor establishing a trust during life to which the settlor transfers most if not all of the settlor's property. The settlor is most often the trustee of the trust during life. The trust may be revoked at any time without the consent of the trustee. [See UTC 103(14), definition of "revocable"]. Thus, the settlor retains virtually the same control that she had over the property before the transfer. The trust usually contains dispositive provisions that direct the distribution of the property at the settlor's death. After the settlor dies, the property may continue in trust or be distributed outright to those named as remainder beneficiaries. If all of the settlor's property has been transferred to the trust during the settlor's life, there is no need for a probate procedure because the trust property is already owned by the trust and thus is "non-probate property." [See Ch. 16].

The efficiency of this transfer is deemed by many to be an attractive feature of the use of revocable trusts as will substitutes. Other attractive features are: privacy (a will is a matter of public record while a trust is not); efficiency of administration (because there is no probate and no on-going involvement by the probate court); and lower cost (in those states that charge a probate fee that is based on the size of the probate estate). As noted above, under UTC Section 505, a revocable trust is not a device for the avoidance of claims by the settlor's creditors. Nor in most cases will the use of a revocable trust avoid federal estate tax as the Internal Revenue Code causes trust property to be included in the settlor's taxable gross estate if the settlor retained the power to control, amend or terminate the trust. [I.R.C. §§ 2036, 2038].

Sometimes a settlor will not transfer all of her property to the revocable trust during life. This settlor might also execute a "pourover will" that would direct the settlor's personal representative to transfer any property remaining in the settlor's ownership at death to the revocable trust. [See § 6.05(B)]. In this situation, it would be necessary to engage in a probate procedure. However, the dispositive provisions of the trust need not be revealed during that procedure, so the privacy of the ultimate disposition of the settlor's property would be maintained.

Another common use of the revocable trust is for the management of the settlor's property in the event the settlor becomes incapacitated. Although settlors will typically serve as the trustees of their revocable trusts during life, the trust usually names a back-up trustee who will serve in the event the settlor becomes incapacitated. Because the trustee will manage the settlor's property, there may be no need for the court to appoint a conservator to take over the incapacitated settlor's estate. [As defined in UTC 103(5). a "conservator" is the person who is appointed by a court to manage the property of a minor or an incapacitated individual This term is usually bracketed wherever it appears in the UTC because states use different terms to describe this appointed individual.] The appointment of a conservator usually requires a finding of incapacity, which can be traumatic for the settlor, and results in the deprivation of a large number of rights from the settlor. The appointment involves a time-consuming and sometimes costly court procedure and conservators usually must post a bond, which adds an additional expense. Thus, the revocable trust provides a seamless and helpful tool for the continuation of the management of the property of the settlor without court intervention. A settlor may also execute a power of attorney with the intent that the agent for the settlor will transfer the settlor's remaining property to the trust if and when the settlor becomes incapacitated. Powers of attorney are also helpful because they may be used to empower an agent to perform some acts that a trustee typically is not authorized to perform, such as applying for government benefits. [UTC 602, Comment]. However, if a settlor has both a revocable trust and a power of attorney, it is more than likely that the settlor intends for the trustee, not the agent under the power of attorney, to engage in the overall management of the settlor's property. [English, UTC Significant Provisions, pp. 190–91.] It is against this background on the use of revocable trusts that the provisions of Article 6 must be examined.

A. CAPACITY TO CREATE
A REVOCABLE TRUST

It is a basic tenet of Anglo–American law that an individual cannot engage in a valid, enforceable transaction unless that individual possesses the required level of legal capacity. The requisite legal capacity may vary from transaction to transaction, depending both upon the complexity and the consequences of the act. [Frolik & Radford, Sufficient Capacity, p. 304]. UTC Section 402(a)(1) provides that a settlor must have the capacity to create a valid trust. However, the only place in the UTC in which the requisite capacity is addressed is in UTC Section 601. Consistent with the treatment of a revocable trust as the functional equivalent of a will, UTC Section 601 provides that the capacity needed to create a revocable trust is the same as that required to execute a valid will. This capacity is sometimes referred to as "testamentary capacity." [See § 6.02(A)].

This approach, while consistent with the Restatement (Third) of Trusts, § 11, is a change from the common law. At common law, the capacity requirement for creating a valid trust was more stringent than that required to create a will. At common law, a settlor had to have the capacity to make a valid *inter vivos* transfer of property, which is sometimes equated to the capacity to enter into a contract. [See Restatement (Second) Trusts, § 18.] The lowering of the capacity level for the creation of a revocable trust is justified, according to the UTC drafters, by the fact that the revocable trust is most likely being used to transfer the settlor's property at the settlor's death. [UTC 601, Comment]. The drafters did not feel it necessary to address the capacity to create other types of trusts because no "uncertainty exists with respect to the capacity standard for other types of trusts." [UTC 601, Comment]. The Comment notes that the capacity to create a testamentary trust (a trust that is created by will) is the same as that needed to execute a valid will while the capacity to create an irrevocable trust is the same capacity as would be required to transfer the property free of trust. [UTC 601, Comment].

The concept of testamentary capacity, while the subject of thousands of cases, is not spelled out in either the UTC or the UPC. UPC 2–501 requires only that the testator be "of sound mind." [See § 6.02(A)]. A longstanding and commonly used test of testamentary capacity asks the following questions:

1. Did the testator understand the nature of the act he or she was performing?

2. Did the testator know the nature and extent of his or her property?

3. Did the testator know the identity of those who were the "natural objects of his or her bounty"?

4. Did the testator understand the will's disposition of his or her property?

[Frolik & Radford, Sufficient Capacity, pp. 307–08].

The drafters point out in the Comment to UTC Section 601 that even though the capacity level for the creation of a revocable trust has been lowered to that of testamentary capacity, a trust is not required to be executed with the same formal execution requirements as are required of wills. [See § 6.02]. However, the state of Florida, which adopted portions of the UTC including the lowered capacity requirement of UTC Section 601, also requires that the "testamentary aspects of a revocable trust" are not valid unless executed with the same formalities that are required for the valid execution of wills under Florida law. [F.S.A. § 736.0403(b)].

UTC Section 601 applies the same capacity requirement not only to the creation of a trust but also to any amendment, revocation, addition of property to the trust or direction by the settlor of the actions of the trustee. This is important to note if the settlor who created a revocable trust should become incapacitated and in need of a guardian or conservator. While in many states, a finding of incapacity automatically denotes a finding that the individual lacks contractual capacity, that same individual may retain testamentary capacity even after a guardian or conservator is appointed. [Frolik & Radford, Sufficient Capacity, p. 311]. Thus, an individual who has been found to need a guardian or conservator to manage his or her affairs due to a lack of the capacity to enter into contracts may still retain the capacity to create, amend or revoke a revocable trust. However, as noted in the next section, the guardian or conservator of this same individual may not exercise the settlor's power to revoke without court approval. [UTC 602(f)].

The Comment states the capacity requirement of UTC Section 601 cannot be waived or modified by a settlor in the trust instrument because it is a requirement related to the creation of a trust. [Art. 6, General Comment; 105(b)(1), Comment; see § 17.01(C)].

B. REVOCATION OR AMENDMENT OF A REVOCABLE TRUST

UTC Section 602(a) reverses the common law rule by providing that a trust is revocable (that is, it can be revoked or amended) unless the terms of the trust expressly provide that the trust is irrevocable. At common law, a trust could not be revoked or amended unless the settlor expressly retained that right in the trust instrument. The drafters justify the reversal of common law doctrine by once again assuming that most revocable trusts are meant to act as will substitutes and were "likely drafted by a nonprofessional, who intended the trust as a will substitute." Thus, if a trust is silent as to its amendability or revocability, the UTC presumes that the settlor meant to retain the right to amend or revoke the trust. In the Comment, the drafters added that "[b]ecause professional drafters habitually spell out whether or not a trust is revocable, subsection (a) will have limited application." Because this provision reverses the rule that was in existence in most states, UTC Section 602(a) provides that the rule is not applicable to trusts that were created prior to the effective date of the state's enactment of the UTC.

Although not expressly stated in UTC Section 602(a), the Comment confirms the common law rule that a power to revoke includes the power to amend and an unrestricted power to amend may include the power to revoke or terminate the trust. [UTC 602, Comment].

Subsection (b) of UTC Section 602 applies if a trust is created or funded by two or more settlors. These trusts, which are referred to in the Comment as "joint trusts," are often created by a husband and wife. If the couple lives in a community property state, they may place their community property into a trust in order to ensure that the property retains its community property character even if they move to a separate property state. Due to the increasing mobility of clients who may have acquired property while living in a community property state, the drafters recommend that the provisions in UTC Section 602 relating to community property be adopted even if the enacting state is not a community property state. [UTC 602, Comment]. Specifically, UTC Section 602(b)(1) provides that if the trust contains community property, either spouse acting alone may revoke the trust but the trust may be amended only by the joint action of both of the spouses. If the trust does not contain community property, UTC Section 602(b)(2) provides that each settlor may revoke or amend the trust "with regard to the portion of the trust property attributable to that settlor's contribution." This subsection does not address the many complexities inherent in determining exactly what proportion of jointly-owned property is owned by each of the tenants, particularly property owned as tenants by the entireties. [UTC 602, Comment]. Also, the Comment emphasizes that the provisions of UTC Section 602(b)(2) should not be interpreted as an endorsement of the use of joint trusts in non-community property states. In fact, the Comment notes that the use of these trusts for non-community property is widespread but editorializes that there is no compelling reason for such joint trusts, that they are often poorly and confusingly drafted, and that they may result in unintended tax consequences. [UTC 602, Comment]. UTC Section 602(b)(3) requires prompt notification to the other settlors of any amendment or revocation of the trust. The Comment explains that such notification would allow the other settlors to protect their interests in the event, for example, a contract not to revoke the trust has been breached.

Subsection (c) of UTC Section 602 spells out the methods by which a settlor may revoke or amend a trust. If the trust contains direction as to how a revocation or amendment is to be made, the settlor can revoke or amend the trust by "substantial compliance" with this direction. [UTC 602(c)(1)]. The Comment emphasizes that the compliance need not be complete, so that if some "technical requirement," such as notarization, is not met the revocation should still be honored. [UTC 602, Comment]. If the trust contains no direction or there is a method spelled out but the trust does not expressly state that this is the exclusive method of revocation or amendment, the settlor may revoke or amend the trust by a subsequent will or codicil that refers expressly to the trust. Alternatively, if a subsequent will or codicil expressly devises property that would otherwise pass under the trust, this constitutes a trust amendment or revocation. [UTC 602(c)(2)(A)]. The Comment explains that the mere disposition of trust property in the residuary clause of the will is not sufficient to revoke the trust. Rather, the revocation by will must expressly refer to the trust or the will must make specific bequests of the trust property. [UTC 602, Comment]. The Comment provides that a revocation or amendment by will or codicil will becomes effective only upon the probate of the will or codicil. [UTC 602, Comment; see Restatement (Third) of Trusts, § 63, Comment h.]

The original version of this subsection spoke of a settlor revoking a trust by "executing" a later will or codicil. The word "executing" was removed in 2001 to avoid confusion about whether the revocation becomes effective on the date of execution or the date the will becomes effective. [UTC 602, Comment]. The Comment also notes that the UTC drafters did not mean to encourage the revocation of a trust by will, but realized that in some deathbed situations it may be the only practicable, as well as the most reliable, method of revocation. [UTC 602, Comment].

Finally, if the trust is silent or contains only non-exclusive means of revocation or amendment, UTC Section 602(c)(2)(B) provides that the settlor may revoke or amend a trust by "any other method manifesting clear and convincing evidence of the settlor's intent." This provision reflects that of the Restatement (Third) of Trusts, § 63, Comment h, which suggests as an example of such evidence a letter written by the settlor to the trustee manifesting an intent to revoke the trust. [See In re Trust Created by Isvik, 741 N.W.2d 638 (Neb.2007)]. When the trust is revoked, UTC Section 602(d) provides that the trustee is to distribute the trust property in accordance with the settlor's direction.

Subsections (e) and (f) of UTC Section 602 address the ability of a surrogate to revoke the trust on behalf of the settlor when the settlor is no longer able to do so. Both of these sections are grounded in certain assumptions that are described in the Comment. Subsection (e) deals with the power of an agent under a power of attorney of which the settlor is the principal to exercise the settlor's power to revoke or amend the trust or order a distribution of trust property. Pursuant to this subsection, the agent may do so only if given express authority either in the trust instrument or in the instrument that creates the power of attorney. The presumption underlying this rule is that a settlor who has taken the trouble to create both a revocable trust and a power of attorney intends the trustee to be the primary manager of the settlor's property, with the agent serving only as a back-up, as described above. [UTC 602, Comment; English, UTC Significant Provisions, p. 190].

The basic presumption underlying subsection (f) of UTC Section 602 is that a settlor who has created a revocable trust wants the trustee of the trust, in accordance with the terms of the trust, to be the person who manages the settlor's property rather than a guardian or conservator or other court-appointed entity. [See English, UTC Significant Provisions, p. 190]. In fact, as noted above, revocable trusts are often touted as offering an alternative to conservatorship; if all the settlor's property is being handled through the trust, there is no need to have a conservator appointed. Consequently, subsection (f) of UTC Section 602 prohibits a court-appointed conservator or guardian from revoking or amending the trust or directing the distribution of property from the trust without the approval of the court that is supervising the conservatorship or guardianship. Whether the court may authorize such an act is a matter of state law. [See, e.g., UPC 5–411, § 15.09(C)]. The drafters recognized that the settlor most likely established the revocable trust at least in part with the settlor's potential incapacity in mind and thus would prefer that the trust remain in place and the trustee continue management of the property. [English, UTC Significant Provisions, p. 190]. Thus, the Comment recommends that "this power should be exercised by the court reluctantly." [UTC 602, Comment}. The Comment also offers alternatives to revocation in the event that a conservator fears the trustee is abusing its discretion, such as bringing an action to remove the trustee [UTC 706, see § 19.01(E)] or bringing an action to enforce the terms of the trust.

Subsection (g) of UTC Section 602 addresses the question of the potential liability of a trustee who acts without knowledge that the trust has been amended or revoked. As noted in the Comment, the revocation of a trust differs from the revocation of a will because the former implicates the actions of a trustee who has a continuing fiduciary duty to carry out the settlor's direction as set forth in the terms of the trust. For this reason, the Comment notes that many drafters include in the trust a requirement that the trustee be given written notice of any revocation or amendment of the trust. [UTC 602, Comment]. However, the UTC does not require such notice and thus must address what would happen if a trustee continues to act after a revocation or amendment has occurred. Subsection (g) of UTC Section 602 relieves such a trustee from liability to the settlor or the settlors' successors in interest for actions taken or distributions made when the trustee assumes that the trust is still in effect.

C. SETTLOR'S POWERS WHILE TRUST IS REVOCABLE

UTC Section 603 reinforces the extensive control and power that a settlor has over the trust property while the trust is revocable. Subsection (a) of UTC Section 603 essentially provides that the only person who has rights while the trust is revocable is the settlor. Any notices that are required to be given to the beneficiaries in other trusts [see UTC 813, § 19.02(M)] are required only to be given to the settlor and the only person to whom the trustee owes duties is the settlor. [UTC 603, Comment]. Thus any other named beneficiaries not only have no power to enforce the trust while it is revocable, they do not even have the right to know of its existence. This rule prevails regardless of whether the trustee is a third party. As a practical matter, however, in these trusts the settlor usually acts as trustee and also is the primary beneficiary during his or her life. [UTC 603, Comment]. Subsection (b) of UTC 603 provides that the holder of a power of withdrawal is treated for purposes of these rules as the settlor of a revocable trust for as long as the power is exercisable. [See § 18.02(B)(5) for a discussion of powers of withdrawal.]

The controversial question addressed in UTC Section 603 is what happens when the settlor becomes incapacitated and thus is no longer able to exercise the revocation power. Should the beneficiaries be notified at that point of the existence of the trust and given the power to enforce it? As originally enacted, the rule of UTC Section 603(a) applied only so long as the settlor had the capacity to revoke the trust. After the settlor lost capacity, the rights of the beneficiaries prevailed over those of the settlor. [UTC 603, Comment]. However, as pointed out in the Comment, this provision may be amended by the settlor so a settlor who did not want the beneficiaries to have enforcement powers or to know of the trust's existence until the settlor's death could so state in the terms of the trust. This approach was deemed to be a "compromise" position reached only after "extensive" debate. [English, UTC Significant Provisions, p. 188]. The debate continued even after the original promulgation of the UTC. Some felt that to be consistent with the treatment of a revocable trust as the functional equivalent of a will, the UTC should not give the beneficiaries any greater rights if the settlor lost capacity. They pointed out that those who are named beneficiaries under a testator's will are not vested with additional rights, including the right to know the will's terms, simply because the testator becomes incapacitated. The proponents of this position also noted that it is no easy to task to determine whether and when a settlor has become incapacitated. [UTC 603, Comment]. On the other side, the argument was made that the beneficiaries of a trust the settlor of which had become incapacitated would not be able to enforce their rights if they did not know of the existence of the trust. In 2004, UTC Section 603(a) was amended to bracket the language that related to the settlor's incapacity. The drafters had concluded by that time that "uniformity among the states on this issue is not essential." [603, Comment].

D. ACTIONS CONTESTING THE VALIDITY OF A REVOCABLE TRUST

The final issue addressed in UTC Article 6 is that of causes of action brought in an attempt to invalidate a revocable trust. As the Comment to UTC Section 604 points out, such actions may be brought on a number of different grounds similar to those on which a will may be challenged. These include lack of capacity on the settlor's part [see 402, § 18.01(A)(1)] and fraud, duress, or undue influence [see 406, § 18.01(A)(1)]. The probate codes of most states contain statutes of limitations beyond which such actions may not be brought to contest the validity of a will. [See, e.g., UPC 3–108, § 10.01(B)(5)]. These statutes provide finality in the distributions from a decedent's estate after a specified period of time. Consistent with the theme that a revocable trust is the functional equivalent of a will, UTC Section 604 provides a statute of limitations that reflects many of the state statutes pertaining to wills. Subsection (a) of UTC Section 604 provides that an action to contest the validity of a revocable trust must be brought within three years after the settlor's death or 120 days following the delivery of a notice "informing the person of the trust's existence, of the trustee's name and address, and of the time allowed for commencing a proceeding." Both of these time periods are bracketed and the drafters encourage enacting states to adopt time periods that reflect their own statutes relating to the contest of wills. (For example, three years is the period set out in UPC § 3–108, see § 10.01(B)(5)). [UTC 604, Comment]. The Comment also notes that subsection (a)(2) of UTC Section 604 allows a trustee to accelerate the statute of limitations by giving notice that would alert any potential contestants to the existence of the trust of their right to proceed against the trustee within a certain specified time. [UTC 604, Comment].

The Comment notes that most trusts will not be challenged and thus it is important that the UTC contain provisions to protect trustees who distribute trust property without knowledge of a pending lawsuit. At common law, the trustee was liable for any distributed property even if the trustee was not aware of any reason why the distribution would be improper. [UTC 604, Comment, citing Restatement (Second) of Trusts, § 226]. Under UTC Section 604(b), the trustee is liable only if the trustee knows that a judicial proceeding to contest the trust's validity is pending or if the trustee has been notified by a potential contestant that a proceeding will be filed and such a proceeding actually is filed within 60 days of the notification.

Beneficiaries, on the other hand, do not receive the same protections as trustees. If trust property is distributed to them and an action is filed timely pursuant to UTC Section 604(a) and is successful, the beneficiaries must return the trust property. [UTC 604(c)]. The Comment notes that state statutory law relating to restitution should be consulted to determine the details of this return of trust property, such as whether the beneficiary is also liable for interest. [UTC 604, Comment].

CHAPTER 19
TRUST ADMINISTRATION

§ 19.01 UTC Article 7: Office of Trustee

Article 7 of the UTC addresses the administrative aspects of the office of trustee, including the trustee's acceptance of office, the actions of co-trustees, and the filling of vacancies in the trust. Almost all of these provisions, with the exception of those relating to a court-ordered bond [UTC 702], are default rules that may be varied by the settlor in the terms of the trust. As some of these administrative items are also covered in Article VII of the UPC, the UPC will be discussed also in this section.

A. ACCEPTANCE OF OFFICE OF TRUSTEE AND BOND

A person who has not yet accepted the office of trustee cannot be compelled to serve as trustee. [See Restatement (Third) Trusts § 35; comment (a)]. UTC Section 701 contains the methods by which the office of trustee is accepted or declined. The rules in this section set forth explicit methods for the acceptance of the trust. In addition, the section contains provisions that recognize that the designated trustee may decline the office and states the presumption that prevails when a designated trustee has neither accepted nor rejected the office.

The provisions of this section reflect some of the provisions relating to the revocation of revocable trusts because of the need in both situations for certainty so that trust property can be protected. [UTC 701, Comment; see § 18.03 on revocable trusts]. The basic rule for accepting a trusteeship mirrors the rule for revoking a revocable trust [UTC 602(c), see § 18.03(B)]. Just as a settlor may revoke a revocable trust by substantial compliance with whatever method is set out in the trust agreement, a trustee may accept the office of trustee by substantial compliance with whatever method of acceptance is set out in the trust agreement. [UTC 701(a)(1)]. In the event there is no method spelled out in the trust or if the expressed method is not the exclusive one, the acceptance may be accomplished if the designated trustee: 1) accepts delivery of the trust property; 2) starts exercising the powers or performing the duties of the trustee; or 3) in some other way indicates acceptance of the trusteeship. [UTC 701(a)(1)].

These broadly-worded methods of acceptance are qualified by UTC Section 701(c). Under UTC Section 701(c)(1), a designated trustee who wishes to decline the trusteeship may act to preserve the trust property without actually being deemed to have accepted the trusteeship if the designee sends a rejection of the trusteeship to the settlor within a reasonable time after acting. If the settlor is dead or incapacitated, the rejection should be sent to the qualified beneficiaries. [See § 17.01(B) for a discussion of qualified beneficiaries.] This provision promotes the maximum protection of trust property by allowing a designee to engage in any necessary intervention without fear that such action will be deemed to be an acceptance. Subsection (c)(2) of UTC Section 701 also allows a designee who is uncertain about whether to accept the trusteeship due to potential liability connected with the trust property, such as environmental issues, to inspect or investigate the property in advance of accepting the trusteeship. The mere actions of inspecting or investigating will not be deemed automatically to be an acceptance of the trusteeship.

UTC Section 701(b) recognizes that a designated trustee may choose not to serve and thus may "reject the trusteeship." The Comment to this section recommends that the designee who has decided not to serve make a "clear and early communication." However, subsection (b) of UTC Section 701 does not describe any formal method of declination nor does it specify to whom the designee should communicate the decision not to serve. The Comment states that "[t]he appropriate recipient of the rejection depends upon the circumstances." The Comment offers the following as possible recipients, the settlor (in the case of a revocable trust), a beneficiary who has a significant interest in the trust, the person who notified the designee of the trusteeship, or the court if the trust was created pursuant to a judicial order. If the designee neither accepts nor rejects the trusteeship, the uncertainty that would prevail could endanger the trust property. Consequently, UTC Section 701(b) provides that a designee, who has taken no action to accept or decline the trusteeship "within a reasonable time after knowing of the designation, is deemed to have rejected the trusteeship." The term "reasonable time," according to the Comment, is to be defined in conjunction with the prevailing facts and circumstances.

UTC Section 702 covers the unusual situation of a trustee bond. Typically, because the settlor has chosen as trustee someone in whom the settlor has confidence, a protective bond is not required to be posted by the trustee. However, a settlor may provide in the trust instrument that a bond should be posted. In this case, the bond will be required under the terms set forth in the trust instrument unless the court overrides the settlor's wishes and dispenses with the bond. [UTC 702(a)]. Perhaps recognizing that the settlor would not have required a bond without good reason, the Comment advises that a court should "rarely dispense" with a bond that has been prescribed by a settlor. A court may independently order a bond if the court deems it necessary to protect the interests of the beneficiaries. [UTC 702(a)]. This too would be a rare occurrence as the removal of the trustee would usually be the better approach if the trustee is jeopardizing the trust property. If the court does order a bond, under subsection (b) of UTC Section 702, the court has discretion to fix the amount, to determine whether a surety is needed and to modify or terminate the bond at any time. UTC Section 702 does not contain any details relating to the amount or parameters of the bond. The Comment points out that such matters are dealt with in the Uniform Probate Code sections that cover bonds for personal representatives [3–604, see § 10.01(B)94)(e)] and conservators [5–415, see § 15.09(B)].

UTC Section 702(c), a bracketed section, precludes the need for a "regulated financial-service institution qualified to do trust business" in the state to post bond. According to the Comment, the section is bracketed not to indicate that it is optional but to signal to enacting states that such a law may already exist in other portions of their state codes.

B. COTRUSTEES

UTC 703 covers a variety of issues that may arise when a trust has more than one trustee. It is not uncommon to have cotrustees, as settlors sometimes wish to include more than one family member in the trust administration or take advantage of both the experience of a professional or institutional fiduciary and the knowledge and sensitivity to the beneficiaries of a family member. [UTC 703, Comment]. Despite the fact that having cotrustees is common practice, the Comment advises that "[c]otrusteeship should not be called for without careful reflection." [UTC 703, Comment]. Although a settlor is free to outline in the trust instrument the sharing of responsibilities and duties among the cotrustees, such meticulous drafting is not the norm. [English, UTC Significant Provisions, pp.

195–96]. Thus, UTC Section 703 provides back-up procedural provisions for those trusts that are silent. Generally, these provisions are modeled after relevant provisions in the Restatement (Third) of Trusts, the Restatement (Second) of Trusts, and § 405 of the Employee Retirement Income Security Act of 18874 (ERISA) (29 U.S.C. § 1105), "which in recent years has been the statutory base for the most significant case law on the powers and duties of cotrustees." [UTC 703, Comment].

Subsection (a) of UTC Section 703 provides that cotrustees may exercise their powers by majority rule if they are unable to act unanimously. The subsection, which is modeled after § 39 of the Restatement (Third) of Trusts and reflects the majority of state statutes that deal with the issue, overturns the common law rule that cotrustees have to act unanimously. Obviously, if there are only two cotrustees, they must act with unanimity.

Subsection (b) of UTC Section 703 addresses what happens if one of the cotrustees resigns, dies or is otherwise unable to serve. Under this subsection, the remaining cotrustees may continue to act without the need of filling the vacancy. This rule is repeated in UTC Section 704(b) which goes on to say that there is no need to fill a vacancy until there are no trustees remaining in office.

Subsection (c) of UTC Section 703 requires all cotrustees to participate in the management of the trust. However, a cotrustee may be excused for doing so if the cotrustee is temporarily unable to participate. This inability could be caused by absence, illness, disqualification under other law or other reasons. According to the Comment, two examples of laws that may disqualify a cotrustee from acting are federal securities law and the ERISA prohibited transactions rules. [UTC 703, Comment]. Subsection (d) of UTC Section 703 allows the other cotrustees to act if one cotrustee is temporarily unable to perform and prompt action is needed.

Alternatively, under subsection (c) of UTC Section 703, a cotrustee need not participate in certain functions if those functions have been properly delegated to another cotrustee. In keeping with the theme of supporting the settlor's intent, subsection (e) of UTC Section 703, which is modeled after Restatement (Second) of Trusts, § 171, prohibits a cotrustee from delegating to another trustee those functions that the settlor expected the cotrustees to perform together. Because it may be difficult to discern such intent, the Comment suggests that the better practice is to delineate any allocation of trustee functions in the trust instrument. Delegation under subsection (e) of UTC Section 703 is distinguishable from delegation under UTC Section 807, which allows a trustee to delegate functions to an agent who is not serving as a cotrustee. [See § 17.08(G)]. Any delegation made under UTC 703(e) can be revoked by the delegating trustee at any time.

A cotrustee who does not agree with a proposed action may either refuse to participate in the action [UTC 703(f)] or participate but indemnify herself by filing a written dissent [UTC 703(h)]. Subsection (h) of UTC Section 703 is helpful because there may be times when a cotrustee disagrees with a proposed action but still participates in the action at the direction of the majority of the cotrustees. This may occur if another party to a transaction, such as a sale of trust property, demands the consent of all the cotrustees. [UTC 703, Comment]. In this case the dissenting cotrustee will not be liable if the cotrustee registered the dissent in writing with another cotrustee before or at the time of the action. This protection will not apply, however, if the action is a serious breach of trust. In the case of a serious breach of trust, all cotrustees are required to "exercise reasonable care" to prevent the breach or to redress the breach by another cotrustee. This provision reflects §§ 184 and 224 of the Restatement (Second) of Trusts.

C. VACANCY IN TRUSTEESHIP AND APPOINTMENT OF SUCCESSOR

UTC Section 704 describes the circumstances that can lead to a vacancy in the trusteeship and the means of filling that vacancy. This section provides default rules that apply only if the trust instrument does not address these issues.

Unlike UTC Section 703(c), which contemplates a cotrustee being temporarily unable to function as a trustee, UTC Section 704(a) describes what can cause a permanent vacancy to occur. A permanent vacancy will occur if the trustee who was appointed in the instrument refuses to accept the trusteeship [UTC 701]; the person designated to serve as trustee cannot be found or does not exist; the trustee is disqualified or removed [UTC 705]; the trustee resigns [UTC 705]; or the trustee becomes so incapacitated that a guardian or conservator is appointed for him or her. The Comment offers as an example of disqualification the loss by a financial institution of its eligibility to act as a trustee or a move of the principal place of administration of the trust to a place in which the trustee is not qualified to act. [UTC 704, Comment]. If the trust has cotrustees, subsection (b) of UTC Section 704 provides that a vacancy only needs to be filled if there are no remaining trustees who are capable and qualified to act. [See also UTC 703(b)].

If a vacancy must be filled, subsections (c) and (d) of UTC Section 704 set forth the priority of persons who should be appointed to fill the vacancy. If the trust is noncharitable, subsection (c) of UTC Section 704 provides that the new trustee shall be, in this order: the successor trustee designated in the trust instrument; a person selected unanimously by the qualified beneficiaries (without the need for court approval); or a person appointed by the court. As to court-appointed trustees, the Comment, citing the two Restatements, provides that "the court should consider the objectives and probable intention of the settlor, the promotion of the proper administration of the trust, and the interests and wishes of the beneficiaries." [See Rodriguez–Tocker v. Estate of Tocker; see also 1001(b)(5)]. The duties of a successor trustee are outlined in UTC Section 812. [See § 19.02(L)].

If the trust is charitable, a 2001 amendment to UTC 704 added a priority list that is basically the same as that for noncharitable trusts, except that the second priority is a person who is selected by the charitable beneficiary. This subsection also includes language requiring the consent of the attorney general. The language was bracketed due to the same 2004 amendment that modified UTC Section 110(d), which provides that the attorney general has the rights of a qualified beneficiary with respect to charitable trusts. [See § 17.01(B)]. States that have not adopted or have modified UTC Section 110(d) should adjust the last sentence of UTC Section 704(d) accordingly.

D.   TRUSTEE RESIGNATION

At common law, a trustee could resign only with the permission of the court. The Restatements provide that a trustee need not get the consent of a court if all the beneficiaries consent to the resignation. [Restatement (Third) Trusts, § 36; Restatement (Second) Trusts, § 106]. UTC Section 705(a) provides that a trustee may resign either with the court's permission or upon giving at least 30 days notice to the qualified beneficiaries, the settlor if the settlor is still living, and any other cotrustee. If the trust is revocable, the notice to the qualified beneficiaries is accomplished by giving notice to the settlor as the settlor has sole power to enforce the trust. [UTC 603]. Prior to the 2001 amendment, notice to the settlor was required only if the trust was revocable. As with most provisions of the UTC, these rules for trustee resignation may be varied by the settlor in the trust instrument.

If the trustee seeks court permission to resign, UTC Section 705(b) states that the court may require whatever actions are reasonably necessary to protect the trust property. UTC Section 705(c) makes it clear that a resignation by a trustee does not automatically discharge the trustee from liability for acts committed by the trustee while in office. In addition, as is pointed out in the Comment, the sheer act of resigning may subject a trustee to liability if the trustee resigned in order to aid another cotrustee in a breach of trust. [UTC 705, Comment, citing Ream v. Frey, 107 F.3d 147 (3d Cir. 1997)].

E. REMOVAL OF TRUSTEE

The settlor, in the trust instrument, may spell out the circumstances under which a trustee or cotrustee should be removed from office. [UTC 105]. In the event the trust instrument is silent, UTC Section 706 describes the circumstances that could prompt removal of the trustee by the court and names the persons who have standing to request the court for such removal.

According to UTC Section 706(a), the removal of the trustee may be requested by the settlor. The right of the settlor of an irrevocable trust to petition for trustee removal did not exist at common law. [Section 706, Comment]. If the trust is revocable, the right to request removal lies only in the settlor as the settlor has exclusive control over the trust. [Section 603]. Removal may also be requested by a cotrustee or a beneficiary. The term "beneficiary" has been interpreted broadly by at least one court which allowed a widow who was not a named beneficiary of the trust but who was eligible to take an elective share that was potentially payable from the trust to file a petition for the removal of the trustee. [See Rodriguez–Tocker v. Estate of Tocker, 129 P.3d 586 (Kan.App.2006)]. Finally, the court may remove a trustee on its own initiative.

UTC Section 706(b) lists the grounds for removal of a trustee by the court. [See also Restatement (Third) Trusts, § 37 cmt. e]. This list broadens the rule in many states, which provides that a trustee may only be removed for breach of trust. [English, UTC Significant Provisions, p. 197]. UTC Section 706(b)(1) states that a trustee may be removed for a breach of trust, but only if the breach is "serious." The Comment points out that the breach may be a single act or a series of small acts that, when considered together, constitute a serious breach. As an example of the latter, the Comment specifies a failure on the part of the trustee to keep the beneficiaries reasonably informed or to respond to their request for information. [See UTC 813, § 19.02(M); see also *In re* Wells Revocable Trust, 734 N.W.2d 323 (Neb.App.2007)].

Under UTC Section 706(b)(2), one or more or all of the cotrustees may be removed if there is a lack of cooperation among them that seriously impairs the administration of the trust. The Comment points out that this may occur if the cotrustees are deadlocked on an important issue. As noted above, if there remains in office at least one cotrustee who is qualified and able to act, the vacancies of the removed cotrustees need not be filled. [UTC 703(b), 704(b)]. The Comment notes that this subsection does not apply to friction between the trustee and the beneficiaries which is in itself typically not a ground for removal. [UTC 706, Comment].

Under UTC Section 706(b)(3), a trustee may be removed because the trustee is unfit or unwilling to act or fails persistently to administer the trust. Removal for these grounds can occur, however, only if the court finds that the removal serves the best interest of the beneficiaries. "Interests of the beneficiaries" is defined in UTC 103(8) as "the beneficial interests provided in the terms of the trust." A trustee may be found "unfit" for a variety of reasons, ranging from lack of physical or mental capacity to sheer inability to administer the trust. [Restatement (Third) Trusts, § 37, cmt. e.] The Comment to UTC Section 706 suggests that in the latter case, the problem may be remedied by the less drastic measure of a delegation of some of the trustee functions rather than by removal. A trustee may be found "unwilling to act" if the trustee refuses to act or is consistently indifferent to the trustee's duties under the trust. [UTC 706,

Comment]. A "persistent failure to administer the trust effectively" requires showing of more than one instance of ineffective management.

UTC Section 706(b)(4) provides that a court may remove a trustee in the event of a "substantial change of circumstances" or if the removal is requested unanimously by the qualified beneficiaries. In these cases, the court must make three findings: 1) the removal is in the best interest of all the beneficiaries; 2) the removal is not inconsistent with a material provision of the trust; and 3) there is a suitable cotrustee or replacement trustee available. According to the Comment, the "change in circumstances" language was added to balance the court's normal tendency to give great weight to the settlor's choice of trustee (under the theory that the settlor knew of any weaknesses the trustee had but chose that person anyway) with the possibility that that choice may eventually prove to be unwise or unworkable. The Comment and the Restatement describe possible changes that may warrant removal, such as a change in the level or quality of service provided by the trustee or its location. [UTC 706, Comment; Restatement (Third) Trusts, § 37, cmt. f]. The Restatement also points out that a conflict of interest that was unknown to the settlor at the time of choosing the trustee may reveal itself later, thus justifying the removal of the trustee. [Restatement (Third) Trusts, § 37, cmt. f(1)]. The ability of the qualified beneficiaries to request the removal of the trustee is consistent with UTC Section 411(b), which allows the beneficiaries to agree to a modification of the trust. [See § 18.01(B)(1)]. As with UTC Section 411(b), the court may only remove the trustee if so doing is not inconsistent with a material provision of the trust.

UTC Section 706(c) incorporates the court's powers under UTC Section 1001(b) to engage in other actions in lieu of removing the trustee or while the removal decision is pending. [See § 19.04(A)]. These include, among other things, compelling the trustee to perform, enjoining the trustee from committing a breach, ordering an accounting, and appointing a special fiduciary to protect the trust property.

F. DELIVERY OF PROPERTY BY FORMER TRUSTEE

UTC Section 707 addresses what happens to trust property when a trustee has resigned or been removed from office. Subsection (a) of UTC Section 707 makes it clear that even though the trustee is no longer in office, the trustee retains any powers necessary to protect the trust property until the property is turned over to the successor trustee. If there is still a cotrustee in office, however, there is no need for the former trustee to retain this authority and UTC Section 707(a) provides that the trustee does not do so. If there is no cotrustee but for any reason the former trustee should not retain the powers granted by this Code section, the Comment points out that the court may instead appoint a special fiduciary pursuant to several other Code sections, including UTC Sections 704(e), 705(b), 706(c), and 1001(b)(5).

Subsection (b) of UTC Section 707 directs a trustee who has resigned or been removed to "proceed expeditiously" to turn over whatever property remains in the former trustee's hands to whomever is entitled to receive it. The recipient may be a cotrustee, a successor trustee, or any other person who is entitled to it.

Although this Code section deals with trustees who have resigned or been removed, the Comment points out that the UTC does not require the personal representative of a trustee who has died while in office to wind up the administration of the trust. The same is true of the guardian or conservator of a trustee who has become incapacitated.

G. COMPENSATION OF TRUSTEE

UTC Section 708 is a fairly short section that deals with trustee compensation. Despite its brevity, the Comment contains an extended discussion of numerous issues relating to trustee compensation. Subsection (a) of UTC Section 708 provides simply that, if the trust is silent as to the trustee's compensation, a trustee is entitled to "compensation that is reasonable under the circumstances." [See In re D.M.B., 979 A.2d 15 (D.C.2009)]. As many states already had adopted the concept of "reasonable compensation," the factors to be considered when determining what compensation is reasonable have been fleshed out in a number of cases and in both the Second and Third Restatements of Trusts. The Comment summarizes these factors as including "the custom of the community; the trustee's skill, experience, and facilities; the time devoted to trust duties; the amount and character of the trust property; the degree of difficulty, responsibility and risk assumed in administering the trust, including in making discretionary distributions; the nature and costs of services rendered by others; and the quality of the trustee's performance." UTC Section 708 does not specify the time at which the compensation must be paid. [See Lyons ex rel. Lawing v. Holder, 163 P.3d 343 (Kan. App. 2007)].

Subsection (b) of UTC Section 708 addresses adjustments in compensation if the compensation is specified in the trust. This subsection allows a court to adjust the compensation upward or downward if the trustee's duties turn out to be "substantially different" than those that were contemplated by the settlor when the settlor set forth the compensation amount in the trust instrument or if the specified amount would be "unreasonably low or unreasonably high." The Comment elaborates on this second subparagraph by noting that a trustee who delegates work to an agent may be entitled to less compensation than specified while a trustee who has special skills (the example given is that of a real estate agent) may receive greater compensation because the trustee performed a task that would otherwise have been delegated to someone else for a fee.

The Comment to UTC Section 708 includes a discussion of compensation when there are cotrustees, concluding that in most situations the combined compensation paid to cotrustees should not exceed what would be reasonable if there had been a single trustee. However, the Comment says that the "totality of the circumstances" must be considered in determining what is an appropriate amount of compensation for the cotrustees. Again, the Comment lists factors to be considered which are derived from the Restatements. The listed factors are "the settlor's reasons for naming more than one trustee and the level of responsibility assumed and exact services performed by each trustee." The Comment then notes that the combined fees to cotrustees may be higher than that of a single trustee "because of the duty of each trustee to participate in administration and not delegate to a cotrustee duties the settlor expected the trustees to perform jointly." The Comment states that cotrustees are entitled not necessarily to an equal share of the total compensation.

H. REIMBURSEMENT OF EXPENSES

UTC Section 709 allows the trustee to be reimbursed with interest from the trust for any expenses that were property incurred in the administration of the trust. Usually a trustee is not entitled to reimbursement for expenses that are not properly incurred. However, subsection (a)(2) of UTC Section 709 allows a limited reimbursement of such expenses if the expenditures benefitted the trust. As is pointed out in the Comment, the purpose of this subsection is not to ratify the trustee's unauthorized expenditures but rather to avoid the trust being unjustly enriched.

Subsection (b) of UTC Section 709 provides that any advances of money made by the trustee for the protection of the trust result in a lien on the trust property to secure reimbursement. UTC Section 802(h) contains a list of transactions to which the rules of UTC Section 802 do not apply, provided that the transaction is otherwise fair to the beneficiaries. Advances of the type described in UTC Section 709(b) are included on this list. [802(h)(5), see § 19.02(B)]. The Comment to UTC Section 709 points out that subsection (b) is not a blanket authorization as there may be many reason why a court would delay or even deny reimbursement of such advances.

§ 19.02 UTC Article 8: Duties and Powers of Trustees

Article 8 spells out the duties and powers of trustees. Prior to the enactment of the Uniform Trust Code, many of these same duties were set forth in the Uniform Prudent Investor Act and the Uniform Trustees Powers Act.

The duties that were set forth in the Uniform Prudent Investor Act were described specifically as they related to the trustee's investment function. The Uniform Prudent Investor Act was promulgated in 1994 and had been adopted by about two-thirds of the states by the time of the promulgation of the UTC. As explained in § 19.03, the drafters of the UTC suggest that states that have adopted the

Uniform Prudent Investor Act should incorporate it as Article 9 of their new trust code. [Art. 8, Gen. Comment].

Part 4 of Article VI of the UPC, which dealt with trustees' powers, was intentionally left blank under the assumption that states would adopt the Uniform Trustees Powers Act. However, the Uniform Trustees Powers Act was adopted by only a very few states so UTC Section 816 sets forth in detail the powers of a trustee.

A. DUTY TO ADMINISTER THE TRUST

UTC Section 801 describes the general duty to administer the trust that devolves upon a trustee when the trustee accepts the trusteeship. This section contains four guidelines for the trustee. The trustee must administer the trust: 1) in good faith (a term which is not defined in the UTC); 2) in accordance with the trust's terms and provisions [see, e.g., In re Betty G. Weldon Revocable Trust, 231 S.W.3d 158 (Mo.App.W.D.2007)]; 3) in accordance with the interests of the beneficiaries as they are set forth in the terms of the trust [see UTC 103(8), defining "interests of the beneficiaries"]; and 4) in accordance with the other relevant provisions of the UTC [see, e.g., UTC 802, 804, 813]. The first three guidelines cannot be overridden by the terms of the trust [UTC 105(b)(2)]. The trustee will not be obliged to follow any term of the trust that would direct it to perform an act that is illegal, impossible or contrary to public policy. [See Restatement (Second) Trusts, §§ 164–69].

B. DUTY OF LOYALTY

UTC Section 802 addresses the trustee's duty of loyalty, which is "perhaps the most fundamental duty of a trustee." [UTC 802, Comment]. The blanket rule is that a trustee must administer the trust "solely in the interests of the beneficiaries." [UTC 802(a); see also Restatement (Second) Trusts, § 170(1)]. The definition of "interests of the beneficiaries" set forth in UTC § 103(8) clarifies that their beneficial interests are those "provided in the terms of the trust" rather than those determined by the beneficiaries themselves. [UTC 103, Comment]. Stated differently, the rule set forth in UTC Section 802(a) requires that the trustee not place the trustee's own interests or the interests of third parties above those of the beneficiaries. Duty of loyalty issues arise most often in the context of transactions relating to trust property. Thus, the remaining subsections of UTC Section 802 set forth specific rules governing these transactions.

UTC Section 802(b) states generally that a beneficiary may void any sale, encumbrance or other transaction involving trust property that has been entered into by the trustee for the trustee's own personal account or that is otherwise affected by a conflict between the trustee's fiduciary and personal interests. Under this rule, the transaction is voidable without any further inquiry as to whether the trustee entered into the transaction in good faith and even if the trustee did not profit from the transaction. [UTC 802, Comment; see Restatement (Second) Trusts, 170, cmt b]. Thus, for example, even if the trustee purchased property from the trust at a price above the property's fair market value, the transaction is irrebuttably presumed to have been infected by the trustee's conflict of interest.

The rule in UTC Section 802(b) is subject to some limitations. First, the voidability of the transaction is subject to the rights of persons dealing with or assisting the trustee that are set forth in UTC Section 1012. UTC Section 1012 protects from liability any person who in good faith assists or deals with a trustee without knowledge that the trustee is breaching the duty of loyalty. [See § 19.04(I)]. Paragraphs (1) and (2) of UTC Section 802(b) provide that a beneficiary cannot void a transaction that was authorized by the terms of the trust or approved by the court. [See *In re* Trust Created by Inman, 693 N.W.2d 514 (Neb.2005), in which the court refused to approve a transaction to which seven of the nine beneficiaries objected.] According to paragraph (3) of UTC Section 802(b), a beneficiary can lose the right to void a transaction if the beneficiary does not commence a judicial proceeding within the time limit set forth in UTC Section 1005. [See § 19.04(D)]. Under paragraph (4) of UTC Section 802(b), a beneficiary cannot void a transaction if the beneficiary has consented to the transaction, ratified the transaction or released the trustee in the manner set forth in UTC Section 1009. [See § 19.04(H); see also Mendoza v. Gonzales, 204 P.3d 995 (Wyo.2009)]. Paragraph (5) of UTC Section 802(b) exempts from the automatic voidability rule any transaction that was entered into or any claim that was acquired by the trustee prior to the time the trustee became the trustee or contemplated becoming the trustee. This paragraph, which is modeled after UPC Section 3–713(1), does not insulate a trustee completely. The transaction will still be subjected to scrutiny and a trustee who has doubts as to whether the trustee can complete the transaction without a potential clash of the trustee's personal and fiduciary interests may want to take advantage of UTC Section 802(i), which authorizes the court to appoint a special fiduciary to complete the transaction. [The court's authority to appoint a special fiduciary is set forth in UTC Section 704(e)]. Further limitations on the "no further inquiry" rule appear in subsections (f) and (h) of UTC Section 802, which are discussed below.

Subsection (c) of UTC Section 802 provides that a sale, encumbrance or other transaction between the trust and certain persons with whom the trustee has a close relationship is presumed to be affected by a conflict of interest, although (unlike in UTC Section 802(b)), this presumption is not irrebuttable. The persons named in this subsection include the trustee's spouse and close relatives (the trustee's descendants, siblings, parents, and the spouses of these individuals); an agent or attorney of the trustee; and a corporation or other person in which the trustee or a person that has a significant interest in the trustee has an interest that may affect the trustee's judgment. For these transactions, factors such as the inherent fairness of the transaction or the degree to which the transaction replicates a similar transaction with an independent party may be considered in determining whether the transaction can be voided. The trustee has the burden of establishing that the transaction was not affected by a conflict between the trustee's personal and fiduciary interests. [UTC 802, Comment].

Subsection (d) of UTC Section 802, which is modeled after Calif. Probate Code Section 16004(c), also establishes a rebuttable presumption of a conflict of interest for transactions that do not involve trust property but that take place between the trustee and a beneficiary while the trustee is serving in office or while the trustee who is no longer serving maintains significant influence over the beneficiary. This presumption arises only if the trustee gains an advantage from the transaction. In such a case, the trustee is presumed to have abused the confidential relationship between the trustee and the beneficiary. The trustee may overcome the presumption by proving that the transaction was fair to the beneficiary. The Comment points out that a transaction in which the trustee gains an advantage is not presumed to be an abuse of the confidential relationship if the trustee can show that a third party in an arm's length transaction would have profited similarly.

Subsection (e) of UTC Section 802 imports the "corporate opportunity" doctrine into the Trust Code. This subsection provides that a trustee is involved in a conflict of interest if the trustee, in the trustee's individual capacity, pursues an opportunity that properly belongs to the trust. For example, the trustee may not enter into a business that competes directly with the trust or purchase an investment that rightfully should have been purchased by the trust. [UTC 802, Comment].

Subsection (f) of UTC Section 802 contains special rules relating to mutual funds. Mutual funds, which have become an increasingly popular mode of investment, invest in a combination of stocks, bonds, and other securities and assets. The investor buys shares of the mutual fund rather than purchasing the investments directly. The pooling of assets allows a mutual fund company to make investments that might not otherwise be available to an individual investor. Mutual funds can also provide an expedient form of trust distribution as the trustee can make an in-kind distribution of the mutual fund shares without liquidating the underlying assets. [UTC 802, Comment]. Subsection (f) of UTC Section 802 provides that a trustee does not involve itself in a conflict of interest by investing in a mutual fund even if the trustee or an affiliate of the trustee provides other non-trustee services to the mutual fund company. This subsection, which mirrors statutes already enacted in most states, clarifies that a trustee that provides advisory services and receives a fee for those services from the same fund in which it is investing trust assets is not automatically deemed to be violating the trustee's duty of loyalty. The investment must be a prudent one (in accordance with the principles in Article 9 of the UTC) and the trustee must notify the beneficiaries annually of the rate and method by which its compensation from the mutual fund company is determined.

Subsection (g) of UTC Section 802 contains provisions that guide a trustee who is voting stock held by the trust. The trustee must act in the best interests of the beneficiaries when voting the stock. If the enterprise is owned completely by the trust, the trustee is required to elect or appoint managers who will manage the enterprise in the beneficiaries' best interests.

Subsection (h) of UTC Section 802 contains a list of transactions to which the rules of UTC Section 802 do not apply, provided that the transaction is otherwise fair to the beneficiaries. Included among these are agreements between the trustee and beneficiaries as to the appointment of the trustee or the trustee's compensation; the actual payment by the trustee of reasonable compensation to himself, herself, or itself; a transaction between the trust and another trust or estate of which the trustee is a fiduciary; a deposit of money into a regulated financial institution operated by the trustee; and an advance of money by the trustee for the protection of the trust.

As noted above, subsection (i) of UTC Section 802 allows a court to appoint a special fiduciary to engage in any proposed transaction that would involve a conflict of interest if performed by the trustee.

C. DUTY OF IMPARTIALITY

Often a trust will have more than one beneficiary and the nature of the interests of those beneficiaries may vary. For example, one beneficiary may be entitled only to income while another is entitled only to the remainder or one beneficiary may be entitled to income currently while another may be entitled to income only after the first beneficiary dies. UTC Section 803 requires the trustee to act impartially in dealing with these beneficiaries and managing their interests in the trust. The Comment to UTC Section 803 points out that the duty of impartiality does not require that the beneficiaries be treated equally but rather that they be treated equitably in light of the trust purpose. The Comment recommends that if a settlor wants the trustee to favor one beneficiary over another, the terms of the trust should so state. [See, e.g., Tovrea v. Nolan, 875 P.2d 144 (Ariz.App.1993)].

D. DUTY OF PRUDENT ADMINISTRATION

UTC Section 804 requires the trustee to administer the trust in the same manner as would a "prudent person." In so doing, the trustee must consider the "purposes, terms, distributional requirements, and other circumstances" of the trust and must exercise "reasonable care, skill, and caution." This section is modeled after § 2(a) of the Uniform Prudent Investor Act and Restatement (Third) of Trusts, § 227. The second Restatement of Trusts measured the trustee's duty against that of "a man of ordinary prudence ... dealing with his own property" and did not make reference to the purposes of the trust. Other "prudent man" statutes looked not to the way a prudent man would act when dealing with his own property but rather to the way he would act when dealing with the property of another. This standard is the one set forth for trustees in the UPC. [7–302] UTC Section 804 eliminates this distinction and measures the actions of the trustee as they relate to the purposes of the trust. This standard may be modified by the terms of the trust, subject to the limits set forth in UTC Section 1008 [§ 19.04(G)]. A similar provision relating to investments appears in Article 9 of the UTC. [See § 19.03(A)].

E. COSTS OF ADMINISTRATION

UTC Section 805 limits the trustee to incurring only those "costs that are reasonable...." The reasonableness of the costs is measured in light of the trust property, the trust's purposes and the trustee's skills. This limitation reflects the common law and mirrors § 7 of the Uniform Prudent Investor Act, Restatement (Second) of Trusts, § 188 and

Restatement (Third) of Trusts, § 227(c)(3). The Comment advises that a trustee who is considering delegating administrative duties to an agent for a fee should consider adjusting the trustee's own compensation in order to avoid charging the trust, and thus the beneficiaries, with excessive cost.

F. TRUSTEE'S SKILLS

UTC Section 806 requires a trustee who has special skills or expertise to use those skills and that expertise in administering the trust. The same rule applies if the trustee has represented that the trustee has special skills or expertise and has been named trustee as a result of the representation. This Code section mirrors the Uniform Prudent Investor Act § 2(f), the Restatement (Second) of Trusts, § 174 and UPC Section 7–302.

G. DELEGATION BY TRUSTEE

At common law, as reflected in the Restatement (Second) of Trusts, § 171, a trustee was prohibited from delegating its duties and the administrative functions of the trust. UTC Section 807 mirrors the reversal of common law that first appeared in Uniform Prudent Investor Act § 9 and Restatement (Third) of Trusts, § 227. UTC Section 807 allows trustee to delegate to an agent "duties and powers that a trustee of comparable skills could properly delegate under the circumstances." The trustee is required, however, to "exercise reasonable care, skill, and caution" in selection the agent, establishing the scope of the agency, and monitoring the agent's actions. If the trustee abides by these rules, the trustee is absolved of liability for an action that is performed by the agent. [UTC 807(c)]. The agent, on the other hand, is under a duty to "exercise reasonable care" and to stay within the scope of the delegation. Agents who accept such a delegation submit to the jurisdiction of the courts of the state. The delegation to an agent described in this Code section is distinguishable from delegation among cotrustees, which is covered by UTC Section 703(e). [See § 19.01(B)].

H. POWERS TO DIRECT

UTC Section 808(a) elaborates upon the exclusive control by the settlor of a revocable trust set forth in UTC Section 603(a) by allowing the trustee to follow the direction of the settlor of a revocable trust even if that direction is contrary to the trust terms. [See § 18.03(C)]. Subsections (b) through (d) of UTC Section 808 relate to directions by trust protectors or advisors. These are third parties whom the settlor has authorized to exercise certain powers under the trust, such as the power to direct investment. Subsection (b) of UTC Section 808 allows the trustee to follow the direction of such a third party unless the direction is manifestly contrary to the trust terms or the trustee knows that the exercise of such a power would be a serious breach of the fiduciary duty that the third party owes the trustees. This subsection balances the need for a trustee to feel comfortable in following the third party's direction with the recognition that the trustee retains responsibility for making sure that the terms of the trust are honored. Subsection (c) of UTC Section 808 confirms that a settlor may confer upon one of these third parties the power to modify or terminate the trust. Subsection (d) of UTC Section 808 explains that these third parties are presumptively fiduciaries who are required to act in good faith with regard to the purposes of the trust and the interests of the trust beneficiary. Thus, the third party is liable for any loss that results from that party's breach of a fiduciary duty.

I. CONTROL AND PROTECTION OF TRUST PROPERTY

UTC Section 809 requires the trustee to take reasonable steps to take control of and protect the trust property. This duty, which is modeled after §§ 175 and 176 of the Restatement (Second) of Trusts, is a component of the trustee's duty of prudent administration as set out in UTC Section 804. [See § 19.02(D)].

J. RECORDKEEPING AND IDENTIFICATION OF TRUST PROPERTY

Keeping adequate records of the trust administration, as required by UTC Section 810(a), is another component of the duty of prudent administration

set forth in UTC Section 804. Subsection (b) of UTC
Section 810 prohibits the trustee from commingling
the trust property with the trustee's own property
and subsection (c) requires the trustee to earmark
the trust property so that the trust's interest in the
property will be apparent to third parties. Subsection (d) of UTC Section 810, however, allows the
trustee to invest as a whole the property of two or
more separate trusts so long as the trustee maintains records that clearly indicate each trust's interest. This pooling of trust assets for investment
purposes often allows the trustee to make investments more efficiently and perhaps to take advantage of investment opportunities that would not
exist for a small trust.

K. ENFORCEMENT AND DEFENSE
OF CLAIMS

UTC Section 811, which is modeled after §§ 177
and 178 of the Restatement (Second) of Trusts,
requires a trustee to take steps to enforce claims of
and defend claims against this trust. However, the
trustee is only required to take "reasonable" steps,
which may include settling rather than defending
an action. [UTC 811, Comment].

L. COLLECTING TRUST PROPERTY

UTC Section 812 requires the trustee to take
reasonable steps to compel someone in possession of
trust property (including a former trustee) to deliver that property to the trustee. Also, the trustee

must take reasonable steps to redress any breach of trust by a former trustee that is known to the trustee. [See UTC 104, § 17.01(B), for the definition of "know."] This section is a more specific application of the duty to enforce claims described in UTC Section 811.

M. DUTY TO INFORM AND REPORT

The trustee's duties relating to reporting and keeping the beneficiaries reasonably informed appear in UPC Section 7–303 and in UTC Section 813. Subsection (a) of UTC Section 813 carries forward the requirement of UPC Section 7–303 that the trustee keep the beneficiaries reasonably informed. However, the UTC limits this duty to "qualified beneficiaries" only. [See UTC 103(13), § 17.01(B), for the definition of "qualified beneficiaries."] More remote or contingent beneficiaries must make a specific request to the trustee. UTC Section 105(b)(9) lists this requirement as one that is not waivable by the settlor. [See § 17.01(C)].

UPC Section 7–303 contains a specific direction to the trustee to inform the current beneficiaries of the trustee's name and address and the court in which the trust is registered within 30 days of acceptance of the trusteeship. Upon reasonable request, a beneficiary is entitled to a copy of the trust terms that affect that beneficiary's interest and an annual accounting. The requirements in UTC Section 813(b) are more extensive. The trustee must furnish any beneficiary who requests it a copy of the entire trust instrument rather than just of those provisions that affect that beneficiary's interest. UTC Section 813(b)(2) also requires the trustee to notify the qualified beneficiaries of any trust of the trustee's acceptance of the trusteeship and the trustee's contact information. UTC Section 813(b)(3) requires the trustee to notify the qualified beneficiaries of the existence of the trust within 60 days of the date an irrevocable trust is created or a formerly revocable trust becomes irrevocable. The trustee must also notify the qualified beneficiaries of the identity of the settlor, their right to request a copy of the trust instrument and the trustee's annual report. UTC Section 813(e) provides that these two subsections will not apply to a trustee who accepts the trusteeship before the UTC becomes effective; to an irrevocable trust created before the effective date; or to a trust that becomes irrevocable before the effective date. UTC Section 105(b)(8) lists the requirements of UTC 813(b)(2) and (b)(3) among those that cannot be waived by the settlor as they apply to qualified beneficiaries who are age 25 and older. This segment has been the subject of much debate in enacting states, as some settlors have complained that they do not wish to have their beneficiaries know of the existence of the trust lest this cause the beneficiaries to lose the ambition to become self-sustaining. The age 25 requirement was added as a compromise so that beneficiaries who were still in their formative years would not be inclined to forego educational and career opportunities in anticipation of their being supported later by the trust. The countervailing concern of those who favor the non-waivability of this requirement is that the beneficiaries must have enough information to enforce their interests in the trust. UTC Section 105(b)(8) and (b)(9) are now bracketed as a result of the 2004 amendments, indicating that they are now considered optional provisions.

UTC Section 813(b)(4) requires the trustee to notify the qualified beneficiaries in advance if any changes are to be made to the rate or method of compensating the trustee.

Subsection (c) of UTC Section 813 requires the trustee to send an annual report to the distributees or permissible distributes of trust property, and to any other beneficiaries who request it. The report, which also must be distributed at the termination of the trust, will include a description of the trust property, liabilities, receipts, and disbursements (including the trustee's compensation), and the nature and value of the trust assets. Such a report must also be sent to the qualified beneficiaries if a trustee vacates the office and there are no remaining co-trustees. If the trustee dies or becomes incapacitated, the report may be sent by the trustee's conservator or guardian or the personal representative of the trustee's estate. A beneficiary may waive the right to this report and to any other information that is required to be sent under UTC Section 813.

N. DISCRETIONARY POWERS; TAX SAVINGS

Sometimes a trust instrument will include language that allows the trustee to exercise discretion in certain decisions relating to the trust, such as the discretion to decide how income should be divided among the beneficiaries. Subsection (a) of UTC Section 814 makes it clear that a trustee's discretion is never absolute, but must always be exercised in good faith and in accordance with the terms of the trust, the purposes of the trust and the interests of the beneficiaries. ["Interest of the beneficiaries" is defined in UTC 103(8)].

If a trustee of a trust is also a beneficiary and has the discretion to distribute trust property for his or her personal benefit, federal tax law may construe this "power of withdrawal" as a general power of appointment. [See I.R.C. §§ 2041, 2514; see also UTC 103(11), defining "power of withdrawal"]. Similarly, if an individual has the power to use trust property to satisfy a legal obligation of support that the trustee has, this power will be deemed a general power of appointment. [Treas. Reg. § 20.2041–1(c)(2)]. Holding a general power of appointment over property may cause tax consequences to the holder of the power. If an individual exercises a general power of appointment during his or her life by directing the distribution of the property to a third party, this exercise will potentially be a taxable gift. [I.R.C. § 2514] If an individual dies while holding a general power of appointment over trust property, the full value of the property is included in the decedent's estate for estate tax purposes, even if the individual never exercised the power. [I.R.C. § 2041] Thus, settlers who were not familiar with this tax rule may have unwittingly put their trustees in a position that will cause them to incur gift or estate taxes sheerly by virtue of their fiduciary positions.

Subsections (b) through (d) of UTC Section 814 are designed to remedy this problem. Subsection (b)(1) of UTC Section 814 limits a trustee's exercise of a discretionary power to distribute trust property to himself or herself to a distribution that is made in accordance with an "ascertainable standard." "Ascertainable standard" is defined in UTC Section 103(2) as "a standard relating to an individual's health, education, support, or maintenance within the meaning of Section 2041(b)(1)(A) or 2514(c)(1) of the Internal Revenue Code of 1986...." The Internal Revenue Code provides in those Code sections that a power of appointment will not be considered "general" (and thus will not result in taxation) if it is limited by such an ascertainable standard. Subsection (b)(2) of UTC Section 814 contains a blanket prohibition against a trustee exercising a discretionary power to satisfy any legal support obligation of the trustee. [But see In re Margolis Revocable Trust, 765 N.W.2d 919 (Minn. App.2009), holding that public policy does not bar the enforcement of an exculpatory clause if the trustee violated this statute.] Subsection (c) of UTC

Section 814 allows a majority of the remaining trustees to exercise a discretionary power that is limited or prohibited by subsection (b), or alternatively allows the court to appoint a special fiduciary to exercise this power. Subsection (d) of UTC Section 814 excludes three types of trusts from the application of the rules of subsection (b). The first is a trust in which the power is held by the settlor's spouse if a marital deduction had been allowed for the property when it was transferred to the trust. Under I.R.C. §§ 2056 and 2523, the value of property that is transferred to an individual's spouse is deducted from the value of the gift or estate before the tax is imposed. The value of this property will subsequently be included in the spouse's estate, so there is no need to apply the limiting rule of UTC Section 814(b). The second type of trust that is excluded under subsection (d) of UTC Section 814 is a trust that is revocable or amendable by the settlor. The power to amend or revoke the trust will automatically cause the trust property to be treated as the settlor's own property for taxing purposes. The third type of trust that is excluded is a trust that makes distributions to a minor. Under I.R.C. § 2503(c), this type of trust often will result in property being paid to the settlor's minor children. The trust is purposely structured this way to allow the settlor to take advantage of an exclusion from the gift tax valuation of certain amounts of property (currently up to $13,000 per person per year), so this type of trust is purposely designed to be taxable.

O. POWERS OF TRUSTEE

As noted at the beginning of this section, the UPC did not enumerate the powers of a trustee in anticipation of the adoption of the Uniform Trustees Powers Act by all the states. Most states did not adopt this statute, so the drafters of the UTC took a two-pronged approach to dealing with trustee powers. UTC Section 815 contains a broad grant of powers that states that a trustee has any power given the trustee in the trust instrument; any power over the trust property that an unmarried competent owner of property would have as to his or her own property; any powers appropriate to achieve the purposes of the trust, and any other powers incurred by the UTC. Subsection (b) of UTC Section 815 provides that the exercise of any power is subject to the fiduciary duties set out in Article 8. [Powers of a personal representative are discussed at § 12.04(C)].

The drafters of the UTC were aware that sometimes third parties who are dealing with trustees demand to see a specific grant to the trustee of the power to engage in the transaction at issue. For this reason, UTC Section 816 contains a non-exclusive list of twenty-six trustee powers. Most of these powers deal with handling the trust property in matters such as buying, selling, leasing, repairing, and insuring trust property; borrowing money, pledging trust property for a period that extends beyond the terms of the trust, and lending trust property to beneficiaries; conducting a business that is owned by the trust; settling claims, conducting litigation, and engaging in alternative dispute resolution; and paying expenses, including the trustee's compensation. These powers are similar to those spelled out in the Uniform Trustees Powers Act. New to the UTC is the power under UTC Section 816(13) to deal with any environmental issues that may arise with respect to trust property. [See UTC 103(6), which defines "environmental law" as "a federal, state, or local law, rule, regulation, or ordinance relating to protection of the environment."] UTC Section 816(21) gives a trustee options as to how to pay amounts that are distributable to a beneficiary who is under a legal disability or whom the trustee reasonably believes is incapacitated. These include the options to pay the distributable amounts to the beneficiary's conservator or guardian or custodian or an adult who has custody or care of the beneficiary. A similar provision appears in UPC Section 3–915. [See § 14.01].

P. DISTRIBUTION UPON TERMINATION

The final section in Article 8 deals with the trustee's actions when the trust is terminated. Subsection (a) of UTC Section 817 allows a trustee who anticipates a termination or partial termination of the trust to send the beneficiaries a proposed plan of distribution and to give the beneficiaries a time period (30 days) within which they may object to the proposed distribution. A beneficiary who does not object within that time period loses his or her right to object. A similar provision appears in UPC Section 3–906(b). When the termination occurs, subsection (b) of UTC Section 817 instructs the trustee to proceed "expeditiously" to distribute the trust property. The trustee may retain a reasonable reserve to pay any anticipated debts, expenses or taxes. Upon distribution of the trust property to the beneficiaries, trustees often will ask the beneficiaries to release them from liability for a breach of trust. A release is an affirmative act of the beneficiary and is not accomplished merely because the beneficiary failed to object under subsection (a). Subsection (c) of UTC Section 817 provides that such a release is valid unless the release was induced by improper conduct of the trustee or the beneficiary was unaware of the beneficiary's rights or of material facts relating to the trust and the release. UTC Section 1009 deals more broadly with any releases that a beneficiary might give. [See § 19.04(H)].

§ 19.03 UTC Article 9: Uniform Prudent Investor Act

At the time of the promulgation of the UTC, the drafters took note of the fact that almost all states had adopted the Uniform Prudent Investor Act. This Act deals comprehensively with the duties of a trustee in the investment and management of trust funds. The UTC drafters suggest that any state that enacts the UTC and has already enacted the Uniform Prudent Investor Act should simply re-codify the Uniform Prudent Investor Act as Article 9 of their Trust Code. The drafters noted, however, that some of the provisions in the Uniform Prudent Investor Act would overlap provisions in Article 8 of UTC, which deals with trustees' general duties. To avoid duplication, the drafters' recommendation is that states that have enacted the Uniform Prudent Investor Act should delete from Article 9 those provisions of the Uniform Prudent Investor Act that overlap provisions in Article 8 of the UTC. Chart 19–1 shows the suggested integration of the Uniform Prudent Investor Act into the UTC. The remaining portions of this section discuss the relevant Uniform Prudent Investor Act provisions.

CHART 19–1
INTEGRATION OF UNIFORM PRUDENT INVESTOR ACT INTO UTC

The following provisions will be deleted from the state's Prudent Investor Act because they already appear as shown in Article 8 of the UTC:

Prudent Investor Act	Provisions	UTC Article 8
Special skills	2(f)	806
Loyalty	5	802
Impartiality	6	803
Investment costs	7	805
Delegation	9	807

Once these deletions have been made, the following provisions of the Uniform Prudent Investor Act will be recodified as Article 9 of the state's new Trust Code:

Section 1	Prudent Investor Rule
Section 2 (a)–(e)	Standard of Care: Portfolio Strategy; Risk and Return Objectives
Section 3	Diversification
Section 4	Duties at Inception of Trusteeship
Section 8	Reviewing Compliance
Section 10	Language Invoking Standard of [Act]

A. PRUDENT INVESTOR RULE

Section 2 of the Uniform Prudent Investor Act sets forth the standard by which trustees will be judged when investing trust assets. This section is derived from Restatement (Third) Trusts: Prudent Investor Rule, § 227(a). A similar standard of prudence as it relates to the overall administration of the trust appears in UTC 804. [See § 19.02(D)].

The basic rule is that the trustee is to "invest and manage trust assets as a prudent investor would, by considering the purposes, terms, distribution requirements, and other circumstances of the trust." A trustee is to act with reasonable care, skill, and caution. [Uniform Prudent Investor Act 2(a)]. Subsection (b) introduces the "portfolio theory," which provides that the performance of the trustee will be evaluated not on the basis of each individual investment but rather on the overall performance of the portfolio as a whole. [Uniform Prudent Investor Act 2(b)]. This provision is designed to allow the trustee to take appropriate risks in investing in order to maximize the return. The risk tolerance of a trust will be dependent in many ways upon the trust purpose.

Subsection (c) lists a number of factors that a trust shall consider when investing. These factors are:

1) general economic conditions

2) the possible effect of inflation or deflation;

3) the expected tax consequences of investment decisions or strategies;

4) the role that each investment or course of action plays within the overall trust portfolio, which may include financial assets, interests in closely held enterprises, tangible and intangible personal property, and real property;

5) the expected total return from income and the appreciation of capital;

6) other resources of the beneficiaries;

7) the needs for liquidity, regularity of income, and preservation or appreciation of capital; and

8) an asset's special relationship or special value, if any, to the purposes of the trust or to one or more of the beneficiaries.

Subsection (d) requires a trustee to make reasonable efforts to verify any facts relevant to the trust investments. Subsection (e) allows the trustee to invest in any type of property so long as the investment is consistent with the standards set forth in this article. Subsection (f) provides that if a trustee has special skills or expertise or has been appointed due the representation of such skills and expertise, the trustee is required to use those special skills and that expertise.

B. DIVERSIFICATION

Section 3 of the Uniform Prudent Investor Act sets forth as one of the basic rules of prudent investing the duty to diversify the trust invest-ments. The inclusion of the rule in the Uniform Prudent Investor Act reflects the presumption of Restatement (Third) of Trusts, § 227 that prudent investing ordinarily requires a trustee to diversify the trust assets. The trustee need not comply with this rule, however, if the trustee reasonably deter-mines that, due to special circumstances, the trust purposes are better served by not diversifying. For example, if a trust is established to hold a life insurance policy on the settlor's life, the purpose of the trust would be defeated if the trustee were to diversify that investment. The Comment to the Uniform Prudent Investor Act contains an exten-sive discussion of the "modern portfolio theory" underlying the diversification rule. [Uniform Pru-dent Investor Act 3, Comment].

C. DUTIES AT INCEPTION OF TRUSTEESHIP

Section 4 of the Uniform Prudent Investor Act contains the simple practical direction that the trus-tee is to review the trust assets within a reasonable time after the trust is established or the assets are received. The trustee is to then make decisions about investment of the assets that comply with the provisions of the Uniform Prudent Investor Act.

D. REVIEWING COMPLIANCE

Section 8 of the Uniform Prudent Investor Act, which is an extension of the standard of care set forth in Section 2, provides that a trustee's actions in investing trust assets will be viewed in light of the facts and circumstances that existed at the time the trustee made the decisions. In other words, the trustee's actions will not be reviewed in hindsight.

E. LANGUAGE INVOKING STANDARD OF UNIFORM PRUDENT INVESTOR ACT

Section 10 of the Uniform Prudent Investor Act provides that if certain words are contained in a trust, and there are no other trust words indicating a contrary intent, these words will be deemed to authorize any investment strategy that is permitted by the Uniform Prudent Investor Act. These words are: "investments permissible by law for investment of trust funds," "legal investments," "authorized investments," "using the judgment and care under the circumstances then prevailing that persons of prudence, discretion, and intelligence exercise in the management of their own affairs, not in regard to speculation but in regard to the permanent disposition of their funds, considering the probable income as well as the probable safety of their capital," "prudent man rule," "prudent trustee rule," "prudent person rule," and "prudent investor rule."

§ 19.04 UTC Article 10: Liability of Trustees and Rights of Persons Dealing With Trustees

Article 10 explains the remedies that beneficiaries may pursue if there has been a breach of trust.

Similar provisions for personal representatives appear in UPC Sections 3–712 and 3–713. [See § 12.04(D)]. Article 10 of the UTC also discusses the rights and protections of third parties who deal with trustees.

A. REMEDIES FOR BREACH OF TRUST

UTC Section 1001 lists the sanctions that may be imposed upon a trustee who has engaged in a breach of trust. A "breach of trust" is defined as the "violation by a trustee of a duty the trustee owes to a beneficiary." [UTC 1001(a)]. These duties are spelled out primarily in Article 8. [See § 19.02]. The remedies that a court may impose include both equitable remedies and money damages. These remedies are based on those listed in Restatement (Second) of Trusts, § 199 (1959). [UTC 1001, Comment]. A court may compel a trustee to perform the trustee's duties and enjoin the trustee from committing a breach of trust. [UTC 1001(b)(1), (2)]. A court may require the trustee to redress a breach of trust by the payment of money, the restoration of property, or by any other means. [UTC 1001(b)(3)]. The money paid might take the form of damages, restitution or surcharge. [See UTC 1002, § 19.04(B) for the measure of liability]. The court may compel the trustee to account. The court may appoint a special fiduciary (sometimes referred to as a "receiver") to administer the trust. [See also, UTC 704(d), § 19.01(D)]. The court may suspend the trustee or remove the trustee as allowed under UTC

Section 706. [UTC 1001(b)(6), (7); see § 19.01(E)]. The court may reduce or deny the trustee's compensation. [UTC 1001(b)(8)]. Factors that a court may wish to consider in determining whether to reduce or deny compensation include: "(1) whether the trustee acted in good faith; (2) whether the breach of trust was intentional; (3) the nature of the breach and the extent of the loss; (4) whether the trustee has restored the loss; and (5) the value of the trustee's services to the trust." [UTC 1008, Comment]. Subject to the rights of bona fide purchasers as set out in UTC Section 1012, the court may set aside acts of the trustee by voiding an act of the trustee, imposing a lien or a constructive trust on trust property, or tracing trust property wrongfully disposed of and recovering the property or its proceeds. Subsection (b)(10) of UTC Section 1001 allows the court to order any other appropriate relief.

B. DAMAGES

If a trustee commits a breach of trust, under UTC Section 1002(a) the trustee is liable to the affected beneficiaries for the greater of: (1) the amount required to restore the trust property and distributions that would have occurred absent the breach or (2) any profit made by the trustee by reason of the breach. The term "profit" does not include the trustee's compensation. Even a trustee who has committed a breach of trust is entitled to compensation unless the court specifically limits or denies the compensation under UTC Section 1001(b)(8). Subsection (a) of UTC Section 1002 is based on the Restatement (Third) of Trusts: Prudent Investor Rule, § 205 (1992).

Subsection (b) of UTC Section 1002, which is derived from Restatement (Second) of Trusts, § 258 (1959), deals with the joint and several liability of cotrustees. Cotrustees who are less at fault may be entitled to contribution from other cotrustees who are substantially more at fault. However, a cotrustee is not entitled to contribution from the other cotrustees if that cotrustee committed the breach of trust in bad faith or with reckless indifference to the purposes of the trust or the interests of the beneficiaries. A cotrustee who received a benefit as a result of the breach is not entitled to contribution from the other cotrustees to the extent of that benefit.

The drafters recognized that it may be difficult to measure the comparative degree of fault of cotrustees. They suggest that the following list of factors, derived from Restatement (Second) of Trusts, § 258 cmt. d (1959), be considered in measuring degree of fault: "(1) Did the trustee fraudulently induce the other trustee to join in the breach? (2) Did the trustee commit the breach intentionally while the other trustee was at most negligent? (3) Did the trustee, because of greater experience or expertise, control the actions of the other trustee? (4) Did the trustee alone commit the breach with liability imposed on the other trustee only because of an improper delegation or failure to properly monitor the actions of the cotrustee?" [UTC 1002, Comment].

Even if no breach of trust has occurred, a cardinal rule of fiduciary law is that a trustee cannot use the trust for his or her or its personal advantage. UTC Section 1003(a), which is modeled after Restatement (Second) of Trusts, § 203 (1959), prohibits a trustee from ever making a profit in connection with the administration of the trust. On the other hand, if there is no breach of trust, a trustee is not liable for any loss or depreciation in the value of the trust property or for failing to make a profit.

C. ATTORNEY'S FEES AND COSTS

UTC Section 1004, which is modeled after Massachusetts General Laws chapter 215, § 45, allows the court to allocate, "as equity and justice may require," the responsibility for paying the expenses and costs of any litigation concerning the trust to any party or to the trust itself. These costs include attorney's fees. Contrary to the commonly applied "American Rule" for awarding attorney's fees, there is no requirement that there be evidence of bad faith or fraud on the part of the other party. [See, In re Trust of Rosenberg, 727 N.W.2d 430 (Neb.2007), Heinitsh v. Wachovia Bank, N.A., 665 S.E.2d 541 (N.C.App.2008), Kutten v. Bank of America, N.A., 530 F.3d 669 (Mo.2008), Duke v. Simmons, 2009 WL 1175114 (Tenn.Ct.App.2009)].

D. LIMITATION OF ACTION AGAINST TRUSTEE

UTC Section 1005 contains two time periods beyond which a beneficiary may not bring an action against the trustee for a breach of trust. Subsection (a) of UTC Section 1005 limits that time period to one year, beginning on the date that the beneficiary (or an appropriate representative of the beneficiary, as defined in Article 3), receives a report from the trustee that discloses adequately the existence of a potential claim. The report must also disclose the time period for filing the complaint. Adequate disclosure is defined in subsection (b) of UTC Section 1005 as disclosure that provides information that is sufficient to inform the beneficiary of the existence of the potential claim or that should at least put the beneficiary on notice to inquire into the existence of such a claim. If the disclosure does not meet the requirements of subsection (a) or if no report is given, the time limit for bringing an action against the trustee is five years from the time that the beneficiary's or trustee's relationship with the trust terminated. This will be the earliest of: (1) the trustee's removal, death or resignation; (2) the termination of the beneficiary's interest in the trust; or (3) the termination of the trust. The five-year limitation will also be applicable for a beneficiary who has not received any report. These two time limitations may be overridden if the beneficiary consents to, releases or ratifies a trustee's action. [UTC 1009]. Also, the common law doctrines of estoppel or laches may bar an action. [UTC 106]. Likewise, state law may cause a statute to be tolled for fraud or other actions. [1005, Comment].

E. RELIANCE ON TRUST INSTRUMENT

UTC Section 106(19) defines the "trust instrument" as the instrument that contains the "terms of the trust." UTC Section 106(18) defines the "terms of the trust" as "the manifestation of the settlor's intent regarding a trust's provisions as expressed in the trust instrument or as may be established by other evidence that would be admissible in a judicial proceeding." Thus, it is possible that the words in the trust instrument and the "terms of the trust" may be different. This could happen, for example, if a court reforms or modifies a trust, which may result in the deletion or modification of words or provisions. [UTC 410–417, § 18.01(B)]. A trustee who relies on the terms of the trust as these are expressed in the trust instrument itself is not liable to the beneficiaries for a breach of trust if the breach resulted from that reliance and the reliance was reasonable. [UTC 1006]. This provision, for example, would not protect a trustee who was aware of a judicial proceeding to modify the trust and yet still acted in reliance upon the words in the trust instrument.

F. EVENT AFFECTING ADMINISTRATION OR DISTRIBUTION

Often a trust instrument will direct a trustee to take certain actions or make or withhold distributions only when an event external to the trust itself has occurred. For example, the trustee may be instructed to pay income to a deceased settlor's spouse until such time as she remarries. The spouse, knowing of this provision, may hide the fact of her remarriage from the trustee. A trustee who continues to make distributions is not liable if the trustee has exercised reasonable care to ascertain the happening of that event. UTC Section 1007 speaks of events such as marriage, divorce, performance of educational requirements, or death, but that list is not exclusive. This provision reverses the rule of Restatement (Second) of Trusts, § 226 (1959), which held the trustee liable for any misdelivery despite the trustee's lack of knowledge.

G. EXCULPATION OF TRUSTEE

A term of the trust that exculpates the trustee from liability is not always valid, even though the settlor knowingly placed the clause in the trust instrument. UTC Section 1008(a) provides that an exculpation clause is not valid under two circumstances: 1) if the clause relieves the trustee for liability from an action committed in bad faith or with reckless indifference to the trusts purposes and the beneficiaries' interests; and 2) if the insertion of the exculpation clause was "an abuse by the trustee of a fiduciary or confidential relationship to the settlor." If the clause was drafted or caused to be drafted by the trustee, subsection (b) of UTC Section 1008 states that this clause is presumed to be the result of an abuse of the relationship. The trustee may overcome this presumption only by proving that the clause is fair and its existence and contents were adequately communicated to the settlor. This approach is contrary to early case law that left it to the beneficiary to prove that a clause drafted by the trustee was the result of an abuse of the confidential relationship. The Comment, citing the Restatement (Second) of Trusts, § 222 cmt. d (1959), lists factors that might indicate whether the exculpation clause is fair under the circumstances. These include: "(1) the extent of the prior relationship between the settlor and trustee; (2) whether the settlor received independent advice; (3) the sophistication of the settlor with respect to business and fiduciary matters; (4) the trustee's reasons for inserting the clause; and (5) the scope of the particular provision inserted." The Comment also notes that if the settlor was represented by independent counsel, the settlor's attorney is deemed to be the drafter of the form and thus the subsection (b) requirements are satisfied. UTC Section 105(b)(10) provides that the provisions of UTC Section 1008 cannot be waived by the settlor in the trust instrument.

H. BENEFICIARY'S CONSENT, RELEASE, OR RATIFICATION

Under UTC Section 1009, a trustee generally is not liable for actions if the beneficiary consented to the conduct, released the trustee from liability, or ratified the transaction. This general rule does not apply if the beneficiary's consent, release or ratification was induced improperly by the trustee or if the beneficiary did not know of the beneficiary's rights or the material facts relating to the breach. This section is based on the Restatement (Second) of Trusts, §§ 216–17 (1959). [See UTC 104, § 17.01(B) for a definition of "know"; see also Mendoza v. Gonzales, 204 P.3d 995 (Wyo.2009)].

I. RIGHTS AND PROTECTIONS OF THIRD PARTIES WHO DEAL WITH TRUSTEES

UTC Sections 1010 through 1013 are designed to facilitate transactions between the trustee and third parties in order to maximize the trustee's ability to administer the trust efficiently and in the beneficiaries' best interest. As noted below, some of these provisions reflect provisions in the UPC that relate to personal representatives and trustees. UTC Section 105((b)(11) prohibits a settlor from waiving the rights of parties other than beneficiaries that are laid out in UTC Sections 1010–1013.

1. Limitation on Personal Liability of Trustee

In the course of administering a trust, a trustee may enter into transactions for which third parties may attempt to hold the trustee personally liable. Under UTC Section 1010(a), a trustee who signs a contract is not personally liable on the contract if in the contract the trustee disclosed the trustee's fiduciary capacity. This is a somewhat more lenient version of UPC Sections 3–808(a) [See § 12.08] and 7–306(a), which provide that a personal representative or trustee is liable if the personal representative or trustee "fails to reveal his representative capacity and identify the estate in the contract." According to the Comment to UTC Section 1010, the UPC provisions require a fiduciary both to disclose the fiduciary's capacity and identify the estate or trust, whereas UTC Section 1010(a) allows the fiduciary the option of either indicating the trusteeship in the signature or referring to the trust in the contract. [UTC 1010, Comment].

As in UPC Sections 3–808(b)and 7–306(b), a trustee under the UTC is personally liable for torts or for obligations arising from property ownership and control only if the trustee is personally at fault. [UTC 1010(b); see Biltmore Associates, LLC v. Twin City Fire Ins. Co., 572 F.3d 663 (9th Cir.2009)]. UTC Section 1010(b) includes a specific reference to violations of environmental law. [See UTC 103(6), definition of "environmental law"]. Other provisions that the UTC drafters added in response to the growing problem of property owners being held liable for violations of environmental law by previous owners appear at UTC Sections 701(c)(2) [§ 19.01(A)] and 816(13). [See also § 19.02(O)].

Subsection (c) of UTC Section 1010 repeats the provisions in subsections (c) of UPC Sections 3–808 and 7–306(a) that the claims described in the preceding subsections may be asserted against the trustee in the trustee's fiduciary capacity even if the trustee is not personally liable. The Comment indicates that this reverses the common law rule.

2.   Interest as General Partner

While UTC Section 1010 protects trustees from personal liability for conduct entered into by the trustee in the trustee's fiduciary capacity, UTC Section 1011 applies the same immunity rules if the trustee is a general partner in a general or limited partnership. For contracts, the trustee must identify the fiduciary capacity either in the contract or in the partnership certificate filed pursuant to the Uniform Partnership Act or the Uniform Limited Partnership Act. Subsection (c) of UTC Section 1011 provides that the immunity does not apply if the trustee is holding the partnership interest in a capacity other than a fiduciary capacity or if the interest is held by the trustee's spouse, descendants, siblings, parents, or the spouses of any of them. If the trust that holds the general partnership interest is a revocable trust, subsection (d) of UTC Section 1011 provides that the settlor is liable personally for contracts and other obligations just as if the settlor were a general partner. All of UTC

Section 1011 is bracketed. The Comment indicates that the states who are enacting the UTC should examine their own specific partnership laws and modify this Code section accordingly.

3. Protection of Third Party Who Deals With Trustee

UTC Section 1012(a) specifically protects third parties who in good faith assist a trustee or in good faith and for value deal with a trustee unless the third party knows that the trustee is improperly exercising or exceeding the trustee's powers. [For a similar provision in the UPC relating to personal representative, see 3–714, § 12.05]. Subsection (b) of UTC Section 1012 relieves a third party who is dealing in good faith with a trustee from the duty to inquire as to the extent or proper exercise of the trustee's powers. Under subsection (c) of UTC Section 1012, a third party who in good faith delivers property to the trustee need not ensure that the property is used or applied properly. Subsection (d) of UTC Section 1012 protects a third party who deals in good faith with a former trustee while assuming that the former trustee is still the trustee. The third party is protected as if the former trustee were still the trustee. Subsection (e) of UTC Section 1012 provides that comparable provisions in other laws protecting third parties override the protections spelled out in UTC 1012. The Comment states that the principal statutes contemplated by this provision are the Uniform Commercial Code (Article 8) and the Uniform Simplification of Fiduciary

Securities Transfers Act. [See Alerus Financial, N.A. v. Western State Bank, 750 N.W.2d 412 (N.D. 2008)].

4. Certification of Trust

As noted above, UTC 1012(b) allows third parties who are dealing with a trustee in good faith to presume that the trustee has the authority to exercise the powers in question. Some third parties, however, may prefer to have further assurances of the trustee's powers and demand to examine the trust instrument. On the other hand, there are many provisions of a trust instrument that would not be applicable to the powers in question and that the settlor or beneficiaries would prefer to keep confidential. UTC Section 1013 strikes a balance by allowing the trustee to give the third party a signed or authenticated certification that contains the information necessary for the third party to know that the trustee has such powers. The certification must include the following information: (1) that the trust exists and the date the trust instrument was executed; (2) the identity of the settlor; (3) the identity and address of the currently acting trustee; (4) the powers of the trustee; (5) the revocability or irrevocability of the trust and the identity of any person holding a power to revoke the trust; (6) the authority of cotrustees to sign or otherwise authenticate and whether all or less than all are required in order to exercise powers of the trustee; (7) the trust's taxpayer identification number; and (8) the manner of taking title to trust property. The certification need not contain the dispositive provisions of the trust. [UTC 1013(d)]. The certification must state that the trust has not been changed in any way that would cause the representations in the certification to be incorrect. [UTC 1013(c)]. Under subsection (e) of UTC Section 1013, the third party may demand to see the actual provisions of the trust that name the trustee and confer the required power on the trustee. UTC Section 1013(f) protects a third party who relies on the certification without knowledge that the representations in the certification are incorrect. Further, under subsection (g) of UTC Section 1013, a person who in good faith enters into a transaction in reliance on the certification may enforce the transaction. If a third party refuses to rely on a certification but instead demands to see the entire trust instrument, subsection (h) of UTC Section 1013 provides that that person is liable for damages if the court determines that the demand was not made in good faith. Subsection (i) of UTC Section 1013 clarifies, however, that a third party may obtain a copy of the entire trust instrument in a judicial proceeding concerning the trust.

§ 19.05   UTC Article 11: Miscellaneous Provisions

This article contains provisions that encourage a broad application of the UTC. UTC Section 1101 encourages a construction of the act that considers the importance of promoting uniformity across the states. [See 1–102(b), § 2.01 for a similar provision in the UPC.]

UTC Section 1102 is a provision that is being inserted in all newly-promulgated (2000 or later) uniform acts. This provision preempts the federal Electronic Signatures in Global and National Commerce Act (15 U.S.C. § 7002). That act allows a state to supersede its provisions by a later-enacted state statute that refers specifically to the federal act. The effect of this provision is to leave in place whatever state statutes control the use and validity of electronic signatures.

UTC Section 1103 provides for the severability of code provisions so that the invalidation of one will not affect the other provisions that can be given effect without the invalid provision. [See 1–104, § 2.01 for a similar provision in the UPC.]

UTC Section 1104 provides an effective date for the UTC. However, UTC Section 1106 states that, unless otherwise provided in the UTC, the UTC will apply to all trusts, whether created before or after the effective date of the UTC. An exception to this rule appears in UTC Section 602(a), which addresses the presumption of revocability of a trust and indicates that the law in effect prior to the enactment of the UTC will determine whether a trust is presumed revocable if the trust was established prior to enactment. [See § 18.03 (B)]. UTC Section 1106 provides that all judicial proceedings commenced after the effective date will be governed by the UTC, as will all judicial proceedings commenced before the effective date unless the court determines that the application of the UTC will prejudice the interests of the parties or have an otherwise negative effect on the effective conduct of the proceedings. [See In re Estate of Somers, 89 P.3d 898 (Kan.2004), In re Trust Created by Inman, 693 N.W.2d 514 (Neb.2005)]. This UTC section also provides that any rules of construction in the UTC will apply to trusts whenever created unless the trust clearly indicates a contrary intention. The UTC does not apply to any act done prior to the effective date. If a right is acquired, extinguished, or barred under a statute of limitations that was in effect prior to the effective date, that statute continues to apply. [See Honsinger v. UMB Bank, 2007 WL 4287683 (2007)]. In other words, the claimant is not allowed to take advantage of a longer statute of limitations under the new UTC nor can the new UTC alter a right that became irrevocable prior to the effective date. The UPC has a comparable effective date provision. [8–101].

The UTC was designed to incorporate or supersede certain other uniform laws that dealt with various aspects of trust law. UTC Section 1105 provides that the following uniform acts will be repealed when the UTC is enacted: (1) Uniform Trustee Powers Act; (2) Uniform Probate Code, Article VII; (3) Uniform Trusts Act (1937); and (4) Uniform Prudent Investor Act. States that have adopted the UTC have been somewhat sporadic in their enactment of UTC Section 1105 and thus in their repeal of these related uniform acts.

INDEX

References are to Pages

741

†